PARTNERS IN PROSPERITY

PARTNERS IN PROSPERITY

STRATEGIC INDUSTRIES FOR THE UNITED STATES AND JAPAN

Julian Gresser

McGRAW-HILL BOOK COMPANY

New York • St. Louis • San Francisco • Hamburg • Mexico • Toronto

1 2 3 4 5 6 7 8 9 D O C D O C 8 7 6 5 4

ISBN 0-07-024671-8

Library of Congress Cataloging in Publication Data
Gresser, Julian.
Partners in prosperity.
1. United States—Foreign economic relations—Japan.
2. Japan—Foreign economic relations—United States.
3. Industry and state—United States. 4. Industry and state—Japan. I. Title.
HF1456.5.J3G74 1984   337.52073   83–24925
ISBN 0–07–024671–8

BOOK DESIGN by CHRIS SIMON

To my father,
a man of kindness, patience, and cheer;
may his inspiration be remembered.

Acknowledgments

A book, like a river, springs from many sources. For their continuing guidance, encouragement, and friendship, always selflessly given, I am especially grateful to Professors Oliver Oldman, Carl Kaysen, Lawrence Susskind, Roger Fisher, Karl Case, and Takeshi Hiromatsu; Andrew Osterman of the Intel Corporation; and Rose Moss, who helped edit an early draft of this book.

An undertaking of this ambition requires special financial sponsorship, and in this respect, I have been especially fortunate. The seeds of my two-year visit to M.I.T. and Harvard were planted by the Dana Fund. The project thereafter was supported by M.I.T.'s Program on Science, Technology, and Society, the Harvard Law School, and Harvard's Program on U.S.–Japan Relations. I shall always be indebted to Carl Kaysen, Director of M.I.T.'s Program in Science, Technology, and Society for giving me the time to explore M.I.T.'s scientific and technical treasures; and to Oliver Oldman and Ezra Vogel for the opportunity to test my ideas against the mettle of Harvard's students and visiting scholars.

Many colleagues offered helpful critical comments on specific chapters. In the United States these included Howard Raiffa, Thomas Schelling, Abram Chayes, Douglas Ginsburg, Jack Lozier, Edwin Reischauer, Louis Sohn, Richard Stewart, Detlev Vagts, Daniel Tarullo, Michael Nacht, Milton Katz,

Lester Thurow, George Lindamood, Richard Bird, Alan Liker, Roy Lahr, and Jerrold Guben; in Japan, my law partners, Sumio Hara and Rex Coleman, and other friends, Fumitake Tokuyama, Hideichi Okada, and Toshihiko Tanabe.

For his dedication and skill and for a job well done, I thank my research assistant, Bill Jaaskela, and for her insights and gentle patience, I shall always remember my dearest friend, Angela Marasco.

Finally, I wish to thank my editors, Tom Quinn and Elsa Dixler, for skillfully guiding this craft through the rapids of mighty McGraw; and my agent, Julian Bach, for his interest, confidence, and masterful administration throughout.

This is the first of the Trigger Method series.

Contents

Introduction

In these times no need is more pressing than sustained economic growth. Economic growth will give those who have nothing decent food, housing, education, medical care, and opportunities of advancement. It will allow those with adequate means the luxury to seek loftier goals. It will weaken the influence of those among us who sow dissension, hatred, and conflict.

Economic growth, however, will not achieve any of these ends if its fruits are not equitably shared. For no appeal to growth can command the people's respect if its benefits accrue to only a few, while its pains are borne by many. Hence the primary task of our leaders is to devise a means of sustaining high rates of aggregate and equitable long-term growth.

A great debate is now raging over the future of our economy. The debate is a result of the recent years of American industry's declining innovation, productivity, and competitiveness. The proposed antidote, already an issue in the 1984 presidential campaign, is a new national industrial policy.

What is an industrial policy? By any definition the concept is vague. Is it a call for centralized economic planning? Is it a new appeal to rational laissez-faire? Or is it something in between? The center of the debate is increasingly on whether government ought to be involved in picking basic and high-technology industries. Yet still lacking is a specific method of how to select and launch "critical" sectors, an explicit rationale to justify those choices and, perhaps most important, a description of the process by which public and private resources are to be made available to these and other industries.

In attempting to meet these shortcomings, this book builds on the work of Robert Reich, Lester Thurow, William Abernathy, Bennet Harrison, Amitai Etzioni, Seymour Melman, and many others.[1] The basic proposal is divided into two parts.

The first part is a concrete procedure, called the "Trigger Method," to pick strategic industries. A strategic industry is an industry that is the primary cause of economic growth in a given time and place. The method is derived from the writings of historians about industries that have actually demonstrated this effect. These include cotton during the industrial revolution, the railroads and machine-tool industry in nineteenth-century America, Swiss watchmaking, the German chemical dye industry, and Japan's trigger industries (steel, autos, household electronics, and computers) in the postwar era. The method arranges the key economic, technical, political, and social aspects of these industries. The idea of a strategic industry is important for the current debate on industrial policy, because it suggests that economic growth can be stimulated by an economic lever, without the need for comprehensive government intrusion in the economy.

The second part of my proposal is to use negotiation as a means of concentrating resources in strategic sectors and in supplemental growth sectors to which strategic sectors are linked. The art of negotiation has recently attracted wide national attention, thanks largely to Roger Fisher and William Ury's best-seller, *Getting to Yes*, because it offers a flexible means of resolving a wide range of disputes. The subject has stimulated commentary and critique, business seminars, political initiatives, and many new research programs, all devoted to exploring its subtleties.

On a theoretical level, negotiation also represents an extremely promising, though surprisingly untapped, resource. In a now-famous 1960 article, Ronald Coase showed that bargaining provides the most efficient means of approximating the true interests of parties, and can lead, without government intervention, to an efficient allocation of resources.[2] With information costs at zero and without market distortions, traditional economic theory indicates that the result of bargaining can approximate the theoretical ideal of the free market.

The process contemplated by this book draws on Coase's theoretical insights and applies them to strategic industries. By identifying and removing market distortions and by channeling resources effectively, bargaining can help strategic industries realize their full potential. The Office of Strategic Industries (OSI), a new office in the White House, would evaluate various industries nominated as strategic by interested government agencies, industry spokesmen, and other members of the public. Designations would be based on explicit criteria derived from the method, and would be reviewed by the OSI's Advisory Council. After evaluating and ranking the industries in the order of their strategic leverage, the OSI would tender offers to those industries designated as most strategic.

A bargaining process would then begin among firms in the industry and concerned governmental agencies, congressional committees, and other groups. As the bargaining continued, other interests such as consumer groups, labor unions, environmentalists, and representatives of minorities would intervene. The upshot would be a public contract, in this book's terms, a "negotiated industrial investment strategy" (NIIS). The agreement would be regularly monitored, evaluated, revised, and when appropriate, terminated.

I believe that the institution of NIIS would represent a fair, efficient, and stable means of allocating resources to strategic sectors. It would be fair in that all necessary parties would be represented in the negotiations; efficient in that the process would produce a negotiated agreement at low administrative and other costs; and stable in that the agreement would create a workable precedent, leaving the parties in a good relationship to deal with future change. The NIIS would not require a major restructuring of U.S. government as some enthusiasts for a new industrial policy urge. In fact, it would strengthen existing institutions and processes in a way consistent with American traditions. And furthermore, it could be accomplished at very little cost.

The Trigger Method and the idea of NIIS rest on a new theory of economic growth. Under the conventional model, economic growth is dependent on capital formation, meaning physical capital like buildings or factories. Economic growth occurs when capital is replaced, more output is produced, or the value of outputs increases. It is a simple and well-understood model, and in some cases it has accurately described the growth process. When the economy is working well, there is little need for corrective government action.

The problem with the conventional model is that it fails to account for the importance of technology in economic growth. The character of technology-driven growth is very different from that of capital accumulation. It is explosive, nonlinear, multidirectional, risky, and profoundly uncertain. For the reasons discussed, most mainstream economists have not been comfortable in describing it. The role of government in technology-driven economic growth is also different. Since this kind of growth often involves "external" costs and benefits, even conventional theory dictates that government be intimately involved in assisting or regulating industry.

The theory of strategic industries draws on the writings of various American and European economists spanning thirty years. The basic concept is best classified as a branch of "leading sector" economics, with particular attention to the role of technology in advanced industrial societies. The theory also integrates aspects of the writings of Joseph Schumpeter on capital and economic growth, Robert Solow on technology and the production function, Jacob Schmookler on the economics of invention, Kenneth Arrow on the mathematics of information, James Utterback on technology and innovation, and Nathan Rosenberg on economics, technology, and history. The most recent and important work of this genre is Richard Nelson and Sidney Winter's study, *An Evolutionary Theory of Economic Change.*[3]

The economic principles and the concrete proposals for national industrial recovery described here bear directly on America's relations with its trading partners, in particular Japan. Japan is critical to the United States, first because it is a major source of our economic difficulties; second because it is the only true democracy in Asia and thus secures political stability in the Far East and the Pacific; and third, because Japan can provide a significant stimulus to economic growth in the United States.

Today the United States and Japan are clearly drifting apart. In the language of game theory, each sees the other in a "fading zero-sum game," each believing it can win only by defeating the other. In fact this course will make both countries worse off. If the U.S. continues its self-righteous complaints against Japan's industrial targeting, and if Japan's leaders remain deaf and blind to American's legitimate grievances, the fruits will be deeper mistrust, insinuation, retaliation, and alienation.

The deterioration of the United States–Japan relationship is most tragic because it is wasteful and unnecessary. *Partners in Prosperity* makes three proposals to reverse the present situation. The first provides psychological insight into the cultural perspectives that divide Japanese and Americans. If countries were intelligent couples, they might seek expert advice. They would find that there is no substitute for clear communication, a sense of priority, and a recognition of the inevitability of change. This is also true of nations.

Second, the book advances a new proposal for "joint economic growth." This will require close concerted action between the United States and Japan, as if their respective strategic industries were actually those of one country. Joint economic growth will increase productivity and output and stimulate innovation simultaneously in both countries. Finally, the book shows in detail how a new negotiation with Japan can begin and how joint economic growth can be achieved.

As a practicing lawyer, I have no delusions that the way is easy. Yet I am convinced that care and dedication can make these years of decline and disorder a decade of hope.

Part I

STRATEGIC INDUSTRIES IN THEORY AND PRACTICE

Chapter 1

Strategic Industries in History

This chapter introduces some of the basic characteristics of strategic industries. British cotton illustrates how the
leading sector develops in an industrial matrix. Cotton also
suggests the vagaries that have at times accompanied strategic
industries, since until cotton's rise the British government
persisted in viewing wool as the logical choice for mechanization, promoting this industry to the disfavor of cotton.
Machine tools and railroads introduce the ideas of technological convergence, vertical disintegration, and forward and
backward linkages. These concepts will be extremely helpful
in understanding the basic rationale for Japan's promotion
of semiconductors, computers, telecommunications, mechantronics, and biotechnology in the postwar period. The Swiss
watch-making industry shows how an industry can become
strategic by altering perceptions of a fundamental parameter
of existence, in this case, time. The German chemical industry
illustrates the transition from strategic industries based on
craft to those based on science. With chemical dyes, hands-
on experience was no longer adequate. Education became
the critical factor, and an educated work force was what imperial Germany possessed in abundance. The German Reich's
manipulation of this industry for its military ambitions fore-

shadows a recurrent theme, present today in the rising tensions between the United States and Japan.

The purpose of these studies is not to provide an exhaustive treatment, but rather to give a feel for the variety and richness of the subject. I am concerned with patterns, not with a deep understanding of mechanics. My ultimate aim is to construct from these studies, and from the analysis of Japanese industrial policies in Part II, a coherent method by which to gauge the strategic leverage of any industry past, present, or future.

Technology, not the gods, has governed human affairs since antiquity. The oar, the sail, the hull, and the rudder brought the oceans into man's dominion. By the wheel, the road, and the aqueduct, Rome turned the savage hordes to servitude. In the middle ages the stirrup joined man and steed into a fighting organism that made this plated centaur master of Europe.[1] Upon the heavy plough, the harness, the horseshoe, three-field rotation, the water-wheel, the cannon, the crank and the clock, medieval man built the manorial system, his source of power and the boundaries of his farthest yearnings. But not until the industrial revolution is technology's strategic role in industry most certain, and for this reason it is with cotton and England that the story begins.

Cotton: The Basic Paradigm

David Landes traces the transition of cotton from an industrial backwater in the mid-eighteenth century to the emblem of British might seventy years later.

In 1760 Britain imported some $2\frac{1}{2}$ million pounds of raw cotton to feed an industry dispersed for the most part through the countryside of Lancashire and existing in conjunction with the linen maufacture, which supplied it with the tough warp yarn it had not yet learned to produce. All of its work was done by hand, usually (excluding dyeing and finishing) in the homes of the workers, occasionally in the small shops of the master weavers. A generation later, in 1787, the consumption of raw cotton was up to 22 million pounds; the cotton manufacture was second only to wool in numbers employed and value of product; most of the fibre consumed was being cleaned, carded, and spun on machines, some driven by water in large mills, some by hand in smaller shops or even in cottages. A half-century later, consumption had increased to 366 million pounds; the cotton manufacture was the most important in the kingdom in value of product, capital invested, and numbers employed; almost all of its employees, except for the still large number of hand-loom weavers, worked in mills under factory discipline. The price of yarn had fallen to perhaps one-twentieth of what it had been, and the cheapest Hindu labour could not compete in either quality or quantity with Lancashire's mules and throstles. British cotton goods sold everywhere in the world: exports, a third larger than home consumption, were worth four times those of woolens and worsteds. The cotton mill was the symbol of Britain's industrial greatness . . .[2]

In analyzing the dramatic growth in cotton and explaining why growth in the cotton industry triggered growth in other sectors, Landes stresses the role of technology. He notes that generally two conditions are necessary for technological change to displace established methods and vested interests: prevailing techniques must be inadequate, and the new methods must be sufficiently superior to pay for the costs of change.

Both conditions were satisfied by the congeries of inventions that grew within the cotton industry. "Cotton lent itself technologically to mechanization far more easily than wool."[3] This came as a great surprise since wool was at the time a far more important industry, and the first machines were adapted to woolen production. Landes notes, "Well into the nineteenth century, long after the techniques of mechanical engineering had much improved, there continued to be a substantial lag between the introduction of innovations into the cotton industry and their adaptation to wool. . . . [T]here has remained an element of art—of touch—in wool manufacture that the cleverest and most automatic contrivances have not been able to eliminate."[4]

Mechanization, of course, was the force that drove all the

inventions and innovations to come. "They came," he notes, "in a sequence of challenge and response, in which the speed-up of one stage of the manufacturing process placed a heavy strain on the factors of production of one or more other stages and called forth innovations to correct the imbalance."[5] Kay's fly-shuttle aggravated an already serious disequilibrium and called forth a family of spinning devices including the carding machine, Hargreaves' Jenny, Arkwright's water frame, and Crompton's mule. These major inventions were accompanied by innumerable adjustments and improvements—articulation of parts, transmission of power, and materials employed—before such contrivances worked commercially.[6]

Machines and new techniques meant gains in productivity and a shift in the relative factors of production from labor to capital. Yet this was not all that was in play. Historians of the industrial revolution are perhaps more concerned with the profound changes that took place in the organization of the means of production, specifically the assemblage of large bodies of workers in one place to accomplish tasks under supervision and discipline. These changes, originating in the cotton industry, came to be known as the "factory system," a social and economic innovation as important as any technical breakthrough of its time.

In seeking to explain the leverage of a strategic industry, it is covenient to view it in a matrix with other industries. An innovation in the former then can be seen to release expansionary forces in closely allied, supplemental growth sectors, and later throughout the economy.[7] In explaining why the threshold of the industrial revolution was crossed first in cotton and not in wool, Landes notes that there was strong domestic demand for cotton that proved more elastic than for wool. Cotton enabled the masses—not only the wealthy— to enjoy the comfort and hygiene of body linen where before they wore only coarse outer garments. The domestic industry was also driven by the pull of vast untapped markets of the tropics. Where wool had previously reigned, cotton came to dominate.

W.W. Rostow suggests that society must also be capable of generating sufficient capital to activate the takeoff, and there must also be a high rate of investment by the private or state entrepreneurs who control capacity and the new techniques.[8] By the late eighteenth century Britain was particularly well situated to satisfy this condition. By the time of the industrial revolution, Britain's growth rate already exceeded that of its continental competitors, and its people were fascinated by wealth and commerce. Most of these early entrepreneurs reinvested in cotton and the industries that cotton stimulated.

Finally, the leading sector must induce a chain of requirements for increased capacity in other sectors, to which society increasingly responds. From cotton grew other branches of the British textile industry. The need for a cheap means to bleach cloth in turn stimulated the production of chemical agents and thus the chemical industry. The development of a complex of cleaning, carding, and roving machines demanded more and more power and led directly to the improvement of the steam engine.

The case study of cotton has suggested that the leading or strategic sector develops in an industrial matrix allied closely with supplemental growth sectors and that it is through the interaction of all these sectors that economic growth proceeds. The specifics of these alliances have not been explained. The next two cases show that these alliances may be both technological and economic, and illustrate these relationships by the examples of technical convergence, vertical disintegration, forward and backward linkages, and the concept of "dynamic feedback."

The Machine Tool Industry in Nineteenth-Century America (1840–1910): The Principles of Technical Convergence and Dynamic Specialization

In 1820 a separately identifiable machine tool- or machinery-producing sector did not exist in the United States.[9] Although machines of varying complexities were in use, industrial power had not yet begun to see their production as a specialized function. By and large, machines were produced by their ultimate users on an ad hoc basis.

The growth of independent machine tool manufactures is evident in a continuing sequence, between approximately 1840 and 1880. In their earliest stage, machinery-producing establishments appeared as adjuncts to factories specializing in the manufacture of a final product. There were two great branches of this development. The first involved heavier, general-purpose machine tools—lathes, planers, boring machines—used initially by early textile machine shops in response to the demands of their industry. The second involved lighter, more specialized, high-speed machine tools—turret lathes, milling machines, precision grinders—that grew from the requirements of the arms makers. Machine tools proliferated in the 1840s and 1850s, first from the demands of textile and firearms makers, next from sewing machine producers, and at the end of this critical period from the demands of bicycle and automobile manufacturers.

The key to the forces that shaped this development were two interrelated phenomena—technological convergence, and vertical disintegration. "Technological convergence" refers to the way in which the processes and problems of producing disparate commodities become closely allied (technologically convergent) on a technological basis. In preindustrial economies, skills are closely tied to each stage in a vertical sequence of production.[10] By contrast, the decentralization of the sources of power in industrial economies permits similar skills and techniques to be used at "higher" stages of production for a wider range of final products. We see such convergence clearly in the machining and metal-using sectors of an economy. Here there are many common processes, first in the refining and smelting of ores; next, at the foundry, where refined metals are cast into preliminary shapes; later at the machines that convert metal components into final form, prior to their assembly as finished products.

Nathan Rosenberg describes the process as follows:

8

The use of machinery in the cutting of metal into precise shapes involves, to begin with, a relatively small number of operations (and therefore machine types): turning, boring, drilling, milling, planing, grinding, polishing, etc. Moreover, all machines performing such operations confront a similar collection of technical problems, dealing with such matters as power transmission (gearing, belting, shafting), control devices, feed mechanisms, friction reduction, and a broad array of problems connected with the properties of metals (such as the ability to withstand stresses and heat resistance). It is because these processes and problems became common to the production of a wide range of disparate commodities that industries which were apparently unrelated from the point of view of the nature and uses of the final product become very closely related (technologically convergent) on a technological basis—for example, firearms, sewing machines, and bicycles.[11]

"Vertical disintegration" refers to the fragmentation of production into operations undertaken separately by different firms. George Stigler suggests that vertical disintegration and therefore an increasing specialization by process is characteristic of a growing industry:

If one considers the full life of industries, the dominance of vertical disintegration is surely to be expected. Young industries are often strangers to the established economic system. They require new kinds of qualities of materials and hence make their own; they must overcome technical problems in the use of their products and cannot wait for potential users to overcome them; they must persuade customers to abandon other commodities and find no specialized merchants to undertake this task. These young industries must design their specialized equipment and often manufacture it, and they must undertake to recruit (historically, often to import) skilled labor. When the industry has attained a certain size and prospects, many of these tasks are sufficiently important to be turned over to specialists.[12]

The growth of the machine tool industry in the United States depended on the coincidence of technological convergence and vertical disintegration. Indeed, the degree of specialization achieved owed its existence in large part to the fact that certain technical processes were common to many industries. The interaction of convergence and vertical disintegration permitted a relatively small number of similar skills and techniques to be used at higher stages of production for a wide range of final products. For example, firms producing only milling machines, and others specializing in grinding machines, would not have been able to generalize their techniques had only firearms manufacturers employed milling machines or bicycle manufacturers employed grinding machines. With technological convergence milling and grinding became important operations in a large number of metal-using industries, which permitted a degree of specialization at higher stages of production than would otherwise have been feasible.

While technical convergence and vertical disintegration contributed significantly to growth in the machine tool industry, it also fostered new techniques in allied sectors. Rosenberg notes:

For there is an important learning process involved in machinery production, and a high degree of specialization is conducive not only to an effective learning process but to an effective *application* of that which is learned. This highly developed facility in the designing and production of specialized machinery is, perhaps, the most important single characteristic of a well-developed capital goods industry and constitutes an external economy of enormous importance to other sectors of the economy.[13]

Dynamic specialization had several important consequences. The machine tool industry became a center for the acquisition and diffusion of new skills and techniques, a reservoir of technical information that was employed by all machine users. By its strategic role in the learning process, it served as a conveyor belt for new skills. The development of specific customers fostered a rapid sequence of inventions and innovations of increasing complexity and differentiation. These in turn were directly responsible for the sharp rise in productivity within the machine tool industry itself. These mutually reinforcing actions conferred important benefits to other parts of the economy. Reductions in the cost of capital goods raised the marginal efficiency of capital in other industries, which resulted in a significant capital saving throughout the economy.[14]

The process is well illustrated by linkages of machine tools with firearms, sewing machines, bicycles, and automobiles. The firearms industry was instrumental in the development of a whole array of tools and accessories such as jigs, fixtures, taps and gauges, upon which the large-scale production of precision metal parts depended. The milling machine, among the most versatile of all modern machine tools, originated in the efforts of arms makers to provide an effective substitute to expensive hand filing and chiseling operations. Another legacy, the turret lathe, made it possible to arrange operations on a work piece in a sequence and obviated the need to reset or remove an object. It thereby revolutionized all manufacturing processes that required large volumes of small precision components such as screws. A turret screw machine was adopted and modified in the production of watches, typewriters, bicycles, and sewing machines.[15]

The sewing machine industry itself constituted a major source of machine tool innovations, particularly from the 1850s through the 1870s. The manufacture of sewing machines resembled firearm production, an analogy that sewing machine manufacturers were quick to apply. Just as in firearms, the solution of technical problems in the production of sewing machines added to the stock of machine-cutting instruments that were later applied in the production of other metal-using products. Two good examples are the universal grinding and milling machines produced by Brown and Sharpe in the 1860s. In each case an innovation that had been developed as a solution to a narrow and specific range of problems was soon generalized in the manufacture of hardware, tools, cutlery, locks, arms, printing machines, scientific instruments, and a variety of other products.[16]

The large-scale manufacture of automobiles required the application of skills and machines not fundamentally different from those that had already been developed for bicycles and sewing machines. The process of transfer and dynamic specialization is best illustrated by the evolution and adoption of the grinding machine from a tool suited to relatively light operations such as finishing components to one capable of meeting the exigencies of massive automobile production. The relation of machine tools to the automobile reflected a symbiosis of an earlier age. Just as the working action of the Colt revolver had been incorporated into machines used to produce the revolver, so the principles of automobile manufacture were later incorporated back into the design of the machines from which automobiles were fashioned.[17]

The Legacy of the Railroad (1830–1860): The Principles of Forward and Backward Linkage

In his study of the transformation of the ante-bellum economy, Albert Fishlow suggests that the railroad proved to be a critical innovation in three respects.[18] First, by reducing transportation costs, it constituted a formidable social saving. The introduction of the railroad released resources that could then be deployed to other more productive uses. Fishlow notes two associated effects: the displacement effect, which involved the substitution of rail for water transport (the canal), and an overall reduction in cost. The latter involved not only a reduction in direct charges, it also included lower interest, financing, and other cost savings associated with greater speed, freedom from seasonality, smaller risk of loss, and direct routing. Fishlow notes that the direct benefits of the railroad totaled around $175 million, or almost 4 percent of the 1859 economy.

As important as its contribution to cost saving, particularly up to 1860, were the so-called backward linkages or derived demands of the railroad. Here the significant factor appears to have been less the increase in generalized expenditures necessitated by the railroad—outlays for construction or operating equipment—and more the specific demands on other key sectors such as coal, iron, and machinery that themselves were in the midst of takeoff. This was particularly true at the end of the prewar period. By then the railroad industry was consuming large amounts of domestic iron. Bessemer steel production was almost totally absorbed by railroads, and more coal was diverted to the railroads than to any other sector.[19]

Outstripping each of these two effects was the railroad's forward linkages. Fishlow suggests the impact was most pronounced in agriculture, though evident also in the stimulus to coal, machinery, and other industries. The railroad was particularly suited to agriculture, a sector whose products were of low value relative to weight, whose products traveled to distant markets, and whose alternatives involved overland haulage on much worse roads. The railroad made the interior more attractive and encouraged surpluses in originally settled areas. Bulky farm products could now be exchanged over larger geographical areas. This in turn fostered regional specialization and its resulting economies in production.

Rosenberg notes the crucial importance of regional specialization on the coal industry:

Reductions in the cost of transporting coal from the mine to electric generating facilities, due to the development of the unitized train shipment of coal and other transportation improvements, have made it possible to close down less efficient coal mines which had previously survived because of their proximity to markets and to rely increasingly on a smaller number of more efficient mining operations. Finally, reductions in transport costs generally make possible the more intensive exploitation of economies of scale, wherever these economies may be significant.[20]

The development of a national railroad network was also a critical ingredient in the diffusion of machine tool technology. Until 1840, machinery production was not only relatively unspecialized—each producer typically undertaking a wide range of output—but it was also a highly localized operation because of the high cost of transporting machinery. The growing specialization in machine production after 1840, characterized by the emergence of large numbers of producers each of whom typically concentrated on a very narrow

13

range of machines, was closely linked with the improvements in transportation and consequent reduction in freight costs.

The relationship of the railroad to these industries was both dynamic and synergistic, and took place on an increasingly wider geographic scale. Investment in industry A reduced the cost of its product; the profits of industry B, created by the lower factor price of A, called forth the investments and expansion in industry B, one result of which was an increase in industry B's demand for industry A's product.

Perceptions of the profits to be made compounded these effects. Many sought to invest in the railroads in order to harvest the appreciation in land values or the benefits in transportation for manufacturing. With the advent of the iron steamship, the synergism was extended to a truly worldwide agricultural division of labor. By the 1880s and 1890s, as a consequence of reductions in the cost of land and water transport and improvements in refrigeration, western Europe became heavily dependent on a wide range of food products, many of which were supplied by the North American midwest.

Strategic Industries and the State: I. G. Farben and the Rise of the German Chemical Industry

The studies of machine tools and railroads have suggested that industrial growth may proceed through a series of pathways in which a leading, strategic sector is in a dynamic, reciprocal relationship with other supplemental sectors. The issue of causation is somewhat uncertain. The expansionary influence of the leading industry is great, but it in turn is influenced and directed by the economic and technical cues received from firms in linked and converging industries.

This is no more organically illustrated than in the German dyestuffs industry. To Landes, Germany's leap to hegemony in dyestuffs is without historical parallel in its technical virtuosity and aggressiveness. In the late 1860s, the German dyestuffs industry was small, dispersed, and essentially imitative. Scarcely a decade later, Badische Anilin, Höchst, AGFA, and others held almost half of the world market. By the turn of the century their share was around 90 percent.[21]

"It was Imperial Germany's greatest industrial achievement," notes Landes.[22] And in large measure it was due to the preeminence of German science, vigorously cultivated by a hierarchy of state-supported technical schools and special incentives. By the First World War, dyestuffs accounted for well over half of the work force and capital investment of the German chemical industry. Yet dyes were only a corner of the new world: the scientific principles that underlay artificial colorants were capable of the widest application. The fountainhead was cellulose. Nitrocellulose explosives came first, followed by lacquers, photographic plates and film, celluloid artificial films, and sundry other items. And in 1909 Baekeland patented the first of the synthetic resins, the "plastic of a thousand uses," Bakelite.

If German dyestuffs demarks the critical factor of advanced education in the development of some strategic industries, it also raises disturbing questions about the role of the state. In history not every strategic industry has required extensive government intervention. For example, in the early years the British government did everything possible to favor wool and burden cotton. Nevertheless, cotton broke away, Prometheus unbound. In nineteenth-century America, railroads enjoyed substantial dispensations through land grants and regulatory subsidies, although direct tax subsidies were modest. Machine tools stand somewhere between railroads and cotton in terms of a state involvement. Nowhere in history, however, has the state been more omnipresent than in the German chemical industry, where it manipulated the industry to attain its darkest military ambitions.

The focus of German state action was a web of cartels that united the "Big Six" German chemical concerns between 1904 and 1916.[23] By eliminating competition and pooling technical experience and resources, I. G. Farben attained an almost absolute monopoly in organic dyestuffs, pharmaceuticals, explosives, and synthetic chemicals before World War I.

15

In structure the terms "monopoly" and "cartel" fail to describe I. G. It was an agglomeration of monopolies, an aggregation of cartels. It is estimated that I. G. was a party to, or an actual promoter of, several hundred international cartels. It has been suggested that by compounding the ideas of universality and absolute control, "panopoly" would be more fitting.[24]

From the start, German patent law served as principal instrument of state strategy. German patent procedures were designed to solicit as much information from foreign applicants as possible, and thereafter the claims were arbitrarily rejected. During World War I bogus chemical patents were themselves weapons of war. As Sir William Page noted in 1917 "anyone who attempted to repeat the method for manufacturing a dyestuff protected by Salzman and Kruger in the German patent no. 12096 *would be pretty certain to kill himself in the operation.*"[25] Salvarsan, the "healing arsenic," when prepared according to I. G.'s specifications proved so toxic it was the source of many American casualties. German patent law also served as a primary means by which I. G. infiltrated and corroded the economic structures of Germany's supposed or actual industrial adversaries.

In war as well as in times of peace I. G.'s patents, cartels, interlocking affiliations, and network of spies were deployed to interrupt vital supplies. Speaking in support of compulsory licensing in 1883, Joseph Chamberlain noted:

It has been pointed out . . . that under the present law it would have been possible, for instance, for the German inventor of the hot blast furnace, if he had chosen to refuse a license in England, to have destroyed almost the whole iron industry of this country and to carry the business bodily over to Germany. Although that did not happen in the case of the hot blast industry, it had actually happened in the manufacture of artificial colors connected with the coal products, and the whole of that had gone to Germany because the patentees would not grant a license in this country.[26]

A similar view was expressed in 1907 by Lloyd George in his comments on the revision of British patent law:

Big foreign syndicates have one very effective way of destroying British industry. They first of all apply for patents on a very considerable scale. They suggest every possible combination, for instance, in chemicals, which human ingenuity can possibly think of. These combinations the syndicates have not tried themselves. They are not in operation, say, in Germany or elsewhere, but the syndicates put them in their patents in obscure and vague terms so as to cover any possible invention that may be discovered afterward in this country.[27]

Before World War I, I. G. had aborted all American efforts to establish an independent dyestuffs industry, so that by the outbreak of war the entire American industry comprised only five small firms that employed fewer than those at work at a single I. G. laboratory. During the war the German cartels were able to induce acute shortages in dyestuffs, nitrates and potash, medicines, military optical goods, surgical instruments, heavy ordnance, and radio and electrical equipment.

As important as the role of the cartel was in disrupting foreign supplies, I. G. proved even more critical on the domestic front. In fact, I. G. Farben *was* Germany's industrial might and it was basically Germany's supremacy in dyes that permitted her to wage four years of pitiless war.

But dyes is really a misnomer. Although it is true that I. G. grew out of the dye industry, its functions were as unlimited as the scientific application of physics and chemistry to raw materials. There were nearly always a large number of disparate products and processes involved in each of the broad areas integrated as a field of production. In using coal in the manufacture of dyestuffs, for example, there were tens of thousands of different crude, intermediate, and finished materials that fell within this general class. And each new branch of chemistry or metallurgy transformed or affected all other aspects of the field.

Although Germany lost World War I, neither the loss nor the ensuing period of social unrest and inflation checked the growth of I. G. Farben. The war increased the tempo of production, the scope of I. G.'s influence, its diversity, its range of interests, the magnitude and comprehensiveness of its affiliations. Twice reincarnated, I. G. became the advance agent of the Third Reich. In World War II it was the principal architect of its master plan, and the chief manufacturer of oil from coal, rubber from oil, and poison gas.

In the late forties plans were made to smash I. G. into some forty-seven different units, each too small to cause trouble. The cold war swallowed the plan. The main I. G. plants, many of which escaped damage, were divided among three main groups. New top managers were picked, many of them former Farben employees. Although the Allies at first insisted that the ownership of I. G. shares be regulated the policy was never carried out. Among Bayer's first official acts taken in 1955 when freed from Allied control was the reinstatement of bearer certificates. These cloaked the identity of the share's true owners from public view.[28]

The study of the German chemical industry may be summarized in two lessons. First, contrary to common thought, the civilian and military applications of key technologies are often entwined. Second, because of their great public importance, strategic industries are often enmeshed in the interests and ambitions of the state. The Third Reich may be history's grimmest example, although the principle is of continuing relevance as the later treatment of current U.S.–Japanese tensions (Chapter 10) will demonstrate.

Strategic Industries Based on Clocks, Watches, and the Hour

The clock highlights three aspects of strategic industries. The first is that an industry can become strategic by virtue of its technical monopoly over a fundamental parameter of human existence such as time. The second is how a nation, riding the crest of industrial preeminence, at times must cede its position to another. This is the story of British watchmaking in the nineteenth century. The third is how economic and social institutions can help a country preserve a dominant position, even in the face of fearsome competition.

The clock, not the steam engine, in Lewis Mumford's estimation, "is the key machine of the modern industrial age."[29]

The bells of the clock tower almost defined urban existence. Timekeeping passed into time-serving and time-accounting and time-rationing. As this took place, Eternity ceased gradually to serve as the measure and focus of human actions . . . .

But here was a new kind of power-machine, in which the source of power and the transmission were of such a nature as to ensure the even flow of energy throughout the works and to make possible regular production and a standardized product. In its relationship to determinable quantities of energy, to standardization, to automatic action, and finally to its own special product, accurate timing, the clock has been the foremost machine in modern technics: and at each period it has remained in the lead: it marks a perfection toward which other machines aspire. The clock, moreover, served as a model for many other kinds of mechanical works, and the analysis of motion that accompanied the perfection of the clock, with the various types of gearing and transmission that were elaborated, contributed to the success of quite different kinds of machine . . .

The clock, moreover, is a piece of power-machinery whose "product" is seconds and minutes: by its essential nature it dissociated time from human events and helped create the belief in an independent world of mathematically measurable sequences: the special world of science . . . .

But the effect of the mechanical clock is more pervasive and strict: it presides over the day from the hours of rising to the hour of rest. When one thinks of the day as an abstract span of time, one does not go to bed with the chickens on a winter's night: one invents wicks, chimneys, lamps, gaslights, electric lamps, so as to use all the hours belonging to the day. When one thinks of time, not as a sequence of experiences, but as a collection of hours, minutes, and seconds, the habits of adding time and saving time come into existence. Time took on the character of an enclosed space: it could be divided, it could be filled up, it could even be expanded by the invention of labor-saving instruments.

Small wonder that societies that mastered the art of clock-making rose quickly to economic preeminence.

Around 1625 the center of watch manufacturing was southern Germany, in particular Nuremberg and Augsburg. Not coincidentally, this also was the center of trade and finance north of the Alps.[30] Despite its older commercial tradition, Italy had already fallen behind and was dependent on immigrant watchmakers and imported timepieces. After a brief interlude when France replaced Germany as the principal center of watchmaking, Britain seized control in around 1675 and occupied the field for about one hundred and twenty-five years until 1800.

In analyzing the causes of British supremacy, Landes suggests first was British pragmatism. While the French concerned themselves with elegance, the British focused on the time-keeping qualities of their watches and soon earned a reputation for unequaled accuracy and reliability.

Equally important was a succession of major innovations: the balance spring, the repeater watch, the cylinder or "horizontal" escapement, and the lever escapement all date from this period. Even more important was the invention of a technique for drilling jewels to serve as bearings or end stones for the pivots of train arbors, which substantially enhanced the durability and accuracy of English watches. Britain kept its secret and its monopoly until about 1820.

Watchmaking and British naval supremacy were so closely allied that in modern times watches would be considered "dual use" technology. The most significant invention was the chronometer, a device for measuring time in remote places. The British navy soon applied the chronometer to taking accurate measurements of longitude. Although Landes hesitates to credit the chronometer as the critical element of British naval prowess, he notes that throughout the period Britain made wide and creative use of this technology.

Beginning in the second half of the eighteenth century, Landes notes, various premonitory symptoms were already apparent. In spite of the prohibitions of the guilds, a number of enterprising makers began to trade under their own name the finished work of other men.[31] These men and their followers would as soon sell a foreign watch as a more prestigious English watch, so that by the nineteenth century there was already a robust trade in importing or smuggling pseudo–British timepieces from the low-cost havens of Geneva, the Swiss Jura, and Holland.

In the meantime, a revolution in watch design was underway on the continent. The traditional watch was relatively thick. This presented no problem when hung around the neck or suspended from belts, but became inconvenient when worn in pockets. Over the course of the eighteenth century a number of important innovations occurred, particularly in France, which despite Britain's continued dominance, began to set the standard of the day.[32]

Landes reports that the British reaction to continental competition was a mixture of alarm and scorn. The journeymen and subcontractors who produced watches for the master makers and dealers complained that the dealers were importing shoddy work, disguised as British, and were mulcting their customers. The master watchmakers remained passive and complacent, telling themselves that anyone who wanted quality would be ready to pay more for a British article.

This mixture of alarm and scorn checked British industry's ability to capitalize on the opportunities developing worldwide. The first big chance was simply the general increase in wealth that brought watches within the reach of an ever-growing number of people. The second was the construction of the railroads, which depended on timetables and preprecision. British output remained stolidly unchanged, while the continent, in particular the Swiss, and for the first time the United States, rapidly accelerated production.

During the early nineteenth century the Swiss had begun to intensify their efforts to reward inventors and innovators by offering prizes for improvements in watch escapements, isochronism, production techniques, and work procedures. During the same period the spirit of opportunism was waning in Britain. By the mid–nineteenth century British industry had been irreversibly eclipsed, the great names fallen by the wayside, one by one.

Watchmaking also became a strategic industry in the agricultural regions of Jura, Neûchetel, and the Vaud in Switzerland. By the mid–eighteenth century visitors already marveled at the affluence and fashionableness of the area:

> . . . they lack absolutely nothing of the necessities and even the amenities and conveniences of life. The neighboring provinces—the Franche-Compté, the bishopric of Basel, and the lower part of their own country—supply them with what nature has not provided and furnish the wheat, the wine, the vegetables, the fruit, and generally everything that is to be found in happier, more fertile countries. The assurance of being able to sell at a good price all sorts of commodities of necessity and even of luxury in these parts, which industry and trade have so enriched, brings in throngs of purveyors. Some of the inhabitants do a profitable trade in these various commodities. The same thing holds for those articles that serve for the interior decoration of houses and for clothing. Visitors to the area are surprised to see very well furnished apartments and people of both sexes dressed with as much elegance and lavishness as in the big cities.[33]

Why did these insignificant mountain corridors achieve such greatness? Personal initiative, intelligence, and talent provided the spark. But as Landes notes, Britain had all of these. Landes finds his clue not only in technical process or in economic linkages, but also in the communal character of the undertaking, the work of a people delineated by space, climate, social and political institutions, religion, and values. "The skills of watchmaking were transmitted by personal contact,"[34] he notes, and in this closed community contacts were facilitated by blood and marriage. Such ties contributed to the rapid diffusion of knowledge within the group, and also inhibited diffusion outside it. Until the advent of automation, watchmaking in Switzerland remained an indigenous technology that even the industrious German workers within Switzerland failed to imitate successfully.

As noted, the Swiss benefited greatly from the surge in demand for watches that took place during the nineteenth century. The Civil War caused an additional, unexpected boon for the industry. Armies depend on a knowledge of time to organize and synchronize. But now a new system of manufacturing—the so-called American system, based on machine production of standard, interchangeable parts—began to threaten the Swiss industry. In 1858 the small Waltham plant of the American Watch Company was producing 14,000 watches. In 1864 it was up to 118,000. As mass economies set in, by the end of the century the American Watch Company and its imitators were producing about 120 million jeweled watches plus an unknown number of dollar and clock watches. Between 1872 and 1879 Swiss exports to the United States fell from 18,312,511 to 5,292,098 francs.[35]

To its credit, Landes notes, Switzerland was able to respond. Where Britain simply could not acknowledge that the Americans were capable of producing cheaper and better-quality watches, the Swiss moved deliberately toward interchangeable parts, retaining an interest in special finishing, complicated pieces, and high fashion. Switzerland withstood the onslaught and even rose to new success, although it never recaptured its monopoly.

In these times the integrated circuit quartz watch has eclipsed the United States and Swiss industries. Between approximately 1978 and 1982 Japan bestrode the waves, but only for a moment. As of this writing, Hong Kong and others are moving in, creating huge enclaves in the fickle international market.

Agriculture as a Strategic Industry

Not all strategic industries need involve capital goods. At times agriculture itself has served as a trigger to growth. Economists and others have generally regarded agriculture as a source of food. But in some cases, such as Denmark and Wisconsin, this industry has also been a source of special high-value-added products whose manufacture has enhanced skills, raised farm incomes, and thereby liberated resources to other sectors.

Denmark's economic growth during the late nineteenth century is generally attributed to the acumen of Danish farmers in seizing the opportunities afforded by changes in the international prices for agricultural products. Around the end of the 1860s prices shifted in favor of livestock at the expense of vegetable foods. The price of British wheat, for example, fell by over 40 percent, while bacon and butter fell by only about 25 percent. Such changes threw most of world agriculture into depression, but not Danish agriculture.[36]

While Britain and other countries took land out of agriculture, Danish farmers increased it. Their key idea was to modify rotations in order to devote more acreage to root crops. Arable land and output could now be deployed to support a greatly increased livestock population. Thereafter the density of cattle, sheep, and poultry increased by over 80 percent and productivity of milk cows soon surpassed that in Great Britain.

In the 1880s Danish agriculture was revolutionized by the centrifugal separator and other inventions that allowed small farmers to specialize. A high level of literacy and strong demand from cities in England and the continent helped even small farms become successful commercial enterprises.

Exports stimulated a transportation infrastructure. As early as the 1860s, Britain was Denmark's chief export market and by 1868 various North Sea ports had grown up. Technical change so accelerated these trends that by 1913 Denmark supplied 60 percent of all British agricultural products, constituting three times the value of British exports to Denmark. Output and income continued to expand in Denmark, while British agriculture remained depressed through most of the same period.

While these events were taking place in Europe, dairy farming was also proving a strategic industry in Wisconsin. Before 1860 most farmers raised wheat. But wheat was subject to destructive cycles and in the late 1850s the industry was in deep depression. Destitute farmers were leaving agriculture, while a few looked for new opportunities. The solution to the calamities was cheese.

Cheesemaking required a systematic method of production, and this triggered the introduction of the factory system. One commentator notes: "The transformation which followed the advent of factory dairying was in its way no less profound than that which had followed its introduction into textiles and metallurgy."[37] Factory methods applied to dairying involved only small numbers of workers and an insignificant use of mechanical power, thus employing features of organization that had been obscured in other branches of industry.

The factories fostered specialization, and specialization demanded more advanced factories. Between 1860 and 1880 there was intense competition among localities and regions where survival depended on larger and more economical modes of production. Production was also stimulated by the expanding domestic and foreign market for dairy products.

As important was the revolution in farm management. Part of this revolution were new techniques for maintaining the health and feeding of cattle, such as the use of the silo, the introduction of vitamins, the application of experiments in animal digestion, and winter feeding known as ensilage. There were also important changes in breeds.

The increasing supply of dairy products itself fostered an increase in the number and size of processing plants, which stimulated a series of technical advances. Lampard notes "no single innovation had greater significance for factory or farms than the butterfat test introduced by Stephen Babcock in the spring of 1890. . . . It became a barometer of milk values for almost every purpose: for cattle testing, municipal milk inspection, fixing prices paid by creameries, factories, condensories, and city dealers."[38] The butterfat test was surpassed only by the centrifugal cream separator, which assumed great importance in Denmark during the same period. The separator helped Wisconsin's dairy farmers diversify into butter, cream, and other products.

25

By 1890 three-quarters of gross farm income derived from livestock, a substantial part of which was from the sale of milk. Wisconsin had become America's first dairy state. The experiences of Denmark and Wisconsin show that agriculture, stimulated by technological advance, can serve as a strategic industry. As will be seen, this has important implications for the poorer, less technically advanced nations.

Summary and Speculations

The first lesson of these six industries is that technology has a critical influence on economic growth. This conclusion is hardly remarkable if one reads Landes, Rosenberg and other economic historians. As discussed in the next chapter, however, this insight has not adequately been incorporated in existing econometric models or in the general theory of economic growth.

The second lesson is that government's role has varied widely in the history of strategic industries. In some cases, such as German chemicals, it was pervasive; in others, like British cotton, almost nonexistent. This is important because it challenges those who would argue that a strategic industry depends on the eye of the beholder—that industries are strategic when governments claim them to be so. Yet in some cases an industry may have a dramatic impact on growth independent of—and at times in spite of—government action. This in no way suggests, however, that government does not have a legitimate and vital role in shaping the growth of some strategic sectors.

The third lesson concerns the dynamics of strategic industries. Often one strategic industry is the proximate cause of the next. This was certainly true of the complex of industries stimulated by cotton in England, and by machine tools and railroads in the United States. As described in Part II, enhancing the triggering capability of strategic industries has been an explicit motive of Japanese government policy since the early 1950s.

Less clear are the specific pathways through which strategic industries trigger growth in other countries. Yet even here various linkages are apparent. There was certainly a rich exchange between England and the continent during the industrial revolution, not only in cotton but also in textiles, steel, iron, and various power industries. The railroads, shipping, and transportation generally are examples of other industries that display this transboundary triggering effect.

Despite the linkages that strategic industries have at times forged among countries, it is nevertheless true that some nations have seized the opportunities of strategic industries and ridden their tide to fortune. Indeed, leading countries have always enjoyed greater wealth. This was true of fourteenth- and fifteenth-century Italy, eighteenth-century England, nineteenth-century England and Germany, and the United States and Japan today. This pattern of stratification was sometimes purposefully exploited, as demonstrated by the policies of the Third Reich. In other cases such as Switzerland, the benefit was maintained by natural barriers.

There is also a life cycle in the history of strategic industries and economic growth. The mandate of heaven passed from England to Germany, and from Germany to the United States, France, and Japan. Tomorrow perhaps it will pass to the rapidly industrializing countries of today. In each case there has been a transfer of technology and learning from the dominant country to a secondary power. Nations that have followed on the heels of the great have often been uniquely positioned to capture the fruits of the latter's labor and investment.

Is it possible that this cycle of ebb and flow might be broken, and that a leading country, because of neglect, sloth, or incompetence, could fall irreversibly behind? Might such a nation simply not have the human resources, capital, or learning to regain dominion over the pace and direction of technological change? More specifically, are the new electronics-based technologies of semiconductors, computers, telecommunications, robotics, genetic engineering, and new materials to be distinguished in this respect from all other industries before them? Is the learning curve here so steep, the pace of technological change so rapid, and these technologies so versatile, that those who falter might over time falter for good? Perhaps this fear is less plausible in the modern age than in times past when technology was more dependent on craft than on science. Yet the proposition is one with which we must contend, because it claims credence today in the halls of power of Japan, the United States, and Europe.

Chapter 2

The Theory of Strategic Industries

Coauthored with Professor Karl Case,
DEPARTMENT OF ECONOMICS, WELLESLEY COLLEGE

The theory of strategic industries is at its core a theory of economic growth and development. This chapter first defines economic growth and reviews the empirical literature on the sources of recent economic growth. Next it examines critically existing models of growth and the policies based on these models. Finally, the chapter suggests why government must be involved, nationally and internationally, in shaping the direction of economic growth.

Economic Growth Defined

The process by which economic growth is generated and sustained has been the focus of theoretical and empirical research for centuries.[1] Indeed, the discipline of economics probably arose in response to the social changes that accompanied rapid growth. Thinkers from the physiocrats in eighteenth-century France,[2] through the nineteenth-century classical political economists, to present-day neoclassical theorists have all sought to explain the nature, causes, and consequences of economic growth.

Economic growth occurs when a society's output of goods and services increases. The standard of living is improved if real output (output adjusted for inflation) increases faster than the population grows.[3] A sustained increase in real output per capita of 2–3 percent can change the character of a society in a relatively short period of time. For example, after a century of 3 percent real growth, an economy would produce twenty times more goods and services per person than it did initially.

The traditional measure of a society's output is gross national product (GNP). Most economic studies use changes in real GNP per capita as the best yardstick of an economy's rate of growth. GNP is an imperfect measure of the value of what a society actually produces because it excludes numerous benefits and costs that affect individual well-being but which do not pass through the officially recognized market. Household services, child rearing, air and water pollution are examples of nonmarket goods which are often extremely difficult to measure.

Traditional Notions of Growth

Although the causes of growth are complex and difficult to identify empirically, growth is fairly easy to explain. Growth occurs when more is produced. More can mean additional quantities of the same goods and services, or it can mean newly developed goods and services.

More can be produced in one of two ways. The quantity of inputs into production can increase: the labor force grows, natural resources are discovered, and/or the stock of physical capital (new machines or production facilities) increases. Or inputs can become more productive, that is, each unit of labor and capital produces more. Often both occur simultaneously.

The productivity of inputs is enhanced in several ways. Managers may organize production more efficiently, or they may develop and apply new processes or techniques of production. We call the development and application of new processes, techniques, and products "technological progress" or "technological change" and use the terms interchangeably.

30

Each case involves the acquisition of new knowledge. Knowledge itself is information that has been selected, interpreted, and transformed. New knowledge is acquired when what was known before becomes more widely known, or when knowledge apparently never known before is produced.

Economic growth begins when a technological change raises the productivity of inputs in an important sector, say, textiles. Improved productivity makes it possible to produce textiles at lower cost. As the new, cheaper techniques spread, the prices of textile products fall. Households can devote a smaller portion of their incomes to textile products and can now buy more or buy other goods they could not previously afford. They are better off. These changes took place during the industrial revolution in Great Britain.

The process of growth causes different sectors of an economy to expand or to contract over time. With technical improvement fewer resources are needed to produce the same output. This may result in structural unemployment. Over the past 200 years, as agriculture has become more productive a smaller and smaller percentage of the population is required to produce food. Society has more to spend on new products. New sectors expand. In time the labor force adjusts, new skills are acquired, and workers are freed to enter growing sectors.

The expansion and contraction of an economy often inflicts pain. During industrialization, a scarcity of agricultural jobs often drives people to the cities where their agricultural skills have little economic value. Today, steelworkers in Youngstown, Ohio, for example, face many of the bitter choices of marginal farmers in nineteenth-century England.

Empirical Evidence of the Causes of Economic Growth

A number of economists have attempted empirically to untangle the sources of growth in the U.S. economy. The most widely cited study is that of Edward Denison published in 1974.[4] From 1929 to 1948 the expansion of the labor force accounted for half the observed growth, and increases in labor productivity accounted for the rest. Thereafter advances in knowledge (technological change) contributed more than any other factor to observed growth, accounting for 22 percent of the total. Advances in knowledge account for about half of increased output per unit of input, or increased productivity.

During the period 1948–1969, Denison suggests that the contribution of technological change to growth was even greater. Nearly 30 percent of the entire increase in output per unit of input is linked to advances in knowledge. Although capital accumulation accounts for a larger portion of growth during the second period than during the first, its share remains below 20 percent of the total, 50 percent less than the share of advances in knowledge.[5]

Critique of Growth Theory and Policy

While economists have recognized and documented the importance of technological progress as an engine of growth,[6] they have been reluctant to build technology into formal models of growth, or to make it the target of pro-growth policies. Rather the central focus of economic theoreticians, as well as policymakers, has been the accumulation of capital. By "capital accumulation" economists mean physical capital like buildings, plant, equipment, and other heterogeneous items.[7] Capital accumulation accounts for at least 20 percent of observed growth.

The emphasis on capital accumulation is incomplete and not necessarily wrong. The incentive to save and invest (to accumulate capital) involves the routine behavior of many individuals, responding in observable ways, to pure economic incentives. Economists feel they are on strong ground in explaining the rate of growth by the rate of capital accumulation, which itself can be derived from the ways savers and investors respond to economic incentives. Replacing labor with capital in most cases *will* enhance the productivity of labor. There is not much to debate about this. Moreover, tying growth to fluctuations of capital investment ties the process neatly to known fluctuations in the business cycle. From this perspective economists are right to eschew an invasive role for government. The process simply works better without it.

Few economists have probed the factors that influence the character and rate of technological change. Most economic analysis of growth assumes that technological progress is exogenous or determined by factors outside the economic system. A favorite word used by growth theorists in describing invention is "autonomous." R. M. Hartwell notes that assuming technological advance to be exogenous "has made the problem of economic explanation easy: the first cause is a *deus ex machina* and the problem becomes one of explaining the adaptation of the economy to the prime mover."[8]

Most rigorous mathematical models of economic growth make population growth and capital accumulation key variables.[9] Output is related to capital and labor inputs through a "production function." Modern models incorporate the existing state of technological knowledge. Growth is understood to occur when the rate of capital accumulation exceeds the rate of population growth or that of the supply of labor. A fundamental assumption is that time is linear. A leads to B, which causes C, which leads to D. Inputs go in one end of the model and outputs emerge from the other.

So conceived, most such models fail to explore the processes that generate technological change. Technological progress alters the ways in which inputs influence outputs. For example a new technique may require more capital and less labor, or less of both. Although such changes can be modeled and their implications explored by shifting the production function, the initial technological changes that give rise to such shifts are deemed to arise outside the system, or exogenously.[10]

Concern over capital accumulation also dominates debates on public policy. Recent public finance literature is preoccupied with the effects of taxation on the rate of private investment.[11] Economic policies enacted in the United States over the past twenty-five years to stimulate growth have been designed almost exclusively to stimulate the production of new capital. The theoretical focus of President Reagan's not-so-new supply-side economics embodied in the Economic Recovery Tax Act of 1981 is capital accumulation.

Focusing public policy on capital accumulation makes sense if the rate and pace of technical change are exogenous and not affected by economic incentives. But if they are not, such models will not be accurate indicators. Where technical progress renders existing capital obsolete, managers with a vested interest in amortizing capital may actually resist or defer introducing new technology, despite its clear benefits.[12] This is as true of companies as it is of nations.

Although the bulk of writings on economic growth ignores the potential endogeneity of technological progress, it was noted by Joseph Schumpeter in 1950 and later by Kenneth Arrow in 1962.[13] Perhaps the most forthright statement was by Jacob Schmookler in *Invention and Economic Growth*. In the concluding chapter he asserts, "long-term economic growth is primarily the result of the growth of technological knowledge—the increase in knowledge about useful goods and how to make them." He continues:

While our ignorance may dictate the continued treatment of technological change as an exogenous variable *in our economic models,* it is plain that *in the economic system* it is primarily an endogenous variable. Even the state of knowledge at a point in time in "intellectually coherent fields" of technology, and therefore the inventive potentials of those fields, are economic variables, for the rate at which each such field is cultivated is primarily determined by the promise it holds of yielding useful knowledge. The selection of the means for achieving an economic end is itself an economic process. Hence, the present state of an intellectually coherent field is largely the end product of a history of economizing decisions made in the process of achieving economic ends.[14]

The strongest, most recent statement that growth is endogenous is by Richard Nelson and Sidney Winter. In *An Evolutionary Theory of Economic Change* (1982), the two Yale economists build a computer simulation model of the process by which firms search for new knowledge through research and development (R&D). In their model, R&D expenditures increase the probability of a technical breakthrough that shifts a firm's production function and generates cost savings. This process inevitably filters out less successful firms and leads to industrial concentration.

In another study, Pankaj Tandon also linked technical change mathematically to R&D spending.[15] Both models, however, suffer from similar limitations. Neither helps significantly to explain the origins of technological change, the magnitude of responses to economic incentives, or the pathways of its spread. In this sense technological change is still considered exogenous. Also, although these writers describe how each change ramifies in a second- and third-order sequence (Markov chain), time is still assumed to be unidirectional. Also essentially unexplored is the basic question of whether and in what specific ways government ought to be involved in directing the course of technological progress.

Endogenous Technology and the Nature of Information: The Case for Public Involvement

Even if we assume that the rate of production of knowledge leading to technological change is influenced by economic variables, there is no a priori case for public involvement; the market provides the proper incentives for efficient production of most goods. This section argues that the unregulated market fails to generate an optimal rate of technological progress.

First, let us summarize the argument:

1. The failure of the market results in part from the properties of information itself.

35

2. The character of economic growth induced by technological change may be very different from that associated with simple capital accumulation.

3. A central element of technology-driven growth relates to the properties of information.

4. The acquisition and dissemination of information has different consequences from capital accumulation and involves substantially greater uncertainty, risk, and random and at times explosive change.

5. Technology-driven economic growth may demand a different conception of time itself. In this sense it is tied intimately to the structure of knowledge.

Information displays properties that distinguish it from other goods. It is both an input and an output of production.[16] Unlike other goods, information, by being given, increases. It multiplies itself. If I give some information to you, I have increased society's net stock of information, although the value of this information to me may have declined. The production of knowledge where resources are consumed or transformed differs in this respect from the production of all other goods.

Information begets new information by opening new uses and by prompting exploration of the unknown. Information thus creates new pathways of inquiry, although at the same time it shuts off old ones. Information is usually generated in the production of all goods, but in strategic industries the informational component may be more valuable than the specific market value of the good produced.

There are at least four ways in which the generation of information affects the rate of economic growth. First, new information can shift the production function, that is, the relation of expected value of output to inputs. Knowledge embodied in railroad technology allowed more miles traveled at the same cost. Second, especially in cases where the outcome of various activities is unknown, a knowledge of the outcome of one activity may directly affect a posteriori the distribution of inputs and outcomes of all others. Once the textile industry had demonstrated the value of steam power, other industries changed so that they too could use steam power. Third, the rate of this process and its efficiency appear to depend on the rate of diffusion of information through society. A potentially valuable innovation is useless to people who do not hear of it. As Arrow suggests:

> That a nation or class has consistently high productivity implies a successful communication system within the nation or class, so the problem turns on the differential between the sort of communication system within and between classes . . . The available evidence certainly suggests that communication problems are a major and perhaps predominant source of productivity and income differentials.[17]

Finally, the influence of information on economic growth is compounded by the fact that information itself is becoming a commodity of exchange to be marketed by experts and data vendors. This greatly affects its diffusion, and thereby the rate by which its benefits are transferred to other segments of society.

Information, knowledge, and technology can be viewed as public, or social, goods. In a seminal paper published in 1954, Paul Samuelson first described a class of outputs that would not be produced in adequate amounts by the normal operation of the market.[18] What distinguishes these goods and gives rise to the market's failure is that they are "nonrival" in consumption. A's consumption of the good in no way interferes with B's or anyone else's. In consequence additional consumers can be added at no cost to society.

Because of the property of nonrivalness it is often, but not always, impossible to exclude others from enjoying the benefits of public goods once they are produced. National defense is a classic example. We all benefit whether we pay for protection or not. In contrast to public goods, the consumption of private goods is rivalrous in nature, that is, benefits are usually contingent upon payment. This possibility of ex-

37

clusion enables producers to maximize profits. McDonald's profits by producing hamburgers, because if I fail to pay, I do not get to eat.

Information, unlike hamburgers, is nonrivalrous. More than one person can possess the same information and use it at the same time. It need not be carved into pieces. Information, however, differs from other public goods like defense in that in addition to being nonrivalrous, exclusion is also possible. The patent laws are an attempt to restrict access to the use of information.

Richard and Peggy Musgrave argue that when goods are nonrivalrous in nature, but when exclusion is possible, they will be produced in insufficient quantities from the perspective of maximum social welfare. An example is an empty bridge:

> Consider, for example, the case of a bridge which is not crowded so A's crossing will not interfere with that of B. Charging a toll would be quite feasible, but so long as the bridge is not heavily used, the charge would be inefficient since it would curtail use of the bridge, the marginal cost of which is zero. Or consider the case of a broadcast, which (by jamming devices) can be made available only to those listeners who rent clearing devices. Again, the jamming would be inefficient since A's reception does not interfere with B's. These are situations where exclusion *can* be applied, but *should not* be because consumption is nonrival. Since the marginal cost to previous users of adding an additional consumer is zero, no admission price should be charged.[19]

In short, information once produced benefits society fully only if it is shared. Moreover, although the processing of information is not entirely without cost, many may acquire it essentially for free. A technological innovation that permits a product to be produced at a lower cost will benefit society only when the innovation is used by competing firms and the price of the good falls to reflect the lower cost.

The problem, however, is that someone has to produce the good, and once the power to exclude is removed, the economic incentive is also extinguished. In terms of the bridge:

But though the marginal cost of admitting additional users is zero, the cost of providing the facility is not. This cost must be covered somehow, and it must be determined how large a facility should be provided. In the absence of exclusion (either because exclusion is not feasible, or because it is undesirable), this task cannot be performed through the usual market mode of sale to individual consumers. Provision through the market cannot function and a political process of budget determination becomes necessary.[20]

Nelson and Winter focus on the same problem, but take it a step further: "The organizational dilemma posed for a predominantly market-organized economy is that it is efficient to make available information public, but the existence of private incentives for information gathering often requires that the information be private. . . . These information problems permeate virtually all economic processes."[21]

Following Schumpeter, Nelson and Winter view the dilemma from the standpoint of the literature on industrial structure. Firms that are successful innovators can drive out competition when information is not shared. Firms in concentrated industries appear to innovate most rapidly because of their ability to capture the full benefits.[22] Thus there is a natural tendency toward concentration in industries where technological change is rapid. Nelson and Winter suggest that concentration is both cause and consequence of the pace of innovation and therefore an important element in economic growth.

New knowledge may be acquired essentially in two ways: first, what is known is disseminated and becomes more widely known; second, knowledge that at present is not known is generated or discovered.

This second form of acquiring knowledge raises a fundamental problem, perhaps more in the realm of philosophy than economics. If a part of acquired knowledge is discovered, by definition it already exists. Otherwise it could not be uncovered. Similarly, it is not certain what portion of newly created knowledge appears new but in truth is merely a restatement of what has been known.

The border between present knowledge and future knowledge is similarly blurry. As stated, existing knowledge creates pathways or paradigms that imply future knowledge. A good analogy is a Bach fugue, wherein the structure of one harmony can be said to shape the next. In this sense future knowledge is read in the structure of existing knowledge.

What is the relationship of this conception of knowledge to time? A linear notion of time oversimplifies. The acquisition of knowledge involves a reaching backward and forward, at times independently, at times simultaneously, a matrix of future, present, and past time frames. Our notion of time often derives from the metaphor of the clock whose hands move ineluctably forward, and Westerners have come to see the dimensions of life similarly and remorselessly circumscribed.[24]

But the clock, after all, is only a machine, and the dimensions of human experience are richer. Another analogy of the relation of time to the acquisition of knowledge is the motet. We hear a voice as it appears, then a second, a third. At first we hear each note separately, then several together, then all at once. The first voice shapes the second and the third, and it is in turn affected by them. Most significantly, the echo of the first voice in time 1 is itself reshaped in our memory in times 2, 3, and later intervals, as the river of music becomes alive in our mind's ear. The motet, however, is only a first approximation. Possibly the acquisition of knowledge involves a process removed from time entirely, more in the nature of Zen mind, omnipresent and atemporal.

Can we say the same about causation? Did progress in the manufacture of machine tools in nineteenth-century America cause subsequent changes in firearms, bicycles, and the automobile, or were innovations in the former in fact elicited by these other industries? Present technical breakthroughs may be as influenced by the prospect of future events, or driven by past circumstance, as they are affected by the conditions of their existing economic environment. As in modern physics, the problem may depend upon the relative positions of the observer and the object(s) of observation.[24]

Our purpose is not to speculate idly on the meaning of existence, but rather to suggest that a linear notion of time, although perhaps of practical use in thinking about the process of economic growth generated by capital accumulation, seems significantly less helpful in thinking about economic growth driven by technology, that is, information and knowledge. As will be shown in Chapters 5 and 6, the notion of technological change as nonlinear is significant because it suggests that the probability and speed of any breakthrough can be increased and accelerated by structuring the position of the key actors.[25]

To summarize: we propose at least two models of economic growth. The first is generated by capital accumulation and is relatively certain, gradual, monotonic. The second model is driven by technology; it is uncertain, risky, explosive, and nonlinear. The industrial revolution may truly have seemed a "revolution" to those at the time who failed to understand such promethean forces.

Once the properties and character of technology-driven growth are understood, the next important question is the appropriate role of public institutions in shaping and directing it.

One of the ironies of modern economics is that economists have focused their attention on capital accumulation where the case for governmental action is weakest, while ignoring technological change where it is strongest. When investing in a new plant or equipment, a manager can calculate the potential profits and benefits with some degree of certainty. As long as capital markets are competitive and there are good investment opportunities available with reasonable risks, investors need only assess the comparative safety of each opportunity. Moreover, when a firm expands its physical facilities, the benefits accrue to the firm itself and, over time, to its stockholders and customers.

The incentive structure facing decision makers under these

41

circumstances is more or less "correct" in an economic sense. Capital will be attracted to investments and industries likely to yield the highest returns. And it is likely that an appropriate overall level of investment will be made.[26] It can be shown mathematically that if there are no externalities and if the government has not distorted decisions with "partial" taxes, private decisions will lead to an optimal rate of capital accumulation.[27]

The character of technology-driven economic growth is different and implies a different role for government. The benefits and costs are likely to be higher and less certain. Moreover, a larger proportion of the costs will fall upon, and the benefits accrue to, parties not involved in making the technological change.

Let us compare capital and technology growth a bit more specifically. Growth sparked by investment and capital accumulation generally occurs during upswings in the business cycle. Usually it is spread across nearly all sectors. Structural change is not a major factor. Although capital accumulation can cause unemployment when capital is substituted for labor, it generally stimulates output and thus increases employment. Economists call these substitution and output effects.

By contrast, technology-driven growth often causes major structural change, as entire sectors contract and new ones arise. New technologies also impose significant although unforeseen costs that are not detected until years later. Without public involvement, industry will have no incentive to explore the harmful byproducts of new technologies. The idea that efficient resource allocation requires private decision makers to consider the full consequences of their decisions is by no means new. The case for public involvement, however, is far stronger where technology-driven economic growth is likely to produce such costs.

The case for public involvement is equally strong from the perspective of the social benefits of new technologies. We have already introduced the idea of a public good. The firm may have no interest in sharing information with its competitors even though it is in society's interest that it do so. This conflict of private and public interest is itself a strong case for public action.

There is, however, an additional case. Those at the frontiers of science and technology reap the benefits of their labor through the sale of products in the market. At the same time, if information follows the forward and backward pathways described, today's activity can open kingdoms of undreamed possibility. The potential to peek into the future can be of great value to the rest of society, but is one that entrepreneurs bestow essentially free of charge. Since entrepreneurs often capture only a portion of the full economic worth of their labor, the signal they receive from the market may be inaccurate. The problem of public goods stems from the possibility of exclusion. The theory presented here derives from the structure of knowledge.

Remedies for Market Failure

Government has at its disposal many remedies to correct the failures of the market. One solution is simply to provide the public good itself. National defense and a system of justice are examples. Here the political process essentially determines the benefits and transfers their cost to the public.

For a public good like national defense there may be little alternative to direct governmental action. This approach, however, is an inadequate solution to the complexities of technological change. Private decisions are responding to market signals since many benefits are private. But they are failing to consider external costs and benefits. In other words, the market is not working perfectly.

To achieve efficient allocation through public action while preserving market incentives, some advocates have urged a mix of taxation, tax relief, and/or subsidies to various activities. Since Adam Smith, economists have called for taxation of polluting industries and subsidies to industries generating positive social benefits where the tax and subsidy are set equal to the marginal social cost and benefit to society. A variety of legal remedies have been suggested when damage occurs. Strict liability rules as well as properly defined negligence rules coupled with class actions, for example, have been advocated as a good way to internalize some external costs.[28]

All such approaches face the common and enormous problem of measuring public benefits and costs.[29] The problem is most acute with technology-driven economic growth where the uncertainties of technology's positive and negative consequences are often greatest.

In a classic 1960 article, Ronald Coase demonstrated that if interested parties were small in number, bargaining and negotiation could lead to an efficient allocation of resources even in the presence of externalities.[30] If industry A benefits from an advance in industry B, face-to-face bargaining should produce a solution beneficial to both. Even if party A has a right to impose a cost on B, if A and B can bargain face to face, payment by B should properly internalize the cost and would likely still benefit both parties.

In the beginning of a cycle of technological change involving rapid rates of innovation, many beneficiaries will be concentrated in the innovating industry or in closely allied industries. Since their numbers may be relatively small, direct negotiation among the affected parties is usually feasible.

Although a negotiation does not fully solve the problems of evaluating social costs and benefits, it can provide a viable means of assessing these interests, particularly if the relevant government authorities are present. The structure of such public bargaining is the subject of Chapter 8.

Patterns of Governmental Action toward Strategic Industries

Governments throughout history have diverged radically from the ideal arrangements suggested by theory. In fact, government leaders have usually acclaimed the benefits of fashionable new technologies or industries, and depreciated, at times obfuscated, their true costs.

Morton Horwitz ably shows how in nineteenth-century America the law of property, torts, and contracts was harnessed to the needs of the nation's developing industries that included canals, bridges, railroads, insurance, and commerce generally.[31] Public nuisance and other legal doctrines, he charges, threw "a disproportionate share of the burdens of economic growth on the weakest and least organized groups in American society." Technology-driven sectors were almost always ensconced in special rules, exemptions, dispensations, and privileges conveyed by franchises, monopolies, and protections of one form or another.

Throughout history social legislation has tended to reinforce the same pattern. For example, such fundamental rights of labor as the right to unionize, to bargain, and to strike have usually been circumscribed in strategic industries; a grim caricature of this restraint was the slave labor of I. G. Farben. Special worker's compensation systems have been established for strategic industries to reduce the options of employees and to limit their right of appeal and redress. Compensatory systems for victims of these industries have either been nonexistent or intentionally designed to subvert social activism. Environmental standards have generally been weaker than in other sectors and various doctrinal barriers have often curtailed the ability of the public to challenge private and public action.

The biases contained in social legislation also appear in administrative law and practice. Especially where the interests of the government and the regulated coincided, as was often the case in strategic industries, legal doctrine has been interpreted to guard administrative discretion. Special statutes have been created to reinforce administrative procedures and to limit judicial review by giving great weight to the decisions of bureaucrats. Public hearings on administrative action and standing to sue have been similarly circumscribed and firms within these sectors well protected by artful legal defenses.

Strategic Industries and the Theory of Comparative Advantage

In his Nobel address Paul Samuelson noted: "Economics puts its best foot forward when it speaks out on international trade." When asked to name one proposition in all of the social sciences that is both true and nontrivial, he cited the Ricardian theory of comparative advantage: the demonstration that trade is mutually profitable even when one country is absolutely more—or less—productive in terms of every commodity.[32]

What is the relation of this venerable theory to strategic industries? It might be argued that there is an inherent tension between the notion of a strategic industry and the theory of comparative advantage. For example, should not a country forgo its strategic industries and devote its resources to other industries in which it appears more efficient? It could purchase strategic products from its trading partners. Why must the United States have a computer industry, assuming this industry to be strategic? If Japan or Germany produces computers more cheaply, or even comparatively more cheaply (even if in absolute terms our computers are cheaper than theirs—which they are not), is it not in our national interest to emphasize agriculture, or some other industry, and buy computers from Japan or Germany? We will all be enriched by trade.

This static interpretation of comparative advantage produces the following problem. If a country bypasses its growth-inducing strategic industry for the short-term benefits of comparative efficiency, it is possible that that country's long-run productivity would fall, and so also would its standard of living. The country's natural trading partners would grow wealthier by focusing on their strategic sectors. The first country would become poorer. In time, comparative advantage would lead to comparative disadvantage.[33] This was precisely the problem Japanese government officials faced in the early 1950s in deciding whether to support the infant automobile industry (see Chapter 5).

46

In fact the world is not static. Factor supplies and technology change, and one country's comparative advantage today may be another's tomorrow. This point is gradually being recognized by the economics profession. In a classic article, T. M. Rybcznski developed a model of comparative advantage under conditions of growing and changing factor supplies.[34] Economists are also beginning to examine how technological change and economic growth can alter patterns of comparative advantage.[35]

A continuing tension is presented today, however, by the system of international trade rules that actually discourages countries from efficiently subsidizing the development of strategic technologies and industries. The problem arises principally because lawmakers and politicians do not interpret economic theory correctly. To explain this point we must restate the argument about public goods, information, and externalities in the context of international trade.

Consider first an industry that has captured an international market by producing cheaply, but that pollutes extensively. By recognizing the polluter-pays principle, the international community conceded that such a country might not be operating efficiently; in other words, that the costs of its pollution must be internalized by imposing a tax or similar measure.[36] Although internalization of these costs might reduce a country's international market share, or even drive it out of business, if these costs are properly measured, in theory this is an efficient result. Since the benefits of comparative advantage were not being realized, other countries could have produced such goods more "cheaply" when the full costs of their production were considered.

The case is equally persuasive on the benefits side. An industry that grows rapidly, is highly innovative, enhances productivity, and stimulates growth across a spectrum of industries confers benefits not only on its host country, but also upon other countries whose industries are linked to this "strategic" industry.[37] These benefits must also be internalized for full comparative advantage to be realized. If in the long run these industries cannot compete effectively, they appropriately will be driven from the market.[38]

Can two countries possess the same strategic industry? Yes. Two or many countries may possess the same strategic industry, if they correctly assess their dynamic comparative advantage. A method for making such judgments, called the "Trigger Method," is described in Chapter 7.

If several countries pick the same strategic industry, will they not inevitably tilt toward conflict? Are not such countries like scorpions in a bottle, each maneuvering the other for the kill? Not necessarily. A country may decide that a given industry is strategic irrespective of whether that country has any hope of finding a significant international market niche. Semiconductors, computers, and telecommunications may be strategic industries for Hungary, even though Hungary enjoys virtually no international market in these products. Hungary may decide that these industries are strategic for purely domestic reasons, such as their contribution to Hungary's scientific capabilities or their triggering influence on domestic economic growth.

If strategic industries are properly promoted, they will grow rapidly and open rich opportunities for countries to specialize. Intraindustry specialization may be likely and even desirable among countries promoting the same strategic industries. Chapter 11 describes how two or several nations can begin to develop new principles and procedures to capture and apportion the gains from the coordinate development of strategic industries.

A skeptic might ask: Intraindustry specialization works well for the rich countries, but what of the poor nations? Will not the collaboration of the rich and powerful simply permit them to appropriate an even greater share of the world's wealth, by cartels, price fixing, and other means?

Not so. The theory of strategic industries suggests that if every country, rich and poor, correctly emphasizes its own strategic industry, each can enjoy increasing growth rates and surpluses through intraindustry specialization and trade with other similarly situated countries. This increased wealth could then be deployed to purchase necessities, especially higher-value-added (strategic) technologies and other products from countries higher up (more affluent) on the world matrix. Moreover, coordinated growth based on strategic industries should actually be antiinflationary, because intraindustry specialization will reduce costs and increase productivity. It is a hitherto unnoticed winning solution for all.

Chapter 3

The Dilemma of America's High-Technology Industries

We are so absorbed these days with the problems of the automobile, steel, and other mature industries that few of us have studied the serious problems of emerging sectors.[1] In the earnestness of our hopes, or perhaps in collective unwillingness to see, we assumed that all is well. Yet there is ample evidence, albeit scattered, of the difficulties of America's high-technology industries. It is an issue of immense national importance and of continuing public neglect. This chapter suggests that a significant part of this decline can be attributed to our failure to devise an effective growth strategy.

There is a pernicious side in our approach, if this word be used, to the revitalization of the economy. We burden sectors that could otherwise serve as engines of growth, aid those whom the market itself has proved less able, and ask the average citizen, even the poorest citizen, to subsidize these policies. The Reagan administration is perhaps the first to make virtue of such sophistry.

Since at least the early 1960s the international competitive position of U.S. industry has begun broadly to deteriorate. This pattern might not be disturbing if it simply reflected a shift in international comparative advantage. What deserves attention, however, is the evidence of decline even in the country's emerging sectors, across the entire life cycle of technology from research to invention, development, and application. This chapter examines the sources and implications of this decline.

The Evidence of Decline

The most commonly used index of international competitiveness is the share of the export market a country's products maintain over time. From 1962 to 1980 Japan's share of world exports of high-technology products increased from 4 percent to 14 percent, while the German and French shares increased only slightly.[2] The U.S. share declined from 32 percent in 1962 to 27 percent in 1974 and has not recovered since. In third-country markets during the same period, the U.S. share declined from 38 percent to 33 percent, while Japan's share increased slightly, from 5 percent to 6 percent, and Germany and France's shares increased markedly, from 9 percent to 16 percent and from 7 percent to 12 percent, respectively.[3]

Between 1970 and 1980, U.S. industries lost export market shares in virtually all major product groups and categories except in computers, consumer electronics, textiles, and apparel.[4] Losses of market share were greatest in economically significant products, such as steel (4 percentage points) and metal working machinery (5.5 percentage points), followed by high-technology products (3.8 percentage points) and technology-intensive products other than high technology (3.1 percentage points). In specific products, U.S. industries' losses were greatest in aircraft (12.9 percentage points), followed by electronic components (12.2 percentage points), jet engines (8.4 percentage points), metalworking machinery (5.5 percentage points), automobiles (5.3 percentage points), and steel (4.0 percentage points).[5]

Between 1959 and 1978, the international market share of the largest U.S. companies in ten industries declined and U.S. manufacturing and productivity, measured by output per hour, grew at about the slowest annual rate of any major industrialized country.[6] During the recession of 1974–1975, manufacturing dropped sharply in most countries, although most acutely in the United States.

The recovery of U.S. productivity growth has also been among the weakest of the major industrialized countries. In the 1970s U.S. productivity grew the slowest; in East Asia it increased fastest.[7]

The Costs of Adhocracy

Part of these trends can be attributed to the failure of academia, industry, and government to devise and implement sensible policies based on an adequate theory of economic growth. This failing has produced three unfortunate results: existing laws and regulations are generally unresponsive to the needs of high-growth sectors; well-meaning and even beneficial policies are checked by contradicting legislative and regulatory actions; special interests with the greatest political muscle capitalize on the state of uncertainty to secure a disproportionate share of public benefits.

Since the 1960s, the United States has subordinated its historic concern with growth and development to the pressing needs of its minorities and poorest citizens. This has led to a wilderness of entitlements that today threaten to choke whatever momentum the nation's strategic sectors generate. The result is little growth and even less surplus.

The Record of Unresponsiveness

The previous two chapters have suggested that high-growth sectors may have special characteristics and needs. Economic growth driven by technology has often been linked to research. Researchers demand access to a stable supply of cheap capital and a financial environment that tolerates projects that may yield low rates of return in the short run. Firms engaged in research demand effective patent and copyright laws to protect their investment and permit them to appropriate a part of its fruits. Skills and education and the wide dissemination of information have proved critical ingredients for strategic industries, even before the rise of the German chemical industry in the nineteenth century.

The U.S. government has failed to respond adequately to the needs of high-growth sectors relative to the performance of its principal industrial competitors. One example is the vagaries of government procurement and funding for R&D. The U.S. government has displayed little interest during the last decade in focusing government procurement on the needs of emerging sectors. As a consequence many programs have remained haphazard and inefficient, at just the time when Japan and some European powers have begun to devote even greater national resources to these sectors. Between 1964 and 1978, real government R&D expenditures in the United States declined slightly, while between 1964 and 1970, West Germany and France greatly increased R&D spending.[8]

The major proximate factor in declining U.S. government spending for R&D was the sharp cutback in defense and space R&D during the late 1960s and early 1970s. At the same time, other parts of U.S. government R&D failed to offset this reduction.

The vagaries of defense procurement have also had adverse influence. Research has been balkanized by the Defense Department's discouraging large companies from commingling employees involved in civilian and defense work. This has produced one group of researchers who are very concerned about costs and another group who are less so. In 1980 67 percent of U.S. defense procurement was sole source. The system is widely recognized to benefit large incumbent manufacturers at the expense of smaller companies. Defense procurement has also produced surges and declines in the market and sudden surpluses and deficits in engineers and technicians.

The uncertainty of government financial support would present a less acute problem if the capital markets in the

53

United States operated efficiently. In a recent study, *High Cost of Capital,* George Hatsopoulos suggests that the high costs of capital are handicapping American industry, in particular, high-technology industries. From the perspective of national policy, the influence of the high cost of capital on the cash flow of these firms is less important than its influence on their long-term investment decisions.[9]

Dr. Hatsopoulos' most disturbing conclusions are summarized below:

1. Between 1961 and 1973 the real cost of capital services, that is, the cost adjusted for inflation, was practically constant at about 15 percent. After 1973, it rose sharply to over 20 percent and has remained at about this level ever since.[10]

The cost of equity is one of the most important factors affecting the cost of capital services. The pretax cost of equity increased abruptly after 1973 settling around 35 percent per year. The cost of funds is also rising. As bond rates rose from 7 percent to 14 percent over the past decade, the pretax cost of funds rose from 16 percent to 30 percent. In 1961 the cost of equipment, structures, land, and inventories was comparable. By 1981, although the cost of equipment services remained about the same as in 1961, the costs of structures, inventories, and receivables were respectively about 40, 25, and 140 percent higher. For basic industries like steel, which have high fixed costs and small inventories and receivables, these costs are less of a problem. They are considerably more onerous for high-technology companies.[11]

2. As capital becomes more costly relative to labor, firms will forgo investments needed to boost labor productivity. Since 1973, the cost of capital services has increased relative to the cost of labor by more than 20 percent. This adverse trend contrasts with the record of the 1960s when the ratio of capital services to labor declined by 27 percent.

3. Since 1974 the ratio of the return on capital to the cost of capital services has exhibited a severe downward trend, remaining below 80 percent in each of the last eight years, including the years of high economic activity since 1979. More alarming is the decline in the "steady-state" ratio, which av-

erages the cyclical effects of recessions and recoveries. The ratio fell below 100 percent in 1973 and deteriorated to less than 90 percent by 1981. For more than a decade corporate businesses not only in high technology, but also in many other fields, have failed to earn on the average enough to cover their marginal costs of capital.

As a consequence many firms are increasingly interested in acquiring existing businesses, even though a new investment in the same type of business would be uneconomical. Although beneficial to stockholders, such acquisitions contribute little to overall economic growth.

4. In contrast to the United States, the cost of capital fell to about zero in Japan after 1973. This is the pure financing cost net of inflationary gains. Before depreciation this cost is consistently negative. Negative costs arise in profitable firms because interest expenses are deductible from taxable income and the appreciation of fixed assets is not taxed.

In addition to lower capital costs, Japanese industry still enjoys a significant labor cost differential. Hatsopoulos notes that in 1981 the marginal cost per hour for labor in the United States was $10.77 while in Japan it was $6.26.[12] He concludes:

A subtle but very important feature of Japan's industrial financing structure is the way in which banks provide a special impetus to targeted growth industries. By effectively eliminating free market constraints on leverage for companies having large needs for new capital (i.e., fast growth), such additional funds are provided at an artificially low cost during the time when the most long-term and speculative investments must be made. As industries mature and their growth rates subside, Japanese companies generally use retained earnings—a form of equity financing that is far more costly than debt—to retire the loans accumulated during the growth phase.

Thus, we see that Japanese companies enjoy an extraordinarily low cost of capital during the stages when expansion of their market share is most important. The cost of capital increases only after they achieve dominance in a particular industry and can generate high earnings. This aspect of Japan's "target industry" policy has ominous implications for U.S. high technology companies which must rely upon costly equity capital to finance their rapid growth phase.[13]

5. High costs of capital exert a negative influence on the willingness of entrepreneurs to take risks and hence to innovate. Table 1 indicates the amount of government subsidy a U.S. firm would require to offset the advantages Japanese firms enjoy by virtue of their lower costs of funds and capital. Assuming (unrealistically) a government subsidy in Japan of zero, Table 3.1 suggests that for projects requiring 10 years of R&D expenditures (assuming also a product with a market decaying at 10 percent per year), the U.S. government would have to make a subsidy of more than 500 percent of the company's contribution to offset the differential with Japan. The table also indicates that the advantage Japanese firms enjoy increases with a project's length of time. In other words,

TABLE 1

Minimum Subsidy Required in the U.S. Corresponding to Zero Subsidy in Japan Under the Conditions Prevailing in 1981

YEARS R & D	SUBSIDY AS A PERCENT OF CORPORATE CONTRIBUTION
3	40
	160
5	180
	240
10	290
	520

*For profitable firms with past commitments to research and development, substantial the Economic Recovery Act of 1981 provides a marginal R&D subsidy of 25 percent of direct R&D costs. Total R&D costs, which include fringe benefits, occupancy costs, and other overhead expenses, are usually 2 to 2.5 times as high as direct costs. Accordingly, the current R&D subsidy in the U.S. is about 12 to 15 percent of a company's contribution.

Hatsopoulos contends, Japanese firms have an even greater advantage in long-term projects, which are precisely those of greatest importance in most fields of high technology.

An inefficient capital market will induce firms to forgo investments in critical technologies that they might otherwise have sought to develop. Although it is very hard to show a causal link to the cost of capital, there is evidence that private funding for research and development in the United States has declined. For example, between 1964 and 1970, firms in West Germany and France expanded R&D funding at a substantially higher percentage than U.S. firms. Although U.S. businesses surpassed West German and gained on French firms in the 1970s, R&D spending by Japanese firms grew faster than that of U.S. firms by a rate of 50 percent.

The Reagan administration hoped that tax reform would solve the problems high-growth sectors have in financing research. But in fact, the Economic Recovery Tax Act of 1981 is generally conceded to have had only a nominal influence in 1982–1983. In the most acclaimed area of research and development, the tax credit's main impact has been to keep companies from "backing off" on R&D outlays. In other words, some companies are maintaining R&D budgets simply because of improved tax treatment. In a recent survey, few respondents viewed the credit as significant in planning R&D budgets. Indeed, many of those interviewed confessed not even to understand the credit fully.[14]

If the structure of the capital markets frustrates all but the least risky ventures, the uncertainty of legal protection of the fruits of an investment further saps entrepreneurial initiative. The problem is particularly acute in high-technology industries. In part the difficulties are intrinsic to the existing patchwork of protection for intellectual property. Copyright protection is limited to the physical expression of an idea. The entrepreneur must secure patent protection or rely on the tort law of trade secrets to protect the invention itself. Yet securing a patent is expensive and time-consuming. Trade secret protection is surrounded by arcane common law rules and cannot be relied on to vindicate many claims. In many cases, restrictive covenants in employment contracts have not worked effectively and, in any case, do not bind third parties. Finally, the rapidity of technological change and the possibility of imitation by "reverse engineering" render many efforts to seek protection ineffective.

The extent to which patent law even applies to new technologies and products such as genetically engineered microbes or computer programs is also not clear. In *Diamond* v. *Chakrabarty* the Supreme court held that a plasmid, a piece of engineered genetic material, was appropriate for patent protection since it was a "composition of matter" within the meaning of the statute.[15] A second case, *Diamond* v. *Diehr*, decided shortly after, suggested that a computer program could receive patent protection if it was an integral part of an otherwise patentable process.[16] The two cases establish the basic patentability of genetically engineered products and computer programs.

In the area of biotechnology the law is still extremely uncertain. It is often difficult to describe microorganisms and to distinguish them in a legally acceptable manner. Often microorganisms are more complex than chemical or mechanical compounds, and so these analogies are not appropriate. Moreover, many of the processes of isolating and engineering these organisms are not reliably reproducible, further complicating the tasks of description.

Because of the difficulties of description, the Patent and Trademarks Office has often required applicants to place a culture of the microorganism in a permanent cultural depository open to the public. This requirement, however, makes protection against infringement difficult, if not impossible. Since allowing a bacteria to reproduce is not deemed an infringement in itself, there is virtually no way of controlling the distribution of a patented organism. On the other hand, prohibiting the making of an organism can effectively chill many legitimate uses of the depositer's culture.[17]

Although some recent decisions have offered broad protection to computer software, in a number of respects the law here is still unclear. For example, many claims concerning computer programs are rejected on the grounds that they are unoriginal or obvious, despite the fact that they may in fact involve great skill and confer substantial benefits on society.

A central part of the problem is that U.S. policymakers are not accustomed to thinking about new technologies as economically strategic, at least in terms of the patent law. There are no special rules under the patent system to reward inventors who develop technologies that have dramatic effects on industrial growth, particularly where the leap may be marginal, incremental, and ostensibly unexceptional. Computer and other programs are only one of many examples. As noted in Chapter I, most technological improvements are of this incremental character, although many such modest modifications can have profound impacts on economic growth. The patent system seems out of touch with the needs of these entrepreneurs.

A similar insensitivity to the needs of certain technologies is reflected in the antitrust law. The theory of strategic industries suggests that some technologies may have a "communal" character, because these industries confer substantial external benefits, and also because they often require extraordinary investments of expertise, capital, and other resources not easily made by a single firm. As will be seen, the Japanese government's attempts to rationalize the structure of strategic industries, particularly in the early stages of growth, suggests its sensitivity to this issue. The writings of Nelson and Winter offer further theoretical justification for special treatment.[18]

U.S. antitrust law, in particular its application to research joint ventures, may be an important obstacle to the development of institutional arrangements necessary to assure national competitiveness. Collaborative basic research does not pose significant antitrust problems, except where a joint venture substantially forecloses competition. A critical problem, however, is presented when a venture begins to focus on applied research. The antitrust concern is most acute when: one or both parents are already engaged in the research field and each could undertake the research in the absense of the joint venture; there are few other research competitors; and the parents are dominant competitors in the same product market.[19]

From the perspective of industrial policy—in contrast to antitrust policy—collaborative ventures involving even applied research may at times be necessary to assure an industry's competitive position. This is particularly true when a key production technology is involved that may yield substantial economies and technological spinoffs across a range of related technologies and products.

A possible test of this proposition is the Microelectronics and Computer Technology Corporation (MCC), a jointly funded research operation. With start-up funding of $50 million, the cooperative includes Control Data, Digital Equipment, Honeywell, National Semiconductor, Motorola, and Sperry Corporation. Japanese companies have been explicitly excluded.[20] MCC will concentrate on advanced computer architecture, software technology, integrated circuit packaging, and computer-aided design and manufacturing systems. Products will be marketed by its individual members, not by MCC directly.

From a legal standpoint MCC is on the line. The targeted technology stands in a nebulous region between basic and applied research. The subjects are virtually identical to those identified by the Japanese government's research programs. Several of the participants are already engaged in similar research and certainly could undertake it, if necessary, in the absence of the venture. In some cases the participants are dominant companies with few other competitors. As of this writing, the Justice Department appears to have approved the project on an experimental basis. Since this immunity will not insulate the parties from private claims, it is unlikely that the department's position will encourage many firms in other industries to follow MCC's example.

Just as strategic industries may present special problems for financing and organizing research or protecting industrial property rights in rapidly changing technologies, at times they may also demand a particular public infrastructure. One aspect of this infrastructure is often an organized data base. As will be seen in Part II, the first step in the Japanese government's promotion of a strategic industry is the preparation of a systematic statistical record. This helps government tailor incentives to an industry's needs, anticipate adverse effects, and conserve resources. Statistics are also critical in the engineering of consensus.

The U.S. is the only advanced industrialized country that still does not possess a centralized statistical office responsible for compiling basic information about population, natural resources, technology, and other aspects of the national economy and society. The Census Bureau hardly qualifies. As Wassily Leontief notes, the country is a statistical jigsaw wherein each department or agency and most state governments assemble data needed for an immediate purpose. Little attention is given to the uses of these data by other agencies or other sectors.[21]

If the history of strategic industries affords any lesson, it is that the rapid diffusion of information is critical to the process of feedback. Feedback in turn helps multiply technology's benefits from one industry to another, across a wide range of related sectors. Perceiving this process, governments have often sought to accelerate the diffusion of technological information.

During the Carter administration there was a nascent interest in remedying the past failures to capitalize on the products of government-funded research and development. Despite an apparent consensus that the existing patchwork system actually impeded technological diffusion, many creative legislative proposals were permitted to die. One notable exception was the Stevenson-Wydler Act of 1980 that proposed establishing regional centers to coordinate publicly funded research and to diffuse its results. The Reagan administration's budget cuts have effectively repealed this act.

To the extent that technological diffusion even remains of government concern, it exists in scattered, sparsely funded programs. The Experimental Technology Incentives Pro-

61

gram (ETIP) is one example. Administered by the National Bureau of Standards, ETIP was created "to find ways to stimulate R&D and the application of R&D results."[22] ETIP reexamines government procurement and regulatory policies with the hope of promoting innovation and increased productivity. ETIP has done almost nothing to promote technology diffusion in the United States.

There is also a hodgepodge of other uncoordinated efforts. One is the Experimental Research and Development Incentives Program (ERDIP), administered by the National Science Foundation. ERDIP's mandate is to reduce barriers to innovation by helping firms with low levels of R&D link up with federal and university laboratories. The National Science Foundation also directs the National R&D Assessment Program, which studies the role of technology in the economy and makes recommendations. The influence of both programs, as well as the Carter administration's Office of Science and Technology Policy (OSTP) have been nominal.

Another effort is the Department of Commerce's (DOC) Office of Productivity, Technology, and Innovation (OPTI). OPTI's stated objective is to serve as the lead agency in Federal patent policy, to support the Government Inventions Program, to increase productivity in the private sector, and to provide support for the activities related to the Stevenson-Wydler Technology Innovation Act[23] of 1980. The Reagan administration's budgetary allocation for OPTI for fiscal year 1982 was only $700,000, less than one-third of NTDA's appropriations for one of its sponsored research projects.

The remaining program of any significance is that of the National Technical Information Service (NTIS). NTIS disburses technical reports and licenses government patents. With regard to its first function, NTIS acts as a clearinghouse for technical publications. Over one million scientific and engineering reports are on file. In fiscal year 1979, 723,000 paper copies and 2,500,000 microfiche reports were sold at modest prices to permit NTIS to fulfill its congressional mandate of becoming self-supporting.[24]

At present NTIS' licensing activities are in disorder. Although its Office of Government Inventions and Patents (OGIP) is supposed to negotiate exclusive and nonexclusive licenses, it is only one of several agencies so engaged. Other government agencies have an obligation to cooperate. OGIP handles exclusive licenses for the USDA and some exclusive and nonexclusive patents for the Department of the Interior, the National Science Foundation, the Veteran's Administration, and the National Institute of Health.

The Department of Defense (DOD) operates in a world unto itself. Access to DOD patents is difficult for most firms. Licenses are accorded grudgingly, and the terms for royalties, fees, grant-backs, and the like are issued on a take-it-or-leave-it basis.

The cultivation of human skills may be even more important to the future of strategic industries than the dissemination of technological information. During the nineteenth century, imperial Germany vigorously promoted science education. The Japanese Ministries of Education and International Trade and Industry, and the Science and Technology Agency have shown an unswerving commitment to education in science and technology in the postwar period.

The Reagan administration is stripping most of the remaining tissue from higher science education. The National Science Foundation budget has been cut from $70 million in fiscal year 1981 to an estimated $20 million in 1982 and $15 million in 1983. Overall decreases exceeded $1 billion by the fall of 1982. In addition, $6 million in funds for research libraries and about $3 million in funds for college libraries was to be eliminated in 1983.

The retrenchment of government support is paralleled by disturbing demographic trends. Between 1970 and 1979, the number of scientific and technical personnel grew more slowly in the United States than in Japan, France, or Germany. The differences are even more striking when one recognizes that the U.S. labor force increased by 24 percent, the Japanese by about 6 percent, and the French by roughly 5 percent. West Germany's labor force actually declined by 6 percent during this same period. Thus, despite increases in available human resources, science and technology were given correspondingly less weight in the United States.[25]

The character of the technical work force also appears in transition. There has been a noticeable "graying" of America's engineering work force as the percentage of younger engineers in the pool has fallen. Since the obsolescence of knowledge occurs rapidly, especially in areas where R&D is extensive, an aging engineering work force is likely to be less creative.

The structure of government can also have a central influence on the development of strategic industries. In unitary systems, government usually attempts to limit cutthroat competition between producers, particularly where there is a risk of duplication of effort or waste of resources. This is viewed less as an obstruction of technological development and more as a means of correcting market failure.

These days in the federal government, as well as states, cities, municipalities, and townships throughout the nation vie to develop indigenous high-technology industries. The freedom to experiment is one of the strengths of federalism. Yet the current frenzy over high technology is pitting one community against another, and in some cases seducing regions into allocating resources to high technology that could be put to better use elsewhere. "Excess competition" is how most Japanese would characterize this situation and one result, as a recent *Business Week* survey tells us, is too few jobs chasing rising expectations.[26] Although there are some constitutional precedents that recognize the need for interstate alliances, few communities have sought to confederate their interests into mutual gains. This is a failing of national leadership.

Contradictions and Conflicts in Government Policy

When government is remiss in recognizing the importance of certain industries or technologies, it merely denies these sectors the support they need. In some cases, however, by intent or indifference it actively obstructs development.

The point is perhaps most powerfully made by U.S. export controls. For years the U.S. export-licensing system has been criticized by industry, Congress, academics, and many trading partners. Although hard to measure, export controls appear to be having an acute impact on the competitiveness of some high-technology firms engaged in east-west trade. The criticisms can be summarized as follows:

- The system suffers from needless delays and an excessive amount of uncertainty, exacerbated by a cumbersome interagency review process and the time-consuming case-by-case approach to applications.
- Because of the diffusion of responsibility within agencies there is also a lack of administrative responsiveness and forthrightness. This discourages efforts by American business to expand exports.
- The system suffers from a lack of adequate guidance. Too much discretion is allowed to midlevel administrators and too little influence is exerted by those technically qualified and sensitive to the changing environment of U.S.-U.S.S.R. relations and the vital role of exports in the U.S. economy.
- Lists of controlled technologies are too restrictive. By attempting to control items unilaterally, the practice incurs the antagonism of foreign exporters who need reexport licenses for technology of U.S. origin. Unilateral control here puts U.S. businesses at a competitive disadvantage. More products are controlled here than in western Europe and Japan. Moreover, the system fails to consider adequate availability of foreign products.

In assessing these criticisms, a recent study by the Office of Technology Assessment concedes that delays are the most serious problem.[27] Although delayed cases still represent only about 3 percent of all license applications, their number is growing. At the same time the number of exceptions is also increasing, which suggests that the increase in applications has substantially eroded the quality of decisions. The study concluded that better, not more, administrators of the program were required. The situation remains unremedied.

The problem of overrestrictive regulations is also unallayed. The OTA study notes that large corporations engaged in trade with the east incur costs related to licensing of as much as $1 million per year.

The largest costs of U.S. export controls, however, are indirect and not easily measured. The OTA notes that many eastern nations now view the U.S. as untrustworthy and have turned to other suppliers. This has strengthened the competitive position of Japanese and other exporters who already have an advantage from relatively lax enforcement of existing controls.

Export controls are only one part of the more general problem of the impact of regulation on innovation and productivity. Regulation imposes technical constraints, delays, and uncertainty, all of which increase costs and undermine a firm's willingness to accept risks.[28] Neither the federal government nor Congress regularly assesses the impacts on innovation of new or existing legislation or regulations. Although there is little empirical evidence that existing regulations impose greater burdens on emerging industries than on other industries, they cause harmful and needless uncertainty. By saddling mature industries with unnecessary costs they reduce the demand of these industries for the products of emerging high-growth sectors.

In addition to the conflicting demands that regulation imposes on some high-growth sectors, the structure of U.S. labor and trade law may also contribute to a polarization of industrial relations just at a time when adaptation, if not accommodation, is required. In many industries the positions of management and labor are opposed and growing farther apart. To many labor leaders the introduction of microprocessor-driven technologies such as robots, NC machine tools, flexible manufacturing, and electronic offices will have subtle, at times insidious, consequences on the workplace. Some suggest that the new technologies will strip a worker's control over the pace and direction of work, and by surveillance, electronic scabbing, and other means shift subtly the balance of power to management's favor. While some labor leaders cling to existing job classifications and press for new "technological rights," the courts at the same time are encouraging an equally unconciliatory position in management.

In 1981 the Supreme Court in *First National Maintenance Corporation* v. *National Labor Relations Board (NLRB)* held that an employer does not have a duty to bargain over an economically motivated decision to close part of its business.[29] Displaying the usual solicitude for managerial freedom, the court fasioned an apparently per se rule excluding partial closings from the mandate to bargain. Although the case does not deal with the decision to introduce a new technology, its logic would seem even more compelling for such decisions that have less immediate impacts on employment.

The absence of an effective program of adjustment assistance increases the likelihood of conflict. Unlike Japanese law, adjustment assistance under U.S. law is tied to impacts from trade. The United States does not currently have a structurally depressed industries law, nor have adjustment assistance programs ever been effectively used to train a corps of skilled workers demanded by emerging sectors. (The training program established in Massachusetts suggests that not all high-tech industries require high-level skills.) The policy of the Reagan administration is only the most recent example in a history of indifference.

The absence of an effective program of adjustment assistance, judicial preservation of management's entitlements, and labor's insistence on new rights bodes increasing alienation, frustration, and conflict. Although there is evidence of a new groping for more flexible work rules relating to hours, job assignments, seniority, wages, and incentives,[30] the critical question is whether these adjustments will come in time to meet the demands of foreign competition. Moreover, as industrial production systems become more electronically synchronized and dependent, and as rising prices drive high-technology companies like Atari to cheaper cost havens, it is likely that labor relations over new technologies will become even more troubled.

Special Dispensations

Adhocracy not only misallocates resources and imposes needless burdens on strategic sectors, it also permits politically powerful groups to capture an undeserved share of society's wealth.

A criticism often directed against those who would bolster emerging sectors is that special attention smacks of favoritism. Yet for years the United States Congress and the administration have granted special benefits, at times windfall profits, to favored sectors without rhyme or reason. Table 2 indicates the benefits extended in 1980 to particular industries, which totaled $303.7 billion or roughly 13.9 percent of GNP. The table reveals some of the absurdities of current practice: semiconductors received no tax breaks while forest products obtained $455 million in 1980; semiconductors received $55 million in R&D grants, 1 percent of the 5.8 billion allocated to the nuclear industry.

The inequities also include special preferences allowed through the tax system. In general, larger companies within a given industry pay lower effective tax rates than medium and smaller companies. Moreover, these subsidies do not include the additional billions paid by American consumers to industries protected from foreign competition by tariffs, quotas, and orderly marketing arrangements.[31]

If adhocracy generated a significant surplus, its virtues might be conceded. But in fact it appears to be a central cause of the country's present economic difficulties. This has particularly harsh implications for the poor. A recent study by Richard Nathan of Princeton University of the cuts in domestic federal spending under the Reagan administration notes that poor people, particularly the working poor, are more affected than the treasuries of state or local govern-

TABLE 2

Fiscal Year 1980 Goverment assistance to selected industries (in Millions of Dollars)

INDUSTRY	RESEARCH AND DEVELOPMENT	OTHER DIRECT EXPENDITURES	TYPE OF ASSISTANCE — TAX EXPENDITURES	PROCUREMENT	OUTSTANDING LOANS AND LOAN GUARANTEES
Coal	$942	$120	$530	$0	$0
Forest products	14	130	455	49	0
Dairy	11	347	0	448	0
Nuclear	5,810	113	0	1,628	0
Cotton	8	232	0	0	0
Petroleum	273	3	3,350	3,733	0
Commercial Fisheries	24	3	0	0	103
Maritime Industry	16	585	70	4,075	6,342
Railroad Industry	55	2,491	0	3	2,064
Housing Industry	53	6,760	23,225	3,044	157,708
Automobiles and Highways	108	1,394	0	1,217	940
Aviation	1,393	2,994	0	7,159	558
Steel	5	45	50	229	393
Semiconductors	55	0	0	4,600	0
Textiles	0	60	0	428	0

SOURCES: Office of Management and Budget, budget of the U.S. government 1980; Congressional Budget Office. "Tax Expenditures: Current Issues and Five-Year Budget Projections for Fiscal Years 1981–1985," report to the Senate and House committees on the budget. Washington, D.C.: Office of Federal Procurement Policy. *Federal Contract Awards* (1979); General Accounting Office. *A Methodology for Estimating Costs and Subsidies from Federal Credit Assistance Programs* (1980).

ments.[32] Between October 1 and December 31, 1982 in New York City alone, about 12,000 people lost their A.F.D.C. (Aid to Families and Dependent Children) benefits and 39,000 others suffered reductions in benefits. In addition, 42,000 lost their food stamps and more than 1 million had their food-stamp allotment reduced; 4,500 lost Comprehensive Employment Training Act jobs; 33,000 lost training opportunities; 450,000 poor people will pay more for housing, and 30,000 will either lose school lunches or pay more for them.

A special study by the Congressional Budget Office reinforces Professor Nathan's findings. It concluded:

Gains from federal tax reductions rise substantially with household income. In 1983, for example, households with incomes less than $10,000 will pay on average about $120 less in taxes than they would have under prior law, while households with incomes over $80,000 will pay on average about $15,000 less. Total federal revenue losses will be about $82 billion in 1983, and about 85 percent of these reductions will benefit households with incomes over $20,000.

Reductions in federal benefit payments for individuals will be greatest for households with incomes below $10,000. In 1983, households with incomes less than $10,000 will lose on average about $360 in federal benefits, while those with incomes over $80,000 will lose on average about $120. Total federal savings will be about $17 billion in 1983, about two-thirds of which will come from reductions affecting households with incomes below $20,000.

About 60 percent of the savings from reductions in grants to state and local governments will come from programs targeted toward low income individuals or those receiving public assistance. Total reduction in grants to state and local governments (excluding grants for direct benefit programs) will range from $12 billion to $14 billion annually during fiscal years 1982 through 1984.[33]

In 1982 the poverty rate rose to 15 percent, the highest level in the United States since the mid-1960s.[34]

The Reagan administration's cuts in entitlements may not be unfair simply because they deprive the poor of necessities. Many believe these benefits were never deserved and that such sacrifices are now needed to rekindle a national spirit of growth. The real reason present cuts are so unfair is that they are necessitated by national prodigality, for which the poor, of all America's citizens, have been least responsible.[35]

Patterns of Decline and Neglect in Selected High-Technology Industries

There is no in-depth study of the extent to which America's high-tech industries are losing competitive advantage. The 1982 assessment of the Cabinet Council on Commerce and Trade and the 1982 Report of the National Academy of Sciences are superficial and incomplete. We are left to integrate piecemeal assessments of various government commissions and studies. Although the record in no way confirms that a crisis is at hand, it suggests the trends and issues that bear watching, and attests to a decade of official indifference and neglect.

Although the U.S. is still leading in some segments of the semiconductor and computer markets, the rate of growth of Japanese exports has outstripped U.S. exports since 1976 for semiconductors and 1978 for computers. There are also other trends.

First is the increasing costs of production equipment and the financial difficulties of many smaller semiconductor firms. Capital intensity, the amount of dollars needed to produce a dollar of sales, is a continuing problem for many high-technology industries. Expenditures for new plant and equipment for semiconductor devices increased from $61 million in 1965 to $238 million in 1975 to $1,596 in 1980. Moreover, the stock market has not offered a panacea as a source of capital. Second, many American firms are experiencing difficulties in recruiting able and experienced electrical engineers. Finally, the U.S. semiconductor industry has been unable to meet the demand for some memory products. Japanese firms were able to fill a breach in supply by acquiring approximately 42 percent of the 16 dynamic random access memory (16 RAM) market. The event was significant because

71

at the time the 16 RAM was one of the industry's most profitable products and critical to the development of the next generation of memory devices. The major Japanese companies now appear to be moving aggressively into the next generation of memory chips, the 256 dynamic RAMs.[36]

Telecommunications has continued its high rate of growth, although there are signs here too of declining international competitiveness. For example, although the output per employee in telephone communications has steadily increased, the annual rate of change from 1976–1981 was 5.8 percent, whereas the average annual change for 1951–1981 was 6.2 percent.

Profits have also fluctuated. In general pretax profits decreased from a high of $4,423 million in 1967 to a low of $3,194 million in 1972 and remained at that level until 1976 when profits reached $4,518 million. Profits increased to $6,893 million in 1978 and decreased to $6,049 in 1979.[37]

The more serious long-term questions, however, are raised by the reorganization of the Bell System. In the past the integrity of the Bell System contributed greatly to the fundamental breakthroughs in information and systems theory. It is unknown to what extent the divestiture of the operating companies, even in modified form, will interfere with the innovation process.

Nathan Rosenberg in his testimony in the case of *United States* v. *AT&T* touched issues of the reorganization's impact on research which will not be resolved for years.

The nature of the process and product of research and development makes the negotiation and enforcement of research and development contracts very difficult. The outcome of the research and development process is inherently highly uncertain, and thus in many instances it is virtually impossible to define successful fulfillment of a research and development contract at the outset. In order even to perceive the areas in which research and development offers potential benefits, it is necessary for the beneficiary to have substantial knowledge of the state of the technology and its potential. It is therefore necessary to have substantial in-house expertise.

Evaluation and application of the contractual output also requires in-house technical expertise by the client. Thus, any attempt to purchase research and development via contract would result in substantial duplication of scientific and technical staff.

Moreover, to meet the needs of the operating companies for research and development most effectively, any organization providing such research and development should be capable of securing the benefits of cross-fertilization due to information exchange among ongoing research and development projects. It should also maintain sufficient continuity in the provision of these services to benefit from accumulated specialized knowledge. In theory, this could be achieved through use of a single, non-integrated provider of research and development. However, exclusive reliance on a single, non-integrated provider of research and development by a firm exposes it to risks arising from opportunistic behavior on the part of the provider of research and development, who will be in a position to exploit his control over an essential input to the client firm. . . .

Either proposed remedy would have an adverse impact upon the breadth of Bell Labs research. Bell Labs remains a major performer of fundamental research in a wide range of areas. The breadth of Bell Labs' research effort, and the range of disciplines tapped by Bell Labs, are important factors in its innovative performance.

It is highly probable, in fact, that many of the most important scientific research problems are becoming increasingly located at the periphery of established disciplines and are therefore becoming increasingly interdisciplinary in nature. For example, much of present-day materials research, at Bell Labs and elsewhere, is highly interdisciplinary, involving distinctive roles for, among others, chemists, metallurgists, physicists, and ceramicists.

Moreover, the pursuit of a wide range of economic functions within the present Bell System, in both manufacturing and service, increases the likelihood that a research finding in any one of the diverse research areas within Bell Labs will yield a benefit somewhere within the Bell System. Such an awareness underlies the present willingness of Bell Labs to undertake fundamental research in fields as diverse as polymer chemistry, radio astronomy, solid state physics, plasma physics, superconductivity, and acoustics.

Thus, the fragmentation of the Bell System, whether by divestiture of Western Electric and Long Lines, or by divestiture of the operating companies, would cause a narrowing in the breadth of the research activities pursued within Bell Labs and would have a consequent adverse effect upon its research performance. Such an impact reflects the fact that the interdisciplinary, mission-oriented research team is a critical aspect of the successful research process at Bell Labs.[38]

Although it is clearly too early to assess the impact of AT&T's reorganization, AT&T is indisputably under fire. One area in which it appears increasingly vulnerable is in communications gear, an industry in which NEC and other Japanese manufacturers are already making substantial inroads. American Bell's huge fixed costs and bureaucratic structure prompted one marketing official to remark, "It's like trying to turn around a 500 pound marshmallow." In fiber optics, officials at Bell Laboratories already concede that AT&T cannot match Japan in the technology of laser diodes, the light source used in optical communications, and that Japan offers by far the broadest range of optical fiber products. Unanswered questions are whether increased competition will stimulate innovation in both countries and merely lead to a restructuring of the market with an even richer range of products, or whether in the long run reorganization will undermine the Bell System's unique research capability.

Since the early 1970s the machine-tool industry and even the new field of computer-integrated manufacturing have been cited as industries with troubled futures. A study commissioned by the Air Force notes three danger spots in the machine tool industry.

1. *On fragmentation:*

... [T]he historical trend in the U.S. machine tool industry toward fragmentation into relatively small, narrowly specialized companies is slowing down or even reversing. However, fragmentation in the industry remains a handicap to technological advancement. One regrettable concomitant of fragmentation is the holding of technology as company proprietary secrets, to the extent that one can observe the wasteful reinventing of technology already developed elsewhere. The current trend is toward a higher degree of cooperation, but attempts in this direction are still hampered by old prejudices as well as a genuine fear that U.S. antitrust laws might be applied. Even if joint efforts may be successfully defended in court, the prospect of litigation costs deters many companies from attempting cooperation.[39]

2. On the obsolescence of manpower:

Because for decades the machine tool industry has been unpopular among younger workers and has attracted them in declining numbers, the machine tool work force is aging rapidly and going into retirement. Replenishment is slow. Further to the detriment of a trained work force, machine tool technology has been treated largely as an art and has virtually disappeared from the curricula of secondary schools and universities. The National Machine Tool Builders Association (NMTBA) now estimates a 25% shortage of qualified personnel in the industry at all levels. Aggravating the shortage of manpower is the need for retraining the existing work force to learn new skills or technologies.[40]

3. On the inadequacy of information flows:

Many avenues exist for transmitting information within the machine tool community. Professional societies such as the Society of Manufacturing Engineers (SME), American Society of Mechanical Engineers (ASME), and Numerical Control Society (NCS), along with trade associations such as NMTBA and National Tooling and Machinery Association (NTMA), and several trade publications, do excellent work in keeping their members and clients informed. The U.S. Department of Defense supports several information centers. . . . However, all of these means for tying the U.S. industry together seem inadequate. The principal problems are that the community is limited in size, tradition-bound, and fragmented. Moreover, most of the machine tool building concerns are small, discrete operations that, in serving their specialized customers, function apart from government-stimulated organization and the general community. Small businesses are typically owned and operated by people who were originally craftsmen and they do not usually employ engineers or other university-trained people. As a result, they are, with some outstanding exceptions, nonparticipating members of the technology-exchanging community. . . .

One of the potentially significant conduits for information flow, the standardization process, is ignored in many areas and existing standards are not uniformly implemented in the U.S. The Task Force found that U.S. participation in international standards development is generally inadequate and that domestic development of standards is particularly hampered by the absence of sufficient user participation.[41]

Critical data with respect to the machine-tool industry are generally bleak. Profits, for example, have remained weak. Average net income (as a percent of sales) dropped from 12.1 percent in 1967 to a low of -2.7 percent in 1970. Net income remained low in the early 1970s, although it rose slightly to 12.0 percent in 1979 and 12.2 percent in 1981.[42] During the last 15 years profits have generally declined, only recently returning to their 1967 level.

According to the 1983 U.S. Industrial Outlook of the Department of Commerce, high interest rates and low capacity have weakened the demand for machine tools. Industries that use machine tools, such as aerospace, farm machinery, mining machinery, and household appliance manufacturers have cut orders down to only those machine tools necessary for replacement.

Rates of productivity have also remained the same. Output per hour decreased in the early 1970s and returned to 1967 levels in 1977. The average annual percent change from 1976–81 was 0.6.[43]

As in other industries expenditures for capital are increasing. In 1958 the machine-tool industry spent $30.5 million, which increased to $74.2 million in 1965 and $105 million in 1969. Capital expenditures dropped to $39.1 million in 1971, but rose again to $199.4 in 1979 and $241 million in 1980.[44]

Trade statistics with respect to machine tools are equally

dismal. Japan's share of the world market is fast closing in on the U.S. share, and there has been an accelerating penetration by Japanese manufacturers into the U.S. market for two key products, NC machining centers and NC punching machines.

The many troubles of the group of related industries concerned with the development of the oceans rarely comes to public view. John Craven, one of the most experienced and astute students of ocean engineering, offered this critique of federal ocean policy a decade ago. His comments are even more pertinent today.

The organization of the federal government for the management of ocean resources is and has been in a state of flux for the past decade. . . .

As contrasted with science federally-supported ocean technology relating to marine resources is very small and at best parasitic on more generalized resource programs. A corollary of this statement is that the U.S. Navy is essentially the sole repository of federally-funded technology development of relevance to the ocean resource industry. For each resource, therefore, ocean development in the United States is either the result of industry initiative, spin-off from military research, or sweep-up from the National Science Foundation, Sea Grant, the Environmental Protection Agency and collateral agency programs or parasitic developments utilizing operating programs of the Department of Defense, NASA, AEC, Coast Guard as host.

The investment by the federal government for ocean resources is limited to the construction subsidy of the Maritime Administration and the ports, harbor, and waterways development projects of the Army Corps of Engineers. These are the largest single monetary investments by the federal government. . . .

OCEANIC OIL

Of greatest significance is that the United States has virtually excluded itself from exploiting off-shore oil in waters not under sovereignty or competing as a producer (e.g. complete U.S. flag operation) in off-shore waters under other sovereignty. Since oil is still the most competitive energy resource, even at the high consumer cost, demand is essentially unregulated. Thus, national goals for consumption are created by unregulated demand, while the decisions for production are dictated by a profit mechanism which is almost totally unrelated to economic determinism and is, in fact, determined by a rigid and inflexible national security policy. . . .

OCEANIC MINERALS

. . . The development of ocean minerals for the United States' interests is almost entirely dependent on the initiative and risk of private enterprise. This does not seem to be lacking, but when compared with the nationally-supported explorations of France, Germany, Japan, and the USSR, there is some cause for concern.

FISHERIES

The first requirement of systems management is the establishment of national goals for oceanic fishing. In spite of a recommendation by NACOA that such goals be established, they have not been (even on an advisory basis), and they are not likely to be. . . .

The United States fishing industry is unable to react to this potential for reduction of imports for a number of reasons. Among the main reasons are the facts that:

1. Overfishing has depleted many stocks, and an increase in domestic fishing must come as a decrease in fishing by other nations.

2. Over-capitalization is the characteristic of most domestic fisheries, since there is no limit of entry (although there is a limit on catch), and the entry capitalization is low.

3. Foreign competition is efficient, subsidized in many cases, nationally managed, and exists where the fish are to be found, even if it is off the coasts of the United States.

4. Our coastal and inland fisheries are subject to other competition for use of the coastal zone—competition in terms of job effectiveness of land-based occupations as compared with the difficult task of fishing.

A more subtle factor arises from the competition with agricultural food and feed. The Department of Agriculture is an effective

78

manager of United States food production through a complex regulatory mechanism involving, in the past, production controls through the land bank system, and at present by a less complex—but nonetheless effective—system. . . . In 1968, the total consumption of fish in the United States reached a peak of more than 16 billion pounds, because the low price of fish made it attractive as an animal feed. As a result of agricultural regulators, the price of soybeans became competitive on the United States market, and the farmer feed business suddenly switched. Fortunately for domestic fishing and for the export-import balance, the collapse of the United States menhaden market was absorbed by world demand for fishmeal. The essential point is that the United States as a nation was denying itself the economic benefit of a low-cost protein produced by its own industry as a result of its own sub-optimized market protection mechanisms. . . .

The net national system decision, if present national policy continues, is that the United States shall import the great majority of its fish products, maintaining a fixed or nearly fixed fishery in tuna and salmon; will maintain a limited industry for high quality shrimp, lobster, and oyster; and will preserve a quaint set of geriatric fishing fleets of primary interest to tourists and artists.[45]

Although the biotechnology industry is robust and growing, a recent OTA report notes that there are already potential trouble spots. Chronic capital shortages and the inability of many firms to achieve economies of scale may become serious as the cost of equipment rises and the stock market's honeymoon with the industry ends. The OTA report also cites the weaknesses of the industry's productive base, which will have a direct affect on competitiveness once current research begins to yield products. The OTA study cites the underdevelopment of instrumentation and the inadequacy of data bases which, coupled with the constraints many universities have put on faculty participation in private companies, restrict the rate of technological diffusion.

Like many other high-technology industries, biotechnology firms are subjected to many controls, some of which appear to be unreasonable. Laboratory viruses and bacteria are unilaterally controlled. Equipment having genetic engineering applications is controlled if laser-based or if embedded with a microprocessor or a computer. Labware, glasses, mixers, and other equipment are embargoed to some nations. Technical data are exportable if accompanied by a letter of assurance, while all other exports of technical data require a validated license.

For over forty years the U.S. pharmaceuticals industry has been among the most successful sectors of the world economy. Between 1940 and 1960 American firms dominated the world market, controlling one-third of international trade in medicinals, and accounted for the vast majority of research and new products. Since the early 1960s, the U.S. share of the world pharmaceuticals research, innovation, production, sales, and exports has declined. The report of the Cabinet Council on Commerce and Trade notes:

Although U.S.-owned firms' expenditures for pharmaceutical research at home and abroad are large and growing, they are far exceeded by the expansion of foreign research efforts. The share of world pharmaceutical research located in the United States has fallen from about two-thirds in the early 1960s to above one-third today. Throughout the period, research accelerated in Japan, the Federal Republic of Germany, and the United Kingdom.

Innovation in the industry has stabilized for the last two decades although these rates have declined sharply from the 1950s. At the same time the average cost per innovation has risen drastically in the last 20 years. The fundamental reason for the dramatic increase in the costs of innovation lies in the substantially greater number of clinical trials and toxicological tests required to bring a new compound to market. The increase in costs has forced all industrial nations to engage in extensive pretesting and selection in new drugs. The result has been a worldwide decline in the rate of new products introduced. Foreign rates, however, have declined less sharply since the 1950s than U.S. levels.

Pharmaceutical products have traditionally provided a surplus for the U.S. trade balance. Yet, this surplus in absolute terms is not significantly greater than that of Switzerland, the Federal Republic of Germany, or the United Kingdom which export a far larger percentage of their production than the United States. The competitiveness of U.S. exports has also been weakened by non-tariff barriers . . . and by ever burdensome FDA testing and licensing procedures. This lower level of exports as a proportion of domestic production provides the United States with a comparable share of world pharmaceutical exports, a share which has markedly deteriorated since 1950. In part, this low proportion of production devoted to exports is associated with the relatively more extensive multi-national scope of U.S.-owned firms. Equally important is the traditional relative unimportance of exports to U.S. producers, as may be seen by a comparison of total U.S. exports to GNP. From this perspective, the U.S. pharmaceutical industry is typical of other sectors of the American economy.[46]

The early successes of the U.S. civil aircraft industry depended essentially on four conditions: a continuous flow of technological advance benefiting both the civil and military sides of aviation; large domestic demand that could support new programs; expanding foreign markets that could bridge cyclical depressions in the domestic market; and fierce domestic competition among airframe and engines manufacturers and their suppliers, which stimulated the production of superior products. For most of the 1950s and 1960s, the American industry benefited from economies of scale that permitted marketing and production risks to be spread over a large customer base. Virtually all of these key conditions have changed today.

Since 1978 there has been a sharp decline in export sales of civilian aircraft, from 4,399 units in 1978 to 1,850 in 1982. U.S. world market share has also sharply declined as the structure of the international market itself has changed.

Foreign aircraft manufacturers are increasingly willing to offset a competitive U.S. product by offering more favorable financing terms and ancillary benefits to purchasers. These include an offer of other high-technology exports such as weapons or a bilateral agreement favorable to the purchasing nation. Military aircraft export sales are of increasing significance to European manufacturers, particularly the French. Foreign aircraft industries are largely owned and controlled by the government. Linkages have helped mitigate the cost of oil imports and have promoted close cooperation between Europe's civil and military aircraft programs. For this reason foreign producers are willing to trade profitability on a sale of aircraft to achieve a high technological capability or expected returns in other critical industrial sectors.

The U.S. civil industry is unable to respond, as its foreign competitors do, with linked services. Once a U.S. company's proposal is rejected, its product can be "locked out" from an entire regional market for more than 20 years. A progressive lockout from global markets sharply erodes economies of scale. Since 60 percent of U.S. sales are from exports, the American industry is in an increasingly vulnerable position. Deprived of its global market, it will be unable to continue to offer products of the quality and price now available. Some analysts even suggest that the industry will be unable to sustain the level of technology, skills, and manufacturing essential to coping with a national emergency.[47]

From 1970 to 1979 after-tax profits as a percentage of sales rose from 1.8 percent to 5.1 percent, but since 1979 they have declined to 3.4 percent. According to the U.S. Industrial Outlook, the chief causes are the high costs of civilian programs and the expansion of military programs. Expenditures for new plant and equipment have also risen, from $57.1 million in 1972 to $686.1 million in 1981, an annual average growth rate of 4.5 percent.[48]

Productivity and the stock price of major aircraft manufacturers have followed a similar cyclical, generally declining pattern.[49]

Trends in the aerospace industry are equally disturbing. Exports of civilian aircraft units have declined from 4,399 in 1978 to 1,850 in 1982. Although aerospace vehicles and equipment increased, most were of military origin.[50]

Since 1978 deregulation and the increase in world oil prices have placed a premium on fuel-efficient, smaller aircraft, particularly commuter craft serving less than 1,000 miles. Virtually all new projects to develop commuter airlines are now under the control of foreign companies, supported by their governments. The U.S. government will purchase about

5,000 commuter aircraft over the next two decades, almost all of which will be of foreign manufacture. Boeing and McDonnell Douglas are the only U.S. manufacturers that have been financially capable of offering new or derivative products in the short- or medium-size ranges above the commuter plane. Douglas may proceed with a joint venture with Fokker to build a 100-passenger MDF-100. The Saab-Fairchild SF-340 will be manufactured in Sweden using U.S. technology.

The aircraft and missile industries have the highest costs of R&D of any manufacturing industry. During the past decade there has been a general retrenchment in government sponsored research and as a result technical advances have declined sharply. Currently Japan and Germany exceed the United States in R&D excluding expenditures for defense and space.

The U.S. lead in space is also slipping. The number of U.S. launches has fallen steadily from 26 in 1976 to 13 in 1980. The U.S.S.R. launches many more vehicles each year than the United States. Even with its arcane vehicles, France is increasing its commercial as well as military launches each year. The rate of Japanese launches has also increased to 3 per year.[51]

The Cabinet Council's Working Group reached these conclusions on the increasingly weak competitive position of the United States.

1. Payloads and launch dates are manipulated by NASA with more regard to the demands of the military services than to commitments to commercial users. As a U.S. priority, manned space is taking third place behind military and communication satellites. The only manned space activity in the near future will be the use of crews on the Space Shuttle.

2. The estimated requirements for space launch services by the mid-1980s will exceed the capacity of the available shuttles by a factor of 2, yet the United States will not

have modern expendable launch vehicles available to augment the shuttle capacity.

3. The U.S. capacity to meet the future demand for space launch services, whether military or civil, is inadequate.

4. Existing launch services are overpriced because there have been few technological improvements in expendable launch vehicles. The U.S. has wrongly assumed that all launch services would be handled by the shuttle.

5. In the next few years Japan will assume the supporting role for all launches in the Pacific rim.

In contrast to the United States, Japan has pursued a steady, intensifying program of support for the aerospace industry since the enactment of the basic Aircraft Industry Promotion Law of 1958. Lacking any significant domestic market, and hamstrung by constitutional restrictions on rearmament, the Japanese government initially emphasized licensing. This strategy produced a substantial transfer of technology that grew from Japan's first commercial venture, the YS-11 project begun in 1957. Although technologically successful, the lack of a developed marketing network frustrated the profitability of the YS-11.

Since 1978 MITI (The Japanese Ministry of International Trade and Industry) has accelerated its support for the aircraft industry. In 1978 Japan and Italy entered into a joint venture to coproduce the new Boeing 767, a 230-passenger aircraft. The government underwrote 50 percent of the amount needed for Japan's part of the agreement and Mitsubishi Heavy Industries, Kawasaki Heavy Industries, and Fuji Heavy Industries participated. In December 1979 the government put up two-thirds of the initial financing for a tripartite industrial arrangement among Ishi Kawajima-Harima, Mitsubishi, and Kawasaki Heavy Industries to produce a new fan jet engine with Rolls Royce. In the following year the agency commenced support for the YXX, a 100– 150 seat narrow-bodied jet designed to replace the Boeing 707 and the Douglas DC–8. Finally in November 1980 Japan signed an agreement with Fokker to merge development of the XXX with Fokker's F–29.

As in other areas MITI has vigorously underwritten the costs of research and development. The most ambitious project is a five-year developmental program that will construct twenty new facilities including an acoustic wind tunnel, a computer-aided digital experiment simulation for aerodynamic analysis, and a robotic test facility for high-speed propellars. The cost of the project will exceed $220 million.

In February 1983 Japan also launched its first operational communications satellite. The satellites will be the first to utilize the 20–30 gigahertz communications frequency band. This is significant because it will permit Japan to expand its use of available space, squeezing satellites closer together with only about 2 degrees separation in the geostationary orbital arc. The Japanese space program will soon launch a satellite for TV broadcast and an orbiting electron beam accelerator for space experiments with particle accelerators. The National Research Council's report suggests that it is only a matter of time before Japan dominates the launching of satellites throughout the Pacific region.

False Choices and Their Implications

For almost a decade numerous advisors, committees, researchers, and others have asked the U.S. government to review the ways existing policies, rules, and regulations undermine productivity and competitiveness in the country's most important industrial sectors. The warning is clear; these industries are in trouble and their problems will get worse. Although there is now a growing interest in high-growth industries, the proponents of a new industrial policy have yet to advance a coherent theory or method to guide their selection or support.

Past neglect has disturbing implications for long-term economic growth. If some industries act as levers to growth, the reverse might also be true. If a nation's strategic industries are selectively obstructed, their decline may significantly retard growth in other sectors. Shrinking demand for the products of mature industries will further choke growth in strategic sectors, and the economy will spiral downward.

The Reagan administration assumes that energy prices and inflation will be held in check. There is no reason for this assumption. After the next short-term spurt of growth increased the demand for oil and the OPEC cartel consolidates its forces, there may be a sharp demand for energy. The country will be caught unprepared because it will have long since scrapped its most innovative programs to develop alternative sources of energy. Rising oil prices may also raise the price of oil-based exports, principally agricultural goods, and contribute to a deterioration of U.S. competitiveness in these and other goods.

The fruits of adhocracy are despair. As more and more industries flounder, more and more will become supplicants to the fisc. More special deals, more bailouts, more positioning for a shrinking pie. Those who have little now will have even less then. And even if in the darkness some leader sees the light, is it likely that a fair strategy will be devised? The country will be in crisis, and it will be assumed, as it has always been, that the weakest must be thrown from the raft to secure the interests of the rest.

Part II
THE JAPANESE CHALLENGE

Chapter 4

The Theory of Industrial
Development in Japan
in Historical Perspective

For the first time in the postwar period, the prosperity and decline of some American industries depend on the strategies of foreign nations. The world of 1945 when our allies lay stripped and exhausted has passed. Now the industrial policies of these countries, and of our former enemy Japan, must be weighed carefully by any responsible public official.

This is most evident with respect to Japan. If any country has proved its understanding of the potential of technology and appears to grasp the principles of strategic industries, Japan has. Should Japanese planners succeed in tailoring incentives to the nation's strategic edge, so also will others with which they are closely allied. The Japanese challenge will compound the problems of productivity that American businesses are now encountering.

Present adversity has rich uses, however, and Americans have much to learn from Japan. Most important, we can study how Japanese planners have drawn lessons from their own and foreign experience to help them peer into the future. It is easy to look back at history to find the points that leveraged economic change; it is quite another to use these points as a basis for oracular planning.

In the late twentieth century Japan will become a society based on science and technology. The transformation will depend on a few strategic industries that for most of the postwar period have fuctioned independently. Today these industries are converging and by the twenty-first century they and their progeny will constitute a gigantic integrated macrosystem.

Throughout the postwar period the Japanese government, particularly the Ministry of International Trade and Industry (MITI), has played a critical role in the development of the country's strategic industries. In recent years it has emphasized "information-intensive" industries such as semiconductors, computers, telecommunications, machine tools, and genetic engineering, and has developed a unique set of supporting policies, laws, regulations, rules, and institutions.

Part II uses eight case studies to introduce the basic principles of Japan's approach. It credits the strengths of government action and probes its weaknesses, thereby offering a tentative assessment of whether Japan should serve as a useful model for future U.S. government initiatives.

Precepts of Industrial Development

Few people believe there is an explicit "theory" of industrial development in Japan.[1] Yet it appears that many bureaucrats, leaders in industry, and influential citizens possess a common perception of the economy and the role of government that differs radically from neoclassical economic thought in the west.

The core of this perception has been an acute sense of vulnerability. Since the early Meiji era (1858–1911), most Japanese have seen themselves as a poor, insular people, dependent on the outside world for basic necessities, encircled, technologically behind, somehow always different. To westerners accustomed to thinking of Japan as a superstate, this self-image may seem strangely anachronistic, yet it still commands a deep resonance in Japan. The sense of vulnerability was exacerbated by the oil crisis of the early 1970s and today it is intensified by the rumblings of trade war.

The most dramatic concrete evidence of this perception is the association of economic and national (military) security. These terms are sharply distinguished in the United States. Military security or national defense is accorded high priority while economic security has been given less attention except during the Great Depression. In Japanese history the two have been entwined. Between the Meiji era and the end of World War II the slogan *fukoku-kyōhei* (rich country, strong army) well described the alliance of these perceptions that supported most of Japan's prewar development. Even in the pacifist years of the 1950s, 1960s, and 1970s, economic planning has been justified by assertions of national security that would not have been politically persuasive in the United States.

Japan's concern over vulnerability and security has shaped its distinctly pragmatic, instrumentalist view of "free competition," technology, law, and industrial structure. Although most western economists do not delude themselves that free competition is a salutary goal in itself, in practice the Justice Department and other organs of state have come to perceive it so. It is part of American ideology.

Most Japanese by contrast have viewed free competition with suspicion. They note that free trade has not assured Japan a fair, certain, or efficient allocation of the world's resources. The embargo on oil before World War II attested to that. The energy shock of the 1970s demonstrated how undue reliance on the market might strip a country of its existing advantages or even its capacity to respond nimbly to change. The suffering of victims of pollution and the repercussions of the victims' movement (between 1956 and 1976)[2] demonstrated for many Japanese the human costs of government's failure to regulate industry effectively. Bankruptcy, a particularly acute hardship in a less mobile society like Japan, has taught the bureaucrats and politicians the social and political unacceptability of foolish trust in the market.

The upshot has been an intensely pragmatic view of competition. In some cases Japanese government officials and industry leaders view competition as a critical stimulus to innovation, productivity, and growth. In other situations it is viewed as excessive, even destructive, and must be controlled. The point is that competition itself has come to be viewed as a public resource, a policy instrument to be deployed depending on circumstance. Within its life cycle each new industry or technology will demand a different dosage of competition. One of the arts of government is to structure the market and to tailor incentives to acheive an optimal level of competition.

Since the Meiji period the Japanese government has viewed science and technology as critical to national survival. But it has been a particularly Japanese concept of technology, an amalgam of western technique and Japanese sensitivity. Key technologies were closely allied with military strategy, and the government's nurturing of the industrial base was throughout history viewed as a prerequisite to military success. It followed that some technologies were considered more important than others, just as some industries were held to be more basic or "key" than others. Because of their overall importance to military and economic development, these industries have been viewed as national assets, and the technologies supporting them as national treasures. The Japanese government has purposely cultivated these perceptions to justify some planning of industry and to demand public sacrifices for the support of its programs.

In the postwar era the Ministry of International Trade and Industry and other government agencies have sought to position Japanese industry strategically to capture the benefits of trade and growth. Some Japanese economists criticize MITI's policies as violating the basics of economic theory. Under a static concept of "comparative advantage," it is taught that countries rich in labor and poor in capital should emphasize labor-intensive production, while those scarce in labor but blessed with capital should allocate capital primarily to production. For example, MITI's promotion of costly, capital-intensive steel products in the early 1950s invoked such criticism because Japan appeared to have a comparative advantage in labor-intensive industries such as textiles, apparel, and shipbuilding.

The government actually sought to develop labor and capital-intensive industries in parallel. Miyohei Shinohara notes:

Even in the process of postwar industrialization, while such capital-intensive industries as iron and steel and petrochemicals were gaining in competitiveness, many labor-intensive processing industries were also building up their technology and enjoying higher rates of growth than the basic industries.

Of course it can be said that MITI put more emphasis on capital-intensive big enterprises, which required greater protection, in order to strengthen the linkage with processing industries. The point here is the parallel development of big enterprises and small and medium-sized enterprises, as well as of the basic industries and processing industries. One should not hastily conclude that bigger or smaller is better. In the process of industrialization, it was necessary to promote the industrial linkage structure between the two sectors by means of parallel development. In particular in the case of the Japanese economy, with its huge domestic market, it is not hard to envisage that some appropriate development of basic industries with rapidity was necessary for the development of processing industries, which are situated closer to consumption.

Thus, on the one hand, MITI's industrial policies were expected to foster the industries whose demand growth and technical progress were comparatively high. At the same time, they proved successful in strengthening some key industries which took a "backward linkage," position in relation to the processing industries. From the standpoint of inter-industry structure, the "industrial block" often found in advanced countries was formed, in which such machinery-linked industries as automobiles, industrial machinery, and electrical machinery are closely related to such basic metal sectors as iron and steel and non-ferrous metals.

Achieving development up to this stage required a very large domestic market. For Japan, with a population of 100 million, it can be said that a necessary base had already been laid for making this development possible.[3]

In the early 1970s two events forced government policy to change. The first was the oil crisis of 1972-1973. The second was the challenge of exports from rapidly industrializing countries like Taiwan and Korea, which had acquired Japanese technology and know-how a few years earlier. In response to both, the Japanese government began to stress higher value-added, information-intensive industries, particularly semiconductors, computers, and telecommunications.

MITI's attention to these industries entailed several obvious benefits. First, by the late 1960s the computer industry was already growing rapidly and was projected to expand, generating jobs and revenue; by 1975 it was an industry of established excellence. Second, the computer could play a key role in revitalizing Japan's declining industries (shipping) and in strengthening its mature industries (automobiles). Third, semiconductors and computers were becoming increasingly essential to a host of new industries such as aircraft, robotics, ocean engineering, and aerospace. By systematizing and rationalizing manufacturing, the computer, it was hoped, would contribute significantly to energy conservation throughout all Japanese industries.

The emphasis on knowledge intensification was supported by what became known as "3 S" and "3 F" policy. The three S's stood for "software," "systematization," and "specialization"; the three F's stressed "fashionization," "feedback," and "flexibility."

Shinohara describes some of these terms as follows:

Systematization means creating new functions through linking and combining different industries and different technologies. It includes the new field of "mechatronics" and also the computerization of social services like medical care, education, energy supply, waste disposal, and transportation.

Specialization implies using technology in new ways. An example is the search for new materials possessing special thermal, mechanical, chemical, optical, and electronic characteristics to be used in atomic power and liquefied natural gas plants, or in the development of the oceans or outer space.

Feedback systems aim at augmenting the organic linkages between the final demand sector and the intermediate products or raw materials sectors in the design of new products and technologies and "fashionization" implies the tailoring of technology to these uses.

Flexibility implies creating a higher degree of value added by developing methods of production intended to process and fabricate various products with a variety of qualities. In apparel manufacturing, for example, new systems allow flexible and automatic dyeing, cutting, sewing, etc., to meet the demand for various colors, shapes, designs, and materials.[4]

Shinohara's key variables closely resemble those identified in Chapter 1. As will be seen, these and other elements have served as pressure points in the Japanese government's plans for the development of strategic industries.

A Note on Economic and Industrial Planning

Since World War II there have been numerous short-term economic plans.[5] The first group was concerned principally with rehabilitation and to some extent was coordinated with the Marshall Plan in Europe. By 1953, however, Japan's government and industry leaders believed that it was dangerous to depend on foreign aid or windfalls like the Korean War. Since then there have been a series of plans whose cumulative purposes were to strengthen the nation's economic base, improve infrastructure, modernize less productive sectors, and, gradually, to enrich the quality of life.

Among the most interesting recent initiatives is the report of the Economic Council of the Year 2000. The remainder of the twentieth century, the report notes, will be a turning point in Japanese industry. Energy is projected to pose a continuing problem with the country becoming increasingly dependent on nuclear power. The savings rate will decrease and private investment will decline. Economic growth will be moderate. Increasing tensions and strains are expected as one in six persons reaches sixty-five years. The industrial structure will continue to shift to "soft" knowledge-intensive service industries and one out of every two persons will be employed in services by the year 2000.

Paralleling the long-term economic plans are MITI's "visions" of Japan's future industrial structure. The first vision was prepared in May 1971 and set the course of labor, international trade, and industrial policies. The second, prepared in October 1974, identified specific targets for such major industries as iron and steel, chemicals, petrochemicals, paper and pulp, aluminum, textiles, and precision machinery.[6] These coincided with concrete objectives for the regional allocation of industries, environmental pollution, energy conservation, the internationalization of Japanese industry, and the basic goals of technological development.

In large measure these goals continue today. MITI's "vision of the '80s" has established a framework for new information-processing industries such as semiconductors, computers, telecommunications, robotics, machine tools, aircraft, aerospace, nuclear energy, and genetic engineering. The vision serves as a benchmark for legal, administrative, and technical decisions and for medium- and long-term projections of industrial trends.

Deliberations on industrial policy are centered in MITI and the ministry's advisory body, the Industrial Structure Council. Since its 1974 report, MITI has added special sectoral committees to the council such as an aluminum committee, an electronics committee, and an industrial organization committee. Committee members include a diverse array of experts and scholars, key industrial leaders, bankers, executives of trading companies, labor and consumer advocates, and local representatives.

The process of discussion within MITI's sectoral committees and subcommittees is only a small part of a much larger, parallel, and continuing negotiation among the large economic federations, industrial associations, prefectural and municipal governments, and within single firms and their affiliates. The MITI vision serves as a model for more specific visions at each lower tier. The vision of the Economic Friendship Association on the development of technologies critical to the twenty-first century, for example, has refined MITI's basic plan and introduced a level of detail not present in the agency's general prospectus. Even more detailed projections are prepared by various local governments, industry associations, and companies on matters more pertinent to their specific problems and interests.

In sum, planning in Japan is a device to enlighten government, industry, and the public on where the country is tending. It is a tool of prediction, an aid to structural change, a guide to government policy, and a means of overcoming bottlenecks. Plans are benchmarks for industry and industrial firms to set their own targets and standards, and for this reason compliance with government plans is often voluntary and self-executing. Ultimately, planning is a means of binding a broad social consensus.

Law and Planning

Japan's approach to industrial policy has relied on a developed view of law as an instrument of planning. Placing his emphasis slightly differently, Chalmers Johnson writes: "Japan's political economy can be located precisely in the line of descent from the German Historical School—sometimes labeled 'economic nationalism,' *Handelspolitik,* or neomercantilism."[7] Johnson describes the Japanese approach as "plan rational," which he contrasts with the Soviet and American models:

In the Soviet Union and its dependencies and emulators, state ownership of the means of production, state planning, and bureaucratic goal-setting are not rational means to a developmental goal (even if they may once have been); they are fundamental values in themselves, not to be challenged by evidence of either inefficiency or ineffectiveness. In the sense I am using the term here, Japan is plan rational, and the command economies are not; in fact, the history of Japan since 1925 offers numerous illustrations of why the command economy is not plan rational, a lesson the Japanese learned well.[8]

He sees the United States as an example of a "market rational" or regulatory state.

A regulatory, or market-rational, state concerns itself with the forms and procedures — the rules, if you will — of economic competition, but it does not concern itself with substantive matters. For example, the United States government has many regulations concerning the antitrust implications of the size of firms, but it does not concern itself with what industries ought to exist and what industries are no longer needed. The developmental, or plan-rational, state, by contrast, has as its dominant feature precisely the setting of such substantive social and economic goals.[9]

Civil law countries like Japan incorporate the Roman conception of law as a "finished system." It is a cathedral in which all the affairs of man are finely and wisely worked. The codes themselves are hierarchically arranged with each specific statute supplementing, refining, or taking precedence over the more general law. When discrepancies or "gaps" in the law are perceived, they are treated as abnormalities and are quickly mortared over. In Japan, legal concepts and terms of art are accorded the highest dignity, and every effort is made, particularly by the Legal Department of the Prime Minister's Office, to assure their consistent usage and meaning throughout the legal system. Japan's architechtonic approach can be contrasted with the allegedly dynamic character of the American common law.

In Japan, the law itself often serves as a plan, and the legal process as a planning process. Hiroya Ueno notes that many statutes in Japan, such as the laws designed to promote strategic industries, served as basic charters or master plans.[10]

Law, of course, also serves to implement the plans it helped create. This proved particularly important in the 1930s when government sought to rationalize industry. "Rationalize" meant direct government supervision of decision making within the firm. In the prewar period the government actually drew up plans for "the control of enterprises, implementation of scientific management principles, improvements in industrial financing, standardization of products, simplification of production processes, and subsidies to support the production and consumption of domestically manufactured goods."[11] Although this approach proved widely unpopular even before World War II, law continued to play a significant role in the government's efforts to rationalize strategic sectors.

To suggest that the development of strategic industries was planned through specific laws, however, understates the importance of law, because often the promotion laws themselves were organized in a larger system. In this sense Japan may be the best test of Weber's famous thesis that industrial progress is intimately linked to the rationality of a nation's legal system.[12]

This systematic approach to law has had distinct advantages in the planning of Japan's strategic industries. It has significantly expanded the level of government control and facilitated coordination of policies. It has also helped endow institutions and methods of control with legal character that accord them respect and power. Such institutions were thereby converted into powerful tools for planning.

A good example is the use of industrial unions under the Important Industries Control Law (Juyō Sangyō Tōsei Hō) of 1931.[13] The law permitted unions to form treatylike cartel agreements to fix levels of production, establish prices, limit new entrants, and control marketing for a particular industry. Although the cartels themselves were not originally conceived as planning institutions, their integration in a broader planning framework helped to make them so.

Administrative guidance is another example. Simply put, administrative guidance refers to the authority of the government, contained in the laws establishing the various ministries, to issue "directives," "requests," "warnings," "suggestions," and "encouragements" to the enterprises or clients within a particular ministry's jurisdiction. According to Johnson, the development of this institution can be traced to MITI's efforts to preserve its planning prerogatives in the face of liberalization. Although Japanese scholars (and the courts) have at times questioned the "legality" of administrative guidance, without question its effectiveness as a planning tool has been strengthened by its close association with law. Conversely, its power as an instrument of control has been enhanced by its being an integral part of a systematic planning process.

The systematic use of law has also had a direct bearing upon the attainment of consensus. Law prescribes the permissible bounds of bargaining between government and industry and among various industries. During the period of "self-control" in the 1920s Johnson notes that the boundaries were very great. During the war they were less so. In each case they were set by law. Johnson describes how after a brief flirtation with selfish "competition" Japan rejected this experiment in favor of cooperation that was institutionalized through law. Most significantly, law invested the debate over strategic industries with a continuing sense of crisis that proved essential to marshalling consensus. Law made the stakes high, law encouraged perceptions (both real and imagined) of fading opportunities, of uncertainty and limited options, of foreign hostility, all of which helped unify the national effort.[14]

Law also directly influenced the planning process by shaping the structure of the market. By creating incentives and disincentives, law allocated resources from one sector to another directly by preferments and indirectly through the market. Law gave the cartels within strategic industries life and converted them to instruments of planning.

In the postwar era, tax law proved a particularly fertile device for planning strategic industries. Johnson lists some of the most important measures: capital asset reevaluation, special reserves, deductions for royalties paid for foreign technology, rapid depreciation, and exclusion of strategic machinery from import duties.

Beyond all other uses, however, law facilitated structural adjustment, and strategic industries served as the principal means of fostering this adjustment. The targeting of specific industries served different purposes in different periods. In the 1930s the primary purpose was economic domination of Japan's neighbors. During the 1940s the aim was to commandeer all resources to the war effort. The principal ob-

100

jective of targeting during most of the postwar period has been economic recovery and technological independence. By structuring the development of the first generation of industries, the sectoral laws have helped shape the course of second, third, and later generations of strategic industries.

A Social Theory of Industrial Development

Most western observers have neglected to study the social theory underlying Japan's information intensification program. This is a serious failing because the social, political, and philosophical implications of the information society is what gives this vision force. To Naohiro Amaya, one of the principal architects of postwar Japan's industrial policy, man in the beginning is slave to the necessities of life. With the solution of problems of subsistence, he enters a second stage, "the stage of desire for outward extension."[15] For Japan this was the period of the 1950s and 1960s, a time of consumer frenzy for the 3 C's (cars, conditioners, and color televisions) where "Promethean and Faustian desires" were pursued insatiably. Political and economic theories encouraged competition, efficiency, standardization, and mass production. But these are no more than apologies for man's gluttony.

The initial stage of outward extension inevitably gives rise to a period of internal confusion.

At this transitional stage, the phenomenon of growing social entropy will become prominent: open self-assertion such as business egoism, regional egoism or, as apparent in the drama of the rice price determination, "farmer egoism" and "consumer egoism"; the increase of factions or groups actively or passively opposing or indifferent to the establishment, like the radicals or the hippies; the weakening of the spirit to service and sacrifice for the good of the society, accompanied by the intensification of the mixed complex of two contradicting factors, which are (1) dependence upon the establishment, and (2) distrust and resentment against the establishment; and politically, the progression of party-pluralization.

The balance of centripetal and centrifugal forces in society will collapse and social instability will intensify.

When people's main desires are directed towards market goods, the job of adjusting, unifying and systematizing these innumerable desires is carried out mainly by the self-regulating market mechanism. But once human desires rapidly and drastically expand into the area of public goods, such convenient mechanism is no longer available. The situation surrounding the question of what is "social welfare" will be just like that of a crowded intersection without a traffic light: a conflict of interests and selfishness. The situation of Japan, which at present is in the latter period of "outward extension," is just this.[16]

Ultimately, suggests Amaya, the problem of the outward expansion of insatiable demand can be redressed only by a transition to a pursuit of inward fulfillment. He cites Aristotle in support of this view: "The possession of such good things as fortunes or tools will harm man, if excessive, but there is no limit to the possession of good things related to intelligence and virtue; the more one has these things, the closer one approaches the good life befitting the true nature of humanity."[17]

The transition is to be set in motion by increasing emphasis on the education and spiritual development of the people. A foundation for this transition is to be laid by reshaping demand:

Firstly, the approach by way of controlling demand; that is to suppress the unlimited desires for outward extension. Business goals lie in the continual increase of sales and profits; from this point of view untiring advertising, model changes, the encouragement of throwaway consumption, are certainly good. But if one considers the limitations of the earth and Japan, the acknowledgement will grow stronger with time that the introduction of measures to control advertising, model changes, and excessive packaging, or to promote product durability, to say nothing of controls on pollution, are socially necessary.

On the other hand, the consumer must overcome the mentality of "dependence" easily affected by commercial hypnotism, and prior to judging whether something is cheap or not, become a wise consumer who can judge independently what his true needs are. The making of a wise consumer is the most essential task of the consumer movement.[18]

Further steps will include the development of "socially innovative" technology, moderation in the consumption of natural resources and energy, preservation of the environment, and the creation of rejuvenated communities, linked by an active interest in public issues and built from the decay of Japan's crumbling villages and bankrupt enterprises. Then basic human relations of man-to-man, man-to-state, nation-to-nation will develop in a spirit of Confucian sincerity and sympathy.

The evolution of the demand structure is closely paralleled by the knowledge intensification of the supply structure. Essentially, the process traces man's liberation from enslavement as a factor of production to freedom and dominion over machines and capital. The first stage corresponds to the period of the ancient world and Middle Ages where a small number of rulers rose above the level of subsistence and crushed the rest of society.

In the second stage productive capacity increases substantially because of improvements in machinery.

This progress enables the productive capacity to expand by leaps and bounds in proportion to the rapid increase in outward extension desires. Also, with respect to labor, inhuman labor that was widespread at the II (a) stage has come to be largely replaced by machines. Although there still exists a large number of people doing mechanical dull work, a drawback from the viewpoint of bringing humanity to full bloom, their working hours, working conditions, wage levels, etc., have drastically improved compared with II (a) where workers were tightly bound to machines. Accordingly, they have come to assume the leading role in the market of outward extension desires, outgrowing their former role as consumers of simple basic wants.

Furthermore, another salient feature of stage II (b) that attracts attention, is the development of functional occupations corresponding to intellect, emotion and volition, which are the fundamentals of human capacity. For example, the development of the machinery system mentioned above requires, naturally, a large number of workers for R&D programs, designers, operators, and other technicians. To command a mammoth machinery system and to conduct business management, a large number of managers become necessary for the intellectual work and decision-making. The function that had been immanent and undifferentiated, at stage II (a), within the capitalist class resting on the basis of ownership now, at this stage is functionally differentiated into intellectual, emotional and volitional activites and this functional system as a systematic management body, has come to replace the former capitalists. In addition, the development of enterprise groups centering particularly on manufacturing industries has been accompanied by the development of such industries as transportation, communication, banking, etc., and also by the rapid increase of demand for services like police, education, medical care and entertainment. And this has brought about a need for a great number of specialists related to intellectual, emotional or decision-making activities. In this way, from the supply aspect, the majority of men are elevated from the position of being subordinate to machines to that of being the master of machines, and thus their human capabilities ranging from intellect to emotion and volition, flourish. At the same time, from the aspect of demand, white-collar workers, naturally, and even blue-collar workers, as a result of the remarkable rise of their income levels, now constitute a huge demand, thus counterbalancing the enormous supply structure. Thus, it can be said that at this stage, human capabilities are extensively developed and human freedom is expanded by leaps and bounds.[19]

Yet despite its advantages the second stage engenders contradictions. Mass production and consumption breed abnormal concentrations of population that destroy the cities and pollute the environment. In the second stage the market is regarded as too "immature" to provide enough public goods to match the production of market goods. Amaya notes, "this is one of the major causes of the confusion in the later period of outward extension of desires." He concludes that only through knowledge intensification of both supply and demand structures can the "essential qualities of human progress" be unleashed.

Underlying this benign concept of knowledge intensification is a less explicit set of notions about the allocation of the burdens of the transition. The fundamental thesis, of course, is that all of society will ultimately benefit, otherwise the imposition of economic burdens on some people during the stages of transition could not be justified. The intervening period is thus of greatest importance. The theory implicitly suggests that at least some of these burdens might be born as a mortgage on the future; in part it promises compensation, and in part it suggests that the burdens suffered may in fact not be so great. As discussed in Chapter 10, there is also another unstated premise: that during the period of transition the burdens of Japan's industrial development may justifiably be allocated in large part to the rest of the world.

Chapter 5

Engineering a Societal Cerebral Cortex: From Automobiles to the Integrated Development of Semiconductors and Computers

Japan's industrial transformation is like the fashioning of a living brain, a brain organized by seven functions. The first two functions involve the diffusion and communication of information. The third is memory, a form of communication across time. The fourth function is competition; living cells in quest of oxygen and nutrients are like firms in the free market, each in ferocious competition for society's scarce resources. The fifth is the principle of compensation; each cell's claim to the body's resources is offset by a countervailing or adaptive force. This implies a sixth, self-regulatory function. Finally, a living brain integrates information in higher orders of complexity and generalization; its core is creativity.

A brain is a useful metaphor for thinking about Japan's restructuring policies. Yet in an important sense it may be more than a metaphor. We are slowly becoming accustomed to the incorporation of technology within our bodies, in artificial limbs, pacemakers, and aural and visual prostheses. In Japan, perhaps more than anywhere else, machines are incorporating the qualities of people, individuals, and groups, while humans and their institutions are reflecting the attributes and failings of the new technologies. Here is the birth of a new organism, larger than the individual or the community, a societal cyborg, part technology, and part flesh and blood.

This chapter uses the concrete examples of automobiles, semiconductors, computers, telecommunications, mechantronics, and biotechnology to show how the Japanese government has sought to integrate these separate strategic industries within an encompassing macroindustrial system. Some of the principles underlying this development—such as technological convergence, linkages, and synergism—have already been described. I elaborate on these principles and explain why the Japanese government has considered the diffusion of new technologies so important, why it has sought to knit together producers and users, and why it has compiled statistics with such care.

Thomas Kuhn of M.I.T. has identified the elements of scientific revolutions. They are holistic, requiring shifts in a basic conceptual framework, or paradigm. They alter "the criteria by which terms attach to nature" and "massively, the sets of objects and situations to which these terms attach."[1] If Japanese planners succeed in their vision of the twenty-first century, Japanese society will undergo a social and scientific revolution in the profoundest Kuhnian sense.

The Principle of Momentum: An Overview of Japan's Postwar Strategic Industries

All strategic industries generate significant economic momentum. Throughout the postwar period the Japanese government vigorously promoted each new generation of strategic industries in order to assure that the momentum of the previous generation would not be lost. The result was a series of consecutive industrial spurts that were largely responsible for Japan's record of sustained economic growth.[2] The momentum continues today.

The postwar periods of industrial growth can be divided

107

in five stages, each stage the trigger of the next. Each of the first three stages began with high growth but then began to taper off; the point of initial decline of the first coincided roughly with the beginning of the next; and the overall growth rate naturally reflected the cyclical pattern of its components, multiplying by over 6.23 for the period 1947–1978.

The most important characteristic of the first two stages was the integration of production. The Yokkaichi combine (known in Japanese as a "kombinat") typified Japan's industrial development in the 1950s.[3] The complex consisted of six refining, chemical, petrochemical, and power companies, three of these so entwined that the operations of one could not be modified without significantly altering all the others. So closely did the six companies coordinate important decisions with government planners that the kombinat came in time to be viewed as a single unit. It is a harbinger of the integration of manufacturing by computer forty years later.

This unique form of production had a direct bearing on economic growth. It canalized innovation in these separate industries during the 1950s to a common industrial purpose. As these complexes increased in size, they also became more specialized and, with automation, more efficient. The reduction in fuel costs and the huge transportation, harbor, and other support facilities the combines demanded triggered growth in steel and other sectors.

The advent of the Japanese steel industry in the late 1950s brought a sure source of cheap, high-quality, mass-produced materials. The stable supply of these materials, the sharp increases in per capita income, and the expansion of overseas markets were the most important preconditions of the development of the automobile and home electric appliance industries.

The oil shock of the early 1970s and the subsequent decline in the rate of growth constituted a critical threshold for the fourth and fifth stages, whose issue are the electronics industries of today: semiconductors, computers, telecommunications, robotics, machine tools, genetic engineering, new materials, aircraft, and ocean resources.

Case 1. The Fall of Comparative Advantage: The Development of the Japanese Auto Industry, 1946–1970[4]

By the early 1950s when the first stage of Japan's reconstruction had been completed, the government turned to the task of identifying the industries that would serve as a base for the nation's development during the decade. It was the first practical test of the static theory of comparative advantage and it pitted the champions of industrial development against those charged with the nation's financial security.

At issue was whether to foster the development of a domestic automobile industry, in preference to agriculture where Japan clearly enjoyed a comparative advantage. In the early 1940s the Japanese automobile industry was beset with difficulties. The scale of manufacturing was uncompetitive; Japanese technology was underdeveloped; there were virtually no supplies of onshore parts; and Japan suffered chronic shortages of foreign exchange. Despite these shortcomings, the advocates of a domestic automobile assembly and parts industry argued that government assistance would reduce domestic demand for foreign autos and create a new demand for domestic steel, machinery, and tires.

MITI's principal adversary was the Bank of Japan. The bank urged that investment be applied first to agriculture, an area where Japan was already successful. Only later, after high short-term gains were realized and reconstruction accomplished, did the bank suggest that investments be made in industries that would require large-scale and advanced production technology.

The debate was abruptly settled by the Korean War. MITI seized on the war's demand for automobiles and hastily drew up an agenda for the industry's development. Its agenda included domestic production with foreign capital, temporary incentives to foreign firms to transfer advanced technology to domestic manufacturers, and financial assistance to the domestic industry. Under MITI's new "Basic Policy for the Introduction of Foreign Investment in Japan's Passenger Car Industry" of 1952, foreign investment was substantially restricted, repatriation of earnings on capital curtailed,[5] and joint ventures with foreign producers possessing superior parts technology screened.

The quota, tariff, and commodity tax were the principal instruments of control. The quota on foreign exchange for automobile imports had been in place since the war's end. It was applied in varying degrees on passenger cars, trucks, buses, small motorcycles, auto parts, and engines until the end of the 1960s. Tariff rates on autos were set high and geared to the domestic producers' interests. Small passenger cars, the core of the industry, bore the highest rates, while trucks, where Japanese producers were strongest, enjoyed the lowest rates. The commodity tax was levied on all passenger vehicles—domestic and foreign—sold in Japan, to finance road construction. Larger foreign cars paid higher rates.[6]

Although quotas and tariffs had created a market opportunity in the early 1950s, Japanese makers were not technologically prepared to exploit it. In 1951 there were only 4,317 passenger cars, none of which was competitive. In October 1952, MITI issued its "Basic Policy for Technology Licensing and Assembly in the Passenger Car Industry." This policy reflected a trade-off between the need for foreign technology and MITI's desire to encourage domestic production. Foreign licensors were given the right to remit royalties on knockdown assemblies, but only for a limited period. MITI guaranteed remittance, but required that 90 percent of licensed parts be produced in Japan within five years. This gave domestic producers an additional incentive to develop a manufacturing capacity for their licensor's parts.[7]

Within twelve months, six domestic manufacturers had negotiated agreements for knockdown assembly of foreign cars in Japan under license. MITI approved four of these applications, rejecting two on the grounds that the applicants were simply too weak to survive. Even at this early date, MITI

110

officials saw the problems of "excessive competition" in this highly capital-intensive industry.

Financial assistance to the industry remained modest. Between 1951 and 1955 the Japan Development Bank financed roughly nine percent of total investment in production facilities for passenger cars. The bank's reconstruction loans greatly helped auto producers obtain supplemental financing from the private commercial banks and special accelerated depreciation rates were extended to auto producers by fiscal legislation prepared in 1951. Approximately $1 million in direct subsidies were awarded to the Automobile Technology Association during the 1950s. By 1958 nearly every passenger car assembled in Japan was designed and produced domestically.

MITI's efforts toward the auto parts industry, however, proved less successful. In the early 1950s the industry was weak and fragmented. Each manufacturer was supplied by 350 primary-parts manufacturers who in turn dealt with several thousand small subcontractors. Many of these were affiliated through ownership, technology agreements, or simply captive arrangements with primary-parts manufacturers. It was a typical Japanese manufacturing pyramid: product flowed up, credit flowed down.

The system provided a stable yet elastic source of supply for the assemblers. Fluctuations in demand were borne by the marginal subcontractors and labor costs at the subcontract level were usually lower than in the larger firm.

The major problem was the large number and small size of the primary-parts manufacturers and subcontractors. The organization of production among these affiliates was traditionally determined and uneconomical. Scales of production were low and inefficient and rarely were modern production technologies in use. Most of these firms were financially weak.[8]

MITI's reforms of 1956–1966 were aimed at modernizing facilities and concentrating production among a few producers. Although mergers were encouraged, they were not mandated. Specific parts manufacturers were approved for borrowing by a special Auto Parts Committee jointly created by MITI and the industry associations. Large firms were favored over small firms, specialized over diversified, and exporting firms over nonexporting firms.

Although MITI's efforts to concentrate the industry between 1956 and 1966 generally succeeded, its attempts to induce the major manufacturers to form joint research projects and mergers in the third rationalization program proved a dismal failure. Despite annual growth rates of 25 percent to 40 percent that made cheap, long-term financing extremely attractive, borrowing was insubstantial and program budgets were never fully utilized. MITI's other efforts during the 1960s to consolidate the major manufacturers, with exception of the Toyota-Hino and Toyota-Daihatsu ventures, were similarly unsuccessful.

By the late 1950s a stable, fast-growing passenger car industry had been established and Japan's susceptibility to perverse economic cycles through imbalance in trade had been reduced. Domestic production in auto parts advanced the development of steel, machinery, and rubber which, along with autos during the 1960s, enjoyed unparalleled growth. Autonomy in design opened new opportunities for exports that induced a shift in production from labor-intensive, low-technology goods to low-labor, high-technology products. Economic growth engendered by the automobile industry created almost overnight a large consumer market that in turn laid a foundation for the consumer electronics industries of the 1960s and 1970s.

Most importantly, MITI's success established a significant precedent. Although the agency's failure to consolidate either the major manufacturers or the parts suppliers underscored the limitations of government influence, its successes showed government planners that a static concept of comparative advantage was ill-suited to the exigent demands of postwar reconstruction. MITI's dynamic approach to strategic sectors had been vindicated. It would be replayed in all the new industries to come.

Case 2. Strategic Industries and the Principle of Structure: The Integrated Development of Semiconductors, Computers, and Telecommunications

If automobiles confirmed the principle of dynamic comparative advantage, the integrated development of semiconductors, computers, and telecommunications underlined the importance of structure. With these industries, the Japanese government learned that certain technologies demand a very special economic environment. This study explains how the government helped shape the structure of the industry, the capital and trade markets, the organization of research, and the distribution of information to the needs of the new industries. It is a chronicle of the many mistakes, detours, and experiments along the way, of how these problems were addressed, and how the industry rose to become the most formidable challenger the American giants had ever known.

The Structure of the Japanese Industry

The structure of these industries holds the key to the subleties of the government's approach. Unlike the United States, where the semiconductor, computer, and telecommunications industries developed independently, the six major Japanese semiconductor and computer companies were all grown as divisions of the dominant telecommunications companies, and established well before World War II. The distinction is crucial because from the outset it slanted the development of computer technology in Japan in the direction of telecommunications. This permitted computer and communications technology to be integrated closely in design, digitalization, and solid state conversion.

Here are the principal actors. The Nippon Electric Company, Ltd. (NEC) was established on July 17, 1899, as a joint venture between Western Electric of the United States and Nichidan Shokai, a trading company. In 1932 NEC was renamed the Sumitomo Communications Industry Company and has since been closely associated with the Sumitomo group. NEC is the world's third largest manufacturer of semiconductors and a preeminent manufacturer of computers, earth stations, and microwave communication equipment.

Fujitsu, Ltd., began as the telephone division of Fuji Electric (a joint venture of Furukawa Electric and Siemens). From 1935 to 1960 Fujitsu remained a small communications equipment manufacturer and supplied most of its products to the telephone monopoly, the Nippon Telegraph and Telephone Public Corporation (NTT). In the early 1960s Fujitsu began an intensive program of computer R&D and today it is Japan's leading computer manufacturer.

Hitachi, Ltd., began in 1910 as an electrical equipment repair shop for the Hitachi Mining Company, from which it was separated in 1920. During the Great Depression of 1929 the firm secured financial support from the Nissan group with whom it has since retained close business relations. Hitachi's hallmarks are its diversity, technological versatility, and independence. The company conducts comprehensive R&D for its various divisions, which include electronics, heavy electrical machinery, household electrical appliances, industrial machinery, nuclear power, and transportation equipment. Hitachi is today Japan's third largest company after Nippon Steel and Toyota, and is the nucleus of its own conglomerate, the Hitachi Group.

Toshiba Corp. was established in 1879 as Tanaka Seisakusho, Japan's first telegraph equipment manufacturer. In 1893 it obtained the financial backing of the Mitsui Bank and has since remained a member of the Mitsui group. In 1978 Toshiba was the second largest manufacturer of heavy electrical machinery (after Hitachi) and ranked first in nuclear power, steam and hydraulic power, fluorescent lamps, and medical instruments. In recent years Toshiba has virtually dropped out of the large computer market, although it remains very strong in semiconductors. In early 1983 it was added to the NTT's "inner circle" of suppliers.

Mitsubishi Electric Corporation began in 1910 as the electrical machinery plant of Mitsubishi Shipbuilding, a precursor of Mitsubishi Heavy Industries. Mitsubishi Electric Corporation was formed in 1921 as part of the Mitsubishi group, an agglomerate of eleven major Mitsubishi companies. Mitsubishi Electric was the last of the six major firms to enter the computer field.

Oki Electric Industry Company, Ltd., began in 1881 as a telephone equipment manufacturer and has continued as one of Japan's three major communication equipment companies. Like NEC and Fujitsu, Oki has enjoyed the consistent support of NTT.

The Nippon Telegraph & Telephone Public Corporation is a government-owned corporation established in 1952 under the jurisdiction of the Ministry of Posts and Telecommunications (MPT). The budget, services, tariffs, and overall policies, as well as the appointment of its top officials, are subject to the review and approval of the Japanese government. NTT holds a legal monopoly over Japan's domestic telephone, telegraph, data communications lines, and switching networks. It designs its own equipment, which is built to its specifications, usually by its major contractors, NEC, Fujitsu, and Hitachi. NTT maintains three electronics communications laboratories for research on computers, very large scale integration (VLSI), optical fiber cable communications, and other advanced technologies.

It would be a mistake to view these firms as isolated entities, for each is a longstanding member of one or two cohesive corporate groups called *keiretsu*. These groups are bound by equity, management, financing, and buying/selling relationships. For example, NEC belongs to the Sumitomo group and is largely dependent on Sumitomo for its loans. NEC also has its own group consisting of 142 companies that generated total revenues of ¥700 billion in Japanese fiscal year (JFY) 1976. Fujitsu belongs to the Furukawa group, which in turn belongs to the Dai-ichi Kangyō Bank (DKB) group. Hitachi leads its own independent *keiretsu*.[9] And so forth.

NTT's keiretsu is known as the Denden group. The family consists of NEC, Fujitsu, Oki, and Hitachi, and these companies have continued to supply NTT with its important

115

executives. In 1977 the four major suppliers filled nearly 70 percent of NTT's requirements for communications equipment.

In many cases the *keiretsu* creates business opportunities for its members. In the mid-1960s the Dai-ichi Bank (now the Dai-ichi Kangyō Bank) replaced its IBM online banking system with a Fujitsu product. Hitachi introduced its HITAC system at the Sanwa Bank and the Industrial Bank of Japan. The Sumitomo group favors NEC customers and Oki sells huge quantities of terminals to the Fuji Bank.

Each of the major computer companies has also launched cooperative ventures with one or more of the other principal firms, and there are numerous affiliations between their respective *keiretsu*.

Within the *keiretsu*, the banks often take the initiative in encouraging, rather than restraining, a client company's actions. This behavior, which has often puzzled western bankers, can be explained as follows. First, the major banks compete to secure a steady, expanding outlet for depositors' funds. Competition is particularly intense because of the strong Japanese propensity to save and because of the Japanese investor's preference for savings deposits over stocks or other securities. Second, Japanese companies are heavily leveraged, which perpetuates their dependence on borrowed money to meet their financial needs. Third, because the banks in Japan are closely regulated by the government, expanding the volume of lending is the most viable source of revenue growth. The banks tend to select high-growth companies, preferably firms belonging to a designated priority industry that will benefit from tax and other privileges. Fourth, equity money is twice as expensive as borrowed money at the present corporate tax rate (about 50 percent). Since dividend payments are counted as profits while interest payments can be deducted as expenses, many companies favor debt over equity. Equity financing is also less attractive because Japanese companies issue new stock to existing stockholders at par value rather than at its market price.

The pivotal position of the banks and the interlocking

directorates of the major companies within the *keiretsu* networks have dwarfed the influence of the individual Japanese stockholder, The dominance of the corporate shareholder explains why stockholders in many of the large Japanese companies tolerate low profit-to-equity ratios for long periods.

The Stages of Protection

The history of the Japanese computer industry in the post–World War II period can be divided into three periods. In the first period (1951–1963) the industry received modest governmental attention and grew slowly. In the second period (1964–1975) the industry gained increasing strategic importance, received extensive governmental protection and support, and grew rapidly. In the third period after 1976 the government's liberalization program simply extended the policies of an earlier era, but there was now a crucial difference: the semiconductor and computer industry was repositioned to the center of a matrix of new "flagship" industries.

As in the automobile industry, Japan turned to the computer to avert technological domination by the United States. The first projects began in the early 1950s (approximately ten years after the development of the Mark I digital computer in the United States) and were based at the universities and NTT. In 1951 scientists at Tokyo University and the Tokyo Shibaura Company, Ltd. (Toshiba), began full-scale computer development using a large number of vacuum tubes. In 1954 the parametron was invented by Dr. Eiichi Goto of Tokyo University, an event that greatly encouraged government support.

Shortly after this event two new projects were launched. One project administered by the Agency for Industrial Science and Technology sought to formulate computer logic using transistors. A second effort was located at Tokyo University, the Communications Research Laboratory at NTT, and at NTT's international affiliate, the Kokusai Denshin Denwa Co. (KDD). NTT focused on electronic switching using

117

the parametron, while KDD began developing code conversion equipment. These projects laid the foundation for Japan's first commercial computer products.

The arrival of the first American computer exports in 1954 underscored for many Japanese observers the need to develop an independent industry. The principal transistor manufacturers turned to the government for help and in 1955 MITI organized a research committee at their behest to consider the future of the computer industry. The committee followed the pattern of close government-industry collaboration set by the automotive industry, and its members included MITI and NTT officials, prospective manufacturers, and various scientists. Its budget for the first year was $2,200.

The committee's conclusions sketched the course of future policy by three principles: industrial growth should be encouraged; foreign technology should be acquired; and imports of computers should be limited.

The government immediately began to implement the first of these objectives. To encourage industrial growth the Electronics Industry Provisional Development Act of 1957 authorized direct subsidies for the research and development of promising technology, loans to products just entering commercial production, accelerated tax depreciation on plant and equipment and a special tax credit for research and development, and selective exemptions from the antitrust laws to permit cartels for the control and allocation of raw materials, production, and joint research.

In addition, a new electronics industry division was established within MITI's Heavy Industry Bureau, and an Electronics Industry Deliberation Council was created to serve as a liaison with the industry.

Although the government's program was principally under MITI's jurisdiction, MITI did not attempt to regulate directly. Instead, market forces, lubricated by government support, were to drive the industry's development. The total subsidies awarded the computer industry during 1957–1961 were extremely modest (approximately $1 million). One commentator notes that total subsidies, tax savings, and loans from the Japan Development Bank (a long-term credit institution under the jurisdiction of the Ministry of Finance) were less than $25 million.

The cooperation of industry and government that had marked the first stage continued as the industry developed. In 1957–1960 the first commercial Japanese computer projects were introduced and in 1957 both NEC and Hitachi began marketing a series of small business computers using the parametron (known as the NEAC-1200 and HIPAC-1 series, respectively). In 1958, NEC and Hitachi introduced refinements of these models at the first International Information Processing Conference (AUTOMAS) held in Paris under the auspices of UNESCO. These machines may have been the world's first commercial computers that used transistors. Not long after, however, IBM introduced its IBM-1401 model, which influenced the second generation of computers.

Despite their progress, many Japanese industry leaders still feared a foreign takeover. By 1960, foreign imports claimed 70 percent of the Japanese digital computer market, and IBM (and to a lesser extent, Sperry Rand) controlled the basic patents to electronic data processing equipment. IBM, it was felt, would unduly influence the development of Japan's computer industry. To repel this threat, the Japanese government raised the basic tariff rate, as it had done for automobiles, from 15 percent to 25, It also toughened allocations of foreign exchange for imported computers, and inaugurated vigorous buy-Japan procurement policies. MITI conditioned IBM's right to manufacture in Japan and remit profits on the company's agreement to license its basic patents to all interested Japanese manufacturers.

Financing remained a problem. Although the six domestic manufacturers enjoyed easy access to commercial credit and a special tax exemption for strategic industries, the development of the computer was an expensive and risky undertaking. MITI encouraged the industry to pool its resources. This was a new tactic. Its success would encourage similar tactics for other industries. The FONTAC project, sponsored by the Agency for Industrial Science and Technology, served as a prototype for later efforts. Fujitsu took responsibility for software, and Oki and Nippon Electric shared the burden of hardware development. The project lasted three years.

In 1961 MITI, adopting another new tactic, also persuaded the industry to establish a $3 million joint venture called the Japan Electronics Computer Corporation (JECC). The corporation was financed by private industry and by loans from the Japan Development Bank. JECC purchased computers from the manufacturers and rented these computers to end users; the manufacturers agreed to repurchase obsolete equipment. Losses resulting from the repurchase of obsolete equipment could then be partially offset against a special tax reserve fund.

The establishment of JECC gave substantial relief to the Japanese industry, particularly in the early years. IBM and the other foreign firms had been renting their machines at one-fortieth to one-sixtieth of the purchase price (including maintenance costs) per month, and this practice had enticed many Japanese firms to purchase foreign machines. JECC thus served two functions. It met the financial needs of its Japanese members and it discouraged foreign competition. IBM and other foreign manufacturers were excluded from JECC (indeed, many firms like IBM did not need to participate) and, more important, Japanese systems containing more than an established percentage (approximately 25 percent) of foreign-made components were ineligible for JECC financing.

In 1964 IBM announced its production of a new third generation of computers, the system 360, and around the same time General Electric acquired the largest French manufacturer, Machines Bull. Despite their most valiant efforts, Japan's government and business leaders felt the nation was falling farther and farther behind.

MITI's first action was to ask its advisory body, the Electronic Industry Deliberation Council, to strike a course of action. These were the council's recommendations: achieve independent technological excellence, increase domestic

120

market share, expand government industry cooperation, initiate development of a super computer, strengthen JECC, rationalize production of peripheral equipment, and educate new technicians. Most of these goals would be accomplished.

Having set its strategic targets, MITI next turned to the problem of establishing a data base and coordinating its own policies more effectively. The agency first established a data analysis center within its bureau for intelligence and also organized a subcommittee on the information industry in the Industrial Structure Deliberation Council. Thereafter it urged the six computer manufacturers along with JECC to establish a private clearinghouse, the Japan Information Processing Development Center (JIPDEC). In 1965 the Japan Federation of Economic Organizations (Keidanren) formed its own computer policy review committee. These constituted the basic infrastructure that remains critical for the promotion of the industry today.

Between 1966 and 1975 the government also worked closely with the industry to develop target technologies. One important effort (1966–71) was the development of a super-high-performance computer. The project was under MITI's Electro-Technical Laboratory (ETL) and cost ¥10 billion. The participating companies divided responsibilities just as had been attempted in the automobile industry, only this time it fared better. Hitachi (the prime contractor), Fujitsu, and NEC took computer mainframes; Toshiba, Oki, and Mitsubishi took responsibility for optical character recognition (OCR), kanji display and graphic cathode ray tubes (CRT) displays; Hitachi and Fujitsu developed disk drives; Tokyo University began researching highspeed logic circuits; and software was developed through the Japan Software Company, a consortium of the major computer firms.

A second target was the NTT Information Processing System (DIPS) project initiated in 1968 by NTT in collaboration with Fujitsu, Hitachi, and NEC. The project was to connect large-scale on-line (time-sharing) computer systems to electronic exchange and transmission systems. In 1973 NTT announced that the project had developed a model with three times the power of other existing Japanese systems. Since 1973, DIPS has advanced through two new generations of products, the most significant being Fujitsu's DIPS 11/45 in 1982. Fujitsu's newest model, the M382, is virtually identical to the 11/45, a fact that underscores the continuing close relationship of the major manufacturers with NTT.

A third target, the ¥35 billion PIPS (Pattern Information Processing System) project (1971–1980), continued the work of the earlier super-high-speed performance project. PIPS was charged with developing a "fourth generation pattern information" system that could recognize Japanese characters, three-dimensional objects, and human speech. The DIPS, PIPS, and super computer program contributed greatly to closing the gap with IBM in hardware.

Having perceived that growth in one industry often requires corresponding changes in other linked industries, MITI officials carefully coordinated their policies toward the semiconductor and computer industries. This was aided by the fact that the major computer manufacturers were also the major semiconductor producers. In semiconductors MITI's overriding objective was to limit foreign competition and to acquire foreign know-how and technology. From the start the government discouraged foreign purchases of stock in Japanese semiconductor firms; generally limited royalty payments to a single rate, thereby preempting competitive bidding; rejected all foreign requests to establish wholly owned manufacturing subsidiaries and joint ventures with over 50 percent foreign equity; and discouraged foreign purchases of stock in Japanese semiconductor firms.[10]

Texas Instruments' (TI) travails during this period are illustrative. In the early 1960s, TI petitioned the Japanese government for a wholly owned subsidiary and was offered a minority-share joint venture, which it rejected. Its chief bargaining chip during these negotiations was its continuing refusal to license its critical IC patents to Japanese firms without gaining a substantial production subsidiary in Japan in return. NEC and the other firms' sublicensees were in fact producing ICs based on technology developed by TI and

122

Fairchild through an NEC-Fairchild licensing agreement. However, because the TI-Fairchild patent accord explicitly excluded Japan, these Japanese firms were not protected, as Fairchild licensees in Europe were, against patent-infringement suits brought by TI.[11] The Japanese government delayed its approval of TI's patent application in Japan. This action helped NEC and the other firms to catch up, and forced TI to negotiate for quicker access. After the Japanese government restrained Japanese exports of IC-based systems to the United States when TI threatened an infringement action, a compromise was finally reached. TI got a 50 percent share of a joint venture with Sony, and in return TI agreed to license its IC patents to NEC, Hitachi, Mitsubishi, Toshiba, and Sony, and to limit its future share of the Japanese semiconductor market to no more than 10 percent.[12] TI bought Sony's share of the joint venture in 1972, and through 1980 remained the only U.S. semiconductor firm with a wholly owned manufacturing subsidiary in Japan.

By 1969 it was obvious that the six major computer and semiconductor manufacturers were operating inefficiently. MITI understood that if the Japanese firms continued to produce similar systems for a domestic market a fraction of the size of the U.S. market, the Japanese industry would be unable to compete internationally, despite the most generous government assistance. MITI therefore decided to expedite the development of core technologies and to realign the industry.

The basis for MITI's effort was the 1971 Law for Provisional Measure to Promote Specific Electronic and Machinery Industries, which provided legal authority for targeting state of the art technologies. Three categories were designed as strategically important: technologies demanding a special R&D investment (including all technology where Japan was substantially behind the United States—for example, digital computers, integrated circuits); technologies where it was thought a large volume of production would yield economies of scale (magnetic disks and facsimile equipment); and technologies where modernized production techniques were becoming increasingly necessary to improve quality and performance and to reduce production costs.

MITI's policy of realignment had two objectives: first, to reduce the risk of foreign takeovers once capital liberalization began (which even in 1969 was deemed inevitable); and second, to expand production and encourage specialization in order to increase exports and diversify markets.

Realignment, however, did not please the industry. Independent, proud, and fiercely competitive, each of the manufacturers resisted relinquishing autonomy. There were other reasons: the companies' inability or unwillingness to dismiss lifetime employees; the difficulty of restructuring relations with commercial banks; rigidities of vertical integration that inhibited mergers and spinoffs; and the restraints imposed by licensing arrangements with American producers.

Despite these impediments, MITI's policies eventually prevailed. In 1969, exercising its authority under the 1957 Electronics Act, MITI cartelized the production and design of some peripheral equipment. The principles of the cartel are instructive because they show MITI's understanding of the technology. Punchcards and paper tape equipment were cartelized, since further innovation in this sector was considered unlikely. Magnetic disks and tapes were not, since Fujitsu and Hitachi were both compatible with IBM. Later, at MITI's urging, Fujitsu and Hitachi formed the Nippon Peripherals Company, which subsequently competed successfully with IBM in these products.

In 1971 the six major manufacturers also agreed to form three groups to produce the "3.75 generation computer series": Fujitsu and Hitachi, NEC and Toshiba, and Mitsubishi Electric and Oki. During 1972–1976 each group received subsidies totaling ¥7.47 billion for research and development, and an additional ¥4.63 billion was paid to the peripheral equipment manufacturers (which included the six major companies). On the eve of liberalization in 1975 the industry again regrouped. Mitsubishi joined Fujitsu and Hitachi, while Oki Electric split off to specialize as a terminal manufacturer.

The industry groupings were purposeful. The Hitachi-Fujitsu association paired two technically and financially strong companies. In the NEC-Toshiba alignment, the relationship of the American cross licensees may have been more important than the financial strength of the companies. In the United States the computer division of General Electric, the Toshiba licensee, had merged with Honeywell, NEC's licensee. The Mitsubishi-Oki arrangement linked the financially strongest company, Mitsubishi, to the firm with perhaps the closest ties with the United States via its joint venture, Oki-Univac, in which Mitsubishi has since acquired an equity interest.

The alliances also produced a shake-out. Although the Oki-Mitsubishi collaboration produced the COSMOS computer series, Oki withdrew in 1975 (noted, Oki has since concentrated on peripherals and is reported to be doing well). Some observers view Mitsubishi's current pairing with Hitachi and Fujitsu as temporary and limited to the purposes of the VLSI project. Although Mitsubishi has not yet withdrawn, some analysts expect it to do so, perhaps restricting its cooperation to research on data processing and small business systems. The NEC-Toshiba alliance has produced the ACOS computer series (100, 200, 300, 500, 700, 900) and is reported to be proceeding well, although Toshiba may soon withdraw and transfer its employees to other divisions.

Fujitsu's and Hitachi's attempt to build the M series illustrates the conflicts that have at times attended MITI's efforts to promote intraindustry cooperation. Initially Fujitsu was to be responsible for the M-160 and M-190, and Hitachi was to develop the M-170 and M-180 models. The arrangement collapsed when Fujitsu announced its new M-180-II model and Hitachi retaliated with the M-160-II and later the M-200H.

The Fujitsu and Hitachi's cooperation, however, was not entirely fruitless. In September 1973 the two companies formed a 50-50 joint venture, Nippon Peripherals, Ltd. (NPL), to conduct R&D and to manufacture and market peripherals and terminals. NPL has since signed agreements on an original equipment manufacturer (OEM) basis with Memorex, NCR Japan, BASF (Germany), Mitsubishi Electric, and other domestic Japanese manufacturers, and in recent years has greatly expanded its overseas sales.

The third phase of Japan's rationalization of the computer industry began on December 24, 1975, when the Japanese government inaugurated a new round of trade liberalization. Foreign capital investment was greatly expedited and the burdensome import quota system was eliminated. Trade and investment in computers were completely liberalized on schedule by April 1976. On the eve of the announcement of its new policy the cabinet released the following statement:

> Because the computer industry is becoming increasingly important to the future of our economy, society, and the people's daily life, we have tried to foster and strengthen this industry. On the occasion of the import liberalization, to go into force on December 24, 1975, the Government [will continue to] cherish the independence and future growth of Japan's computer industry, and will keep an eye on movements in the computer market so that liberalization will not adversely affect domestic producers nor produce confusion. The Government and the local public organizations, industrial and financial circles shall endeavor to recognize and understand this situation correctly.[13]

This resolution set the tone for the government's liberalization countermeasures policies that continue today. To mitigate liberalization, the government expanded its support for research and development of core technologies and foreign penetration of the Japanese market was checked, principally by limiting foreign procurement opportunities. Japanese planners reasoned that these administrative restraints could gradually be relaxed because market forces naturally would limit foreign participation when Japanese industry became more competitive. By the early 1980s it was hoped that Japan's industry could begin its own drive for the world market.

The most famous and controversial project since liberalization has been NTT's and MITI's collaboration in very large-scale integrated circuits (VLSI). In April 1975 NTT formed

126

a VLSI group with Hitachi, Fujitsu, and NEC to maintain telecommunications at a high level, at a cost of 20 billion. Once the project was underway, MITI proposed consolidating NTT's efforts with MITI's own research, which was at the time conducted jointly with five major manufacturers at MITI's Electro-Technical Laboratory. Initially NTT rejected the idea, primarily because it was reluctant to alter its telecommunications research to suit the more general needs of computer development. Nevertheless, on July 15, 1975, MITI and NTT agreed that part of the two efforts could be joined and in March 1976 the VLSI Technology Research Association was formed, commencing a 4-year program with a budget of ¥70 billion. Basic research was conducted at the joint laboratory of the association, while the Joint Computer Development Laboratory and the Information Systems Laboratory took responsibility for applied research.

The stated aims of the VLSI program were to develop long-term, high-risk process technology and in this regard it succeeded admirably.[14] Even more significant than the technical results of the VLSI program were the economic consequences of Japan's emphasis on production technology. A major portion of the program's initial funding was spent in the United States to purchase electron beam technology and other production and test equipment. The VLSI program substantially reduced the cost of acquiring these technologies at a critical point in the industry's development, but it also helped displace foreign, particularly U.S., imports that until then had dominated the domestic market.[15]

Benefiting from public subsidies, and structured to avoid reduplicative research, Japan's largest computer manufacturers were now free to expand capacity and concentrate on the U.S. market. In 1977, the top six Japanese semiconductor producers spent $116 million on new plant and equipment. That figure rose to an estimated $212 million in 1978, with NEC accounting for $66 million and Fujitsu for $42 million. Most of the investment made by NEC and Fujitsu went to build ICs, especially a production capacity in MOS RAMs.[16] In 1979, spending by the top ten semiconductor producers in Japan climbed to an estimated $420 million. The manufacturers' heavy spending responded to the increasing demand in the domestic Japanese market and to the rapidly growing export opportunities.

The U.S. market was a particular target. During the first two years of the VLSI program, the major Japanese firms (led by NEC and Fujitsu) built up a distribution system in the United States. Prior to 1976, major U.S. distributors had been hesitant to serve Japanese producers who could not meet commitments for large volume and continuous supplies of high-margin memory and MPU devices. This situation changed as the Japanese rapidly expanded production capacity and advanced their technology. By the middle of 1977, NEC, Fujitsu, Hitachi, and Toshiba were all moving toward broad-based distribution channels, which were frequently managed by marketing experts recruited from U.S. companies. By the beginning of 1978 when MOS memory demand jumped in the United States, Japanese firms were well placed to take advantage of the situation.

The strength of the Japanese in MOS production was due largely to the demands of the domestic computer industry, which pulled the technology away from the consumer market and toward higher value-added products. This had three important consequences: it stimulated domestic innovation in design and production, which was soon applied across a broad spectrum of complex products; it displaced foreign imports, forcing U.S. firms to shift to less technologically advanced products; and it prepared the Japanese industry for its onslaught in 1978 into the U.S. market for MOS memory and microprocessor devices.[17]

In exploiting the fruits of VLSI, Japan's growing telecommunications industry, centered at NTT, played as important a part as the computer industry. Historically, NTT bought almost all of its equipment from the Big Four—NEC, Hitachi, Fujitsu, and Oki. NTT would make all decisions on technical specifications. Engineers of the major manufacturers would then be invited to develop new equipment, partly after the basic research had been completed by NTT's own engineers.

Until the end of the 1970s, NTT's procurement was completely closed to foreign firms: the entity even prohibited the four major domestic manufacturers from using imported semiconductors in the equipment they supplied.

Under NTT's guidance the production value of communication equipment rose steadily from under $2 billion in 1973 to over $2.6 billion in 1977. A study by the Bank of America estimates that communication equipment consumed approximately $235 million worth of semiconductors in 1978, with NEC and Fujitsu together accounting for about 35 percent of that total.

NTT also helped to finance exports. Negotiating its equipment purchases on a cost-plus basis, it acted to provide "monopolylike" prices in a manner similar to U.S. military purchases. The exclusion of foreign procurement helped stabilize prices and production volumes while NTT advanced part of the purchase price in the form of interest-free loans to the manufacturer. As a result, Japanese telecommunications exports climbed from 8 percent of sales in the 1970s to 18–20 percent today.

Aiming at Supremacy: Technologies of the Next Generation

The history of Japan's targeting of electronic technologies shows a subtle transition from the immediate dictates of the market to a broader, perhaps deeper, concern with basic research. As described, the early emphasis was on key products just entering commercialization, while the VLSI project and the 1978 Law of Provisional Measures for the Promotion of Specific Machinery focused on production technology. Today the government is interested in basic technology. Its focus of attention is the ten-year, ¥1,128,000,000 project administered by MITI's Agency for Science and Technology to develop "new electronic devices" for the next generation.

The project is subdivided into three distinct areas and it is important to grasp the basic ideas involved. The first is superlattice devices. These are electronic devices of extremely fine, crystalline structures, that can operate at ultra-

129

high speeds. The material itself has the capacity to generate light, so this new technology may play a critical role in opto-electronics and telecommunications generally. Bell Labs, NEC, and Thomson CSF are at present the world leaders in this technology.

The second area involves the development of three-dimensional integrated circuits. Three-dimensional ICs are constructed by alternatively layering active elements and insulation. Three-dimensional integration is expected to reinforce the development of ultralarge-scale ICs and monolithic ICs and to assist in the integration of such functional elements as sensors, processors, memories, and display. Three-dimensional ICs will also accelerate the miniaturization of computers.

Although the IC market is very advanced, the development of cost-effective three-dimensional ICs could have further dramatic effects on cost and efficiency. A primary initial market will be robotics, in particular the development of an artificial eye.

The third project involves the development of "fortified" ICs that can withstand extreme conditions of intense irradiation, temperature, vibrations, and shock. The most likely applications of these devices will be in aircraft, space, nuclear power generation, automobile engines, and defense. Outside of Japan, RCA, Rockwell, Hughes, and the French Atomic Energy Commission are world leaders in this field.

These technologies may be understood as "basic" in at least three ways. First, they aid Japanese IC makers in continuing along a learning curve that has caused the density of IC chips to double virtually every two years since 1960. This fact alone has been responsible for the dramatic decline in cost of IC products.

Second, these technologies are directly targeted at industries that themselves represent the next frontier—advanced computers, robotics, aircraft, and space. Technical breakthroughs in targeted technologies will be transformed into productivity gains in these linked industries.

Third, new functions are basic in a less deterministic sense. There may be a whole range of industries that will benefit in various ways from technological advances in new functions. The project represents an educated stab into the unknown, an investment at high risk, with uncertain payoff. In this sense it departs from the more cautious targeting of technologies of the past, and as later case studies will show, may signal an important new trend in Japan's industrial policies in high technology.

The Development of the Software Industry

In the early years of the Japanese computer industry, manufacturers would usually donate software as an ancillary service in the sale of a computer, believing it to be of little value. As a result the market for software remained less developed.

Around 1970, the Japanese government began to realize that the technology demanded a systems approach. If software were not as vigorously promoted as hardware, the former would increasingly constitute a limiting factor in the computer industry's overall development. MITI embarked on one of its most famous efforts at "structural reinforcement."

The first step was to establish a specialized quasi-public entity known as the Information Technology Promotion Association. IPA has three functions: consignment, credit, and registration of special purpose programs.

The main objective of consignment is to mitigate the risks of developing key software products and to upgrade the quality of these products. To qualify, consignees must satisfy three conditions: there must be a special need for government promotion of the software; the fruits of each development must be viewed as widely usable in business (general utility); and independent development by the private sector is deemed difficult. For the ten-year period ending in fiscal 1979, ninety-seven such programs were developed.[18]

Many of the products of the consignment program were inferior. Efficiency was low, storage difficult, programs unreliable, and similar programs had to be developed for each computer.

To boost the reliability and efficiency of software production, IPA in 1976 started a 6-year program to upgrade production technology. At the center of this development was the Kyōdō Systems Development Company financed by seventeen software firms. Four systems formed the nucleus of the project: a CPL-A language system to help the design and production of software; a CPL-B language system; a data base system to control program modules; and systems relating to peripherals. To date fourteen such subsystems have been completed and four new subsystems are under development.

A second program designed to foster diffusion of software was the system of credit guarantees. Credit guarantees were intended to alleviate the burden that many small software companies encountered receiving adequate financing. The criteria were restricted to:

1. Funds needed to introduce computer mainframes and accessory devices that could increase the efficiency of business operatons.

2. Funds needed for the purchase and development of programs to improve information processing service operations and the technology involved, and for the purchase and development of general purpose and advanced programs.

3. Funds needed to train and educate information processing personnel.

4. Funds needed for other purposes, such as starting on-line information processing services.

In order to encourage the wider use and development of general-purpose programs, the tax system was amended in 1979 to institute a reserve fund system for the development of such programs.[19] Under this system up to 50 percent of the income on arrangements involving general-purpose programs registered with the IPA could be set aside as a program reserve fund. Both private and juridical persons were permitted to register programs. Registered programs had to demonstrate a high level of proficiency and had to fall within a category designated by MITI's Computer Utilization Improvement Plan. Moreover, the applicant had to demonstrate that the program would be transferred to a number of customers without any basic change, and would likely be widely used. Finally, the maker would have to establish that the program was developed with Japan.

In sundry other ways, the Japanese government has sought to develop an infrastructure conducive to software development. Government agencies began to expand their procurement of software programs and the Japan Development Bank soon placed a major emphasis on training EDP engineers, extending loans to promote computer security, and underwriting the developemnt of systems of high social value related to medical care, transportation, disaster prevention, labor and environment, and enhanced line use.

MITI's proposal for a new law for the protection of computer software culminates the agency's 13-year program of promotion. Modeled on the patent system, the law will protect holders of registered software for a period of 10 to 20 years. Mandatory licensing will be required when MITI judges transfer crucial to the objectives of industrial policy. Holders of software rights will be entitled to injunctive relief and damages and a special mediation system will be established to facilitate early settlement of disputes. The bill is one of the most sophisticated approaches to the needs of the software industry formulated by any country.

Lessons of the Case

The history of the development of semiconductors, computers, and telecommunications in Japan illustrates some of the key variables identified earlier and discussed in greater length in Chapter 8. The distinctive features of these industries have been the economies resulting from chip density

133

and learning, the rapidity of technological change by product and process, the speed of technological convergence and diffusion of innovation, and finally, the forward and backward linkages between users and suppliers.

The criteria used for the promotion of the industry established a basic paradigm for the promotion of other strategic industries. In the early days the basic aim was largely to accelerate commercialization of promising technologies and to reduce the costs of plant and equipment. By the 1970s the focus was on costly production technology, and with the passage of the second Electronics Promotion Law attention was placed on technology that promised significant collateral social benefits, such as energy conservation or reduction of pollution. The project for the next generation significantly extends the trend of governmental willingness to support higher-risk, longer-term, increasingly speculative projects offering hope of fundamental scientific and technological breakthrough.

From the outset the targeting of specific technologies was never a purely technical decision. MITI officials well understood that any project they sought to promote would first have to run the gauntlet of bureaucratic acceptability and public understanding. Consensus has thus posed a fundamental constraint upon government action.

The support of software development between 1970–1979 is a good example of the relation between the criteria and consensus. A successful consignee has had to prove that the social benefits of a proposed system justify public expenditure under conditions where the firm cannot expect a reasonable return on its investment. Japan's approach may be among the world's most advanced formulations of the relation of technological development to the public good.[20]

The key to understanding Japan's strategy is the concept of structure. Since the major companies supplied a part of their necessities from their own divisions, vertical integration greatly facilitated convergence and the integration of product and process technology.

MITI reinforced the effects of vertical integration by repeatedly attempting to rationalize the industry. As illustrated by the peripheral cartel and many other examples, MITI demonstrated an acute understanding of the potential and limitations of technology. Moreover, MITI's approach was not to focus on a single technology, but rather on a series or family of related technologies. In this way rationalization could be tailored to the needs of the technology, the market, and the industry as a whole.

A direct consequence of rationalization was intraindustry specialization, not only in semiconductors, but also in computers and telecommunications. Intraindustry specialization enabled rationalized firms to achieve optimal economies of scale that substantially covered the costs of producing these systems' products. Economies of scale in turn helped a rationalized firm move more quickly down the learning curve in each of its devices than would have otherwise been possible. The major firms slanted their production mix to meet the needs of the different domestic and international markets their systems products served.

Contrary to expectation, rationalization did not substantially retard competition. In part this was because the markets were growing fast enough to permit serious competition over increasing shares in segments where the systems products of the major firms overlapped. Despite vertical integration, consumption by the largest firms of their captive production remained relatively low, for example, 10 percent on average among the top four firms in 1979 in MOS devices.[21] The juxtaposition of low internal with high overall consumption may indicate that Japanese firms engaged in significant amounts of intercompany trade.

MITI's policies at times demanded sacrifices. For example, Fujitsu could have penetrated the U.S. market in the 1960s but, it is reported, MITI discouraged this initiative. Even in the early 1970s MITI officials apparently felt that Fujitsu's success would have caused the U.S. government to demand liberalization of the home market before the Japanese industry as a whole was ready to meet intense foreign competition. In another episode, Oki lost favor with NTT because of its close relationship with UNIVAC. Oki eventually withdrew from the computer business in the mid-1970s in order to concentrate on peripherals and communications equipment, where it still remains strong. These events underscore the importance of larger consideratons of industrial policy in the government's specific assistance to the information industry.

The structure of the research effort supported MITI's efforts at rationalization. Although the VLSI project has been widely scrutinized from a technical perspective, it may prove more significant as an institutional innovation. VLSI represented the most elaborate governmental attempt before the fifth generation computer project to orchestrate collaborative research between fiercely competitive firms. In organization the project was without precedent both in terms of the number of participants, the coordination of governmental and private laboratories, and the management of the project through the VLSI Association. From a legal perspective the project posed new problems of protection of trade secrets and the allocation of property rights among the private companies and between the private companies and the government. From the government's perspective the project facilitated diffusion of basic know-how among the participants and their affiliates, and established an esprit de corps at the critical period of liberalization. This contribution alone assured its success, irrespective of the attainment of any of the project's specific goals.

From the beginning the government did everything it could to structure the domestic and later the international market to favor the domestic industry. Foreign penetration of the home market was managed at least until 1976 by high tariffs, quotas, registration requirements, merger policy, and other controls on direct foreign investment, customs practices, and procedures, as well as by "buy-Japan" and other exclusionary policies and practices (such as NTT's procurement policies), and administrative guidance of pricing and the diffusion of technology.

A complex of subsidies designed during most of the 1960s

and 1970s helped push technological development. These included preferential government procurement, credit allocation, and tax incentives. Tax incentives included depreciation for productive facilities, depreciation for purchases, tax credits for R&D, tax provisions relating to JECC, tax breaks for the software industry, including a deferral, a warranty system, a tax credit for the expenses of training information processing engineers, a special depreciation for users, and various tax incentives to promote the export of high-technology products. Market protection and subsidies further supported the dominant position Japanese firms enjoyed in any case by virtue of vertical integration.

The triple objectives of technology-push, user-pull, and market protection were combined in the 1960s and 1970s in the second significant institutional innovation, the Japan Electronics Computer Corporation. JECC purchased state-of-the-art computers from manufacturers (technology-push) and leased these at lower than market rates to users (technology-pull). The government acted as a market maker, matching producers and users, and facilitating the flow of information. Protection was assured, since foreign firms and domestic firms using more than 25 percent foreign components were excluded from JECC.

The combination of domestic subsidies, vertical integration, and structural adaptation gave the Japanese makers a powerful base from which to launch an offensive pricing strategy. By the late 1970s, Burros charges that the major firms were implementing a two-tier pricing strategy that purposely set domestic prices at high levels in order to subsidize dumping, particularly in the U.S. market.[22] More importantly, he notes that the Japanese makers intentionally relinquished a part of the home market in 16k RAMs in order to deflect U.S. producers' attention from the U.S. market. (Exports of 16k RAMs to Japan actually rose in 1979.) Because the major Japanese producers of 16k RAMs were also the principal consumers of this product—a structural advantage U.S. firms did not enjoy—the Japanese firms were able to recapture control of the domestic market in 1980 while still maintaining their dominant position in the U.S. market. The 16k RAM debacle is a warning of the devastating effects of leverage in the rapidly expanding international markets for new technologies.

Despite its early emphasis on MOS memory, the Japanese industry has not neglected bipolar logic circuits. And independence in other areas is also becoming important. The VLSI program contributed significantly to the industry's mastery of production technology. The next step will be to originate its own microprocessor designs or architecture that will succeed Intel's 8086. Although the Japanese industry remains almost entirely dependent on licensed and unlicensed copies of American microprocessors, by leaping from 16- to 32-bit systems, some original Japanese designs may emerge. The most likely source will be NEC's 32-bit processor developed jointly with NTT. A related area will be custom logic circuits built for large computers and other applications. As of this printing all of the major Japanese companies have secured production capabilities in the United States to pursue the markets for custom and gate arrays, where the turnaround time for design and production may be more critical than price cutting.

As noted, the major Japanese computer companies, perhaps with the exception of Matsushita, recorded interest-bearing bank debt-to-owner's equity ratios of between 150 and 400 percent. Ordinarily, high debt-equity ratios of this order imply greater risks to lenders, especially in an industry as volatile as semiconductors. High risk in turn suggests instability in capital sources. In fact, the risks were offset in several ways.[23] First, interest payments were deductible, as they are in the United States, which reduced the theoretical cost of capital. Second, and more important, most obligations were as short as 90 days, which permitted their renegotiation on a regular basis. This introduced an element of flexibility not otherwise available.[24] The Japanese government viewed capital requirements of the computer firms to be as important a problem as its trade and restructuring policies.

Throughout the period, the total supply of Japanese funds

138

was controlled by the Bank of Japan, interest rates were regulated by the Ministry of Finance, and private capital was allocated by the city banks under the guidance of public financial institutions. Since the collapse of a highly leveraged firm threatened the banks, and since a bank collapse could spread throughout the economy, company troubles became a matter of national concern. In exchange for their virtual monopoly, the city banks came to view their commitment to the computer industry as a matter of collective responsibility.

As with the structure of research and the capital markets, the Japanese government recognized early on that an industry as important as electronics would demand new, specially tailored public institutions. Accordingly, it created a new Machinery and Information Industries Bureau within MITI, established new advisory bodies and governmental laboratories, and helped organize various specialized institutions such as the Information Technology Promotion Agency. Finally, government and business leaders recognized the transcendent need to cultivate a cadre of experts and technicians for the information age.

The case study poses three important theoretical questions. First, does the existing capital structure in most countries adequately support the information industries? More specifically, are the information industries special, whether because of the time required for research, their complexity, cost, and risk, or perhaps because of the uncertain magnitude of their benefits? Chapter 3 suggested that the U.S. government has largely been insensitive to the special institutional imperatives of these technologies. The history of the computer industry in Japan shows that that government has at least been grappling with such questions since the 1960s.

Nelson and Winter note that a relatively concentrated industry, particularly in the early days of its development, may be a better shelter for research and development, and may prove more conducive to innovation and productivity than a more competitive, fragmented industry.[25] At the same time concentration demands trade-offs. One is higher prices and restricted output,[26] another is "static inefficiency" that results when "best technology" is monopolized by the market leader. Other problems are higher production costs and greater reduplication of research efforts. A final problem is the tendency of skillful and aggressive firms to capture the profits of the industry's principal innovator through imitation, a serious disincentive to innovation in the long run.

The Japanese government's approach to rationalization and the measures designed to assure the stable supply of capital largely mitigated these trade-offs. Competition in expanding markets tended to drive down prices. Market segmentation avoided reduplication and prevented a single firm from monopolizing key technologies. The structure of the industry also helped diffuse the benefits of technological development. The strengths of the major firms rested on segmented but overlapping final markets, which in turn promoted even more sophisticated specialization. The government's rationalization policies accelerated this process and helped each firm maximize scale economies and descend the learning curve. The results were cheaper devices and cheaper systems using these devices.

Chapter 6

Engineering a Societal Cerebral Cortex: Telecommunications, Mechantronics, and the Marriage of Biotechnology and Electronics

Case 3: Planning Telecommunications: The Problem of Overmanagement

Most strategic industries require government involvement at some point during their life cycle. Telecommunications is no exception. In the United States the telephone system has been operated as a regulated private monopoly since the turn of the century. In Japan telecommunications are owned and managed by the Ministry of Posts and Telecommunications and NTT.

When technologies change, this change challenges preexisting forms of management. The challenge is often from new competitors who want to enter the system. In theoretical terms, the availability of new, cheaper products draws into fundamental question the original justification for monopoly prerogatives. The monopolies in both Japan and the United States today face new demands from competitors and have begun to reorganize and to reform.

It now appears that Japan's strategy is to maintain government ownership and control of the monopoly while phasing in competition at the local area and in certain industrial segments. NTT's recently proposed twenty-year information network system suggests that the agency may be placing even greater reliance on planning and a systems approach to this industry.

This study reviews the key elements of this strategy: the plan itself; rationalization of circuit use; the restructuring of the monopoly; accelerated development of fiber optics, lasers and related technologies; and the fifth-generation computer. The fundamental question is the extent to which Japan's systems approach will positively reinforce technological change and market forces, or whether, by restricting the entry of new firms and in other ways by dominating this industry, the monopoly will smother innovative opportunity and obstruct Japan's transition to an information-based society.

The Plan: The Information Network System (INS)

NTT's 20-year plan will integrate computer and tele-communications on a scale unparalleled in history. In essence the INS links home and business telecommunications with congeries of information-processing centers and a highly sophisticated network. Users will select from a broad array of customized consoles including telephones, facsimiles, and data and video terminals. The telephone will assume new functions as an answering machine and relay.

When completed, the network will be totally digitalized and constructed with optical fibers. Information will flow from video to facsimile and continue on to data terminals. The network will store, process, and transmit various types of information by large-scale and decentralized processing units. Customers will be able to use any terminal for multiple functions simply by connecting the terminal to the available circuit. This will allow businesses to transact business away from the office or at home.

The INS will be implemented in four steps. The first will introduce and promote visual communication services; the second will establish an experimental digital network; the third will extend these experiments to the existing network;

142

the fourth will develop a comprehensive system for information processing.[1]

The essential premise of the development of visual communications services is that communication is more effectively delivered visually than aurally. An important element of the INS will be the facsimile, which permits high-speed transmission of types of information that are difficult to present orally. Facsimile also provides a convenient mode of communications for those who have difficulty speaking or hearing. Other nontelephone services will include telemeter and telecontrol. Telemeter systems use communications circuits to monitor remote locations. Telecontrol permits remote operation of instruments via electronic signals. Telemetric and telecontrol systems will increasingly be used for remote process control in factories.

A natural consequence of the rapid progress already achieved in semiconductors, VLSI, and processing of digital signals is digitalization of communications. NTT intends to promote digitalization through the more effective and economical use of communications networks, to digitalize existing telephone and telex systems, and eventually to link the entire NTT service by a single digital network.

The origins of this concept are in the 1971 amendments to the Public Telecommunications Law that opened telephone and telex networks to data processing. These networks were based on analog systems ill-suited to data communications. To remedy the situation, in December 1979 NTT developed a tailored data communications system known as DDX (Digital Data Exchange Network) to permit circuit switching, and in 1980 NTT introduced its packet switching system. NTT intends to promote digitalization by creating regional facsimile communications networks at competitive rates and by phasing digital switching facilities into the existing telephone network.

NTT's plan also envisions adding new communications processing functions, upgrading the efficiency of each step, and integrating the whole system. In the past the principal obstacle to constructing a telecommunications network was

Partners in Prosperity

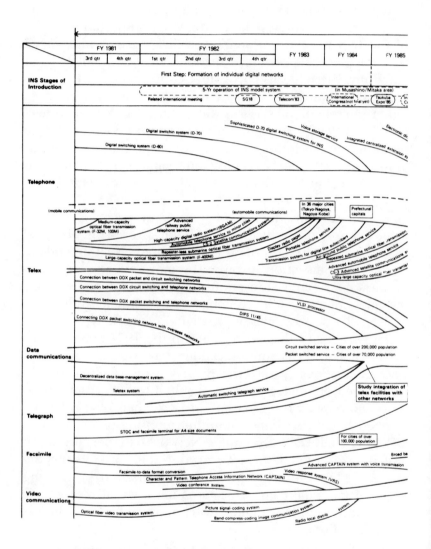

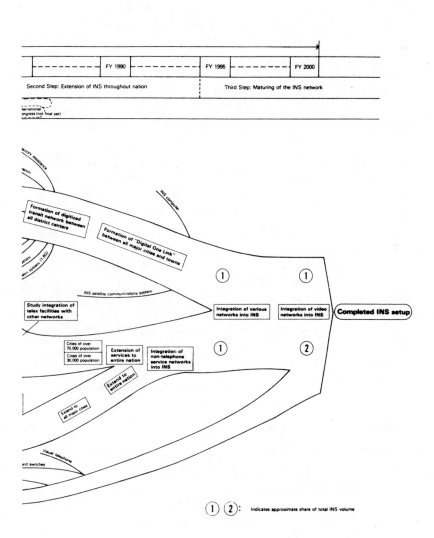

| | FY 1990 | | FY 1995 | | FY 2000 | |

Second Step: Extension of INS throughout nation

Third Step: Maturing of the INS network

ternational
ongress (not final yet)

ctory assistance

rism

Formation of digitized transit network between all district centers

INS computer

Formation of "Digital One Link" between all major cities and towns

rism

ion system (1.60)

INS satellite communications system

Study integration of telex facilities with other networks

Integration of various networks into INS

Integration of video networks into INS

(Completed INS setup)

Cities of over 70,000 population

Cities of over 30,000 population

Extension of services to entire nation

Integration of non-telephone service networks into INS

Extend to entire nation

Extend to all major cities

Visual telephone

and switches

① ② : Indicates approximate share of total INS volume

145

the effective transmission of information. Today this problem has largely been alleviated by the advent of VLSI technology. Streamlining storage, exchange, and processing of information are now principal concerns. The INS will make maximum use of network architecture, essentially a system of rules to ensure the smooth operation of the entire system as new functions are added to existing terminals and as linkages among computers proliferate. Network architecture will permit computers to share data files and distribute processing functions, contributing substantially to the system's efficiency.

INS will involve massive storage and retrieval, which in turn will depend increasingly on advances in information-processing technology. Users will be able to access data at reasonable prices through interlinked terminals at home or in the office. A prototype will be constructed at Mitaka by mid-1983.

Although the overall impact of the INS will greatly exceed the sum of its individual parts, its various components are themselves far more than simple subsystems. The INS should be conceived of as an administrative framework that helps organize various research areas deemed critical for a host of reasons, some quite apart from the requirements of the INS itself. This principle is particularly true of the national projects on fiber optics and the fifth-generation computer.

Rationalization of Circuit Use

The second key element of Japan's telecommunications strategy is the deregulation of circuit use. A complex of arcane rules and regulations has cramped the development of communications by retarding MITI's efforts to infuse the computer throughout industry and society in general.

Message switching is defined in Japan as the "mediation of information by computers without changing its content." The concept is somewhat broader than in the United States, since it involves value-added data processing, packet switching, and store and forward data processing.

In the past, message switching was prohibited. For example:

An electric products company (G) plans to introduce a sales-inventory system between itself and (H), a warehouse company. In the past NTT would have rejected the system because the transfer of receipt-shipment data would constitute message switching. As a result, G would have had to establish a branch office in the warehouse company and applied for permission to use the circuits for data communication as a single user. G would have had to bear the extra costs of unnecessary personnel.[2]

When a data-processing company or computer service bureau in the past connected its patron to its computer by a communication circuit, it was considered to be subletting the circuit for third-party use. There was no additional charge. However, two basic conditions were imposed: the computer of the service bureau could not be used for message switching, and only terminals of the same company or companies having a specific business relationship were permitted to communicate via the computer bureau.

Formerly, when a computer of one company was connected to an input/output device of a second company, the circuit was considered to be in shared use by the two companies. Although at present there is no additional charge, joint use is still subject to specific restrictions. The most onerous requirements are: the companies must conclude a joint-use contract with NTT or KDD; message switching is not permitted; and the companies must be affiliated in a specific business relationship designated by the regulations.

The limitations on business use are the most cumbersome. If a company is not within one of the prescribed relationships, it must apply to NTT for special permission. However, NTT continues to obscure the criteria for permission and still does not disclose fully the kinds of past relationships it has approved. Given the cost of developing a complex data communications system, and the uncertainty of approval, many companies have been forced to abandon their plans after introducing new systems.

Approval of the Ministry of Posts and Telecommunications is required before interconnecting a specific-use circuit to a switching public network circuit via a computer or concentrator. Such interconnections have in the past been authorized without charge if the conditions for joint computer use were met, and if a public network terminal in a location was not connected to a public network terminal in a second location. In practice, an additional charge continues to be levied in various circumstances to compensate the carrier for losses of its trunk call revenues.

In early 1980 demand for the removal of the use restrictions began to mount with the opposition centering in MITI. The focus of MITI's attack was the interim report on June 15, 1981 of the Subcommittee on Information Policy within the Council on Industrial Structure. After stressing the overriding importance of the government's information intensification policies, the report identified three areas of attack. The first was the restrictions in the telecommunications laws pertaining to message switching, joint use, and circuit interconnections. The second was the differential in rates, particularly long-distance rates which, the report alleged, would destroy all incentives for data processing. The third were the policies and practices of MPT that depressed competition in the private sector. The report concluded by recommending that NTT and MPT:

• Immediately amend the telecommunications laws

• Clarify or remove all restrictions on message switching and joint use of circuits

• Facilitate the introduction of Digital Data Exchange (DDX) and packet switching, and

• Stimulate competition in the private sector

MITI's views were soon echoed by the Keidanren (Japan Federation of Economic Organizations). In its proposal of July 28, 1981, the Keidanren offered these recommendations:

148

1. Liberalize the telecommunications laws:
   (a) abolish restrictions on joint use of circuits, except where essential; (b) permit incidental message switching; (c) liberalize restrictions on public-private interconnections; (d) promote a broad interpretation of international telecommunications agreements; and (e) remove the differential in long-distance rates.

2. Promote software and the increase of productivity:
   (a) establish a clearinghouse to help users gain access to computer programs; (b) strengthen existing assistance programs to the software industry; (c) clarify the copyrights of developers of software programs; and (d) establish subsidies to facilitate the unbundling of software and hardware systems.

3. Develop data bases:
   (a) strengthen national data bases, particularly in the energy field; (b) facilitate the transfer of government-held data bases to the private sector; and (c) open government-held information to public review within the limits of smooth administration.

4. Establish a social information system that is open to public review, yet protects individual privacy.

NTT was further castigated by the recommendations of the Administrative Management Agency. This constituted the strongest indictment to date of the inefficiencies in the Japanese telecommunications system. The recommendations censured the MPT (Ministry of Posts and Telecommunications), particularly for its sloppy budgetary practices, the unreasonably high rates of telephone service, and its use of telephone revenues to subsidize computer services. The report demanded a thorough investigation and separate accounting of the agency's computer and telecommunications services.

Although the computer industry stood in many ways to be the principal beneficiary of liberalization, the industry remained largely silent. Some commentators explained this reticence by the close links of the six major computer makers, the Denden family, with NTT.[3] Indeed, in 1980 the group supplied approximately 92 percent of the nearly $400 million total sales of data communications equipment to NTT. Other voices, such as the small, uninfluential on-line data processing service, also remained silent. These companies well knew that MPT and NTT could easily retaliate by rejecting or delaying applications of interconnection or joint use.

NTT and MPT have vigorously fought off their opponents. NTT cites the mandate in its charter of 1982 that promised better service for customers. It notes that the agency has pioneered the development of on-line services and therefore deserves to continue to play an important role. Both MPT and NTT have stressed the national importance of the INS project and the need to maintain a monopoly over communications circuits to "preserve national security."

The results of the debate are still uncertain. Joint use, including message switching, will probably be liberalized for companies in close association, and joint use without message switching will be permitted for unaffiliated companies. A permit system will probably be introduced to allow third-party use, including message switching. All other cases will be liberalized but a notification will be required to the Minister of MPT. Intracompany and public-leased connections will be significantly liberalized, except for those involving message switching. Interconnections with private lines (public-leased-public) will most likely be approved on a special basis.

Restructuring the Monopoly

A third element in Japan's strategy is the proposed reorganization of NTT. Besides the complaints over the circuit use restrictions, NTT has had to cope with the forces demanding its restructuring. One problem has been its declining credit balance on telephone services, which accounts for over 90 percent of its overall income. Another issue has been inefficient management of personnel. A third has involved NTT's long-standing inflexible labor agreements that have limited the agency's efforts to rationalize operations.

On July 30, 1982, the Second Ad Hoc Committee on Administrative Reform released its final report that has framed

150

the debate over NTT's reorganization. The report focused on three issues: rationalizing management on the lines of private industry; setting competitive rate structures sensitive to technological change and innovation; and restructuring the agency to maximize its efficiency despite its cumbersome organization.

The report urged that NTT be broken up into a central company and several local services within five years. The central company will own stock of the local companies, will be responsible for the construction, maintenance, and operation of trunk lines, will own and manage the Electric Communications Laboratory, and will make arrangements for the separate accounting and division of revenue of the local companies. The local companies will construct, maintain, and operate the circuits and provide services within their operating areas.

In time the central company will sell its stock to the public, taking account of market conditions. Similarly, the government might gradually divest a part of its shares in the central company.

Under certain conditions companies offering satellite communication and optical fiber cable will be permitted to enter the network. New entrants may offer limited as well as nationwide service. In addition, these parties will be permitted to offer telephone and other services to certain users through their own circuit facilities and, by linking their own trunk lines, to the circuits of local companies under conditions as determined by the central company.

The rate structure will also be reviewed and reformed.

NTT's customer equipment section, its data communications supply section, and part of its maintenance section, will all be made independent. Labor disputes will continue to be regulated and restricted by three labor laws. All existing NTT labor-management agreements will be reviewed and new procedures established for disputes involving maintenance workers. Personnel rationalization in the telephone operator and other operation sectors, maintenance sector, and telegraph sector will also be encouraged and measures taken to correct

151

the credit deficit, including the abolition of nighttime delivery. Finally, measures will be taken to avoid tariff differences between service areas due to variations in profitability. Rate differences caused by distance will be corrected and an appropriate charge system established as in the United States to divide revenue equitably among service areas.

As of this writing, NTT and MPT are still vigorously resisting reorganization.[4] A strange coalition of the Liberal Democratic Party (LDP) and factions of the Socialist and Communist parties are supporting NTT on the grounds that divestiture will raise telephone rates and cause regional gaps in services and rates. The business community and the press favor divestiture because they believe it will best stimulate the industry's long-run development.

Accelerated Development of Technologies

Japan's fourth strategy is to accelerate the development of critical technologies. Optical fibers permit information in the form of packets of light to be transmitted at speeds and quantitites far exceeding the capacities of copper wire. These bundles of fibers can transmit pictures from one surface to another, around curves, and into otherwise inaccessible places, with an extremely low loss of definition and light, by a process of total reflection. Lasers are essentially devices to transform random light particles of various frequencies into a very narrow, intense beam of coherent light.

At the heart of the INS concept is the transformation of communications by fiber optics. The development of fiber optics in Japan is part of a broader national effort including lasers, optical ICS, optical computers, communications, machine tools, and systems that combine these components that include computer-controlled systems, optical communications systems, optical information processing systems, and optimal energy use systems.

The rationale for government support of the optical industry is identical with that of other new industries. MITI's report states: "In the development of an optical technology

152

industry, free competition has a basic role; however, because of the great risks involved, it is also necessary for government to play a part. This is particularly necessary in this early stage of the industry's takeoff. It will also be necessary to prepare a suitable environment for its development thereafter."[5]

The elements of MITI's promotion follow the orthodox pattern of other industries: support for joint research, large-scale national projects, government assistance in the diffusion of technology, and construction of a statistical data base.

The central financial agency involved is the Japan Development Bank. All the projects will last seven years and are designed to achieve the three objectives of the Law for the Promotion of Certain Information Based Machinery: the promotion of research, industrial rationalization, and accelerated technological change. In accordance with the "public" objectives of the law, all projects qualifying for loans must demonstrate that they will contribute to the protection of the environment, the prevention of hazards, or the rationalization resource use.

The government has also launched two long-term, large-scale national projects to establish closer cooperation with industry and the academic community. The first, an eight-year project, will develop fiber optics in the context of advanced computer systems at a cost of ¥18,000,000,000. The second, a 7-year project, will cost ¥13,000,000,000 and will develop advanced laser systems.

The Fifth Generation Computer

If the INS will constitute the veins and arteries of Japan's future communications system, information will be its blood, and the fifth-generation computer its heart. It is helpful to discuss briefly the synergism in the information industry to understand this point fully.

Perceiving the synergism between computers and telecommunications, the Japanese government is promoting software in general and the fifth-generation computer in particular. The first synergism is the software-hardware connection. The design of VLSI technology is now so complex that software tools such as computer-aided design—especially computer graphics—are now indispensable. Telecommunications provides the means of accessing data that will help perfect the next generation of designs for microprocessors, switching circuits, and other products.

The second synergism derives from the hybridization of computers and telecommunications. The telephone is no longer solely a telecommunications device. Its power is now largely dependent on the microprocessor, a computer or chip contained within it. Telephones increasingly will perform various data-processing functions, and the telecommunications circuit itself is being transformed into a network of computers. These high-powered computer networks are themselves increasingly essential to the advanced engineering of software.

Third, the computer and telecommunications today are involved in a kind of technological dance with each limiting and stimulating the other. Each new breakthrough in computer hardware or software opens opportunities and imposes pressure for a corresponding, "sympathetic" adjustment in telecommunications. Each advance in telecommunications creates an incentive for a technological breakthrough in computers.[6]

Finally, the development of the automated office, particularly the intelligent work station, is dramatic evidence of the synergistic and integrated development of computer software and hardware.

The project will extend ten years, cost over $400 million, and involve NTT, MITI, and eight private companies, Fujitsu, Hitachi, Nippon Electric, Mitsubishi, Toshiba, Oki, and Matsushita. The project is located in a new organization, the Institute for New Generation Computer Technology (ICOT).

The project's basic purpose is to develop a knowledge information-processing system endowed with very advanced problem-solving capacities. Intelligence will be greatly improved; the relation of man and machine will mimic a human interaction. The machine will understand problems and questions, analyze information, and formulate and communicate a response.

The elements of the system are: basic software;[7] an intelligent support system;[8] an intelligent utility system;[9] a basic knowledge base;[10] a basic applications system;[11] and various applications systems.[12]

In brief, the fifth-generation computer will be a congeries of small and large machines integrated by a common language (PROLOG).[13] The system's architecture will all be new, involving a network of subsystems based on advanced VLSI. A prototype is planned for 1990.

The project will stimulate six fields of technical development. The first is VLSI. Although these devices have already been introduced into memories, the aim of the Fifth-Generation Project is to combine them in storage systems involving memories and logic. Today's microprocessors are a first step toward linking these two functions. One objective of the project is to construct an intelligent computer-aided design (CAD) system to permit reuse of data from past designs.

The second is the development of new materials for high-speed devices. Examples are optical technology, Josephson junctions, and gallium arsenide devices that, it is thought, will outstrip silicon as a medium for electronic transmission. Although the development of these devices is not a direct objective of the program, the demand for advanced VLSI will indirectly stimulate their development.

The 1981 White Paper notes: "The progress of the development of these devices mut be watched so that they can be incorporated into the project at some intermediate stage . . . should these devices prove sufficiently practical and capable of superior performance."[14] The report emphasizes the attractiveness of Josephson junctions because they require virtually no energy in storing information.

A third field is software development. One of the major objectives of the project is the construction of highly intelligent support systems, or in other words, programs that will automatically rewrite themselves to prepare new programs or to adjust changed specifications.

A fourth is the development of artificial intelligence and pattern recognition technology. According to MITI officials, a computer system geared to artificial intelligence will be developed at an early stage of the project along with computers that will be able to understand patterns such as graphics, images, speech, voice, and characters. This in turn will be achieved in part by further development of parallel-processing technology such as SIMD (Single Instruction Information Multi-Data) systems that will greatly enhance the capacity of control systems to draw inferences that are critical for artificial intelligence.

Finally, the project will accelerate the integration of computer and telecommunications technology. The White Paper continues:

It is necessary to establish a technology which can connect a local network associated closely with a computer to a global network used for communication, and then to establish a system for allowing jobs and data bases to be distributed readily. Attempts have steadily been made to provide a foundation for realization of the foregoing technology and system, the technology of optical communication being an example. A wide variety of efforts ranging from technological research and development to standardization should further be made by those concerned.

One ideal to be realized toward and in the 1990s is either a nationwide or worldwide information system which utilizes a communication network for making correct and precise information readily available elsewhere.[15]

Some foreign critics have challenged the Fifth-Generation Project as grounded on an uncritical acceptance of various programatically dubious, avant-garde concepts. Such comments in many respects reflect ignorance of the real significance of the project.

Although the project's ultimate goals, if attained, will certainly constitue a remarkable scientific accomplishment, the stated technical goals are only part of the objectives. As with other "revolutionary" technologies, the societal benefits of the fifth-generation computer effort may greatly exceed the

156

market value of the final product. In this light the project is a practical means of training a cadre of young (many of the key scientists are under thirty), farsighted software engineers. It will join several important fields of research and through the exchange of ideas and experience will accelerate the convergence and diffusion of groups of important technologies. The fifth-generation computer project is far more complex than its VLSI predecessor in the number of participants, the length of time, and the project's scale and ambitions. If successful, it will create a new vocabulary, a form of communication among scientists and between scientists and the rest of society that will profoundly influence Japan's transition to a technology-based society.

Lessons of the Case

Telecommunications today is rapidly converging with computer and semiconductor technology. The Japanese government has adopted a systems approach to accelerate this development by focusing on key synergistic relationships. Its approach involves public ownership and controlled access and use of the circuits, unified management, and targeting of key technologies all in the context of the INS plan.

There are real costs to a systems approach. Virtually all countries subsidize local rates via long lines. In Japan, however, users of long-distance lines pay forty times what local users pay, and the tariff schedules are difficult to amend because the Diet sets the tariff. The rate is substantially less in most other industrialized countries. NTT's policies adversely affect consumers, time-sharing and data-processing firms, and specialized carriers, whose entry continues to be limited. Here the burden may fall most heavily on foreign firms, since most of these firms cannot meet the requirement of close "affiliation" that would bring them within the ambit of permitted data-processing activity.

The most serious consequences of NTT's approach may be its influence on industrial policy itself. Professor Kenichi Hirai, for example, notes the serious impediments NTT's

157

"technology first" strategy presents for the development of the telecommunications industry, for regional experimentation, diversification, innovation, and the diffusion of computer services throughout the country.[16]

A theoretical challenge underlies his and other criticisms that has not been fully addressed. In the early days of telecommunications, the Japanese government, as other governments, considered it inefficient to permit many companies to compete in stringing telephone wires to each household. Because of the need for orderly administration of this critical sector and also because of clear economies of scale, telecommunications was viewed as a natural monopoly. Due to recent breakthroughs in communications technology and intense competition in this market, treatment of telecommunications as a natural monopoly no longer seems valid.

How then is NTT's strategy to be justified? The INS, like the VLSI, the fifth-generation computer, and the various projects of the next generation, provides a framework for action and as such is a powerful tool to organize consensus. In Japan this is a significant attribute. From a systems point of view there may also be something to be said for NTT's efforts to preserve the integrity and stability of the research. It was just such an environment in the old Bell system that led to the development of systems and information theory, the transistor, and a range of now familiar, fundamental innovations. What is unclear is whether NTT will smother by overprotection the industries it seeks to foster. If so, telecommunications policy will prove the Achilles' heel of Japan's strategy for the information industries.

Case 4. Toward Mechatronics: A Detailed Look at the Systems Approach

Since the 1950s the Japanese government has been concerned about productivity in the workplace and has actively fostered technologies that promised to make manufacturing more efficient. The machine tool industry has been the strategic industry of longest standing, although in recent years robotics and flexible manufacturing have also become important. In these new modes of production the computer dominates, and it is the long-term implications of the integration of electronics with mechanical engineering (mechantronics) with which I am here most concerned.

The Japanese Machine Tool Industry, 1955–1982

As early as the mid-1950s, the Japanese government recognized the coming importance of machine tools. To this end it followed a strategy similar to those for the automobile and computer industries: it commenced a well-coordinated effort to concentrate its fragmented domestic machine tool industry into a cartelized oligopoly, comprising the most successful manufacturers. Once it achieved cartelization, the government induced the cartel to focus on higher value-added numerically controlled (NC) machine tools and sustained the cartel by tax breaks, concessionary loans, grants for research and development, and a protected home market.[17]

As discussed in case 2, the First Extraordinary Measures Law established a basic framework for concentrating and promoting the Japanese electronics industry. In the early days the key provisions were Article 2, which directed MITI to prepare a "basic rationalization plan" for each of the machinery industries designated by Cabinet Order, and Article 6, which authorized the Minister of International Trade and Industry to "instruct" persons engaged in one of these industries to take concerted action deemed "specially necessary for achieving the rationalization target." Concerted action could include imposing restrictions on the kinds of products manufactured, setting production quotas, adopting restrictions on technological development, and establishing arrangements for jointly purchasing parts and materials.

To expedite rationalization, the law established two forms of antitrust immunity. The first was a formal, de jure immunity for actions conducted under an instruction from MITI. The second was an informal, de facto immunity for cases where the industry voluntarily complied with MITI's basic rationalization plans. The statute placed clear limitations on formal immunity. For example, Article 7 provided that joint activities should not exceed those "necessary . . . for attaining the rationalization target as set forth in the basic rationalization plan." Activities could not be "unduly discriminatory" nor "unduly detrimental to the interests of consumers in general as well as persons engaged in related enterprises."

The Minister of International Trade and Industry was to survey the joint activity conducted under his instructions and to revoke permission for violations of the conditions of the immunity. Companies acting in concert were obligated to file timely reports with MITI. Firms voluntarily complying with MITI's policies, however, could virtually ignore all these restrictions. Not surprisingly, some of the subsequent concerted actions were based on this second form of immunity.

On July 20, 1956, MITI identified "[m]etal cutting machine tool[s]" as one of the categories of "Specific Machinery" encompassed by the First Extraordinary Measures Law and on March 15, 1957, issued a Notification of its Basic Rationalization Plan. The general purposes and strategies of this plan resembled plans for other strategic industries. They were "to promote the modernization of facilities as well as . . . to increase the manufacturing quantity per product of each manufacturer by centralizing the varieties of manufactured products," and "to advance quality and performance and to reduce . . . manufacturing costs." Elsewhere MITI announced its goal "[t]o promote specialization in manufacturing and to seek . . . centralization of manufacturing by product, to seek standardization of parts, to rationalize the method of purchasing thereof," and finally, to establish collaborative research institutions for the advancement of these technologies. According to MITI officials, the latter goal was never achieved.

In August 1957 the Japan Machine Tool Builders Association established a Manufacturing Shares Deliberation Committee chaired by Mr. Koiwai, then vice-president of Mitsui Seiki. The deliberations of the committee produced the first scheme for market allocation, an "Agreement Concerning Concentrated Manufacturing" concluded in November 1960, later amended on May 20, 1966, and again on November 9, 1967. According to the Houdaille petitioner, the last amended version set forth its basic purposes: "to achieve coexistence and co-prosperity of the industry by arranging to keep the size of companies appropriate, making efforts to rationalize management thereof and cooperatively establishing an orderly production field allocation system by means of concentrating those manufacturing on products already being manufactured" (p. 62).

The agreement provided that:

Each of the members of the association shall not manufacture types of machines [the] manufacturing of which may cause disorder in the production field allocation system of the industry, other than those types of machines which are currently manufactured (types of machines which were actually manufactured for the years 1962 and 1963 or types of machines which were manufactured after the year 1964 and were reported to the association (p. 63).

The extent of concerted activity mandated under the agreement was exemplified by the directive of paragraph 4:

So far as it does not cause any disorder in the production field allocation system, each of the members shall concentrate its manufacturing on the type[s] of machines which are exchanged or transferred through technical or business cooperation among the members of the association for the reason that such exchange or transfer is advantageous to the members or contributes to the development of the industries (p. 64).

Finally, each member of the association was obligated to give notice to the association when it planned to commence manufacturing "types of machines other than the current types of machines."

On July 1, 1968, MITI updated the Basic Promotion Plan for the metal-cutting machine-tool manufacturing industry. Specific production goals for fiscal year 1970 were set at

¥135 billion worth of metal-cutting machine tools, ¥22 billion of which were targeted by MITI for export.

Small-scale production of machine types was discontinued in order to further the establishment of "a specialized production system by concentrated manufacturing." By notification, MITI prescribed the "[a]ppropriate production scale" for each of twelve types of metal-cutting machine tools, divided by the types of tools to be produced by each company per month. Each company was to stop manufacturing types of machines when its share was "less than 5%" and production "less than 20%" of the company's total production. Companies were to concentrate manufacturing on the "main machine types, whose production might attain the appropriate production size."

The notification also stated:

With respect to machine tools, . . . adjustment of kinds of manufactured manufactured machines [shall be conducted] within the group of companies manufacturing such machines, and if the proper production size cannot be reached by means of adjustment within the group . . . adjustment with other groups or other enterprises, or rearrangement of the groups [shall be made] so that the proper production size can be reached (p. 65).

Other provisions of the notification stressed the importance of industry-wide collaboration in research, production, marketing, export, and technical development toward the goal of attaining a rational market structure. On April 1, 1969, after some debate among the members of the association and its board of governors, the association complied with the directive in the Basic Plan.

Although in every case the association ultimately capitulated to MITI's directives, there was always intense debate. Both with respect to these disagreements as well as to conflicts among its members, the cartel agreement served as a powerful means of dispute settlement. The agreement contained the following provision:

When it is difficult for individual members of the association to achieve [proper production quantity and to stop manufacturing certain specified machines], such members shall make efforts to achieve the target by trying at first to rearrange among member companies of the group the types of machines manufactured and then technical or business cooperation should be planned with other groups or among members of the association; provided, however, [that] the number of member companies manufacturing each type of machine shall not be increased (p. 70).

Under the revised agreement each member wishing to produce a new type of machine was obligated to report to the association. These reports were then reviewed by a special production field (market allocation) committee. After completing its deliberations the committee tendered the report to the board of directors of the association, which transmitted its views to the concerned member. The board of directors was empowered to make final determinations on whether the member's "report" would be granted or denied.

In August 1970, a "questionnaire on concentrated manufacturing" was sent to sixty-eight cartel members soliciting their views on whether "free competition should be completely allowed." In their responses, sixteen members advocated abolishing the cartel agreement in favor of competition, and fifty-two supported continuation in its current or some varied form. The majority prevailed. The association's "Machine Tool News" described this result in its March 1971 issue:

This will mean that the current agreement, although not uniformly enforceable because it was based on joint private action and is not mandated by law, deserves support on the merits of its contribution toward maintaining order in the industrial system by restraining the members' will to easily advance into the manufacture of other types of machines[s] . . . Accordingly, even after liberalization measures are taken, to maintain fair competition, industrial groups should cooperate to some degree to avoid excessive competition (p. 72).

On January 14, 1971, the board of directors approved a revised "Standard Agreement" that was still in force in 1983. Its preamble states:

Each of the members of the association shall make efforts to promote a rational production system by taking such measures as effective development of new products and concentrated manufacture of main products, in order to accommodate itself to [the] development of internationalization and perform its responsibility as a supplier of machine tools which are fundamental equipment for machinery industries and shall seek its development by maintaining the co-existence and co-prosperity of the industries.

In order to perform the responsibilities described above, it is desirable for the members of the association always to develop new products and to know the production situation of other members. Therefore, each of the members of the association shall cooperate in making notification regarding new products.

If any of the members of the Association manufactures new products using its own technology or as a result of technical or capital cooperation (including joint ventures in which such member participates) with foreign companies, such member shall make a notification thereof to the association with respect to each of the new products (p.74).

Under this arrangement, any member wishing to manufacture a new product can submit a notification of intent to the association. The association then circulates a copy of this notification to all members, any of which may submit written comments to the association within one month. All such comments are promptly conveyed to the notifying member. When the association believes a member's opposition will hinder the sound development, co-existence, and co-prosperity of the industry, the association was authorized to negotiate with the member after hearing the views of the competent authorities.

Since the first cartel, MITI officials have clearly understood the need to stimulate numerically controlled (NC) machining centers. As a result, these products were exempted. Other NC tools were controlled and allocated only to those firms with demonstrated substantial production.

Several months after enactment of the Second Extraordinary Measures Law in 1971, the Japanese Cabinet issued an Enforcement Order implementing this law. Article 2 of this order specifically designated "[m]etal cutting machine tools" and "[h]igh efficiency, computer controlled metal cutting machine tools" as well as certain "[n]umerically controlled metal forming machines" as machines targeted for production.

On August 13, 1971, MITI released its "Elevation Plan for the Metal Cutting Machine Tool Manufacturing Industry." The plan focused precisely on NC metal cutting machine tools. The introductory paragraph of the plan states that it is "limited only to enterprises that manufacture numerically controlled metal cutting machine tools and computer-controlled metal cutting machine tools." Paragraph 3 of the plan exhorts Japanese manufacturers of these products

[t]o try to increase the degree of specialization so that the production share of numerically controlled metal cutting machine tools and computer controlled metal cutting machines tools in each manufacturing enterprise is increased to approximately 50 percent of the total production of the metal cutting machine tools manufactured (p. 79).

As in earlier MITI notifications, concerted activities were explicity encouraged. The machine-tool manufacturers were exhorted "[t]o further promote joint operation of enterprises concerning technology, production, materials, marketing, exportation, etc." Moreover, the notification urged these metal-cutting machine-tool manufacturers: "[t]o strengthen connections with related industries such as the control equipment manufacturing industry, the conveying equipment manufacturing industry, the industrial robot manufacturing industry and the tool manufacturing industry as well as connections with the industries which purchase goods from such industries (pp. 79–80).

Other forms of collaborative activity were also identified. These included: "establishment of a joint research system concerning basic research on adaptable control technology, etc.," "establishment of a data bank concerning metal working in cooperation with related industries," and promoting "standardization of machines and tools for numerically controlled metal machine tools, such as tooling, pallets, etc." According to MITI officials, these plans also never reached fruition.

MITI's circular acknowledges the impact of rationalization on the international market. Accordingly, plans were made "to provide a system for overseas after-sale services," and an export value of ¥15 billion for NC and computer-controlled metal-cutting machine tools was set as the production target for fiscal year 1977.

MITI's strategy of "elevating" the machine tools industry by concentrating on NC machine tools was continued in the Third Extraordinary Measures Law enacted in July 1978. Article 3(1) of the law entrusts MITI with establishing an "Elevation Plan" for enterprises that manufacture certain machines. By Cabinet order, the following NC machines were designated:

1. Numerically controlled metal cutting machine tools which can simultaneously control multiple spindles

2. High-performance adaptive-control metal-cutting machine tools

3. High-performance module structure numerically controlled metal-cutting machine tools

4. Numerically controlled metal-cutting machine tools which automatically dispose of cutting scrap.

The Elevation Plan also prescribed "[m]atters concerning appropriate production scale, joint operation of enterprises, or specialization of types of goods to be manufactured." As before, there were constraints: rationalization was not to be "unduly discriminatory" nor "to exceed the necessary degree for attaining the rationalization target" nor "to be unduly detrimental to the interests of consumers or persons engaged in related enterprises."

Elevation also required rationalization of the distribution system. In one circular, MITI urged NC firms "[t]o seek collection of information regarding metal working [machine tools] and improvement of the distribution system thereof and to consider establishment of a service organization for the purpose of effective use of the machines concerned." Cooperation between manufacturers of NC metal-cutting machine tools and "manufacturers, and customers of computers, controlling devices, conveying devices, industrial robots, measuring instruments, tools for machines," was to be "strengthened"; and the "standardization of numerically controlled metal-cutting machine tool devices, such as tooling, pallets, etc.," was to be promoted. Although the Elevation Plan adopted in 1978 continues in force today, MITI officials note that consensus could never be reached on the service organization and standardization of numerically-controlled tools.

As with all of Japan's postwar strategic industries, overt protection of the domestic market was deemed necessary. The principal means of accomplishing this was a system of direct approval. By law, applications for approval to import machines into Japan were to be rejected if there existed Japanese-made machines of the same kind or of equal efficiency, or if of a different kind, where domestic machines could be used for the same purpose. Although the system was formally abolished in 1970, the domestic market is still protected by government procurement policies and by other means.

In addition to promoting the domestic market, MITI also orchestrated a legal export cartel of certain NC machine tools destined for the United States and Canada. According to the Houdaille petition, on March 1, 1978 an agreement was established under the Export and Import Trading Law to regulate prices in the exporting trade of NC lathes and NC machining centers. Nonmembers were also included. Every exporter (cartel member or outsider) was required to obtain specific approval from MITI for the price of each export.

167

Under the amendment, the Japan Machinery Exporters Association was deputized as the administrator of the price-approval scheme. The association was to act for MITI on "[b]usiness matters concerning" the "receipt of applications for approval," "comparing and verifying the submitted applications for approval with the standards for approval" set up by MITI, "notification that approvals have been granted," "acceptance of reports to be collected pursuant to," and the conduct of certain surveys. By subsequent Cabinet order, the association was granted the power to approve applications.

Although neither the Cabinet Order nor subsequent ministerial ordinances identified criteria to approve export applications, agreement was reached on standardization of prices. An internal guideline published by the Machinery and Information Industries Bureau and MITI's International Trade Administration Bureau stipulated that such approvals are to be given "when the export trading price [FOB price] is above the price to be set forth separately." The "price to be set forth separately" was kept secret by the government and the Japanese exporters. In fact it was set by MITI based on consultations with the machine-tool industry, and information provided by it. Although this reference price is portrayed in the internal guideline as a floor price, the Houdaille petition suggests that it constituted a ceiling. MITI officials assert that the petitioner's interpretation is incorrect. In any event, the effect of the scheme was greatly to encourage cooperative action.

Throughout the twenty-five years of the industry's promotion, the Japanese government made particularly creative use of tax incentives. In private interviews MITI officials have expressed substantial doubts that either the tax incentives or concessionary loans had much influence on either the growth or competitive position of the industry. Although this is an empirical question, the existence of these special incentives is undisputed.

One of the most important tax advantages enjoyed by the Japanese manufacturers was a special "bonus" depreciation deduction. These deductions were generally permitted over and above normal depreciation.[18]

Export subsidies were also important. Until 1964 the Japanese government allowed all or a significant part of export income to escape tax entirely. In addition, an exporting trading company was for a time permitted to reduce its domestic taxable income by special depreciation deductions charged against a special "reserve for cancellation of export contracts," and for expenses of overseas offices. The Houdaille petition charges that the latter was a subterfuge because the deduction was allowed whether or not there was a realistic possibility that export contracts would ever be canceled. Together these measures gave Japanese machine-tool makers the advantage of being able to export their products virtually tax free. At the same time, the Japanese tax system also weakened the position of U.S. producers in the Japanese market. A U.S. machine-tool manufacturer exporting to Japan could not receive the exemption from tax enjoyed by his Japanese competitor. U.S. exporters were also not allowed artificial deductions for canceling of export contracts. The Japanese machine-tool maker's competitive position was further enhanced, in Japan and in other markets, by the cost advantages of high-volume production that the export tax incentives made possible.

Another export subsidy of long standing was the partial exemption from tax of income from the export of technology. The exemption was calculated on a percentage of all royalties and other revenues received in foreign currencies for industrial property rights, copyrights, or technical services.

Japanese exporters were thus able to protect export earnings by selling through a foreign subsidiary and requiring the subsidiary to repatriate in the form of "royalties" for technical property rights or services. Although these royalties were not subject to the Japanese income tax, all taxes paid on these royalties were credited against the manufacturer's tax on income from sales in Japan.

Another governmental program in effect from 1964 to 1974 gave Japanese manufacturers a special additional depreciation based on a formula that increased ordinary depreciation deductions by the ratio of the company's export income to total income. Further increases ranging from 30 to 60 percent of such special depreciation were allowed by a 1968 amendment to the program. The additional "depreciation" was not confined to export-related assets, but increased depreciation on all of the exporter's assets, including those used to manufacture and sell goods in Japan. This program not only gave Japanese manufacturers a cost reduction on products sold abroad, it allowed extra deductions against domestic income. These deductions gave Japanese manufacturers distinct advantages over their U.S. competitors.[19]

In 1956, the Japan Development Bank began to provide special loans to certain machinery industries designated under the First Extraordinary Measures Law. Continuing in the 1960s, the Small Business Finance Corporation supplemented these loans by providing special funds to small- and medium-sized companies in the same machinery industries identified under the three Extraordinary Measures Laws. These special loans, set at favorable long terms and low concessionary interest rates, significantly helped promote the industry, particularly in the 1950s and 1960s.

As in other strategic industries, a system of direct government grants and indirect assistance for research on machine-tool production reinforced the loan and tax incentive programs. It is estimated that total research and development grants from all Japanese government sources provided the machinery industry with ¥8–¥10 billion ($36 to $45 million) each year between 1965 and 1975.

In addition, some funds were diverted to the machine tool association from the Japan Bicycle Rehabilitation Association and the Japan Motorcycle Rehabilitation Association. Under the 1948 Bicycle Race Law, "the Tokyo Metropolitan government and prefectures as well as cities, towns, and villages which are designated by the Minister of Home Affairs . . . can sponsor bicycle racing in order to contribute toward (i) improvement of bicycles and other machines, promotion of trade and rationalization of the machinery industry [and to provide other public benefits]." The municipalities so designated, defined in the law as "Bicycle Racing Sponsor[s]," are granted an exclusive monopoly to manage wagering on these races.[20]

Seventy-five percent of the wagering proceeds from these races is returned to those who bet on the winners, but 25 percent of all race wagering proceeds is retained by the designated municipalities that sponsor the races. By the express terms of the law, the racing sponsors are obligated to share a specific portion of their winnings with the Japan Bicycle Rehabilitation Association.

The Bicycle Race Law prescribes as one of the purposes of the Bicycle Rehabilitation Association the "promotion of industries related to . . . machines." The Japan Bicycle Rehabilitation Association is directed by law "[t]o make loans to banks and other financial institutions in order to provide necessary funds for promotion of industries related to bicycles and other machines," and [t]o render assistance to the undertakings for promotion of industries related to bicycles and other machines." Each designated municipality, or "bicycle racing sponsor," is permitted to retain the lion's share of the wagering proceeds. The law directs the recipients to "make efforts to allocate the profits arising from its sponsored bicycle racing to the funds necessary for carrying out measures for the improvement of bicycles and other machines and rationalization of the machinery industry . . . ." According to MITI officials, only ¥100 million or $500,000 was diverted from racing to the machine-tool industry in FY 1978 and each year after. The Houdaille petitioner asserts that the amounts appropriated were in fact much greater.

During the 1950s the Japanese government at times supported its export industries by deploying funds raised from unrelated sources. The practice is called "linkage" and it has been applied to machinery at least since the mid-1950s.

During this period a quota was imposed upon imports of sugar as a device to protect Japanese sugar farmers from international competition and also as a foreign exchange control to protect Japan against an excessive drain from the yen abroad. Since the sugar import quota raised the price of sugar in the domestic market significantly above the prevailing world price, licenses to import sugar into Japan were extremely valuable. These licenses were allocated to the support of the machine tool industry.[21] A publication of the Japan Machinery Exporters' Association, notes:

This system was in effect from February 1954. It was the most effective encouragement policy, being a system where the losses from construction and plant exports were compensated by the margin between the import price of raw sugar from Cuba and the domestic price. . . . The amount corresponding to 50% of the loss [from dumping the export products abroad] was divided by $30. . . . The number thus obtained represented the tonnage quantity of raw sugar that the exporter was entitled to import through allocation of an import license.[22]

According to the Houdaille petition, ships were exported at a 10 percent loss, while construction and plant exports were sold abroad at a 15 percent loss. The machinery exporters' article notes that 37 percent of all construction and plant exports from Japan in fiscal year 1953 were subsidized by means of this linking system. This meant that in fiscal year 1954 the subsidized share of Japanese construction and plant exports rose to 58 percent. The price of domestic Japanese sugar was reported to be actually $40–50 per ton higher than the world price when the system began in February 1954. Later in fiscal 1954, the article continues, a "reduction in the foreign exchange allocation for imports of raw sugar caused a sudden rise in the domestic price, resulting in margins of more than $100 per ton, and margins of something like $150 per ton were reported in November 1954." The Houdaille petition suggests that at least toward the end of this program, Japanese exporters actually made a profit by dumping goods abroad and receiving the sugar subsidy.

Why was the Japanese government so preoccupied with preserving order in the development of the machine-tool industry? As noted in Chapter 4, Japanese bureaucrats have historically distrusted the capricious, irrational, and often inefficient workings of the market. The machine-tool industry was thought simply too crucial a sector in which to waste scarce resources.

Rationalization represented the government's attempt to stave off the forces of unreason. Rationalization meant agreement among manufacturers on promotion, price, quantity, quality, and export targets. As in other areas, rationalization was extended to customers, distributors, and other industrial users. In other words, the government sought to encompass the principal forward and backward industrial linkages of the machine-tool industry in its rationalization program.

The elevation plans show that rationalization was also a dynamic concept. Elevation meant the intensified production of higher value-added NC machines. Elevation plans brought the concept of targeting, used by the government in cooperative research, down to the level of production within the individual firm.

The study of the semiconductor and computer industries noted the attention to public benefit in the criteria used to identify core technologies, which is reaffirmed by this history of the machine-tool industry. Throughout, the focus of rationalization was on the communal benefit to the association and to the industry as a whole. This was matched by corresponding communal responsibilities, namely the participating firms' obligations to cooperate and to achieve rationalization targets. In the study of the development of the computer industry I noted how MITI discouraged Fujitsu's untimely entry into the U.S. market, even when from a technical perspective the firm was ready to seize this advantage. The code of responsibility in the machine-tool industry, as in other areas, was both a means of achieving consensus and an expression of it.

The study illustrates again the importance of law in Japan, particularly as a tool of planning. It is no coincidence that the basic law for the promotion of the machine-tool industry was the same one that served as the basis for the semiconductor, computer, and telecommunications industries. In both cases, law served as a master plan.

Throughout administrative guidance served as a powerful legal means of attaining compliance with the plan. The cartel itself was little more than an extension of the administrative process. This insight makes the various deputations to the cartel over pricing, production, and export quotas of great interest, because it shows the western observer how various "unrelated" institutions are transformed in Japan into quasi-legal vehicles of state planning. The various tax and other financial incentives are additional illustrations of this legal-planning approach.

Rationalization then implied at least three layers of control: rationalization of technological development, rationalization of industrial structure, and rationalization of corresponding policy instruments. In each case, rationalization was accomplished and legitimized through law.

The Promotion of Robotics

The government's promotion of robotics has followed a very different course from that of machine tools. NC tools were from the start targeted on foreign export markets. Not so with robots. At least in the short run, domestic demand has been so strong that it has more than saturated existing supplies. Robots, moreover, are most useful when tailored to a specific setting, a fact that at least initially undercut their attractiveness as exports.

More to the point, robots have begun to exert a profound influence on domestic industrial structure. Robots are perceived to humanize work by relieving humans from more monotonous or dangerous tasks. Robots enhance quality, improve management, and increase productivity. Robots, it is thought, will create economies of scale by integrating assemblies, replacing costly labor, rationalizing low-volume parts production, and inducing reallocation of labor to more productive uses.

174

By contributing to productivity throughout the industrial base, the government's promotion of robots is designed to increase the international competitiveness of all user industries, in particular small- and medium-sized companies. The development of robotics will also support a host of other policies. For example, long-term forecasts for the technological development of robots show that they are conceived as a means of conserving energy and other resources, and also as a critical technology for exploring the oceans, outer space, and other new environments.

Flexible Manufacturing

The development of NC machine tools and industrial robots, along with sensors, automatic warehouses, unmanned carriers, and computer-aided design, reflects the underlying demand for flexibility, quality, and high productivity in manufacturing. But in a sense these are only piecemeal developments, part of a much more important revolution in manufacturing. To appreciate the Japanese government's plan to develop a "flexible manufacturing complex," it is important to grasp the industrial significance of the systems of production underway.

Japan's intense interest in flexible manufacturing is a product of a much larger, worldwide decline in mass production. In the early days of the automobile industry, Henry Ford's invention substantially cut production costs, reduced prices, and improved productivity. The Model T sold remarkably well and Ford prospered. Later General Motors, not Ford, became the preeminent auto manufacturer in the world. While Ford continued to manufacture single types of automobiles on mass-production lines, GM regularly altered models and surpassed Ford. In so doing, GM demonstrated the benefits of flexibility and quality, particularly when at the time rising labor costs placed a premium of labor-saving devices.

Until the mid-1970s, Japanese manufacturers focused their energies on process innovations, but most of these innovations concentrated on only extreme lines or a single part of

175

manufacturing. In the automobile or electrical/electronic industries, for example, the focus was a marked streamlining of transfer lines, particularly through the introduction of numerically controlled machine tools, and later machining centers.

Innovations at either of these extremes, however, had limitations. Although mass-production transfer lines were highly efficient, they often sacrificed flexibility. While NC machines could be adapted to a wide variety of assignments, their productivity was low. A need developed for manufacturing systems that could offer both productivity and flexibility, at low to medium volumes of production. In Japan such production accounts for over 70 percent of total machinery output in value.

The answer was flexible manufacturing. Flexible manufacturing systems (FMS) combine the technologies of numerically controlled machine tools, computers, materials handling systems, and more recently, industrial robots. At times they may include computer-aided design systems or automatic warehouses.

The FMS is a bridge between transfer lines and stand-alone NC machine tools. FMS applies to medium- and low-volume manufacturing that is currently machined on poorly utilized transfer lines, or to overutilized stand-alone NC machines that are dedicated to a single part.

FMS brings a number of important concrete benefits to the manufacturing process. For example:

1. It reduces inventory. FMS eliminates work in progress and thereby minimizes lead time.

2. It reduces labor costs. In FMS neither machines nor the material handling system is manned. Both are directed completely by a central computer.

3. It maximizes the use of equipment. The universality of FMS equipment leads itself to maximum use of equipment. FMS equipment is rarely down for setup, and need not be dedicated to particular parts.

4. It maximizes flexibility. It can be adjusted to changes in the market, changes in product, changes in engineering, and changes in technology. It can be installed at nominal cost and expanded or contracted as production dictates. The machine and computer units and the materials-handing system can be replaced as modules.

In sum, FMS address the needs of manufacturers who are searching for a means of producing related, but not identical, parts in medium-range volumes. This class of products and the means of producing them are expected to enjoy a substantial spurt in growth.

A number of flexible manufacturing systems have already been introduced in Japan. One example is Fujitsu Fanuc's ¥10 billion factory. The Fuji factory, constructed in 1980, is Fanuc's production center for a wide variety of electronic machine systems, including industrial robots, CNC (computer numerical control) wire-cut EDMs (electro discharge machinery), and mini CNC machine tools. It is the result of the company's long years of experience in the CNC field—an unmanned machining factory incorporating the FMS based on its own comprehensive CNC technologies.

The nucleus of the FMS is the machining cell. Each machining cell is composed of CNC machine tools, an industrial robot, and a monitor. Transfer of workpieces from these cells to the automatic warehouses of materials and parts is carried out by unmanned carriers. Total operation control is handled in the central control room, where central control and monitoring systems and production computers provide support.

By installing FMS, the Fuji factory can produce ¥18 billion in products annually with only 100 employees. The company claims this is one-fifth of the employees required for similar output of a conventional factory.

Although FMS includes almost all flexible systems in a factory, introduction of FMS has so far been limited to machining processes or material handling processes. To distinguish FMS introduced so far and more complex and complete

FMS to be realized in the future, MITI uses the term "FMC" (Flexible Manufacturing Complex) for the future FMS. MITI is promoting a ¥13 billion FMC project known as "Flexible Manufacturing Complex Provided with Laser."

Each FMC cell consists of five fully automatic, interactive operations: fabricating parts in special flexible dies, machining these parts, treating and machining by laser, assembly of the machined parts by robots, and automated inspection. The entire operation will be controlled by a hierarchy of computers, and workers will be needed only to act as safety observers. The project started in 1977 and is scheduled to end in 1983. At least twenty major robot and machine tool companies are participating.[23]

The budget of JFY for 1978–1983 has been:

JFY 78	¥	384 million
79	¥	2,272 million
80	¥	2,824 million
81	¥	2,718 million
82	¥	3,310 million
83	¥	1,200 million

The first two years (1977–1978) were spent in setting and refining the project's targets; the next two years (1979–1980) in developing details; the major investments were made in 1981 and 1982, as individual developments were combined and an experimental FMC plant constructed. The final year will be for operation and appraisal. In October 1983 MITI unveiled its first prototype factory, an aggregate of laser-equipped machine tools performing such sundry tasks as turning, drilling, and milling, that will reduce the number of production processes by 60 percent.[24]

MITI's flexible manufacturing program resembles the Fifth-Generation Computer Project in that it is an experiment in industrial learning involving the convergence and integration of multiple technologies. Irrespective of its outcome, it will yield important insights into the organization of production.

Except in the most general terms, it is hard to foresee the impact of the development of flexible manufacturing systems. If labor continues to acquiesce, productivity should increase. The coordinated development of NC tools, robots, and other flexible manufacturing will stimulate innovation in each of these related sectors. The link of flexible manufacturing to communications will compound and distribute these benefits on an even larger scale. The beneficiaries will be not only the mature and successful industries, but also shipbuilding, textiles, construction, and other industries now in decline.

Lessons of the Case

Flexible manufacturing systems promise an optimal mix of high productivity traditionally associated with mass production (transfer lines), and the flexibility and versatility of stand-alone NC machine tools, so-called single-part manufacturing. Four important conditions underly this development: integration, systems organization, increasing importance of computers, and telecommunications.

Flexible manufacturing, and its natural extension, the flexible manufacturing complex, is the product of the combination of various separate technologies, NC machine tools, robots, transport systems, and so forth.

The integration of these technologies is governed by distinct principles of organization. Specifically, the machines are arranged with buffers to allow upstream and downstream machines to keep operating when an intermediary machine fails. The grouping of machines is organized *redundantly*, with alternative processors and production paths to permit production to continue while a machine is under repair, and information on the state of various machines is repetitively distributed to identify the pathways of production in cases of machine failure.[25] The deployment of any given machine is thus subordinated to the overall needs of the system.

Flexible manufacturing systems depend on a hierarchy of computers, and increasingly on telecommunications. In March 1983 Yamazaki Machining Works began operations at its Nagoya plant, consisting of sixty-five computer-controlled ma-

179

chine tools and thirty-four robots linked to a telephone with a computerized design center in its Nagoya headquarters.

The target of flexible manufacturing is small-scale "batch production" where over 75 percent of all machinery is produced. Batch production is basically associated with high initial costs, and for this reason manufacturers tend to make a number of initial runs to minimize this cost. A resulting problem, however, is excess inventory. Flexible manufacturing permits the cost reductions of successive runs of batch production, while avoiding much of the high initial sunk cost.

"Economies of scope" is another way of describing the benefits of flexible manufacturing systems. This concept is a new and important criterion in selecting a strategic industry. Where before an initial investment could be amortized by mass production of identical parts, here the same level of investment can be recouped by production of an equal or greater volume of *different* parts. Flexible manufacturing thus yields greater variety at declining costs. (Compare the history of machine tools in Chapter 1, pp. 7–12.)

Flexible manufacturing complexes have presented an important structural problem. Because of their cost very few individual firms will undertake this development, although long-term putative gains would dictate that this investment should be made. This is the identical question, at the level of production, of whether to initiate a long-term program of research.

Many small, even innovative companies in the United States are reluctant to manufacture these systems because their costs are prohibitive, and users are similarly constrained by the depressed state of demand for their products. To many American firms, flexible manufacturing, for all its promised benefits, is not a profitable investment.

In Japan, the government's efforts to rationalize the industry have partially transferred the locus of decisions from the firm to the group. This has substantially reduced individual risk, expanded the range of potential applications, and extended the length of time a firm need wait for a return on its investment.

Equally important is the attention paid to the development of the market. Although the market for these new technologies is largely untested and unexplored even in Japan, the Japanese government has considered the development and rationalization of the industrial user market to be equal in importance to the promotion of the technologies themselves.

In all this the legal system has played a critical role. Fundamentally it has brought decisions that would otherwise have remained narrowly technical or scientific into the light of public debate and scrutiny. This is an important role of law in all advanced industrial systems.

Case 5. The Marriage of Biotechnology and Electronics[26]

If NC machine tools and robots are the descendants of industries based on craft, biotechnology is the next frontier. It is the result of a great transition, beginning with chemcial dyes in the nineteenth century to industries based on science in the twentieth. Here Japanese planners are peering into the recesses of life itself and designing incentives for a technology whose implications are profoundly unknown.

Technological convergence has been a dominant motif in the development of semiconductors, computers, and telecommunications, industries that are increasingly being linked with machine tools, robots, and integrated manufacturing. What of biotechnology? To what extent will the principles of electronics be incorporated in biochips, gene libraries, or other bionic hybrids? To what extent is the Japanese government aware of the economic implications of this grand convergence, and in what ways is it actively seeking to promote it?

The Development of an Industrial Policy

By comparison with electronics, biotechnology like other life sciences developed late in Japan. The paucity of able scientists, the complexities of orchestrating multidisciplinary

181

research within the universities, and the existence of more pressing priorities all contributed to the backwardness of the life sciences until the early 1970s. Not until the Asilomar conference in January 1973, which called for a moratorium on research, did the Japanese government give serious attention to biotechnology. Among the first agencies to take an interest were the Science and Technology Agency, the Ministry of Education, and the Japan Science Council. The upshot of their deliberations was a set of guidelines covering experiments at national universities and government laboratories. These guidelines were modeled closely on those of the U.S. National Institutes of Health.

The award of a basic process patent on recombinant DNA to Stanford University shocked many Japanese into realizing how far behind Japan was. In addition to pharmaceuticals, there was growing concern over the wide applications of biotechnology to agriculture. Agriculture is one of Japan's less competitive industries, although it has always had a deep religious significance. To many Japanese, agriculture is the mother of all industries, since rice has been, and may always be, their staff of life.

During the 1950s the media began to suggest that an alliance of American seed companies and biotechnology firms were attempting to monopolize the basic technologies applicable to agriculture and thereby seeking to gain control over the Japanese industry. Although these fears were vague and many of their fundamental premises were unchallenged, the U.S.–Japan "seed war" as it came to be called was portrayed to extend even to the developing countries. Here U.S. firms were depicted as using their lead in biotechnology to lay claim to the natural resources of these poor areas. Such vague fears, reminiscent of Japanese sentiments about IBM in the 1950s, have helped shape the perception of biotechnology as a strategic industry, and the course of subsequent policy.

At about the same time, many in government and industry began to recognize the significance of Japan's indigenous strength in fermentation technology, since fermentation held the key to mass production. The debate widened in August

1980 with the publication of the report of the Science Council of the Prime Minister's Conference, which served as the blueprint for the industry's development.

The report emphasized the profound implications of progress in the life sciences and stressed the need for collaboration among government, industry, and the universities. Following the paradigm of previous targeted technologies like automobiles, computers, and mechatronics, the report set out a scheme for government action. Foreign technology would be acquired; subsidies granted; public laboratories would be jointly used by industry and government, and industry urged to form research unions to target specific technologies. The government would take responsibility for facilitating intra-industry cooperation. By designating biotechnology as strategic, the Science Council's report helped promote broader understanding of its importance, and clarify the responsibilities of various segments of society.

The Problem of Organization

From the start, the organization of the industry and the orchestration of its promotion have posed critical problems. Unlike electronics, biotechnology criss-crosses traditional administrative jurisdictions and interests. As with other key sectors, MITI asserted primary jurisdiction, and the locus of activity became the Basic Industries Bureau charged with the promotion of steel, nonferrous metals, and chemicals. The organization of the effort within the Basic Industries Bureau reflected MITI's initial concern with the adjustment and elevation of these basic industries, in particular the chemical industry.

Biotechnology soon became an important interest of other agencies. The Ministry of Agriculture and Forestry began a series of projects involving the nitrogen fixation, biomass conversion, and new biological resources through cell fusion and nucleic transplant. The Ministry of Health focused on clinical testing, approval, manufacturing, and marketing of pharmaceuticals, while the Ministry of Education and the

Science and Technology Agency released guidelines for research.

The various projects lacked coordination. In June 1982 MITI organized a new biotechnology office that is now taking the lead in marshalling a national consensus.

There has been close cooperation between government and the private sector. An important private body is the Biotechnology Council in the Council of Economic Federations (Keidanren). The council includes more than eighty of the major companies involved in biotechnology and is the locus of intraindustry discussion. It is also an information clearinghouse and serves as a lobbying group for government assistance. A number of members of the Biotechnology Council are also key actors in the Industrial Structure Council, MITI's principal advisory body. In 1982 a new advisory group to the Ministry of Agriculture and Forestry was established to address the legal and policy problems in the international trade in seeds. Each major industry association, such as chemicals and pharmaceuticals, also has its own research group on biotechnology, and some conglomerates such as Mitsubishi have consolidated their development of biotechnologies.

Consolidation is now perceived as a critical impediment to success in the industry. Fifty-nine percent of firms interviewed in a recent survey of 159 firms noted that they were consolidating their research staffs, 60 percent (of 157 firms) suggested consolidation of research expenditures and 48 percent (of 158 firms) intended rationalization of research structure.[27] According to this survey, there has been a sharp increase in research personnel. This is most evident in textiles, followed by food and pharmaceuticals. The greatest areas of commitment have been enzyme utilization technology, fermentation, cell fusion, and recombinant DNA technology.

Targeting Biotechnologies of the Next Generation

The development of the bioindustry turns on certain key technologies. The development and commercialization of these core technologies are the objectives of a collaborative effort among government, industry, and the private sector.

The government's research program will proceed in three stages over the next ten years. The first stage will involve the acquisition of key technologies such as recombinant DNA and cell fusion. Pharmaceuticals, especially higher value-added pharmaceuticals like monoclonal antibodies, reagents, insulin, and interferon, will be top priorities as products.

The second stage will emphasize the application of basic technologies. Here the focus will be on fermentation and fuel chemicals including enzyme technology.

The third round will involve upgrading mass-production technology, breeding of high-level plants and chemicals, and a transition to a systems approach. The wide exploitation of biomass and the structural transformation of the chemical industry will be important.

The best-known collaborative effort is MITI's program for the development of technologies of the next generation. It includes bioreactors, large-scale cell cultivation, and recombinant DNA. Bioreactors are microorganisms used as enzymes and catalysts. Biological reactions involving enzymes or microorganisms, it is suggested, may have an advantage over conventional chemical reactions, since enzymes can function under normal temperatures and pressure. The primary purpose of developing bioreactors is to reduce energy and pollution-control costs in the chemical industry. Because bioreactors permit greatly expanded volumes of production at reduced costs, they constitute a critical process and production technology.

Large-scale cell cultivation involves replacing serum in the media for various cell lines, thereby making submerged cell cultures possible. A serum-free medium and/or a submerged culture will drastically reduce the cost of large-scale cultivation and the time for purification of the product. A primary beneficiary of this new technique will be the pharmaceutical industry.

Recombinant DNA technology is the best-known technology. The project involves the screening of useful DNA, the study of its structure, isolation of various DNA types and their transformation, and purification of products based on recombinant DNA. The technology's importance stems from its versatility. It is now possible to engineer specific characteristics or capabilities into new microorganisms that can be used in the production of chemical, agricultural, and other industrial products.

As in electronics, the structure of the government's research program may be as important as the targeted technologies themselves. From the outset the projects were closed and the participants tightly screened. The project for the next generation originated in the Biotechnology Forum, a study group organized by five of the major chemical companies. With the award of the process patent to Stanford University, the group began lobbying for government assistance. MITI, it is said, sent questionnaires to two biotechnology associations to survey their members' activities and needs. Approximately fifty companies were selected and the project was put out to bid in August 1981. At first, four research targets were identified—bioreactors, recombinant DNA, mass cell culture, and cell fusion—but during subsequent budget negotiations with the Ministry of Finance, the last was dropped.

All the participants are major companies or institutes (see Table 3). Although a few small businesses have ventured into biotechnology, the majors are all huge conglomerates. The companies are also organized to capitalize on their existing strengths. For example, Kyōwa Hakko and Ajinomoto, leading fermentation manufacturers, can use their lead in this field to exploit advances in mass cell culture. Mitsubishi Chemical and Mitsui Toatsu are leading petrochemical manufacturers, who will be primary beneficiaries of advances in bioreactors.

In general, the project for the next generation is modeled on the VLSI format, with one critical difference. The VLSI project involved direct subsidies, which in several cases permitted the inventing company to retain the patent rights. The present project involves contracted research that gives the government, under existing law, title to all patents. MITI officials note that the patents will be licensed openly to all. The participants will pay a slightly reduced royalty.

186

TABLE 3

Next-Generation Basic Industry Projects on Biotechnology, Sponsored by MITI

TYPE OF STUDY	MEMBER COMPANIES
Bioreactor	Mitsubishi Chemical, Mitsubishi Gas, Kao, Daicele, Mitsui Toatsu, Denki Kagaku
Mass cell culture	Kyōwa Hakko, Asahi Chemical, Ajinomoto, Takeda, Toyo Jozo
Recombinant DNA	Sumitomo Chemical, Mitsui Toatsu, Mitsubishi Kasei, Institute of Life Sciences

In other respects the VLSI model is closely followed. Each company focuses on a specific preassigned project. Research is conducted in its own laboratory and the results are, in theory, shared with the other participants. Since the research is very narrowly focused and under MITI's careful supervision, trade secrets are adequately protected. Like the VLSI, the flexible manufacturing, and the fifth-generation computer projects, the biotechnology research program is an efficient means of educating a cadre of scientists and technicians.

Although the project for the next generation deals with technologies basic to the industry's development, the technologies and some of the products deriving from them are not far from commercialization. For example, MITI officials expect commercialization and production of insulin and interferon by 1987, of cattle and human growth hormones by 1988 and 1989 respectively, and a cancer vaccine using recombinant DNA technology by 1997.

MITI has encountered numerous difficulties in coordinating the biotechnology research program. As with computers in the late 1960s and early 1970s, some large companies have been unwilling to collaborate in group research. Others have been dissatisfied by the terms. Only direct expenses such as a researcher's time and expenses in operating a laboratory are covered; overhead is not allowed, and capital equipment purchased during the program remains the property of the government.

Although the mode of compensation has discouraged some companies, the system does preserve incentives for others. For companies that are behind, the subsidy constitutes a benefit and the collaborative research is a means of acquiring learning and know-how. When left to its own resources, a company would tend to buy the least expensive capital equipment possible, although often it will splurge on a higher grade for a government project. Especially where the equipment is already close to being fully depreciated, the government is often willing to allow a company the right to retain it. Government assistance also gives support and prestige to the proponent of biotechnology.

Indirect Government Support

Until recently, funding has not been as critical a problem in biotechnology as in other sectors. Nevertheless, to the extent that corporate research and development budgets have increased, scarcity of capital is becoming gradually more serious. This is particularly true for smaller, non–publicly held medium-sized ventures. Although there are few explicit tax incentives for biotechnology, a variety of measures have been designed to facilitate the adoption of the new technology by users. This is particularly evident in special tax exemptions for businesses converting to new technologies, for incremental increases in research and development, and for accelerated depreciation of equipment for industrial R&D associations.

As a strategic industry, biotechnology qualifies for particular low-interest government loans. The principal governmental source of these loans for research facilities has been the Japan Development Bank through a fund for technology promotion. For the past four years this fund has remained fairly constant around ¥100 billion, or approximately 10 percent of its total loan portfolio, at interest rates between 7.5 percent to 8.4 percent. A secondary, increasingly important source is the commercial banks that have recently been offering loans at the same or sometimes lower rates than government-related banks. A third source is the $4 million BioIndustry Promotion Fund established in 1981 under the auspices of the Science and Technology Council. In FY 1981 the fund supported three projects designed to extract, analyze, and synthesize DNA, evaluate the safety of rDNA technology, and use rDNA technology to produce vaccines for influenza and B-type hepititis.

Although direct government procurement has not constituted a significant source of support for biotechnology, indirect support by guidance over the price structure of certain industries has. This is particularly evident in the pharmaceutical industry. Approximately seven-eighths of the drugs in Japan are sold by prescription under the national health plan. The key to the system is the standard price determined during the clinical testing period. The standard price is then discounted by physicians that sell these designated drugs directly to their patients. After a drug is placed on the market, the price is adjusted every year to reflect its market price. The market price may vary from the standard price due to heavy discounting by the pharmaceutical manufacturers.

In the 1970s the Ministry of Health made special allowances in standard prices to pharmaceutical manufacturers that used fermentation technology. Although use of this particular subsidy appears to have been reduced, if not eliminated, by the recent reductions in pharmaceutical prices,[28] assistance through the price structure continues in agriculture, energy, and other heavily regulated industries.

While biotechnology received subsidies indirectly through price support of pharmaceuticals, it also benefited from special promotion accorded it. This produced a stream of foreign complaints over testing, procedures for approval, guidance, import licenses, designations, distribution, customs uplift, limitations on membership in industrial associations, abuse of confidential data, property rights, and preferential treatment of domestic joint ventures over foreign subsidiaries. The government's aid to the infant pharmaceutical industry also bolstered firms beginning to enter biotechnology.

An important objective of the government's strategy is to strengthen the industrial base that will support biotechnology.[29] The first area of attention involves seeds and plants.

Until recently the Ministry of Agriculture and Forestry has not been fully sensitive to the fundamental implications of the marriage of plant genetics with biotechnology. Inventories of plants, seeds, and plant genes, as well as the cultivation, production, and dissemination of information have been haphazard. A special Diet Committee on the biosciences has proposed the development of a comprehensive program to rationalize the entire field. This would involve an accelerated financial commitment, expanded development of a computerized data-retrieval system of plant genes, and intensified measures to protect, preserve, and cultivate microbes, plants, and other organisms.

A second area is the development of biomass technology. This is a seven-year project begun in 1980 at a total cost of ¥80,000,000,000. The project's basic aim is to develop technologies for the efficient conversion of undeveloped cellulose to ethyl alcohol by using microbes. The project emphasizes technologies involving systems engineering, energy-saving methods of distillation, liquid waste processing, fermentation, and electronic-ray, physical, and chemical processing technology.

The third and fourth areas, not directly related to biotechnology, involve the development of new materials and their introduction into currently depressed industries such as chemicals. The new materials being developed under sponsorship of MITI's Agency for Industrial Development are high-performance ceramics, synthetic membranes, synthetic metals, high-performance plastics, advanced alloys, and advanced composite materials.

The Marriage of Biotechnology and Electronics

The analogy has often been drawn between the processing of electronic information by computer and the processing of genetic information contained in the DNA helix in cells. The code of life depends on only four bases (adenine, cytosine, guanine, thymine) from which the twenty-one fundamental

190

amino acids derive. These in turn are the building blocks of proteins that govern metabolism.

Since biological information is transmitted chemically and electrolytically, the fields of biotechnology and electronics would seem to have a natural affinity. This insight has not escaped the theorists. The "sequantor," an automated machine used to carry out sequential degradation of peptides and proteins, heralds the new field of "biotics," a term coined by Maturama, Pitts, and McCulloc, who attempted to copy the organs of the body or senses with the aid of electronics.[30] Futurologists such as Jöel de Rosnay foresee the advent of gene libraries, text processing of genetic information, biomolecular programming, microbiomachines, biochips, and biological autoassembly—all from the convergence of microelectronics and biology.

As we have seen, convergence is a key promoting factor in the development of most strategic industries, and it is often allied with forward and backward linkages and high rates of innovation. In the United States small companies such as EMV have begun to forge a creative alliance of the two fields and, not surprisingly, the subject is of considerable interest in Japan.

The signs of the beginning of such convergence are already apparent. The design of the project for technologies of the next generation that integrates electronics, new materials, and biotechnology implies this. As already described, the program will develop key electronic and biotechnologies in tandem. The project focusing on synthetic membranes for new separation technology promises major breakthroughs in large-scale energy conservation and the reduction of pollution in chemical factories. The technique will also greatly assist in the purification of products derived from genetic engineering. In this way the program for the next generation will stimulate exchanges and inventions within each field and among these different areas.

The subsidized development of automated cell sorters and DNA synthesizers is a second area. Such research is being sponsored by the Science and Technology Agency and will permit the analysis of infinitesimal quantities of biological substances such as hormones. In Japan it is said the system inaugurates the new field of "microchemical robots."

A third field is the various applications of biomimetic technology to the development of artificial enzymes, biocompatible materials, biomembrane artificial organs, and the like. One part of this work is the current research on bioholonics under the auspices of the Science and Technology Agency's Program on Exploratory Research on Advanced Technology (ERATO). The aim of the project is to clarify the mechanism by which living cells aggregate and organize holonic elements, with particular interest in developing autonomous molecular machines, and other applications of engineering to material science.

Fermentation is a fourth category. Japan has traditionally enjoyed an advanced level of fermentation technology. Since approximately 2 percent of Japan's GNP (about $50 billion) is made up of products using industrial microbiological processes, there is a growing demand for fermentation technology. After the 1973–1974 oil crisis, the industry made great efforts to upgrade its technology in batch fermentation and to develop continuous fermentation processes. The economic rationale of biological batch production closely parallels that in flexible manufacturing systems. Numerous companies have also begun to specialize in the design and construction of large-scale fermentation facilities and in providing instrumentation.

A collateral area is computer control of fermentation. Computers can memorize various chemical changes in fermentation as well as physical changes such as temperature and process the data at high speed. Hitachi and Fuji Electric, for example, sell fermentation equipment with full instrumentation and control. One report notes that the Japanese government has supported over 200 projects in this general field at a cost of approximately ¥8 billion since 1975.

Sensors are a fifth field. Sensors address the need of the bioprocessing industry for sensitive instruments. The use of sensors has so far been limited to measurements of gases, usually in combination with some measurement of liquid conditions such as turbidity. There is a need for sensors that can take direct measurements of liquid concentrations of products, byproducts, and reactants, as well as enzymes and microorganisms.

Several Japanese companies are working on the development of direct-measuring sensors of this kind that use an immobilized enzyme to convert the measured compound into a product, which can be detected by conventional—for example, electrochemical—means. Large companies (Matsushita Electric), and small (Denki Kagaku Keiki K.K.) are working on the development of such biosensors, and a large market for these products is expected.

Software is a sixth area. Software will be necessary to enhance hardware applications. Currently the government is considering the development of specialized software under the consignment program discussed in case 2. Although a formal program on the development of biochips has not yet been organized, its creation is only a matter of time.[31]

Lessons of the Case

Viewing the Japanese government's promotion of biotechnology from within Japan, some domestic specialists are forthright in pointing out the weaknesses of current action. The first problem is the cumbersome administration of industrial policy. Although the applications of computers are broad, the potential uses of biotechnology may be even broader. Biotechnology's applications cover almost every industry and for this reason the new science has exacerbated ministerial rivalries. Such problems were less acute during the early development of the computer industry, which developed largely under MITI's sponsorship.

The Ministry of Agriculture and Forestry (MOAF) has set up particular impediments. Traditionally the ministry has maintained jurisdiction over seeds as part of its several responsibilities over agriculture. With the advent of biotechnology, however, the ministry has taken particular pains to dominate not only trade in seeds, but also the development of basic research on plant genetics and the diffusion of this information. The ministry's action runs counter to MITI's own effort to promote the new technologies. MOAF's actions can be understood only as a parochial effort to preserve its own monopoly and to protect agricultural interests.

Some critics also suggest that in many ways MITI officials fundamentally misunderstand the nature of living systems by assuming that the promotion of biotechnology can simply repeat the approach developed for the computer industry. In seeking to develop general principles for the promotion of the basic technologies of recombinant DNA, cell fusion, and bioreactors, MITI officials assume that these principles can be universally applied. Some commentators note that this strategy misjudges the specificity of living organisms, and that the program is wasteful of scarce governmental resources. In criticizing the government's strategy, these scientists urge that greater attention be paid to training bioengineers and in developing a national gene bank, two fields in which the government thus far has been remiss.

Despite the weaknesses of its approach, the Japanese government must be credited for mounting a vigorous national effort to capitalize on the strategic potential of biotechnology. The first line of defense has been structural adjustment. Biotechnology is of national importance to Japan today not so much for the international markets it will someday dominate—this may be a decade away—but for the direct impact the development of this new industry will have on other sectors. By reducing the costs of batch production of interferon and other drugs, genetic engineering is proving a key factor in the growth of the Japanese pharmaceutical industry. Biotechnology will also help revive weaker although structurally important industries such as chemicals and petrochemicals. The new technology, it is hoped, will seed important new alternative energy industries.

As before, government action has focused both on demand and supply, on users as well as producers of biotechnologies.

194

The measures applied have been tailored to the needs and circumstances of each industry.

Again the best illustration is the pharmaceutical industry. The pharmaceutical industry is quickly becoming a leading sector, a trigger to structural adjustment. Various regulatory and other incentives were granted the pharmaceutical industry to encourage its development which, incidentally, were passed through to fermentation manufacturers and firms entering biotechnology. The passthrough bound the manufacturers even closer to users.

The strategy behind the promotion of the supply structure is different. Here the focus is "core" technologies that display many of the characteristics identified in Chapter 1, convergence, flexibility, linkage, and so forth. Of these, convergence may be most important, because it permits the most effective deployment of subsidies.

When a core of technologies is essential to several important industries, the benefits of affirmative government action are multiplied. The most immediate example is again the pharmaceutical industry. As the pharmaceutical industry expands, it will demand advanced fermentation equipment, sensors, and computerized equipment. As these technologies develop they in turn will help the pharmaceutical industry acquire larger market shares through incremental gains in productivity. Looking to the more distant future, the Japanese government has already embarked on measures to hasten the integration of biotechnology and electronics. This cannot help but spur innovation, rapid technological change, and productivity gains throughout the industries these basic technologies serve.

Acute concern is expressed about the government's financing of research and the form its efforts to rationalize the industry are taking. The major areas of targeted research, although certainly of basic importance, are all areas that the private sector is undertaking separately at its own expense. In biotechnology there is yet no high-risk, long-term research program such as the fifth-generation project. This is a reflection of differences in the two industries' stages of development and the government's assessment of the industry's position.

The structure of public research differs from past strategies toward electronics. There are no existing antitrust exemptions for intraindustry collaboration. Yet the potential for anticompetitive conduct in biotechnology may be even greater than in electronics or the machine-tool industry. The number of large firms actively involved is great and their activities within the Biotechnology Council are on a broader scale than that of the early days of the semiconductor or computer industries. The bioreactor, recombinant DNA, and mass cell cultivation projects involve only strong leading firms. There is little time or opportunity for the weaker firm or newcomer to participate. Japan's lax enforcement of the antitrust laws in this sector may be explained as an effort to assist the major firms in rapidly building economies of scale.

The project for the next generation is structured as contracted research rather than as a subsidy. The basic intention seems to be to permit the government to control the pace of technological development and the transfer of technology. Although the main participants in the project are large powerful companies, the government is taking pains to assess the needs of the industry as a whole. Like their U.S. rivals, Japanese companies are fiercely competitive and jealously guard trade secrets. But in biotechnology, as in electronics, the government has until recently delayed strengthening the protection of industrial property rights whether by patent, copyright, or tort law. The effect if not the intent of such actions has been to make advanced technology more accessible to firms in less-favored market positions. The liberal terms of royalty and the government's guidance over technological diffusion will also stimulate a flow of information among dominant and weaker firms, and among producers and users.

The other idea behind all these measures is to build on existing strengths. The expansion of the fermentation industry and the current emphasis of the Fermentation Institute on recombinant DNA research is a good illustration. The attention to the integration of biotechnology and electronics is another. Such strengths will be played in more intricate variation throughout the 1980s.

Conclusion

This chapter has drawn a portrait of how Japan has nurtured and guided its strategic industries since the early 1950s. As Chalmers Johnson has ably shown, the basics of this approach were crafted as early as 1925. The roots may lie in the Meiji era.

Westerners, in attempting to explain Japan's industrial policies, often err in two important respects. First, they tend to overstress the importance of cooperation and to downplay the role of competition. Second, they portray the Japanese government as engaged in picking winners and losers. In fact, competition has been at least as important as communitarian action, and as the case studies show, the two need not be in irreconcilable conflict. Moreover, although firms in Japan may win in one instance, rarely are they permitted to aggrandize themselves at too great a cost to the rest of society. In other words, in time, the surplus generated by an activity must be conveyed back to those whose sacrifices brought the surplus about.

This creative tension is built into the structure of Japanese business. Miyohei Shinohara notes:

In current research on industrial organization in Japan, too much emphasis has been placed on seller's monopoly; buyer's monopoly (monopsony) as a unique characteristic of the business hierarchy or subcontracting has rather been disregarded. Enterprises are linked hierarchically in this monopsony network with big corporations above and subcontractors under them. . . . When the secondary and tertiary networks underpinning the affiliates and subcontracting are considered, there is a strong orientation toward buyer's monopoly or monopsony, an important characteristic probably unique to Japanese industrial organization.[32]

Flexibility is supplied by the intragroup and interindustry.

197

The claim is often made that each group takes unified control over any new industry in its ranks and that group banks give priority in financing their fellow companies; thus the tendency to compete between business groups financially supported by the group network is often pointed out. But there is actually much greater flexibility than this, and the link within each group is loose enough so that each company can display great "capacity to transform" by itself. Thus, the structure of the Japanese business group is rather flexible, and there is always continual feedback between MITI and industry. The business groups as a whole have even greater flexibility, providing a cushion against rapid change in the economy (p. 42).

Shinohara concludes:

There are those who contend that this combination of rigidity and flexibility worked to hinder growth, but in my opinion the ingeniousness of the system played an important role in providing a base to accelerate economic growth. The Japanese postwar economy's record of higher growth rates than in many other countries, a record that lasted for almost thirty years, was achieved by offering a type of economic development quite different from the static, atomistic variety described in modern economic theory. Success was achieved by harnessing the economy to a dynamic combination of flexibility and rigidity. A situation leading to an atomistic dissolution of the system would have meant the loss of dynamism. This system was of course not developed out of direct planning but came about naturally, spontaneously, producing a structure appropriate to high growth. A totally rigid system is a barrier to growth, as the experience of the socialist nations suggests. Japan's unique combination of rigidity and flexibility was very effective and highly successful (p. 43).

The tension between structural rigidity and flexibility parallels the national concern over balancing collective responsibility with individual initiative.

Chapter 2 discussed the unique properties of information and some of the ways the organization of information can contribute to economic growth. Since the 1950s the Japanese government has taken great pains to overcome the domestic industry's strong concerns over corporate secrecy in order to assure the broad dissemination of information deemed vital to the rapid development of strategic industries. This policy can be viewed from sociological, technical, and commercial perspectives. As in other countries, access to information is a critical ingredient of power and influence. Access to information in Japan, however, may be even more important than in other societies, because it is closely related to face. To be excluded from the information loop implies to one's peers that one is insignificant and unimportant, and results in serious embarrassment. Conversely, inclusion in an information loop is essential to obtain support for any position and to bind a strong consensus.

Anthropologists have noted in studies of primitive societies the concept of "stimulus diffusion." Typically, a tribe will hear of a technical breakthrough in a distant territory, for example, the invention of a canoe. Without further information, beyond that such a breakthrough is possible, the first tribe will soon discover canoe making. The policies of the Japanese government to promote cooperative research and the diffusion of technical information can be viewed as a very sophisticated way of fostering stimulus diffusion.

The integration of various sectoral subsystems into a gigantic macrosystem entails benefits that escape most western analysts. Imagine a matrix. The principal policy tools employed to promote strategic industries since the early 1950s are represented on the X axis. The Y axis plots the key industries and strategic sectors that will form the macrosystem of the twenty-first century. The Z axis represents technological change over time. It is easy to see that the benefits of any governmental intervention are multiplied throughout the system. The case of biotechnology described how the government permitted some pharmaceutical companies to set higher prices. This constituted a triple subsidy to the pharmaceutical manufacturer, the makers of fermentation equipment, and to the nascent biotechnology industry. The integration of these various subsystems substantially increases the prospects of multiplying the positive effects of any governmental intervention across a spectrum of related industries.

This matrix also suggests another interesting aspect of the Japanese approach. It is customary to refer to new industries as "infant"; indeed this term is often employed by MITI officials and some Japanese economists. Actually, to call biotechnology, artificial intelligence, or fiber optics infant industries seems a misnomer. In Japan they appear to arise naturally from the industrial momentum generated by the industries preceding them. They are buds of a common trunk, a common infrastructural base. In this sense the situation of Japan on the eve of the twenty-first century appears vastly different from that of a developing country searching the industrial landscape for its appropriate leading sector.

There is an interesting parallel between Japan's policies toward the information industries and the Swiss watchmaking industry a century ago. Just as the Swiss mountains provided a natural barrier to foreign access to the domestic industry that helped sequester the art of watchmaking, so today Japanese industry enjoys a natural advantage conferred by the ignorance of most westerners about Japanese scientific developments. Very few westerners, for example, read and understand Japanese technical or scientific journals or even know of their existence. On the other hand, Japanese scientists and industrialists generally keep well informed about western technical developments. The Japanese government's careful attention to the diffusion of technical information greatly reinforces the industry's natural linguistic advantage.

I have emphasized the strengths of the Japanese approach to strategic industries. But what are its vulnerabilities? There is a darker, less publicized side to these policies and it is their impact at home and abroad. The next chapter explores whether Japan's imaginative strategies can succeed without substantial cost.

Chapter 7
False Choices and Tragic Choices

The Principles of Adjustment

All societies change. In the modern age nations that fail to adjust to change cripple economic growth and fall behind their competitors. How successfully Japan copes with the costs of structural transformation will determine to some extent its competitive position with the United States, Europe, and the rapidly industrializing countries.

In some cases adjustment requires unavoidable sacrifices. These are true tragic choices. Other costs of adjustment, however, are avoidable, although nations may fail to mitigate these costs because of incompetence, corruption, ideology, or tradition. To conceal their inadequacies, or to secure public acquiescence, governments will often call such choices tragic. In reality they are false choices.

Japan's policies of structural transformation may demand harsh sacrifices. Communities may be disrupted; workers thrown from their jobs; the computer poses new, unprecedented risks of invasion of privacy and usurpation of liberty; there are unassessed costs in genetic engineering and in radiation from electronic media; the deeper, more disturbing

201

consequences of computer imperialism are virtually unconsidered.

In the 1960s and 1970s Japan developed a unique method of allocating the social costs of industrial development. This integrated systems approach was developed in tandem with the targeting strategies discussed in Chapter 5. In those days national attention focused on pollution, particularly from oil refineries and power and chemical plants. These were the strategic industries of the 1950s, and already by 1970 they were in decline. Although the solutions of the courts, the Diet, the administrative agencies, local governments, and citizens groups were designed for the exigencies of that period, it is useful to abstract from them general principles relevant to our subject.[1]

The first set of principles concerned the relation of law and policy to science, and the specific issue was the causes of pollution disease. The diseases were various pulmonary disorders (emphysema, bronchial asthma, asthmatic bronchitis, and asthma), Minamata disease, mercury poisoning, and itai-itai ("it hurts, it hurts") disease or cadmium poisoning, so called because of the frightful pain its victims suffered. During the 1950s and 1960s the industry and most of the scientific community insisted, despite ample evidence to the contrary, that the causes of the victims' injuries were unproved. Later the victims' appeals were upheld.

As a result of political agitation, people became aware that the issue of causation was not only technical or scientific, but was also a complex political and institutional question. Citizens groups, then the courts, the Diet, and the administrative agencies began to understand how the polluters' defense of scientific uncertainty was a device to obscure responsibility and to stave off the victims' suits. Many began to see that no issue in science is "certain," that all scientific problems arise within a spectrum of "uncertainty," and that the critical public choice is who must bear the burden of such uncertainty. In the early 1970s the Japanese courts, reflecting a broad consensus, decided that the companies would bear this burden.

The courts left to them the burden of disproving that they were not the cause of the victims' injuries.

These decisions had an enormous influence on the course of subsequent policy. In the early 1970s both Japan and the United States enacted air pollution laws that imposed stringent auto emission standards and deadlines for compliance. Curiously the law's principal backers had little sense of whether its targets were technically feasible, or what the cost of compliance would be.[2]

By 1975 United States industry had persuaded the courts that the deadlines were "technically unfeasible." In that year Japanese industry met the same targets. To many observers the case suggested that technical feasibility, like scientific uncertainty, was only partly a technical problem; that technical breakthroughs also are as dependent on their legal and institutional setting as on the details of technical analysis.

The second set of principles concerned the responsibility for the harms of industrial activity. Here the courts, the Diet, and the administration held industry and the government to the highest duty of care for human life, and, in later decisions, for the natural environment. The standard of conduct was unequivocal. The costs of harm were imposed on industry by court decisions, administrative fines, emission charges, local ordinances, and mediated private settlements between industry and local citizens groups.[3]

The third set of principles answered the question of how the costs of pollution should be distributed. In some cases the government bore these costs fully, especially where its liability was determined. In others, the government initially paid for cleanup, and was later indemnified. Japan may be among the few major industrialized countries of the world to have actively implemented a comprehensive program of pollution cleanup and control on the theory that the government bore this duty irrespective of its own liability, as part of its affirmative sovereign responsibility.

Collective responsibility was also the principle governing the allocation of costs across industries. The most famous example was the system enacted in 1973 for compensating victims of pollution-related disease. Under the law, polluters were charged an emission fee that was used to compensate victims. Emission fees were collected locally, pooled in a central fund, and redistributed to areas in need of relief. Although some of these victims had become ill from exposure to pollution in the past, the law still imposed the charge on present polluters. The theory behind this exaction was that present polluters were exposing today's population to the same level of risk as in the past. Collective responsibility and cross-indemnification within industry were thus mirror images of the cooperation and collective action that had spurred these same industries' development.

The final principles set the criteria for entitlements. It was generally conceded that the victims had borne a disproportionate share of the hardships of industrial growth, and for this reason they deserved benefits over and above those accorded ordinary citizens.[4]

My study reached these conclusions:

1. Although Japanese environmental controls were among the world's most stringent, they had little adverse effect on economic growth, and even less on employment.

2. Pollution controls actually stimulated growth in some depressed sectors, such as the steel industry.

3. Pollution injury came to be viewed as a necessary, if tragic, incident of industrial development and for this reason the society had concluded that measures had to be devised, along with the promotion of industry, to care for its victims. From this perspective Japan's approach may be fairer than that in the U.S. or Europe, where the suffering of victims of pollution is largely ignored.

4. A more subtle, deeper consequence of Japan's strategy to control pollution was its influence on the victims' movement. In effect it ensnarled the victims in judicial procedures that sapped their energies and spirit. It paid great attention to the face of their complaints, but little heed to

their true hopes. Today the victims' movement is all but dead and Japan's industrial drive continues unabated.

This chapter surveys the extent to which this model conceived and implemented in the late 1960s and 1970s will be applied again to the controversies of the information age. As new injuries and new problems appear during the next twenty years will they be denied or obfuscated as others were a half-century ago? Or will the same approach permit Japan to adjust nimbly to the inevitable pains of its transition?

Structural Problems and Their Adjustment

In the 1980s and 1990s Japan may experience severe economic, social, and political hardships.[5] Although it is unlikely that these hardships will actually have been caused by the diversion of national resources to information processing industries, they certainly have the potential of disrupting significantly the Japanese government's approach to these high-growth sectors. This section focuses on the problems of economic stagnation, in particular the difficulties of the basic materials sector and the influence of economic distress on local communities.

At present Japan, like the rest of the industrial world, is emerging from recession. Current projections suggest that apart from electronics and some other high-technology industries, basic materials, manufacturing, and processing and assembly industries will continue to decline. The greatest imbalance is in basic materials.

After the first oil crisis in the fourth quarter of 1973, production significantly decreased in both the basic materials and the processing and assembly industries. A bottom was reached in the first quarter of 1975, and thereafter the processing and assembly industries began a continuous climb toward recovery. By the second quarter of 1981 they had attained an index level exceeding 200. In contrast, the basic materials industries, which also hit bottom in the first quarter of 1975,

205

continued to decline after the second oil crisis and after a brief recovery. By the second quarter of 1981, their production index had fallen to 115. The imbalance between processing and assembly industries and basic materials industries is widening. There are several reasons.

The principal cause of problems of supply has been the rising cost of raw materials and energy resulting from high crude oil prices. Increased raw material and energy costs have led to an increase in total costs for all industrial sectors. Basic materials industries such as petrochemicals and aluminum refining (electric power-related) have been the most seriously affected because raw materials and energy account for much of their total costs.

One result of the rise in the price of raw materials has been a decline in international competitiveness. An example is the displacement of domestic naphtha sources by Canadian and domestic products. Another is the declining competitiveness of the Japanese aluminum industry. Still another is the steep import of petrochemical products such as ethylene derivatives.

Some Japanese commentators believe that "excess competiton" is a cause of the difficulties of the basic industries. Kenji Miyamoto writes:

A unique structural feature of Japan's basic materials industries is their lack of either vertical or horizontal integration as compared to their U.S. and European counterparts. The resulting excessive domestic competition makes it difficult for the basic materials industries to pass on increased costs in the form of higher prices for their products to the downstream industries which depend upon them. Their problem is one of costly raw materials and low product prices.[6]

Another primary problem for the basic materials industries is sluggish domestic demand.

Processing and assembly industries are heavily dependent upon exports and private investment in equipment and plants. In contrast, the basic materials industries rely to a greater extent on final demand such as housing investment, public works spending, and individual consumption. The recent stagnation in housing and public investments has been a direct cause of the slump in domestic demand. The rise in relative cost of basic materials, as compared to that of other materials, has also resulted in decreased demand for these materials.

As discussed in Chapter 4, the first step in invigorating a depressed sector is often the preparation of a vision, a generalized indicative plan of future trends and actions. MITI has recently prepared such a plan for the basic materials sector.[7]

The vision emphasizes the strategic functions of the basic material industries. First, this sector functions as a buffer. It helps to cancel out price increases for imported basic materials and support stockprices at home.

Second, it strengthens Japan's bargaining power. The world's supply of primary products and basic materials is based on oligopoly. To ensure steady supply, MITI considers it important to diversify Japan's sources of imports. MITI's more important aim is to maintain a strong bargaining position in international negotiations over the volume and price of basic materials.

Third, it maintains technical prowess. Japan's basic materials industries play an important role in the overall accumulation of know-how and in increasing the value added to end products. Basic materials industries are expected to make major contributions to future innovation. Existing technology relating to fine ceramics, organic high polymer chemistry, metallurgy, and crystallization are all important to the development of new fields such as materials engineering and biotechnology.

Fourth, the basic materials industries contribute to improving the quality of products. The Japanese steel industry's rolling technology, for example, is one factor behind the competitiveness of Japanese-made automobiles.

Finally, basic materials are linked to basic security and for this reason a domestic stockpile is maintained, irrespective of any domestic lack of raw materials.

207

The problems of the basic materials industries, as well as other depressed sectors, are being addressed through the Temporary Measures Law for the Stabilization of Specific Depressed Industries, enacted in 1978.[8] Basically the law helps ailing industries overcome stagnation and stabilize management. The first step is the designation of a candidate industry. Steel, aluminum refining, synthetic fibers, and shipbuilding have been so designated. Designation is based on the request of a majority of the members of an industry and the recommendations of the relevant ministry's advisory council. The minister in charge next prepares a basic stabilization plan. The plans include targets for the disposal of excess capacity, regulation of newly built and expanding facilites, conversion of businesses, disbursements from a special depressed industries credit fund, loan guarantees, and other benefits. The plans help the government stabilize employment, target assistance, and negotiate schedules for the voluntary compliance of firms in the designated industries.

Although the fragmentation of local communities has progressed for many years, the stagnation of the basic material industries will exacerbate the present situation. The disruption of communities is the result of increased social mobility, the reduction in the size of agricultural communities, breakup of kinship groupings, and the decline in local self-sufficiency.

The technopolis program is conceived in part as an antidote to such problems.[9] The program will involve a partnership between MITI's office of regional industrial development and various local governments. Local governments will offer land, clean water, various grants, loans, and tax-related subsidies. These will be supplemented by MITI and other concerned agencies of the central government.

Fourteen industries will be integrated in the technopolis: (1) aircraft, (2) space, (3) optics, (4) biotechnology, (5) medical electronics (ME), (6) industrial robots, (7) integrated circuits, (8) computers, (9) word processors, (10) metal-based new materials, (11) fine ceramics, (12) medicine and medical supplies, (13) industrial machinery, and (14) software. By integrating so many industries the technopolis will accelerate the convergence, diffusion, and other key factors discussed in Part I.

The technopolis program is also an ingenious means of regional development and in this sense is intended to reverse the dissolution of local communities. One aim is to foster regional autonomy. Another is to equalize the distribution of industries and the distribution of national wealth. A third is to extend to the millions of Japanese who cannot afford to live in the major metropolis the cultural and social benefits of the cities.

The first prototype is Tsukuba Science City near Tokyo. Tsukuba has been in the planning and building stages since 1963 and represents an investment of about $5 billion. Administratively the city is divided into institutes for higher education and training, construction, science, engineering, biology, and agriculture. Each institute is managed by the parent university or agency. Tsukuba is the locus of a number of MITI's large-scale national projects including the "flexible manufacturing system complex." Its closest parallel may be the science city at Akademgorodok and the related university of Novosibirsk in the Soviet Union.

The construction of technopolis will be the responsibility of local governments as part of their existing regional development plans. The central government will make direct grants and offer tax incentives and other attractive financing to promote the project.

The program depends strongly on Japan's land-use laws of which the most important is the Industrial Relocation Promotion Law. The law divides the country into three distinct zones. Excessively concentrated regions such as the tri-city megalopolis of Tokyo-Osaka-Nagoya are designated as "removal zones" in which new plant construction is restricted and outward plant relocation is encouraged. Less concentrated urban centers such as Sapporo, Sendai, and Fukuoka are classified as "neutral zones" in which new capital formation is neither strongly promoted nor discouraged. Outlying, relatively undeveloped regions such as Hokkaidō, Tohoku, Kyūshū, Shikoku, and Okinawa are designated "establishment zones" in which plant formation and direct investment are vigorously encouraged by both national and local governments.

A company relocating a factory from a "removal zone" to an "establishment zone" qualifies for special loans, depreciation allowances, and an industrial relocation promotion subsidy. Relocation, however, is not necessarily a prerequisite for preferential treatment under Japanese investment laws. Any new construction in an establishment zone, regardless of the sites of affiliated plants, will generally entitle the investor to take advantage of a variety of special programs. Industrial siting in Japan is also regulated under laws and regulations that typically require new facilities to maintain a green belt equivalent to at least 20 percent of a factory area.

One of the most interesting aspects of the technopolis policy is the government's effort to encourage foreign firms to set up operations. Foreigners now qualify for tax incentives, subsidies, and special financing on the same terms as domestic companies. The long-term implications of technopolis policy for coordinated planning between the U.S. and Japan are discussed in Chapter 11.

Westerners have long asserted that Japanese lack creativity, particularly in matters of science and technology. "A nation of copycats." "Innovators, perhaps, but not true originators!" Now that Japan has become a technological superpower, many westerners are naturally interested in whether Japan's technological drive will slow down, particularly as it reaches the cutting edge of many technologies.

Assuming for the moment a basic lack of originality in Japan—an assertion with which I do not agree—will not the pervasive involvement of government and the domination of research by huge industrial conglomerates aggravate Japan's creativity problems? If new industries such as semiconductors, robotics, and genetic engineering require flexibility and initiative, will not bureaucracy's heavy hand put out the spark, if the spark be even there?

Can a society engineer creativity? This is the experiment on which Japan has embarked. As suggested, the VLSI, the fifth generation, flexible manufacturing, and next-generation projects should be viewed as explorations in industrial learning. The most important motive is to stretch the minds of the participants, to train Aristotles for the next generation's Alexanders.

If such experiments shape creativity within existing governmental and industrial structures, the breeding of a new generation of bold risk takers represents a counterpoint to it. Since the oil shock of 1973 MITI has doggedly sought to nurture a cadre of new businessmen and venture capitalists. In the words of a MITI official:

The free economy can only remain sound if new businesses which actively fulfill new needs through new methods (new management) are constantly being formed.

The appearance of innovators will effectively keep market mechanisms from becoming inflexible in the hands of the oligopoly. In order to achieve a mobile market structure, strong competitors must be created. Thus oligopolistic enterprises should be split. To convert industrial structure smoothly, new businesses for new industries should be developed.

Schumpeter said it is new men and new firms who lead new industries. Existing enterprises will not necessarily become the leaders of new industries. To some extent change in industry is linked to change in enterprise. Although venture businesses are not only the developers of new industries, they are certainly very important.

Venture businesses have excellent technical capabilities, a fact that may suggest a new direction for the management of small and medium-sized enterprises, with their limited managerial resources. A positive, determined, entrepreneurial spirit, characterized by a willingness to take risks, can be a strong stimulus to the knowledge intensification of small and medium-sized enterprises in general.

The growth of venture businesses means greater economic activity. In coordination with existing enterprises, they can revive and regenerate productivity in existing enterprises. The growth of venture business can thus be said to have multiple effects.

In the future, the government will play a greater role in many fields. Thus the oligopolistic structure of industry may increase and

211

the economy will become more bureaucratic. For this reason, the energy of the venture businesses, though they are only a minority, will be important. This minority will thus have an impact on our industrial society and it is important to encourage them.[10]

Japan's venture business can also be viewed as a reaction to the principles of mass production. Manufacturing today demands new combinations of technologies, drawn from diverse fields, tailored more closely to the needs of users. Large enterprises in Japan, accustomed to dealing with routine work in bulk, have not been adept at custom work, and the rigid, highly specialized system of research and development has impeded versatile combinations. Within the large enterprises, however, there is now a cadre of able scientists and entrepreneurs yearning to try their teeth on new opportunities. This untapped core is the focus of MITI's promotional efforts.

Although "venture business" is an English term, it has indigenous roots in Japan. According to a MITI survey, the new entrepreneurs are highly intelligent, usually men in their early thirties who have worked primarily in large or medium enterprises. Their businesses tend to be knowledge-intensive, dynamic, highly market-oriented, a portrait of their founders. Most venture businesses are involved in specialized research and development and tend not to have facilities for production and assembly.

Despite the increasing recognition of the economic and social importance of the new entrepreneurs, serious obstacles frustrate their development. Concern for community has often discouraged industrial initiative. Lifetime employment and seniority undercut the need to strike out on one's own. Cultural biases against quick and easy capital gains check the development of an over-the-counter (OTC) market. One still hears the perjorative *kuinige* ("eat and run") for someone's seeking an easy windfall.

On a more concrete level, there are also serious legal and institutional impediments. One is the underdevelopment of the over-the-counter market. In Japan the OTC is principally a circulating market for stocks that are no longer listed, while the standards for new listings have been steadily raised for the protection of investors. In the United States approximately 4,300 stocks are currently traded over the counter, whereas in Japan only 137 are listed. Listings on the major exchanges in Japan are similarly circumscribed. In the United States, 2,367 stocks are listed, whereas in Japan only 1,700 are currently listed on all the major securities exchanges.

Credit is also a problem. Although there are many private financial institutions including city, regional, and long-term credit banks, and various financial organizations specializing in financing small- and medium-sized enterprises, these institutions have hitherto been closed to venture businesses. The Japanese banking laws and guidelines of the Ministry of Finance prohibit extensions of credit to enterprises of high risk and untried management. Moreover, existing financial institutions have virtually no technical expertise by which to evaluate these enterprises.

There are also numerous government-affiliated financial institutions in Japan, but these too have been impediments to financing. In some cases loan limits are excessively high. Other institutions require a guarantor for security. Finally, most government organizations are very conservative and, like the private banks, lack technical expertise to screen proposals.

These obstacles have helped frame the Japanese government's response. MITI's first action was to found the Center for the Development of Research and Development Oriented Enterprises (VEC) in July 1975. VEC acts as a surety for unsecured debts on loans for research and development, arranges seminars and other meetings, and channels funds and technology to small and medium enterprises.

A primary task of the center is financial aid. Affiliated with VEC is a special advisory committee headed by Soichiro Honda, president of the Honda Motor Corporation. Its task is to evaluate promising enterprises. The criteria emphasize independence, resourcefulness, creativity, and individual initiative. The guarantee system covers 50 percent of the amount of a loan and has a ceiling of ¥80 million. Security is unnecessary and the period of a guarantee is eight years. VEC's fee is 2 percent of guaranteed principal with a bonus of 5 to 10 percent to be paid if the project is successful. Since its establishment VEC has handled 121 cases of secured debt, covering loans amounting to ¥3.1 billion.

VEC has also been instrumental in the development of a number of venture capital companies (some of the major companies are set forth in Table 4). All have started with less than ¥600 million in capital and almost all have encountered difficulty in obtaining adequate funds and in installing effective management.

The most enterprising Japanese venture capital company is the Japan Associated Finance Company (JAFCO) established in 1973. Closely affiliated with the Nomura Reserach Institute and the Nomura Securities Company, JAFCO performs a broad range of consulting and financial services, only a part of which concern new enterprises. For example, JAFCO is involved in long-range financial planning, mergers, acquisitions, divestitures, as well as a whole array of financial services for promising small and medium enterprises. In its venture activities JAFCO has concentrated on profitable high-technology companies whose shares may or may not be sold over the counter.[11]

The government is well aware that the key to vitalizing venture capital in Japan is reform of the existing over-the-counter and securities markets. Only when investors are able to capture sizable capital gains will there be sufficient incentive to invest. A special government investigatory committee has proposed creating a special registration system modeled on the U.S. National Association of Securities Dealers (NASDAQ) to expand the volume of sales. The committee has also urged removal of many existing restrictions, such as stipulations on the level of profits, capital requirements, limitations of new issues, and dealing by brokers on their own account. In addition to its specific recommendations, the report urges expanding the volume of funds available for venture capital financing, strengthening VEC, removing existing

TABLE 4

Venture Capital Companies as of Spring 1983

COMPANY	DATE ESTABLISHED	PRINCIPAL FINANCIAL LIAISON	NO. COMPANIES INVESTED IN AFTER ESTABLISHED	AMOUNT OF INVESTMENT, YEN	NO. COMPANIES WITH PUBLICLY TRADED STOCK AFTER INVESTMENT
Nihon Enterprise Development	11/72	Long-term Investment Bank	100	3 billion	20
Japan Godo Finance (JAFCO)	4/73	Nomura Securities	90	8.6 billion	19
Universal Finance	12/73	Yamaichi Securities	***	***	14
Central Capital	1/74	Nikkō Securities	***	***	8
	4/74	Kangyō Bank & Kakuman Securities			10
Tokyo Venture Capital			70	1.7 billion	
Diamond Capital	8/74	Mitsubishi Bank	100	2.7 billion	12
Japan Investment Finance	8/82	Daiwa Securities Co.	8	250 million	0
Sanyo Finance	8/82	Sanyo Securities Co.	3	130 million	0
Yamaichi New Ventures (Nuben)	11/82	Yamaichi Securities	0	0	0
New Japan Finance	12/82	New Japan Securities	0	0	0
Wako Finance	12/82	Wako Securities	1	10 million	0

impediments to technology transfer, establishing new tax incentives for venture businesses and venture capitalists, building educational programs to train venture capital managers, and in many other ways fostering the diffusion of what is perceived as new financial and managerial "technology."[12] The positive reception given the report by MITI, the industrial and financial community, and even within many parts of the Ministry of Finance, offers strong reason to believe that many of its recommendations will be vigorously implemented in the coming years.

There is an interesting parallel between Japan's attention to its new entrepreneurs today and actions of the U.S. government twenty years ago. Venture capital in the United States was largely the product of the Small Business Investment Company Act, generous capital gains treatment, NASDAQ, and a vital national securities market.[13] These laws and institutions were well conceived and they have had a positive impact on the overall development of technology. Japan's strategy for the promotion of venture business, on the other hand, is targeted on more specific national objectives. The contrast in the two programs is yet another test of whether a more guided approach to the development of key sectors is more compatible with the exigencies of the postindustrial age.

Strategic industries exert an important influence on innovation by helping to diffuse technological information. As the studies of the Japan Electronics Computer Corporation and the Japan Robot Leasing Corporation suggest, the Japanese government has made technological diffusion a central policy objective. It is an underlying motive of all the major publically funded joint research programs and the explicit mandate of the New Technology Development Agency (NTDA).

NTDA deserves attention. The agency was established in 1961 to stimulate technological diffusion by serving as an intermediary between innovators and industry, and by sponsoring selected research projects. As a mediator, NTDA conducts a continuous search for new technological developments.

216

Industries, universities, and independent research labs are asked periodically to submit their latest findings. Private individuals are also encouraged to tender their discoveries.

The results of this search are divided into two categories: discoveries suitable for immediate mediation to an appropriate industry, and discoveries that require further refinement. Inventions eligible for mediation are reviewed and, if necessary, are patented by NTDA on behalf of the inventor. Because of its position as a government agency, NTDA has some influence over the decisions of the patent office. Next, the invention is aggressively marketed to appropriate users. Marketing includes direct contact with interested companies, symposia, and various commentaries in leading newspapers. When an interested party is identified, NTDA serves as a true mediator between the inventor and the third party, attempting to bring the two together. Upon agreement, NTDA will serve as an information clearinghouse and will collect all royalties. NTDA is paid 10 percent of the royalties for its services.

Companies participating in an NTDA mediation may at times request further support for research and development, and in such cases NTDA will offer low-interest loans. Loans are repaid within five years and in some cases NTDA receives a commission of 20 percent.

Besides mediation, NTDA also supervises a special "entrusted technology development" program. In the first stage, it canvasses industry, universities, research institutes, and companies to identify promising new technologies. Technologies contributing to pollution control, energy conservation, medical care, or other important policy objectives are of particular importance. Next a comprehensive financial analysis is made by the agency in cooperation with its advisory council. High-risk, long-term projects that promise strong future demand are of greatest interest.

When a given technology is identified, NTDA invites the prospective developers to attend a discussion on the problems and opportunities of the technology. At this point one or a group of companies is identified to assist in developing the technology. In some cases development is done jointly, in some cases delegated to a single firm. The next step is to prepare a specific financial and technology development plan. Often research projects are undertaken within NTDA's own facilities. In such cases NTDA recruits elite scientists and engineers from industrial and university laboratories. Costs of personnel, material, and research are shared with the agency. When the research is completed, the agency consults with its advisory body to determine whether the project was successful. If successful, the firm must repay the agency for its expenses over a five-year period without interest. If unsuccessful, the debt is canceled.[14]

When a project is successful NTDA concludes a contract to facilitate diffusion of the technology. In such cases the agency as a rule tenders one-half the price to the inventor. In cases where there is a strong demand for the technology, the developing company is permitted to monopolize it for three years. Proceeds of the sale are divided between the inventor and the sponsoring company.

NTDA's annual budget has grown from $6.4 million in 1972 to $23.6 million in 1981, an increase of more than 268 percent. Of the annual budget, 69 percent was allocated to entrusted development.

Some Potential Adverse Consequences of Japan's Information Policies

The protection of personal privacy from the intrusion of computers is a matter of increasing concern in Japan. In a 1981 survey, 57 percent of a sample of 3,000 persons confessed concern about invasion of privacy and 79 percent favored greater government protection.[15] Most respondents stated that domestic peace would be disrupted. Some were concerned about bugging or that the police would keep dossiers and other records on their movements. Others were anxious about investigations into their past. Still others feared publication of intimacies or harassment by solicitors. The

218

protection of privacy poses complex and unique problems in Japan, given its cultural sensitivities to shame and disclosure, and its recent memories of midnight searches and state control.

Although the Japanese government has yet to pass a comprehensive privacy law, various laws protect individuals from the intrusions of administrative action. The Japanese constitution, for example, guarantees citizens the right to freedom from interference in their private lives. Various statutes require civil servants to protect official and personal secrets. Other laws permit individuals to inspect official records pertinent to their activities. Finally, various statutes impose obligations upon certain professionals to protect matters disclosed by clients in confidence.

At present there are more than fifty local ordinances protecting privacy by regulating the operation of computer systems.

The Tokyo ordinance, a typical example, contains the following provisions:

1. Private Information Protection Committees. The ordinance establishes committees of local citizens to oversee the disposition by local government entities of computer-held records on private citizens. The committee is empowered to investigate all intrusions on the privacy of local citizens. The scope of the committee's authority is coextensive with the jurisdiction of local government's to compile tax, electoral, and other information.

2. Restrictions on the Uses of Local Computer Systems. The ordinance prohibits the compilation of records relating to a person's thoughts, religious beliefs, individual characteristics, past crimes, or other information that could be used for purposes of discrimination.

   Local governments are also forbidden to furnish information in their possession to national or other public entities through interconnecting local computer systems with national data banks.

3. Citizens Administrative Actions. Local citizens are entitled to review files on their activities, and in cases of error, to have such records corrected or expunged.

4. Accompanying the average citizen's concern about privacy is an increasing sensitivity to computer security. In January 1976 the government formulated a set of "Guidelines for EDP Security." The guidelines require the appointment of a "security manager" within each computer division. The security manager is responsible for overseeing all safeguards on computer systems including the protection, sanitization, and storage of tapes, programs, and data. Regular audits are required. There are various restrictions on the transmission of data to private parties to preserve confidentiality.

The guidelines establish general rules upon which the ministries and agencies have based specific regulations. Several ministries have also formulated guidelines to protect privacy in the private sector. The guidelines differ depending on the industry concerned and the circumstances of the supervising ministry.

Of all Japan's targeted industries, the risks of genetic engineering have been most widely debated. No consensus, however, has been reached since the industry's risks are still so poorly understood. The uncertainty of existing legal controls reflects this failure to achieve consensus. No statute directly regulates genetic engineering and the application of the toxic substances, air, water, and other pollution control loans is unclear. Few local controls exist either by ordinance, pollution control agreement, or otherwise, although experiments involving genetic engineering may be included by implication in some local guidelines.[16]

There are two sets of explicit guidelines at the national level that cover recombinant DNA experiments, and MITI is currently preparing a third to govern genetic engineering at factories and other industrial sites.[17] The principal guidelines (issued by the Prime Minister's Office on August 27, 1979; subsequently amended in part on April 7 and November 7, 1980, and April 1, 1981) apply to research at government laboratories. The Ministry of Education has also issued guidelines covering research at public and private universities. The guidelines closely resemble the NIH safety standards. They include both biological controls and physical controls at the same four levels (P-1 to P-4) as in the United States. The United States and Japanese guidelines are basically similar with some important differences concerning physical containment, practices, inspection, and equipment.

Recently the guidelines have been relaxed to align them more closely with U.S., English, and German standards. For example, P-2 facilities can now be used for experiments involving transplants of human hormone genes into escherichia coli (E. coli). Prior to the amendments, university researchers had to register test plans with the Ministry of Education. Now the university president and recombinant DNA safety committees may make final determinations. Similarly, the regulations pertaining to mass cell cultivation have been relaxed. Although the guidelines are not legally binding, they generally command greater respect than in the United States. This is particularly true in genetic engineering where the industry's development is tied intimately to the government's strategic economic planning. In addition, the guidelines establish a standard for the Japanese Patent Office in its determinations under the Patent Law of whether a given application endangers public health.

There are also numerous judicial precedents that bear directly on the industry's development. The courts' decisions in the four great pollution trials involving mercury, cadmium, sulfur, and nitrogen oxide poisoning have firmly established the principle that compliance with a regulatory standard or guideline will not shield a negligent party from liability in tort. These decisions, particularly the Yokkaichi case,[18] have assigned collective responsibility to industry for pollution-induced injuries and have used statistics to surmount various

221

technical barriers to proving causation. The precedents established by the courts may be applied to cases of injury resulting from DNA experiments.

Apart from genetic engineering, other high-technology industries also pose risks. Various toxic substances are used in the production of silicon wafers and there have already been several cases of contamination of water supplies throughout the world. Electronic media, in particular video display terminals (VDT),[19] have been associated with high rates of fetal abnormalities in pregnant operators regularly exposed to these machines. Flexible manufacturing and other automated systems are the source of continuing accidents in Japan as in other countries.

The media have not played upon such risks and the public seems largely unaware of them. There are few epidemiological studies of diseases relating to toxic substance poisoning of semiconductor facilities or VDT terminals, and experimental research on these subjects is limited. Since no one perceives a problem, there are no funds for victims of these diseases or their offspring. Few direct regulatory standards have been set and there is virtually no litigation in this area.

Automation will breed conflict in Japan as in other countries. Various studies, however, suggest that direct government action and the structure of Japanese industrial relations will mitigate these conflicts to some extent.

A recent cross-cultural study, *Jobs in the 80s*,[20] identifies a number of serious "mismatches" that would be aggravated by the government's promotion of the information industries. The first mismatch involves Japan's graying population. Average life expectancy in the mid-1930s was 50; today it is 70. According to the Economic Planning Agency, each senior citizen today is supported by fifteen working people; in 2015 he or she will be supported by three. Most commentators predict a backlash among younger workers who increasingly protest the cost of supporting older citizens. The Japan Youth Research Institute projects increased unemployment among the middle aged and elderly, increasing demand for jobs in higher age brackets and among women, a decline in the number of jobs for youth, a gap between the number of highly trained persons and the greater demand for jobs requiring less education, an obsession with "desirable" jobs, and an increasing reluctance to accept "dirty" jobs.

The second mismatch is among those now employed. Here the study finds increased alienation over meaningless and overpowering jobs; dissatisfaction with work conditions—salary, working hours, and fringe benefits; complaints arising out of "organization-centered" patterns of life; dissatisfaction arising out of competition for status, position, and promotion; and an increasing gap between big business and middle and small businesses.

A third mismatch results from changes in the industrial and occupational structure. The study cites the instability in employment in the service sector, shortages in occupational training facilities, the gap between academic training and the needs of the workplace, and the tensions resulting from the decline in seniority and lifetime employment.

The final mismatch is the decline in the work ethic—greater concern with leisure and intergenerational conflicts over the goals of work.

In recent years the Japanese government has attempted to study the impact of microelectronics on employment. A special MITI subcommittee reached the following conclusions:

Manufacturing

1. Manufacturers of equipment appear at present to be suffering the most adverse economic impacts from the introduction of microcomputers. This is less so in those departments that have been able to retool. In general, manufacturing departments are losing personnel, while marketing departments are expanding personnel due to an increase in demand. Parts suppliers are beginning to forgo work as the number of parts required declines.

223

2. In development departments: conventional engineers are beginning to be reeducated; there is a strong emerging demand for application systems engineers and programmers; engineers are beginning to provide in-house technical training for their company manufacturing and marketing.

3. Engineers appear eager to learn new technologies and to adapt. Consequently they are not suffering any substantial reduction in employment.

4. Many divisions must be relocated. Although in the short run these divisions will maintain existing personnel, a decline is inevitable in the long run. Workers will need to be retrained, and their job categories changed.

5. Parts manufacturers will be affected by the requirements of equipment manufacturers, who are increasingly offering technical guidance to facilitate adjustment.

Users

6. It is likely that there will be an attrition of jobs, particularly those involving measurement, testing, analysis, and instrumentation. However, since enterprises are expected to control the expansion of personnel, significant changes are not anticipated.[21]

Microelectronics will force significant changes in the office. A recent survey of 429 firms suggests that most expect that almost all types of businesses will be conducted through home terminals, volumes of transactions will increase, and support personnel will be significantly reduced.[22]

Although some people will lose their jobs, MITI's study suggests that there will also be demand for a new generation of software engineers. One prediction suggests the demand for applied software engineers will total 795,600 by 1985, representing an increase of 715,300 jobs since 1975.

The Ministry of Labor predicts similar "positive" impacts for the NC machine-tool industry:

1. Businesses that have introduced NC machine tools, account for nearly 50 percent of all businesses.

2. More businesses have increased the number of regular employees than have reduced them.

3. Changes in the number of regular employees are attributable not only to a "change in the volume of orders received," but also to "labor-saving" and an "increased number of new types of jobs" through the introduction of NC machine tools.

   Businesses both with and without these machines gave "increase in the volume of orders received" as the primary reason (68.1 percent and 66.3 percent respectively) for the increase in the number of employees. Others responded that "expansion in the scale of business" was responsible. Among those who introduced machines, 29.8 percent answered that they needed more workers as "new types of jobs increased through the introduction of NC machine tools and new techniques." The percentage of those citing this reason is highest among the smaller scale businesses.

   Asked the reasons for a reduction in the number of workers, the percentage answering "employment adjustment due to decline in the volume of orders received" was high in both types of businesses. The primary reason for reducing employees was to save labor costs. This percentage has risen as the scale of operation has increased.

4. Changing the types of job and the reassigning of workers were the main measures taken to cope with the introduction of NC machines. Few establishments were found who dismissed their employees. Most managers interviewed responded that job changes were the most frequent measure adopted (65.2 percent) followed by "transferred employees to other departments (25.3 percent)" and "employed new hands as necessary (24.4 percent)." Those who reduced employees was lowest, 3.9 percent.[23]

The ministry made these observations regarding the prospects of future employment:

1. Although declines are anticipated in some divisions dealing with the administration, an overall increase in employment is anticipated.

2. The number of regular employees will increase by 4.6 percent (about 29,000 workers) from 1980 to 1983 although a 0.4 percent decline is expected in "administration and management." Increases are expected in "planning, research and designing" (7.2 percent), "marketing, sales and transportation" (6.0 percent), and "manufacturing" (5.3 percent). The larger the scale, the lower the rate of increase. A decline of 0.7 percent was recorded for establishments with more than 1,000 employees.

3. The number of NC:MC machine tool operators is expected to increase. The percentage of business establishments employing NC:MC machine tool operators is 44.2 percent. Among these businesses, 62.7 percent stated that "the number of these operators will increase in the next three years." With regard to the number of engine lathe and milling machine operators, 34 to 35 percent expected an "increase," while 57 to 60 percent anticipated a "levelling off." Changes are consequently anticipated in the function of metal machine tools operators.[24]

Not all sectors of Japanese society are as sanguine as the Ministry of Labor and MITI, agencies that, after all, may wish to understate the adverse effects of information intensification. The Federation of Japanese Automobile Workers, the industry most directly affected by robots, has recently expressed its concern about the impact of automation. The All Japan Federation of Electric Machine Workers has cautioned that it will soon be impossible to absorb surplus labor through job transfers, noting that part-time workers will most immediately be affected. At its general convention in 1982, the Japanese Federation of Labor (Domei) demanded that management consult prior to introducing new robots.

The best test may be the automation of the Asahi Newspaper. After over 200 formal negotiating sessions, and far more informal sessions, agreement was finally achieved. Although production has been fully automated without a single employee being discharged, many Asahi workers apparently remain frustrated, confused, and alienated.[25]

One imaginative approach the Japanese government has taken to deal with the dislocations of microelectronics has been to construct an industry-employment matrix. Table 5 suggests the impact of microprocessors by industry and type of work between 1970 and 1975. MITI officials note that the matrix has proved useful in predicting future trends, designing incentives for technological development, and rationalizing structural transformation policies to mitigate their impact on employment. Wassily Leontief has recently advocated a similar use for input-output analysis, citing the experience of Austria and other countries.[26]

The principal direct means by which the government has attempted to alleviate the pains of information intensification is through adjustment assistance to workers, communities, and firms in ailing or otherwise adversely affected sectors.[27]

In 1977 the Japanese government enacted the Temporary Measures Law Governing Unemployed Workers in Specific Depressed Industries (Employees Law) to deal with the problems faced by workers in the newly threatened industries. The law engrafted adjustment assistance onto earlier statutory programs for unemployment insurance.[28]

Under the present system, displaced workers are required to participate in the government's training and placement programs. In 1958 the Diet authorized the government to establish special training programs, and in 1960 it amended the law to help place workers from economically depressed communities in distant, economically growing areas of the country.

To qualify for unemployment benefits, a worker must report to the local Public Employment Security Office to obtain certificates. If a worker agrees to take any job assigned to him, the government will attempt to find him work. Workers

TABLE 5

Percentage of Increases in Number of Workers, 1970–1975 (Unit %)

TYPE OF WORK \ INDUSTRY	AGRICULTURE, FORESTRY, FISHERY	MINING	FOOD	TEXTILE	PAPER, PULP	CHEMICAL	PETROLEUM, COAL PRODUCTS	CERAMICS, STONE & CLAY	IRON & STEEL	NON-IRON METAL	METAL PRODUCTS
Scientific Workers											
Mechanical Engineers											
Electric Engineers											
Information Processing Technicians											
Other Technicians											−6.5
Medical and Health Care Technicians											
Judges, Lawyers, etc.											
Other Law-related Occupation											
CPAs											
Other Professionals				7.0							
Corporate Directors			−1.7	−0.5	−1.9	−1.7			1.3	0	0.9
Managers			2.1	1.8	0	0.8			2.4	1.0	3.0
Clerks	1.3	−5.9	2.1	0.8	1.7	2.5	4.2		2.5	1.9	3.1
Salesperson			0.7	4.9		3.1					
Other Sales-related Occupation			6.2	9.5		10.2					14.0
Agriculture, Forestry, Fishery	−6.1										
Mining and Ore Extraction		−12.4									
Transportation	1.4	−3.0	−2.9	−3.0					3.4	4.0	−2.3
Communication											
Metal Ore Works										−2.2	0
Metal Processing								−5.1		−1.5	−1.0
General Machinery Manufacture and Repair				−3.8		−1.5			2.6		
Electric Appliances Manufacture and Repair									1.9		
Transportation Equipment Manufacture and Repair											
Precision Instruments Manufacture and Repair											
Filature and Spinning				−5.9		−6.7					
Tailoring and Cutting				3.3							

TABLE 5

Percentage of Increases in Number of Workers, 1970–1975 (Unit %) (*continued*)

GENERAL MACHINERY	ELECTRIC APPLIANCES	TRANSPORTATION EQUIPMENTS	PRECISION INSTRUMENTS	OTHER MANUFACTURING	CONSTRUCTION	UTILITIES	COMMERCIAL	FINANCE, INSURANCE, REAL ESTATE	TRANSPORT/ COMMUNICATION	SERVICE	PUBLIC SERVICE	UNCLASSIFIABLE	TOTAL
													−7.7
−3.0		−4.2								7.0			−2.6
	−6.6				−1.4					6.4			−2.4
										19.7			13.0
					2.3	2.9			1.5	−3.3	1.7		−0.7
							5.1			4.0	1.5		4.0
													3.1
										3.1			1.9
										6.8			6.8
				−1.4			1.2		0	4.1	10.0		4.0
−0.6	0	0		−7.7	7.8		1.8	5.8	2.6	3.8			1.5
−1.0	0	0		−6.2	8.5	3.1	0	1.3	0.8	3.8	2.6		1.3
1.4	0.2	3.1	2.3	2.3	8.4	3.5	4.4	5.9	2.2	5.2	3.3		4.0
5.4	1.9			3.3			1.8			−4.8			1.7
14.1	14.0			2.1	19.9		1.8	4.9	6.1	6.5			3.1
										1.1			−6.1
					4.2								−9.8
	0			−8.4	2.7		−1.6	−3.0	1.4	1.7	1.3		0.8
							3.6		−0.6	−2.9	0		−1.5
−2.8		−0.8											−2.1
−4.6	−5.1	−1.2	−4.9	−3.4	5.2		1.2			−1.8			−1.6
2.4	3.1	6.5		1.9	9.7		6.2			7.5			3.5
5.9	−2.6						−0.8			3.5			−1.8
		3.7					−0.4		−1.1	3.3			1.7
	−2.1		2.5				−1.5						1.2
										−14.7			−6.2
				−49.5			−6.6			−6.8			−9.1

TABLE 5

Percentage of Increases in Number of Workers, 1970–1975 (Unit %)

TYPE OF WORK \ INDUSTRY	AGRICULTURE, FORESTRY, FISHERY	MINING	FOOD	TEXTILE	PAPER, PULP	CHEMICAL	PETROLEUM, COAL PRODUCTS	CERAMICS, STONE & CLAY	IRON & STEEL	NON-IRON METAL	METAL PRODUCTS
Other Textile-related Works				0.2							
Wood, Bamboo Processing (except woodworking)											
Wood Working											
Paper, Pulp Industry					−2.5						
Printing, Bookbinding					−1.7						
Rubber, Plastic Works											
Leather and Leather Goods											
Ceramics, Stone and Clay								−1.1			
Food and Beverages			1.3								
Chemical Products						1.4	5.9				
Construction Workers											
Machine Operation		0					−1.1				
Electricians										0	
Other Skilled Workers (except woodworking)		0.9									
Painter and Decorator											0.7
Draftsmen											4.2
Wrapping and Packaging			−2.4	0	−4.8						
Warehouse Workers											
Other Unskilled Labor			−1.2	−2.6	2.7	−3.0		−3.5	−5.0	−2.5	
Security											
Service			1.3	−6.5							
Unclassifiable											
TOTAL	−6.1	−10.0	0.8	−1.5	−1.5	1.0	4.8	11.2		−0.8	−0.05

*Box highlighted indicates basic workers of the industry
*No entry denotes a very small number of workers. (under 10,000 in either 1970 or 1975)
SOURCE: *The Diffusion of Microelectronics Technology and its Influence on Industrial Structure* (Microerekutoronikusu gijitsu no fukyū sangyō kōzō e no eikyō), Industrial Research Institute, August, 1982.

TABLE 5

Percentage of Increases in Number of Workers, 1970–1975 (Unit %) (*continued*)

GENERAL MACHINERY	ELECTRIC APPLIANCES	TRANSPORTATION EQUIPMENTS	PRECISION INSTRUMENTS	OTHER MANUFACTURING	CONSTRUCTION	UTILITIES	COMMERCIAL	FINANCE, INSURANCE, REAL ESTATE	TRANSPORT/ COMMUNICATION	SERVICE	PUBLIC SERVICE	UNCLASSIFIABLE	TOTAL
							5.6		−5.3				−9.9
		−7.2		−3.1			4.8						−2.6
				−1.7									−3.5
													−2.0
				−0.1									−0.3
				−0.4									−0.5
				−1.2									−1.1
					0		7.4						−0.9
													1.9
													1.9
		1.9		−3.8	[2.2]	−1.1	2.8		−2.2	−5.0	−13.8		1.4
		4.6			9.2				4.4	8.0			4.1
					4.0	0	1.9		1.4	5.3			2.6
				−1.8			4.1		−2.6				−0.5
		0.8		−2.8	3.1				−1.7				0.2
8.2	10.2	6.1			11.6					7.5			8.0
					3.9		10.5			−0.9			−1.5
					3.4		7.8	5.0					2.5
−5.6	−4.1	−2.2			−9.0	1.1	6.5		−5.1	3.5	5.6		0.03
							0		−1.1	9.6	2.4		2.7
					−1.7	2.4	3.7	8.5	1.9	[0.9]	1.2		2.1
												25.9	25.9
−0.8	−2.0	1.1	0.9	−6.3	3.8	1.6	2.6	−3.1	1.0	2.6	2.3	25.9	0.1

*Box highlighted indicates basic workers of the industry
*No entry denotes a very small number of workers. (under 10,000 in either 1970 or 1975)
SOURCE: *The Diffusion of Microelectronics Technology and its Influence on Industrial Structure*
(Microerekutoronikusu gijitsu no fukyū sangyō kōzō e no eikyō),
Industrial Research Institute, August, 1982.

who refuse government-assigned jobs jeopardize their right to unemployment benefits.

Workers laid off from industries that are certified as structurally depressed receive special allowances if they participate in the government's retraining programs. Workers over forty receive special extensions of their employment insurance benefits, and employers who retrain rather than discharge workers are also subsidized. During the past six years, the government has designated twenty-six industries, including portions of the textile, steel, and aluminum industries, as structurally depressed.

The Employees Law and related legislation encourage large firms to continue to retain permanent employees even during recessions. Such assistance, however, is possible only in diversified companies. Smaller firms that deal almost exclusively in one industry have no place to remove workers once their industry becomes depressed. In such cases, workers must look to the government's unemployment insurance programs.

In several respects the Japanese approach facilitates adjustment. By tying the program's benefits to workers' participation, the law creates incentives for workers to relocate to more productive sectors of the economy. And, by establishing facilities for placement and for training, the law helps relocate these workers on a nationwide scale. Finally, by incorporating these elements in its basic unemployment program, rather than seeing them as a countermeasure to the impacts of trade, the government retains the option of retraining workers in response to changes in domestic, as well as international, industrial structure.

In late 1978 the Japanese government also initiated a program of adjustment assistance for communities whose industries had lost competitiveness. Firms in over thirty communities received low-interest loans, loan guarantees, extensions of existing loans, and various tax advantages to encourage their expansion into new growth sectors. At the same time workers were retrained and supported with other benefits.

Japanese companies in industries designated as depressed

232

are entitled to various forms of assistance. In addition, a host of special subsidies are accorded small and medium enterprises. Since these enterprises account for as much as 99.4 percent or 6,230,000 of Japan's 6,269,000 private establishments, and employ 81.4 percent (32,206,000 of 45,720,000) of the work force, such subsidies constitute a substantial transfer payment.

New technologies at times demand new ways of organizing work. When production is nonroutine, it is also inherently unpredictable. A premium is placed on flexibility. Problem-solving now requires collaboration among people at all stages, and often the key to adaptability is how rapidly information can be shared within the group.

In some ways the structure of Japanese labor relations also facilitates adjustment and even catalyzes technological change. Much has been written about how custom and law sustain lifetime employment and seniority in Japan. Equally important, however, are joint consultation, quality circles, job rotation, and the role of first-line supervisors. Although these institutions are now undergoing change, they still constitute a buffer against the dislocations caused by the government's transformation policies.

Until the mid-1950s Japanese labor-management relations were far from harmonious. But during this period of crisis a group of farsighted, relatively middle-of-the-road labor leaders began to acknowledge the need for cooperation with management. This group, which included labor leaders within strategic industries, gradually won both the support of management and their fellow unionists.

Although in the early postwar period joint consultation was first proposed by management to frustrate the attempts of radical workers to seize control of production, the consultation system did not develop fully until the mid-1950s. Joint consultation today represents the principal means of labor and management communication on critical issues. It is more a species of joint problem-solving than a direct negotiation. Topics vary from large problems of investment and production to the specifics of a housing allowance. At times

233

management offers confidential information to obtain a union's assent before a formal discussion commences. In other cases, workers disclose plans to management to express grievances or to clarify their interests. Over 70 percent of private enterprises with 100 or more employees have established such channels for consultation.

First-line supervisors developed during the 1950s in response to management's desire to restore order at the workshop level, in particular in strategic industries. The supervisors perform two functions: they represent the lowest level of management, and at the same time are the apex of production on the work floor. The supervisors resemble the American foreman system, introduced into the Japanese steel industry in 1956 (Yawata) and 1959 (Nippon Kokan).[29]

A related, better-known institution is the quality control circles. Essentially these are groups of employees trained in statistical techniques to discover defects and errors. Working together stimulates education, sharing of information, and an optimal mix of human and other resources. Quality circles have grown from approximately 33,000 (with 400,000 participants) in the 1960s to over 115,000 (more than 1 million participants) today.

Job rotation is a fourth important institution. Tadashi Hanami describes the system:

The newly employed labor force is often assigned to the lowest-level job, even in cases of employees with higher education. Starting from the lowest-level jobs, they are gradually promoted through various kinds of jobs. In this way, most workers not only learn various kinds of jobs and are always ready to take part temporarily in other jobs if needed, but also, and more importantly, they learn the whole system and structure of the production process of their company. This gives a strong advantage to Japanese workers, since they avoid finding their present job meaningless within the total, complex production process or feeling themselves to be tiny isolated in a mammoth system.

Furthermore, this practice of work rotation provides a decisive advantage to Japanese companies in coping with technological change, the introduction of new products, the expansion of the

234

scope of business, the introduction of new equipment, or the opening of new plants, because of innovations and changing business conditions.[30]

A recent study by the Ford Motor Company cites several additional factors as contributing to the high rates of productivity in the automobile industry: more economical use of space, greater machine density, more innovative combinations of operations, higher machine yields, minimum inventories, balancing the lines, and careful planning of material requirements. All these techniques are largely dependent on the close cooperation of management and labor.

It is relatively easy to see how lifetime employment, seniority, quality circles, joint consultation, and the other dimensions of Japan's industrial relations system buffer some of the most painful dislocations of structural transformation. Less noticed, however, are the significant incentives these institutions also confer on strategic sectors. These include: (1) job stability and certainty provided by lifetime employment and seniority; (2) economic incentives conferred through the bonus system; (3) flexibility attained through job rotation, low interfirm mobility, and the absence of rigid job classifications in union contracts; (4) workers' loyalty and dedication that reduce the risk of theft of trade secrets; (5) labor's ability to perform multiple tasks facilitated by job training, rotation, and the educational system; (6) rewards for new ideas and strong incentives for communitarian action; (7) attention to group participation in management decisions affecting the workplace and the development of new technologies; and (8) a general appreciation that workers must be included in information loops in order to build consensus and to increase their effectiveness. Although there may be exceptions, the structure of Japanese industrial relations since 1950 appears generally to have been a positive force for innovation and technological development.

In *Computer Power and Human Reason*, Joseph Weizenbaum probes the direct and more insidious ways by which the reification of the computer strips science of its ethical standards, engenders conformity, and separates man from his moral and intellectual responsibilities. His critique focuses on the individual. The computer, he alleges, will intensify man's sense of surrender to the grip of anonymous, baleful forces. By undermining man's sense of control, the computer debases civic courage and clouds the complexities of moral choice. Weizenbaum writes: "What we have gained is a new conformism, which permits us to say anything that can be said in the functional languages of instrumental reason, but forbids us to allude to what Ionesco called the living truth."[31]

Of what relevance is Weizenbaum's book for contemporary Japan? Although it has been translated into Japanese, the book appears to have had little influence. Much has been written about the pressures on the individual to conform in Japan. Could Weizenbaum's fears have their most insidious effects here, particularly as the strains of crowding, competition, and international criticism mount? Will intelligent terminals replace many basic human interactions and with them the cohesive bonds underlying consensus, solidarity, and collective responsibility? Or will the computer, contrary to Weizenbaum's admonitions, actually bind Japanese society to even more powerful collective action?

Conclusion

Despite their many benefits, strategic industries often impose heavy burdens on societies. In promoting the next generation of strategic industries, Japan's leaders will need to address a common core of questions that leaders in other countries concerned with industrial development will in time also face: What will be the standard of care? Who will bear the costs of these industries' development and in what proportion? Who will receive the benefits of governmental assistance and through what process will these benefits be conferred?

It is likely that the next generation of high-technology

industries will cause social, economic, political, and environmental problems. In most respects these will be no different from those eventually confronting other countries. Since Japan is now at the forefront of these new technologies, its solutions to these problems should be closely watched.

Japan's experience is of theoretical and practical importance because it represents a systems approach to handling the problem of social costs in the development of strategic industries. This chapter has offered various examples of this approach: a special statutory scheme to incorporate structurally depressed sectors; incentives to foster the infusion of high technology into these sectors; an imaginative adjustment assistance program to retrain workers and place them in growing sectors where their contribution is most needed; sensible measures for energy conservation that will continue irrespective of perturbations in the world demand for oil; an imaginative program to build cities of science and technology that will stimulate regional growth and carry the benefits of the new industries to the remotest parts of the country.

In many respects Japan appears well buffered against adversity. The government's developed industrial base will serve as an early warning system so that adverse effects, particularly on employment, can be anticipated and met by countervailing action.

The basic values of Japan's communitarian tradition, reliability, trust, loyalty, responsibility, and certainty are also assets that will help to alleviate some of the most severe pains of adjustment. Japan's flexible labor unions and the cooperative structure of industrial relations will probably continue to accommodate the introduction of new technologies at least in the short run.

The transformation of Japanese society will involve a sharing of risks and a sharing of benefits. The government will share with industry the expense and risks of failure of long-term technological development projects. The key firms will capture an important part of these benefits. But the government will assure that an important part, an apparently equitable part, of the benefit of these activities will also be distributed to other firms, competitors, and the public at large.

The participating firms will bear part of the investment costs and may well also be forced by government regulation, administrative guidance, compensation systems, or liability rules to shoulder part of the social costs, the "harms" of its activity.

However, industry will not bear all these costs. Part will be borne by the average citizen. This will be the price for his or her right to live in the information age. In theory this is how the avoidable costs for industrial development will be reduced, and the unavoidable equitably shared.

If these are some of the benefits of Japan's systems approach, what are its chief failings? Although it is clearly too early to judge, Japan may be most vulnerable to issues that lie outside the paradigm, ones that challenge the system's every logic. In other words, if the basic assumptions and values of a system prove unsound, such systems may not as easily be altered as less tidy approaches. Should Amaya's benign vision be seriously flawed, and Weizenbaum's concerns prove correct, Japan's onslaught into the information age may be far more costly than the slower, disorderly, more questioning transition of the west.

I have purposely deferred discussion of the bilateral and international impacts of Japan's structural transformation policies. These too have depended on a fairly precise allocation of burdens and benefits. For its defense Japan has enjoyed the benefits of U.S. support. In matters of international immigration, Japan's borders have been closed, even to the millions who fled the holocaust of Indochina. In international environmental matters, Japan continues to be unsympathetic to the need to protect the commons. Japan's most polluting industries have been rationalized or deposited with the less politically aware nations of the periphery. In economic affairs, except when checked, Japan has paid little heed to the dislocations to foreign markets and countries by the deluge of Japanese products.

These are complex questions and my aim is not to pass

judgment on the morality or immorality of Japanese government's actions. Rather, what should be noted is that the process has been insulated from the cries of protest. The price of such isolation is conflict. Part IV predicts that the protests against Japan's insularity will soon so clamor about her government and business leaders that all Japan has sought to achieve may be lost.

Disorder at home and conflict abroad need not be the fruits of this decade. Part III explains how a concrete approach can be fashioned to the difficulties identified in Chapter 3. Once this approach is launched, the United States will again be able to deal strongly, yet generously, with those whose actions now seem to threaten us.

Part III

THE PILLARS OF
NATIONAL INDUSTRIAL RECOVERY

Chapter 8
The Trigger Method

Parts I and II have introduced many of the factors responsible for an industry's strategic impact. This chapter organizes those indicators into a technique to be used by government officials, businesspeople, industrial analysts, and others interested in evaluating strategic sectors or technologies. I refer to this procedure as the "Trigger Method." This chapter explains the method in detail after summarizing the basic elements of a strategic industry.

A Systems Approach to Determining Strategic Industries

It is time to refine the argument and to show how it might be applied.

Historians suggest that some industries in a given time and

Chapter 8 of this book introduces a procedure for identifying strategic industries and evaluating their impact. Advice on the use of the Trigger Method is part of the consulting services of the author and his associates. An application for a service and trademark registration of the Trigger Method by Julian Gresser is pending. Inquiries regarding the Trigger Method should be referred to the author or to his counsel, Charles R. Brainard, c/o Kenyon and Kenyon, 1 Broadway, New York, N.Y. 10004.

place have been the primary cause of economic growth. I call these strategic industries. Time and place are critical conditions because the strategic importance of an industry depends on the circumstances of the host country, and even, I shall show, on regional blocs.

Government action is critical to the destiny of many strategic industries. Governments can promote industries to strategic candidacy, and governments may declassify industries. In some cases, a country may sense that a given industry is strategic but fail to capture its benefits by the ineptness of its approach. As late as the 1970s Great Britain was the second largest source next to the United States of industrial inventions, yet it failed to commercialize many of them.[1] Sometimes government leaders mistakenly believe that an industry is strategic and favor it to the detriment of an even more important sector. David Landes shows how, despite all impediments, cotton surpassed wool in its impact on growth during an important period of the industrial revolution in England.

The influence of an industry on aggregate economic growth is determined by the action of critical indicators. These core characteristics are in large part empirically based and can be found in the historical record. No core characteristic should be designated unless strong independent historical support is found for it.

An increasingly important element of many, although by no means all, strategic industries is their reduction of the costs of communications, information, and transportation. Similarly many, although again not all, strategic industries are at the forefront of technological change. Strategic industries are not limited to the capital goods sectors. As the example of nineteenth-century Denmark shows, agriculture can be a strategic industry in some cases.

A critical mass of many of the key variables and their synergistic actions is largely responsible for a strategic industry's influence on economic growth. A strategic industry need not possess all these characteristics, but it must possess a critical core.

The core characteristics themselves vary in importance de-

244

pending on time and circumstance. Throughout the period of their influence, however, these factors can be sufficiently powerful to cause the industry to be a significant stimulus to economic growth.

Industries can be arranged along a spectrum, some exhibiting more of the core characteristics and some less. There may be degrees of strategic leverage.

Industries will vary in their degree of strategic leverage. They can become more or less strategic. New strategic industries will appear, and others will no longer deserve the name. A preliminary study of nuclear power suggests that this industry may have been strategic for the United States in the 1960s, although clearly it is no longer so.[2]

Some industries are important but not strategic. The U.S. automobile industry is very important if only because of the number of people it employs. But it might not be strategic according to my criteria. The automobile industry was clearly strategic to the United States during the early part of the twentieth century.[3]

Some industries, although not strategic in themselves, perform important functions for other industries. Nørregaard Rasmussen notes:

It should not be overlooked that in many cases the term a "key industry" is used in a sense widely different from the one mentioned above. In certain cases the term is used when relating two industries no. i and no. j to one another. Industry no. i is then termed a "key industry" for industry no. j if the production in the latter industry is technically dependent on the products of the former industry. In this sense the iron ore industry is a "key industry" in relation to the steel industry. Within the framework of the present model this definition would involve that in the marginal case a certain industry has all the remaining industries as "key industries," or in general the "key industries" for industry no. j would be all those industries, for which $A_{ij} \S 0$, $i = 1, 2, \ldots m.4/$

The demand of the U.S. automobile industry for robots serves an important function for the development of the robotics

245

industry, possibly a strategic industry, as well as a host of other industries.

It is not productive to speculate about which industries are strategic and which are not. A satisfactory answer can be derived only by careful analysis of the core variables and others to be identified as this concept is refined.

The Method

By the following ten-step method, the reader should be able to gauge the strategic leverage of any industry past, present, or future. The first six steps are descriptive and analytic, and are illustrated by the example of the American cotton textile industry in the early nineteenth century. Chapters 4 to 7 have already explained how decision makers in Japan, although not employing the proposed method, are using many of its principles to plan the development of strategic industries to the end of the twentieth century and the beginning of the twenty-first. Chapter 9 describes the final three evaluative steps of the method.[5]

Step 1: Defining the Industry

The first problem in designating an industry as strategic is to determine the boundaries of the industry itself. Chapter 9 addresses the question of *who* should make this decision. The present discussion is concerned with the methodology of definition.

Particularly in capital goods industries, intermediary technological changes often determine the qualities and direction of economic growth. Nathan Rosenberg suggests that in such cases we must rethink our basic notions of an industry as defined by product lines, and begin to focus on interindustry relationships and intraindustry technological flows.

Any consideration of the textile industry would be artificial which did not include the chemical, plastics, and paper industries. Con-

246

sideration of the machine tool industry must now take into account the aerospace, precision casting, forging, and plastics forming industries. These industries are now complex mixtures of companies from a variety of SIC categories, some functioning as suppliers to the traditional industry, some competing with it for end-use functions and markets. "The industry" can no longer be defined as a set of companies who share certain methods of production and product-properties; it must be defined as a set of companies, interconnected as suppliers and market, committed to diverse processes and products, but overlapping in the end-use functions they fill. We can talk about the "shelter" industry and the "materials forming" industry, but we cannot make the assumptions of coherence, similarity and uniformity of view which we could formerly make in speaking of "builders" or "machine tool manufacturers." Similarly, companies are coming to be less devoted to a single family of products and manufacturing methods, and more a diverse conglomerate of manufacturing enterprises, stationed around a central staff and bank, and to some extent overlapping in the markets and functions they serve. These changes are part and parcel of the process of innovation by invasion.[6]

Rosenberg finds in input-output analysis a powerful tool to look inside the "black box" that conceals how the primary factors of production, capital, and labor are transformed into a final flow of output.

The technique makes it possible to study the process of technological change by examining changing intermediate input requirements, by looking, that is, . . . at the coal and ore and steel and chemicals and fibers and aluminum foil; sausage casings, wire products, wood products, wood pulp, electronic components, trucking, and business services that establishments furnish to each other. . . . Many aspects of technological change are visible only at this intermediate level.[7]

Only by examining these intra- and intersectoral relationships at the intermediate levels of production can we begin to grasp the causes of technological change.

Input-output information enables us to predict that cost-reducing technological changes in some sectors are likely to have wider-range repercussions than similar changes in other sectors. It highlights the pervasiveness of cost reductions in such sectors as transportation, energy, services, and communications, and makes it possible to identify and assess the relative significance of such cost reductions in different sectors of the economy. But the problems are far more subtle and complicated and revolve around the essential fact that technological progress in one sector of the economy has become increasingly dependent upon technological change in other sectors. That is to say, technological problems arising in industry A are eventually solved by bringing to bear technical skills and resources from industry B, C, or D. Thus, industries are increasingly dependent, in achieving a high rate of productivity growth, upon skills and resources external to, and perhaps totally unfamiliar to, themselves.[8]

The problem of interindustry relationship or flows is less acute in non–capital goods sectors, although they may still be important. The task is to identify as precisely as possible the core of the industry that appears chiefly responsible for economic growth.

After determining the appropriate technological boundary of the industry, the next problem is to describe it in time and place. If the object is to describe a past or present strategic industry, the decision maker must pinpoint the time period and the geographical area where the industry first began to exhibit its strategic character, how this character changed, and when it began to decline. This will require careful assessment of each stage in the life cycle of an industry. Because the flow of technology may change over an industry's life cycle the definition of the industry itself may need to be revised.

Step 2: Assessment of Economic Indicators

The second step is to assess the target industry from the vantage of specific economic indicators. Some indices can be supported by data easily obtained from historical studies or current statistics. Others may require new in-depth research.

GENERAL INDICATORS

The general indicators (outputs and inputs) are high rates of: (1) growth, (2) exports, (3) employment, and (4) productivity gains. In comparison with other industries, strategic industries display these general indicators at some period in their life cycle. These high rates probably will not all occur at the same time. Productivity gains resulting from technological change may precede spurts in growth, while rising employment and exports may often accompany or be consequences of increasing growth rates.

RESEARCH, INVENTION, AND INNOVATION

Many, although not all, strategic industries involve a substantial commitment to (5) research. In the last forty years such research has been conducted in corporate laboratories. The research was far less institutionalized than it is now, although even then the industries' leaders appear to have been interested in probing technology's frontiers.

Strategic industries also tend to have (6) high levels of investment in human capital. Rosenberg stresses this important variable:

Much of society's "investment" (if the term is used in the only meaningful sense of any current use of resources which increases future output) consists in investment in human capital; and a significant portion of the apparent discrepancy between the growth in output per capita and the growth in measured inputs, referred to earlier, is attributable to the exclusion of all capital which becomes embodied, so to speak, in the human agent. Such investments become increasingly important as an economy achieves higher levels of per capita income and it is apparent that the failure to include the expenditure of resources upon such activities as formal education and on-the-job training has imparted a major downward bias to our measure of capital formation and to our measures of growth-inducing forces generally.[9]

They also exhibit (7) high rates of invention and innovation: "Strategic industries display high rates of invention and the commercialization of these inventions (innovation). As suggested by the machine tool industry there is often a positive feedback between the two. Innovations create a market and a demand that stimulates invention."[10] Invention opens new opportunities for the canny entrepreneur. The process is usually incremental, but in the aggregate, of great importance.

ECONOMIES OF PRODUCTION

Economies of production include economies of (8) scale, (9) specialization, (10) scope, and (11) the learning curve and the product life cycle.

Strategic industries generally display sharply increasing economies of scale; in other words, an increase in output per factor of production (productivity) as a function of scale. As with machine tools in the nineteenth century, such increases in productivity are often more the result of specialization than scale. At times, however, as in the early 1950s in the Japanese petrochemical industry, one industry can capture both type of economies. The synergetic action of many factors tends to multiply the benefits of eonomies of scale and specialization over time (dynamic economies) and in other sectors of the economy.

As was seen in the discussion of flexible manufacturing in Chapter 5, "economies of scope" may increasingly be an important condition for some future strategic industries. Today an initial investment is amortized by the mass production of identical parts. In some emerging industries, such as flexible manufacturing, the same level of investment can be recouped by production of an equal or greater volume of different parts or of the deployment of the same part in multiple uses.

(11) The learning curve and the product life cycle. The learning curve refers to the relation between labor costs and output as a function of experience. After an initial increase, labor costs generally decline as a result of workers' acquaintance with their tasks. The semiconductor industry displays a steep declining learning curve associated with mass production of memory chips; the aircraft industry, a more gently

declining learning curve that reflects batch production. The learning curve appears particularly important in some strategic industries.[11]

A related notion is the product life cycle. In strategic industries the product life cycle tends to be shorter than in other industries, and, the industry's products tend to turn over at increasing rates. This in turn can effect a shift downward in the learning curve. The semiconductor industry displays this phenomenon. For example, in product life cycles, $A, B, C, \ldots n,$ the learning economies of C influence B, B influences A, and so on to the nth permutation. As suggested by the development of the machine-tool industry in the nineteenth century, these economies are augmented by the increasing specialization, complexity, and differentiation that characterize strategic industries.[12]

STRUCTURAL FACTORS

(12) Vertical Integration. Strategic industries often become vertically integrated, in part as a response to technological convergence. This is perhaps best exemplified by the development of the Japanese semiconductor and computer firms that grew from divisions of the early telecommunications companies and in response to the needs of their communications industry.[13]

However, a strategic industry may be "vertically disintegrated" as was the machine-tool industry in the early days of its development in nineteenth-century America.

Step 3: Technical Indicators

DUAL USE

Most strategic industries, although not all, include technologies that have both civilian and military uses. Military uses involve defense, offense, or some other strategic deployment, usually dependent on early availability for use as weapons. In most cases the state of the art is in the military application; but in other cases, such as semiconductor memory chips, it may lie in commercial applications.

251

CORE TECHNOLOGY

Often a core group of technologies plays a critical technological and/or economic role within a strategic industry. In the late 1970s the 64k random access memory (RAM) occupied not only the technological frontier of critical memory components, but because of its suitability for mass production it also constituted an important source of revenue for the industry. Such technologies possess "strategic functions" that mirror, on a lesser scale, the functions of the industry as a whole.

FRONTIERS OF SCIENCE AND TECHNOLOGY

Some high-technology industries such as robotics, semiconductors, and genetic engineering are generating a disproportionately larger percentage of fundamental advances in science and technology, in part because of their commitment to research. As suggested by the history of machine tools, these industries often are guided by a core group of technologies with diverse applications. The strength of users' demands and the versatility of applications have often assured the rapid diffusion of scientific and technological advances to other sectors.

KNOWLEDGE (INFORMATION) INTENSIVE

Strategic industries have often been closely allied with communications. The railroads created a national market and, in concert with the steamship, an international market. The semiconductor, computer, intelligent robots, telecommunications, and even bioengineering are today's information-processing or communications industries. As discussed earlier, the economic properties of information contribute largely to the strategic functions played by these industries.

TECHNOLOGICAL CONVERGENCE

Nathan Rosenberg's study of the American machine-tool industry in the nineteenth century is a good example of technological convergence. The phenomenon is also well illustrated in the convergence between the computer and semiconductor industries, exemplified in the microprocessor (computer), the overlap between telecommunications and computer networks, and the increasing integration between biology and the information industries in the new field of bionics.[14]

COMPLEMENTARIES, INTERDEPENDENCE, AND THE CONCEPT OF TECHNICAL IMBALANCE

In history the productivity of an invention has often turned on the availability of a complementary technology. Enjoyment of the benefits of A had to await inventions B, C, or D. In the past the reduction in the cost of power generation proved critical to the aluminum industry and affected the extent to which fertilizers reduced the costs of food production.

A related notion is "technical imbalance." Often an improvement in one part of a system is constrained by another part of the system. The improvement creates an imbalance placing a "strain" on other parts. This in turn induces changes that make the system as a whole more efficient. The operation of an audio system illustrates this idea.

The auditory benefits of a high-quality amplifier are lost when it is connected to a low-quality loudspeaker. Edison, and later Westinghouse, well understood the idea of technical imbalance in their development of the electrical power industry in the United States.

SYNERGISMS

I use the word synergism in its biological sense: A potentiates B and is itself thereby enhanced, so that the combined potency of A and B exceed their individual effects. Rosenberg's description of the changes in the machine-tool industry is a good case of synergism. Synergism differs from linkage in that it describes a more precise and technical interaction between technologies, suppliers, and industries.[15]

COMPLEXITY AND DIFFERENTIATION

It has been suggested that an important index of technological capability is complexity (the number of parts). For example, countries with less-developed industrial bases generally manufacture machines involving fewer than 5,000 parts; countries at an intermediate level 5,000–50,000 parts; and those at the highest level manufacture machines using 50,000–2,000,000 parts. Only the U.S., it is alleged, has this capacity.[16]

Step 4: Social and Political Indicators

GENERALIZABLE PATTERN OF PRODUCTION

Strategic industries often introduce a new pattern of production that is thereafter generalized throughout the economy. The factory is introduced with the cotton industry in England in the eighteenth century. Henry Ford introduces the mass production of automobiles. Today computer-controlled integrated systems of intelligent robots and machine tools are fundamentally reshaping production. Although less easily described or quantified, such basic changes in how human beings organize their work can be as important to a strategic industry as any of its more technical characteristics.

GENERALIZEABLE PATTERN OF COMMERCE

In addition to its general legacy for economic growth, banking at Bruges and the Italian city-states in the fourteenth and fifteenth centuries created general principles and practices of commerce that continue in many cases unchanged today. The partnership, the branch office, double entry bookkeeping, bills of exchange, marine insurance, and other major evolutionary steps in the development of mercantile law all date from this period.[17]

RELATION TO OTHER CRITICAL NATIONAL POLICY OBJECTIVES

In the eighteenth century there was little relation between the early growth of cotton and Britain's national objectives.

Cotton simply broke through naturally, an unbound Prometheus.[18] Some strategic industries, however, have had a close relation to government's objectives in other sectors. The best example is the German chemical dye industry that well served the Third Reich's ambitions for conquest.[19] A critical feature of Japan's strategic industries today is the perception of some ministries of their contribution to energy conservation, pollution control, technological development, productivity, labor relations, and international political adjustment.

NATIONAL PERCEPTIONS OF WEALTH, PRESTIGE AND POWER

Governments have almost always come to perceive strategic industries as critically important either for prestige, military prowess, scientific advance, or economic success. The interesting question is whether this perception and the consequent preferments that often accompany designation are what *make* the industry strategic, or whether there are forces at play independent of governmental action. The cotton industry in England seems to support the latter hypothesis, since cotton grew and flourished despite sumptuary laws against it, and national dispensations to wool. This in no way discounts the significance of a government's perceptions of the importance of an industry, nor those of the public. National perceptions are always important in the evaluation of an industry's strategic significance.

SCALE RATIOS OF SOCIETY

Strategic industries often have dramatic, at times even sudden, changes in the human, mechanical, and informational scale ratios of society.[20] Change a person's life expectancy from 35 to 75, the onslaught of adulthood from 12 to 20, communicative skills by voice or gesture, the hours of sleep, and you dramatically affect economic performance. These are the human-scale ratios.

Consider the changes on land from donkey to convoy, on sea from the barge of Hatshepsut to the supertanker, the development of air transport, and you find shifts that dramatically influence economic growth. These are the mechanical scales, measured in volume and speed, that pertain to the movement of goods. Finally, consider the transformation involved from the smoke signal to the computer and then to the satellite. These are the scales of communication, measured in bytes, distance, time, and cost. Each major change in the scale ratios of society alters the size and dominance of the social group, the generation and distribution of wealth, and the configuration of land, sea, and air relationships.

Step 5: Secondary and Tertiary Effects

Strategic industries have characteristic secondary and tertiary effects during their life cycle. When concerned with an existing or future strategic industry, we must attempt to predict these effects. They are substantially clear in the analysis of strategic industries of the past.

HIGH MULTIPLIER

An important element is the rapid rate of purchase or use by other industries of revenues generated or output of the strategic industry. Forward and backward linkages are examples of the multiplier in a specific sectoral direction. Strategic industries exhibit high multipliers initially through these sectoral pathways.

DEEP "PENETRATION" OF INPUT-OUTPUT MATRIX

Strategic industries often involve a sharp reduction in cost that is distributed broadly throughout the input-output matrix of an economy. One of the key breakthroughs in the history of British coal was the sharp reduction in fuel costs. With the development of the coal industry, reductions in fuel costs were captured soon after in glass, brick, lime, and metal making. Analogous economies are evident in the ways the railroad helped to reduce the costs of transportation and communications in other industries, and in agriculture.

Some industries, particularly capital goods sectors, penetrate the input-output matrix through technology. A good example is copper wire. An example from high technology

The Pillars of National Industrial Recovery

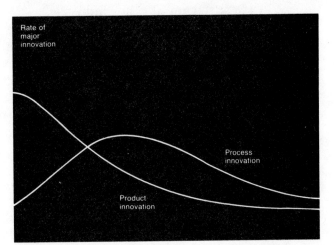

	Fluid pattern	Transitional pattern	Specific pattern
Competitive emphasis on	Functional product performance	Product variation	Cost reduction
Innovation stimulated by	Information on users' needs and users' technical inputs	Opportunities created by expanding internal technical capability	Pressure to reduce cost and improve quality
Predominant type of innovation	Frequent major changes in products	Major process changes required by rising volume	Incremental for product and process, with cumulative improvement in productivity and quality
Product line	Diverse, often including custom designs	Includes at least one product design stable enough to have significant production volume	Mostly undifferentiated standard products
Production processes	Flexible and inefficient; major changes easily accommodated	Becoming more rigid, with changes occurring in major steps	Efficient, capital-intensive, and rigid; cost of change is high
Equipment	General-purpose, requiring highly skilled labor	Some subprocesses automated, creating "islands of automation"	Special-purpose, mostly automatic with labor tasks mainly monitoring and control
Materials	Inputs are limited to generally-available materials	Specialized materials may be demanded from some suppliers	Specialized materials will be demanded; if not available, vertical integration will be extensive
Plant	Small-scale, located near user or source of technology	General-purpose with specialized sections	Large-scale, highly specific to particular products
Organizational control is	Informal and entrepreneurial	Through liaison relationships, project and task groups	Through emphasis on structure, goals, and rules

Reprinted with permission from *Technology Review*, copyright © 1978 is the semiconductor, now an indispensable component in a wide spectrum of other industries.

The concept of penetration and the idea of forward or backward linkages are closely similar—and in some cases may be identical—in that the deeper the penetration, generally the greater the linkage-multiplier-feedback effect. A possible distinction may be that linkages imply both reduction in the costs of supplying a given input and also an *increase in demand* for the output of an industry or its linked industries.

FORWARD AND BACKWARD LINKAGES

Strategic industries display forward and backward linkages in both an economic and technical sense. Just as the railroad engendered the growth of agriculture (forward linkage) and stimulated the coal and iron industries (backward linkage), so today rapid advances in semiconductor technology are changing the size, design, and uses of computers (forward technical linkage), while also increasing the demand for new materials such as gallium arsenide (backward economic and technical linkage).

HIGH RATE OF FEEDBACK

Forward linkages are often in a dynamic relation that Albert Hirschman has termed "pincer cum feedback":

Thus it is quite possible for industry A to be established as a result of final demand for its products crossing the threshold, and then for B to follow suit not only because of demand factors, but also because B intends to use A's products as a principal input. Such a development has a particularly dynamic quality, because it necessitates an expansion of industry A, which was originally set up only in response to final demand and must now satisfy new industrial customers as well. In other words, while the existence of industry A helps to induce the establishment of industry B, this establishment in turn induces the building of new capacity for A.[21]

The feedback may be technical as well as economic, with technological innovations in "downstream" industries influencing technical changes in the "upstream" suppliers.

As noted, strategic industries involve high rates of product and process innovation. In general, a strategic industry's life cycle is described by James Utterback and illustrated in Figure 2. A firm finds an initial use for a major innovation in a small, often vacant market niche. Rising demand for its products and increasing costs and other factors tend to stimulate process innovation, which in turn calls forth new product innovations. A product innovation for one firm may often constitute a process innovation for another. James Utterback notes:

When one examines the relationship between various producer and user firms it quickly becomes apparent that, in this broader sense, most innovation is not product innovation at all, but contributes to productivity directly through the linkage of different firms in the physical flow of production to final demand.[22]

Most process innovations tend to follow product innovations by several years, although the lag tends to shorten as a product becomes standardized.

Strategic industries in most respects follow Utterback's life cycle of product and process innovation. A major difference between strategic industries and other industries, however, is the speed and range of diffusion of technological change, first within the strategic industry itself and then to other sectors; and also the rate of feedback among the primary, secondary, and tertiary sectors.

Economic feedback is illustrated in the derived demand for the primary industry's products. Such demand can itself stimulate additional innovation. Technological feedback is illustrated by secondary or tertiary technological breakthroughs that either stimulate technological change in "upstream" sectors or become inputs of these sectors. Industrial feedback takes place when a principle developed in a linked sector is referred back and adopted by the primary sector. The historical relationship of innovation, diffusion, and feedback is discussed in Chapter 1.

High rates of innovation, diffusion, and feedback are associated with high rates of economic growth. The dynamic relation of product and process innovation, diffusion, and feedback loops suggests that governments employ different measures over the life cycle of any industry.

Step 6: High "External" Benefits, High "External" Costs

Strategic industries confer significant benefits to large segments of society, often far exceeding the market value of their products. To some extent such benefits can be quantified as indicated in Fishlow's study of the railroads. At the same time, these industries often impose significant adverse costs on large segments of the population. The air pollution of the Japanese kombinat in the 1950s and 1960s is a vivid example.

Usually there is a lag between the initial perception of the benefits of a strategic industry and a later realization of its costs. Often the distinction is exaggerated as government and industrial leaders tout these benefits and seek through legal and other means to depreciate their adverse consequences.

The benefits and costs of strategic industries also appear to have a distinct relationship to each other. In many industries the benefits and costs often rise gradually. In strategic industries, however, while the benefits are often immediately evident, the costs are not. Often these may appear in a sudden event. An example is a nuclear reactor. When operated safely, the reactor provides electricity to an entire city. With mishap, it brings catastrophe. At times the costs of a strategic industry appear silently and over a protracted period. This was the case of Minamata (mercury poisoning), itai-itai (cadmium poisoning), and related environmental diseases in postwar Japan.[23] This oscillation of benefits and burdens itself appears an important characteristic of strategic industries.

Steps 7 to 10 Summarized

By the Trigger Method policymakers should be able to identify and, if necessary, assist strategic industries. As explained in the next chapter, after an industry is analyzed according to steps 1 to 6, the applicant submits an analysis to the Office of Strategic Industries. Next, the report is summarized and arranged in a matrix for purposes of comparison with other nominated industries. Each industry is then evaluated with respect to the economic, technical, political, and other indicators noted. This procedure raises the difficult problems of how to perform this assessment, how to weigh indicators with respect to each other, and how to integrate the nominal, ordinal, and cardinal values assigned into a final determination of an industry's strategic significance. Such decisions can be made only partially by technical analysis. Chapter 9 proposes that the ultimate decision about which industrial sector is strategic, and the extent of its strategicness, be determined by a negotiated agreement involving the targeted industry and other affected interests. The next section of this chapter illustrates the retrospective uses of the Trigger Method by the case of cotton textiles in nineteenth-century America.

Cotton Textiles in Nineteenth-Century America— A Historical Illustration of the Trigger Method

Between 1780 and 1840 the cotton textile industry of the eastern seaboard states served as a strategic industry for the region and, to a lesser extent, for the rest of the country. A value from one to ten is used to rate the industry with respect to each of the key indicators. The evaluation is based on an interview with J. W. Lozier, a historian of the industry.[24]

Step 1: Definition of the Industry

We are concerned principally with three classes of cotton mills and their supporting managerial, marketing, and financial institutions: dispersed small rural mills, medium-sized mills of villages and cities, and clusters of big mills intensely operated at large water-power facilities.

261

Step 2: Economic Indicators

1. Rates of growth (10). After 1807 the cotton textile industry was the fastest growing sector in New England.
   Lozier estimates that between 1807 and 1815 the industry grew by over 300 percent. It continued in cycles of
   rapid growth throughout the period.

2. Rates of exports (1). Despite its high rate of growth,
   cotton textiles never developed into a significant export
   industry. England continued to dominate the international market until the late nineteenth century.

3. Rates of employment (10). Few industries employed as
   many people as did the cotton industry. Cotton mills
   were particularly a major employer of women: Lozier
   estimates that 75 percent of the workforce employed by
   the mills in Vermont were women and 81.4 percent in
   New Hampshire were women. Cotton mills contributed
   the first large-scale employment opportunity for women
   outside the home in other than domestic tasks.

4. Rates of productivity
   (a) Labor productivity (10). Throughout the period cot-
       ton textiles demonstrated sustained high returns to
       labor. The mechanization of any process often dou-
       bled, tripled, or quadrupled the output of a single
       worker. A good example is mechanization of looms,
       in which each loom enhanced the output of a hand
       loom by between 300 percent and 400 percent.
   (b) Capital productivity (4). Returns to capital were sig-
       nificantly less.

5. Rates of research and development (10). In the early
   1800s few companies possessed institutionalized research
   laboratories. By contrast, however, cotton textiles involved a considerable amount of experimentation that
   kept the industry far on the technological frontiers of
   the period.

262

6. Rates of investment in human capital (8). In some cases jobs were eliminated as certain manual and other human skills were engineered into the machines. In this sense the industry required disinvestment in human capital. On balance, however, it demanded and created a new generation of skills and mechanical knowledge that other industries quickly incorporated into their own machinery.

7. Rates of invention and innovation (10). Cotton textiles was one of the leading sectors of invention and innovation. One index of new inventions is the comparative rates of new patent filings. Cotton textiles were a subject of intense interest and more new patents were filed here than in almost any other industry. The rate of new patents tracked the period of the industry's sharpest growth.

8. Economies of scale (10) and specialization (10). Lozier
& notes that during the entire period there were no di-
9. minishing returns to scale. Clustered together, the large Lowell-type mill complexes also maximized the return on huge water power developments. Lozier notes: "Through their size and concentrations on one simple coarse product, these mills became so highly efficient that they could easily outcompete both British mills and smaller American mills."

10. Economies of scope. Economies of scope may be a product of the age of numerical control of production, more specifically flexible manufacturing, and for that reason are not applicable to this period.

11. Learning curve and the product life cycle (10). Product life cycle, particularly for the machinery sector, was very swift. In the mills of Dover, New Hampshire, some machinery was considered obsolete within five years.

12. Vertical integration (10) and disintegration (10). Cotton displayed a distinct and pronounced cycle first of vertical integration, and in the latter part of the period, of dis-

integration in Stigler's sense. About 1806 yarn manufacturers, finding it hard to sell yarn by itself, turned to hand weaving. Shortly after, hand weaving was brought into the factory to improve inventories and to control workers. Hand weaving itself was soon eclipsed by power weaving. While these events were taking place, each mill began to introduce and to specialize in its own machine shop. The mills of Providence are a good example of the proliferation of such small specialized machinery divisions.

The pattern of industrial fragmentation generally followed these lines. Some mills in the 1820s built their own machine shops. Soon they were producing machines for other mills. Later the larger, more capable mills, such as those in Taunton and Lowell, were manufacturing machines for industries unrelated to textiles, like railroads. By the 1840s some mills were so diversified they could no longer afford machine shops and spun these off as separate divisions, for example the bleach and dye works.

Step 3: Technical Indicators

DUAL USE (2)

In general there was little direct relation between the cotton and arms industries in nineteenth-century New England. Cotton cloth was of course used to clothe the armies, but this would hardly qualify the technology as "dual use." During the Civil War era, several large textile machinery shops, such as those in Chicopee, Manchester, and Taunton began to manufacture arms.

CORE TECHNOLOGY (10)

Advances in cotton milling in eighteenth- and nineteenth-century America were based on key technological breakthroughs that included the introduction of the Arkwright system of mechanical production of cotton thread (1791); the addition of waterpower weaving (successfully introduced in 1814–1815); the Gilmore Scotch loom (1817); the massive engineering of water power at Lowell, Massachusetts (1822–1840). In addition, there were many core breakthroughs in the machine-tool shops within the larger mills that supported innovations in weaving.

SCIENTIFIC (2) AND TECHNOLOGICAL FRONTIERS (10)

The machinery shops of the cotton textiles industry served as a primary source of technological and scientific advances. As noted, various inventions and innovations were made in the use of water power, although these were primarily of technological, not scientific, character.

KNOWLEDGE INTENSIVE (8)

Although cotton textiles themselves did not maintain formal laboratories, the industry, particularly its machine-tool divisions, quickly became a transmission center, in Rosenberg's terms, a "pool or reservoir of skills and technical knowledge" for the entire economy.

TECHNOLOGICAL CONVERGENCE (8)

Technologies adapted to a specialized use in the mills were soon found to have other uses, and these principles were transferred and applied in other industries. Although machine building shops were the primary locus of convergence, Lozier notes a similar process in the adaptations of the technology of water power.

INTERDEPENDENCE (8)

Cotton textiles demonstrated a significant "push-pull" relationship as one technological advance stimulated another, while at times imposing bottlenecks on new developments. This was true generally of cotton textiles from the development of Kay's flying shuttle that greatly increased the output of weavers, which in turn created a bottleneck in spinning. This in turn was relieved by inventions of Hargreaves, Cartwright, and Arkwright that created a bottleneck in weaving.

The United States quickly outstripped England once the new technologies began to diffuse rapidly. Technological advances in spinning in the United States created pressures that could be resolved only in the development of power weaving. Thus in northern New England machines were quickly adapted to the production of coarse goods in large quantities, using highly integrated process. The emphasis here was on heavy power-spinning machines. The mule was rarely used in this area.

SYNERGISM (10)

David Landes notes that synergism was extremely important to the development of the textile industry, although it took primarily a financial rather than a technological form. Recognizing the importance of the new technologies, entrepreneurs of this period would first organize a closely held corporation, promote the stock within Boston and other cities, and wait for the price to rise. Then they would unload and organize a new corporation. At times the original promoters would continue to manage these businesses, although ownership was transferred to others more willing to invest for the longer term. The technique represented a major innovation of its day and offered essential financing to the mills at a critical point in their development.

COMPLEXITY, NUMBER OF PARTS, AND DIFFERENTIATION (10)

Cotton textile technology became increasingly complex and differentiated. The development of the ring frame and the spinning and self-acting mule are examples of the principle of increasing number of parts and complexity. Only at the end of the period when the industry began to settle down did standardization of parts and process become more significant.

Step 4: Sociopolitical Indicators

GENERALIZABLE PATTERN OF PRODUCTION (10)

Lozier notes: "The most important role of the textile industry in this country was that of a demonstration model for the factory system. Although the paper, flour, and nail industries had something of a factory system early in the nineteenth century, it was the textile industry by its size and geographic range that personified the factory style to the public. Cotton textiles first legitimized, then popularized, the factory system for 19th century America."

GENERALIZABLE PATTERN OF COMMERCE (1)

Textiles did not introduce major new innovations in commerce. Actually, the industry was at the mercy of commission merchants.

RELATION TO OTHER CRITICAL NATIONAL OBJECTIVES INCLUDING PERCEPTIONS OF WEALTH, PRESTIGE, AND POWER (8)

In many ways the factory system was alien to late eighteenth-century notions of how industry should be organized. By the early nineteenth century, however, it had so impressed the country's leaders that cotton textiles were cited as all that was virtuous about Republican technology. The factories, it was said, put lazy people to work, inculcated good morals, and encouraged identity. Cotton textiles also helped keep money at home and encouraged economic independence, primary mercantilist objectives. Hamilton, and later the Jeffersonians, came to view cotton textiles as a prestige industry.

Step 5: Secondary and Tertiary Effects

HIGH MULTIPLIER (5)

In general terms the multiplier of cotton textiles was comparatively less important than that of other sectors, since profits for the industry remained relatively low. A fair amount of the revenues earned by the owners of mills and commission merchants who sold the goods of the mills went into economic development including canals, railroads, and other industries.

DEEP PENETRATION OF INPUT-OUTPUT MATRIX (8)

If the industry is characterized primarily by its capital goods sector, the tools of the machine shops become ubiquitous inputs in most other sectors. Cotton goods themselves were widely used and were a significant input in the commercial and household clothing industries.

LINKAGES

1. Backward technical linkages (10). Although backward economic linkages were also significant, they were not as pronounced as the industry's technological impact. Even at its heyday the industry consumed about 20 percent of southern cotton, the remainder being shipped to England. Other backward linkages included the demand for canals, turnpikes, railroads, and various public works projects.

2. Forward technical linkages (6). In response to the rising demand of other sectors, textile machinery manufacturers soon branched out into other lines such as locomotives, new machine tools, paper machinery, fire engines, pumps, mill work, stationary steam machines, sugar mills, and the like.

3. Forward economic linkages (4). The mills produced a new service industry of commission merchants who helped organize a whole range of other industries and contributed vitally to the cultural life of Boston and other major mercantile cities.

FEEDBACK (9)

The machinery divisions of the cotton textile industry displayed Hirschman's pincer-cum-feedback loop to some extent. Economic feedback was significant to the extent that it stimulated growth in other sectors that, in turn, increased the demand for cotton textiles.

Step 6: High External Benefits (10) and High External Costs (8).

Cotton textiles brought significant, although as yet unquantified, benefits and costs to American society. Among the benefits were the various technical and economic linkages already noted as well as some lesser secondary and tertiary effects. Lozier notes that reduction in the cost of cotton textiles permitted the average household to purchase more cotton goods and, what is significant, to change linen more frequently. This likely contributed to hygiene, in particular to the reduction in lice, which were a primary cause of typhus. Incidence of typhus and other vermin-related diseases dropped markedly at the end of this period.

The industry also imposed great hardships on some communities. The introduction of larger, integrated mills at Lowell eclipsed the smaller-scale mills of the periphery. The rapid turn to power weaving destroyed firms using other methods, and mechanized picking wiped out overnight the household picking industry. Cotton textiles also forced families apart and altered irrevocably a rural way of life. Lozier writes:

The cotton mill altered the life of rural Americans, particularly young women, by replacing highly social home spinning and weaving with less social factory labor. In the factory, while one might work with friends and family, the dispersion of machines, noise, demands on attention, and work rules against unnecessary conversation made socializing less frequent and more difficult. At home the eighteenth-century domestic spinner and weaver had enjoyed a large measure of control over the time and place of her labor, but the mill hand worked in a disciplined system where her hours and work location were dictated by machines, production lines, water supply, and management efforts to maximize the use of her capital. Instead of the familiarity of her own home, she had to stand at a demanding machine for 12 to 14 boring, noisy, lint-filled hours.

Although dislocations resulting from rapid technological change are not true "externalities," the industry imposed significant external costs as well. For example after 1850 brown lung disease resulting from the industry's pollution became a major health problem.

Scale Ratios of Society (not evaluated)

Cotton textiles dramatically affected the human, mechanical, and transportation scale ratios of nineteenth-century America. Although a gap existed between rich and poor in the eighteenth century, the separation was relatively low for most people. The mills substantially widened this gap, creating in their wake a class of economically rich people, the Lowells, the Cabots, Lawrences, Lees, Thorndikes, and others, who came to wield most of the political power throughout the region.

Summary

If the results of a full analysis of the cotton textile industry of early nineteenth-century America were condensed and registered in a matrix beside other industries of this period, cotton textiles would clearly qualify as a strategic industry.

Although it did not display all the core characteristics, it suggested most of them and did so to a significant degree.

Although the importance of some of these indicators changed over the period, a critical core was virtually always present. Lozier cites vertical integration, convergence, and backward technical linkages being among the most important variables, with the industry's greatest significance being the introduction of the factory system itself.

The primary importance of the machine-building divisions indicates the importance of "critical niches" within a strategic industry. The existence of this growing, increasingly important segment suggests some of the problems in defining a strategic industry and in evaluating the core indicators with respect to it.

Chapter 9

Planning Strategic Industries without Plans or Planners

Why Coherence in Government Is Necessary

The time is at hand when the politicians and business and labor leaders must choose between coherence or a jangle of disparate voices each claiming a preference incompatible with the next. There are three reasons why coherence today is imperative.

First, the times themselves have changed. Thirty years ago it mattered little whether other countries protected their home markets. The United States bestrode the world like a colossus, and distortions in trade had only marginal effects on U.S. competitiveness. Today the balance of power has shifted and the interference of other countries in the free flow of technology, goods, and information places a premium on a firm's and a nation's ability to adjust. Incoherence cripples adjustment.

Second, when ordinary industries falter, the consequences may be harsh, but the risks are borne principally by the entrepreneurs, stockholders, bankers, and employees directly and indirectly involved. The decline of strategic industries, however, may affect whole communities, nations, and even

271

groups of countries. Although the potential loss of entrusting a strategic industry to the market is not easily determined, the consequences may be great. There are of course risks to a government's supplementing market forces. But such risks are at least of its own making. Anticipating and reducing such risks is the responsibility of good government.

Third, economic growth is the progenitor of conflict. Simon Kuznets writes:

Economic growth perforce brings about a decline in the relative position of one group after another—of farmers, of small scale producers, of landowners—a change not easily accepted, and, in fact, as history teaches us, often revisited. The continuous disturbance of preexisting *relative* position of the several economic groups is pregnant with conflict—despite the rises in absolute income or product common to all groups. In some cases, these conflicts did break out into overt civil war, the Civil War in the United States being a conspicuous example. Other examples, in the early periods of industrialization among the currently developed countries, or, for that matter, more recently within some less developed countries, are not lacking.

Only if such conflicts are resolved without excessive costs, and certainly without a long term weakening of the political fabric of the society, is modern economic growth possible. The sovereign state, with authority based on loyalty and on a community of feeling—in short, the modern national state—plays a crucial role in peacefully resolving such growth-induced conflicts.[1]

The United States faces three choices. First, it can persist in its existing inconsistent, often contradictory approach to industry. This approach is responsible for the difficulties high-technology industries face today.

Second, it can attempt comprehensive industrial planning. Proposals for a national industrial policy, national economic planning, a fourth arm of government, and a new industrial development bank are all examples. Comprehensive industrial planning has been attempted episodically in American history, even with vigor during the Great Depression and

World War II, but its record of success is mixed. Most Americans are deeply suspicious of it.

The last option is a new approach to public bargaining called "negotiated industrial investment strategies." It is the principal topic of this chapter.

Joseph Badaracco and David Yoffie of the Harvard Business School argue that any attempt to reorder existing political institutions will simply squander the time, energy, and talent of American industry and government.[2] They are right to insist that those who would tinker at existing institutions must demonstrate that their proposals for reform are better.

Why Past Attempts at Coherence Have Failed

To be effective a new approach must be fair, efficient, and stable.[3] Fair in that it is consistent with a nation's notions of equity and justice; efficient in the sense that it represents the least costly allocation of resources; and stable in that government creates a workable precedent for the future, leaving the parties in a good relationship to deal with future change. Why has such an approach been so difficult to achieve?

Part of the explanation lies in America's historic ambivalence toward planning and the confusion in the profession itself. In the days of Frederick Law Olmstead, the preeminent landscape architect of the nineteenth century, planning was tied intimately to the preparation of a "comprehensive" or "master plan."[4] Beginning in the 1950s a furious debate commenced within the planning profession over the concept of "comprehensiveness." By the mid-1960s the master plan was in disfavor. Planners were becoming increasingly aware that no matter how many planners were employed or how artfully planning agencies were fitted into the structure or government, the political system would continue to work incrementally through bargaining and compromise, not by "implementing the general interests," and that the main decisions in any master plan would need to reflect the distribution of power in the community at a particular time.

The challenges to comprehensive planning in the 1960s and 1970s can be grouped within several categories. The first was a frontal assault on the planners' competence. Since planners lacked an adequate theory of the city, some argued, they were "unable to say when a city is performing optimally and when it is not." Others challenged the pretensions of planners as self-appointed arbiters of the public interest. The analysis of physical, social, and economic conditions, they contended, involved normative judgments that planners were no more qualified to make than anyone else. The master planners were accused of being too narrow and ineffective. The critics urged that the most significant issues were concerns about the distribution of wealth, status and power, not issues of the physical environment that preoccupied the planners. Underlying these three objections was a fundamental distrust of planning. Ever since the Standard Enabling Act of 1928, legislators have seen the planners as interlopers and their pretentions to legitimacy as usurpations of the prerogatives of public authority.

The deepest attack came from David Braybrooke and Charles Lindblom, who suggested, in *A Strategy of Decision,* that comprehensive planning conflicted with the incremental, fragmented, and remedial character of most decisions. The attack on comprehensive planning led to a decade of exploration involving "advocacy" planners, utilitarian planners, and "learning-oriented" planners who focused their energies on small-scale experiments in urban development.

The failures of the city master planners have been paralleled by the abortive attempts at national industrial planning. Ellis Hawley writes of Hoover's utopian associative state and his disastrous program for bituminous coal (1921–1928):

Viewed from the altered perspective that took shape after 1929, his emerging private government seemed increasingly undemocratic, oppressive, and unresponsive. Associationalism, once widely accepted as a new and superior formulation of the "American way," became for many a mere facade behind which "selfish monopolists" had abused their power and plunged the nation into depression.

274

And the leaders of this new order, revealed now to be far less altruistic and far less prescient than Hoover had hoped they would be, seemed unable either to sustain expansion, solve festering social problems, or check the greatest economic contraction in the nation's history. As conflict mounted, moreover, demands for more effective "coordination" were soon transforming Hoover's efforts at associational direction and reform into programs and agencies he had never intended. Ironically, by demonstrating that they could not achieve the sustained expansion, rising living standards, and decentralized, non-coercive planning that they were supposed to achieve, he helped open the way for "big government" and state-enforced market controls in the 1930s.[5]

The historical landscape is littered with other failures: the War Industries Board of 1918, the Industrial Board of the Department of Commerce (1919), the National Recovery Administration, the Federal Trade Commission under Warren Harding, the Cotton–Textile Institutes, the Humphrey-Hawkins Bill, and the skein of plans in transportation, communications, agriculture, and defense. Of course, not all such efforts have aborted. The National Reconstruction Finance Corporation and the War Production Board during the crisis of World War II appear to have managed the requirements of war and materials with success. Ironically, America's greatest industrial planning achievements may have been the Marshall Plan in Europe and the occupation of Japan.

Why Comprehensive Industrial Planning Will Fail

Comprehensive industrial planning will fail in the United States primarily for four reasons. First, although George Lodge of the Harvard Business School tells us that we are in the midst of great transition from rights of property to those of community membership, from consumer desire to community need,[6] America's animus against centralized planning is deeply entrenched. Existing examples of active national cooperation among government, industry, labor, and other interests are rare, often silent, in the nature of conspiracies.

275

We are still far from organizing all the parts into a whole.

Second, why suppose that government planners have a better feel of the market than those who deal directly with it? There is no reason to suppose that comprehensive planning will produce fairer results in the 1980s than in the past.

Third, comprehensive planning is unstable and easily assailed by disadvantaged interests. In the past in such cases the President has defended his policies by turning the plan into a public relations document.[7] The Ford administration's comprehensive "plan" for conservation quickly degenerated into an apology for doing as little as possible, and President Carter's tripartite program for collaboration among government, business, and labor similarly went nowhere.

Finally, implementation of the plan would be uncertain. Government planners need not take responsibility for the consequences of their plans. Managers, however, bear principal responsibility. This asymmetry of interests destabilizes the process.

Our task, then, is to construct a fairer and more effective approach, one respectful of America's most basic traditions and institutions, and suited to the challenges of the decade.

Negotiated Industrial Investment Strategies (NIIS)

If strategic sectors can trigger economic growth, comprehensive industrial planning should not be needed. Identifying the strategic sector, promoting it effectively, and assuring that the benefits of growth are widely and fairly distributed to other industrial sectors and throughout the country is all that is required.

A mediated negotiation within industry and across industrial lines can serve as an effective means of attaining these objectives. The purpose would be to reach an agreement reflecting as closely as possible the declared interests of the participants. New institutional arrangements will demand competence, imagination, persistence, and resourcefulness. Painful, perhaps protracted at times, negotiation can offer an effective, fair, and stable means of allocating resources to strategic and other sectors. The following discussion presents a general overview of the proposed process and illustrates each step by the example of the semiconductor industry.

Two points should be clarified. First, the term "negotiation" is a shorthand expression for a number of related ideas. To the average person, negotiation implies conflict. Although the negotiation of actual conflicts may be important, it will be only one aspect of the process described here. The economist or specialist on mediation views negotiation as a form of bargaining in which different interests, rather than true conflicts, predominate. The alliance of divergent interests toward the goal of maximizing joint gains is the primary function of the contemplated negotiation. There is a final class of concerted actions, which are essentially exploratory and creative, that is also included in the idea of a negotiation. Such actions are less concerned with interests, and more with discovery—discovery of the growth potential inherent in all strategic technologies and industries. This creative, exploratory function can motivate domestic and international negotiations alike.

Second, although the focus is on the federal government, the discussion is presented primarily as a model. State and even local governments and municipalities may wish to initiate their own negotiations over strategic industries, and as in other areas, these local experiments can refine and elaborate actions at the national level.

Although negotiating industrial investment strategies may appear alien at first glance, there are in fact numerous precedents and close analogies. One example is the investment strategy negotiated by the cities of Columbus, Gary, and St. Paul. In each case, three teams were assembled representing federal, state, and local interests. A different mediator oversaw each negotiation. In Columbus, the final product was a seventy-six-point agreement involving public and private investment totaling more than $500 million.[8]

A different form of the negotiated investment strategy was used in Connecticut in 1983. Agreement was reached on the distribution of $33 million in federal aid to the state for human services. In fact, the amount represented a 25 percent budgetary cutback. Rather than making this decision arbitrarily, the governor decided to use negotiation. At the initiation of the governor's office, eighteen state agencies, 114 municipalities, and numerous private service agencies participated in a mediated negotiation. Three teams were assembled involving the state agencies, public and private providers of funds, and sundry local officials whose offices would have received these funds. With the aid of a mediator, the teams negotiated a set of commitments that were approved by the governor and later by the legislature.

A third model of negotiated rule making was first proposed in 1982 by the Administrative Conference of the United States. Under the conference's proposal a small group of interests, usually no more than fifteen, would work with a mediator to negotiate the terms of a specific regulation. Negotiated rule making differs from the present practice in that parties must now intervene in a formal administrative hearing to register their opposition to a proposed rule drafted by an agency. The Environmental Protection Agency, the Federal Aeronautics Administration, and the Occupational Safety and Health Administration have all experimented with the conference's new procedures.

Negotiated rule making, however, is simpler than the negotiated investment strategies proposed here. Rule making is a well-known administrative procedure involving established practices and a specific agency with limited power. The object of a rule-making negotiation is clear, and the parties are under special pressure, since if the negotiation fails the agency will promulgate a rule by itself. In contrast, negotiated investment strategies involve multiple interests and objectives. Negotiated rule making overlays only a small part of a negotiated industrial investment strategy.

Beyond negotiated rule making, there are a variety of somewhat less precise analogies. Probably the closest is the numerous standards developed by consensus. Consensus standards are developed though a structured decision-making process among representatives of interests who are substantially affected by the standard. During the negotiation the parties frequently confront difficult value choices involving trade-offs between cost and safety. Virtually every person in the United States daily entrusts his or her life to such negotiated rules, in the form of electrical and building codes, product safety standards, and workplace and health standards. The existence of these standards is evidence that complex public choices can be negotiated.

The environmental field also offers many examples of mediated negotiation among federal, state, and local industry, both public and private. The National Coal Project in which dozens of parties reached agreement on over 200 recommendations concerning the use of coal in the United States is also an important illustration. The various negotiations conducted by independent mediation centers such as the Institute for Environmental Mediation in Seattle, the New England Center for Environmental Mediation in Boston, and ACCORD, Inc., in Denver are other examples.

The Ten Basic Steps Toward the Marriage of Warring Interests

Although these steps in negotiating an industrial investment strategy are for a strategic sector or sectors—in this case the semiconductor industry in particular—the basic paradigm can be used with at least equal effect to supplement government policy toward any industry, strategic, stagnant, or declining.[9]

1. The Office of Strategic Industries (OSI) announces that it will accept nominations for strategic industries.[10] The criteria based on the method described in Part I are published in the *Federal Register*, the leading newspapers, and other media of wide circulation.[11] The nominations are reviewed by an Advisory Council to the OSI. The OSI with the approval of the President designates a strategic industry or a group of strategic industries.

279

2. The OSI next tenders an offer to negotiate to the industry. The offer is published in the *Federal Register* and other public media.

3. The first meeting is convened. The interests and positions of the parties are clarified and a chief mediator, with a team of assistant mediators, is selected.

4. The negotiation begins. The range of affected interests is expanded.

5. The negotiators prepare a "single negotiating text." The text is circulated and amended.

6. A tentative agreement is reached and the draft agreement published in the *Federal Register*.

7. The negotiation resumes. Additional comments are obtained and the negotiators obtain final commitments from their committees, companies, and associations.

8. The agreement is ratified.

9. The agreement is implemented by the responsible agencies and contracting parties.

10. The agreement is monitored and periodically renegotiated.

The OSI would be a new office in the White House, along the lines of the United States Trade Representative (USTR). The OSI could even begin as an independent group in the White House, although in any case a strong presidential mandate would probably be essential for it to be effective. The OSI would be principally responsible for evaluating strategic industries and overseeing and facilitating the negotiations. Its head would be a member of the Cabinet. It would be independent from any industry, agency, or other interest having a stake in the outcome of the negotiation.

If the OSI is to play an innovative role, innovators and entrepreneurs must be its mainstay. The staff must be recruited from industry and other walks of life under a special program, perhaps like the White House Fellows program, that rewarded imagination and creativity in government.

The OSI would have an advisory council,[12] consisting primarily of inventors and, in moderation, scientists, economists, legal scholars, and others with pertinent knowledge. Its members would be appointed by the President and Congress. The Council would screen nominations and generally help to strengthen the functions of the OSI.

The method of identifying and evaluating strategic industries would be primarily a technical process, closely linked to the politics of the negotiations themselves.

Nominations could be presented to the OSI by virtually anybody—an industry association, the National Academy of Sciences, various federal or state agencies, private research institutions, business associations, and other groups and interests. Once presented, however, the nominations would have to satisfy clear and specific criteria for a strategic industry. The criteria would be based on the analysis introduced in Chapter 8.

Only six of the ten steps of the Trigger Method have been discussed at any length. It is now time to link that discussion with the process under consideration. The criteria will include all the key indicators in the method, and perhaps others to be added from time to time. For example, one criterion might require the nominator, if an industry group, to suggest one or several other linked industries whose designation as strategic would most benefit it. This would encourage firms in one industry to explore linkages and to discover mutual gains with other industries. As will be seen, this will be essential to the success of a bargaining strategy.

Once the nominations are collected, the OSI will face the onerous task of evaluation. The first step is to arrange all the nominated industries along the horizontal axis of a matrix with the key variables on the vertical axis as indicated in Table 6.

The staff of the OSI would then summarize the findings for each nominated industry.

The OSI's next task is to assess all nominated industries with respect to an absolute standard of strategic leverage. A simple ranking of "high," "medium," and "low" can be used.

TABLE 6

SELECTING STRATEGIC INDUSTRIES KEY VARIABLES DEFINING THE INDUSTRY	A	B	INDUSTRY C	... n
Assessment of Economic Indicators				
Growth				
Exports				
Employment				
Productivity				
Research				
High Level of Investment in Human Capital				
High Rates of Invention and Innovation				
Economies of Scale				
Economies of Specialization				
Economies of Scope				
Learning Curve and Product Life Cycle				
Vertical Integration				
Technical Indicators				
Dual Use				
Core Technology				
Frontiers of Science and Technology				
Knowledge Intensive				
Technological Convergence				
Complementarities				
Synergisms				
Complexity and Differentiation				

TABLE 6 (*continued*)

KEY VARIABLES	A	B	C	... n
		INDUSTRY		
Social & Political Indicators				
Generalizable Pattern of Production				
Generalizable Pattern of Commerce				
Relation to Other National Policy Objectives				
National Perceptions of Wealth, Prestige & Power				
Scale Ratios of Society				
Secondary & Tertiary Effects				
High Multiplier				
Deep "Penetration" of Input-Output Matrix				
Forward & Backward Linkages				
Rate of Feedback				
High "External" Benefits; High "External" Costs				
Final Ranking				

The analysis would be performed by the staff of the OSI. By this procedure the field of nominated industries could be narrowed to only those demonstrating the most significant strategic potential.[13]

Next comes the comparison of the industries within the "high" category with respect to their degree of strategic leverage. This presents the problem of aggregating nominal and ordinal variables across the matrix. This difficulty is faced by many researchers involved in cost-benefit analyses, environmental impact reviews, and other areas of planning. Although the simplest way to proceed is to assign an equal weight to each variable, there are more sophisticated techniques for handling such problems.[14] The industry whose overall ranking is highest is the most strategic. This method provides the OSI with an initial indication of areas of greatest leverage.

The final task is for the OSI, with the concurrence of the Advisory Council (AC), to begin contracting the industry's representatives or nominators. Contacts are made in the order of ranking. Simply because an industry is ranked "most strategic" would not necessarily mean that it is the best candidate for a negotiation. It is possible that after consultation, the industry's leaders or the OSI or both will conclude that a negotiation is not appropriate. Such insights would prove very useful in other negotiations or at some future negotiation involving the same industry.

As discussed, it would be highly disruptive to permit judicial review of the OSI's determination of strategic potential at so early a stage in the process. Those dissatisfied with a decision of the OSI can appeal to the AC, which would be empowered by statute to make final determinations in those cases.

After evaluating the strategic industries and completing its informal contacts, the facilitator is now ready to tender an offer to negotiate.

Steps 3 and 4 deal with convening the negotiators and with the complexities of representation. The first task is to determine the appropriate range of interests and who will represent these interests.

In general, any interest that might be substantially or materially affected should be represented. At the outset it will be necessary to distinguish those interests which are indispensable, without which the negotiation could not profitably proceed. The participation of others, who are more remotely affected, can be limited to written comments.

Over the life of any negotiation issues may change and

interests will naturally expand and contract. When an issue is resolved, an interest group may wish to remove itself from the negotiation and when a new issue arises, new interests will likely wish to participate.

Once the appropriate interests are identified, the next issue is who will actually represent these interests. Some firms may wish to appear individually. Others, especially where their interests are closely aligned, might elect to appear through an industry association. Diverse, less easily aggregated interests, such as consumer or environmental groups, would be represented by a government agency mandated to act as a surrogate for these interests or by representative organizations of private citizens.

Any representative must enjoy the trust of his or her constituents. In industry the chief operating officer might be appropriate since he or she knows the policies of the company and can predict its reactions. The chief officer is also in direct communication with pertinent interests in the company whom he or she can draw into the negotiation at appropriate times.

Some interests, such as environmental, consumer, or other "public interest" groups, may not be able to afford to participate by their own means. This presents a problem because the political legitimacy of a negotiated agreement rests largely on the concurrence of the significant affected interests.

The OSI would defray these expenses. If an organization's participation is deemed essential to a negotiation, defraying its out-of-pocket expenses actually conserves government resources. Moreover, since collateral interests can be a valuable source of new ideas and information, including these interests produces a more responsive and stable agreement. Although in practice the additional cost of subsidizing such interests has often been minimal, their participation should be underwritten even if the costs are substantial.[15]

In some cases an interest group essential to the negotiation may refuse to participate, hoping to block the conclusions of a negotiation at a later date. In such a case the facilitator can try to convince the group that through participation it would be in a better position to influence the outcome. In addition, the facilitator must first decide whether other organizations whose interests are fairly close to those of the recalcitrant are willing to participate. The facilitator must also determine whether the absent group's interests are significantly or only tangentially affected. Finally, the facilitator must consider whether the group is so important that its failure to participate would undermine the legitimacy of the agreement. Alternatively, the facilitator could decide that the party ultimately would join the discussions and participate in good faith. If the facilitator ascertains that the appropriate interests are willing to participate, he must next ask each party to pledge to negotiate in good faith in an attempt to reach a consensus. Even an abstract commitment can be useful when in the course of a negotiation emotions become frayed. A commitment to mutual gains can convert many conflictive situations into "positive-sum" outcomes.

The next task is to define the initial issues.[16] This is often the most difficult task in a negotiation. As in negotiated rule-making, the facilitator can help to define the issues by asking the parties to define what they deem most important. At this preliminary stage the issues are often framed in general terms to help the parties grasp the overall scope of the negotiation.

After initial parties are assembled and an agenda is defined, the appointment of a team of mediators is the next task. As in other areas, the mediators need to possess neutrality, analytic capabilities, and a commitment to the process. The chief mediator would likely be an independent outsider, appointed by the president and supported by a team drawn from the OSI. Ideally he or she would be familiar with the industry and its problems and respected by the parties. As in other situations, the mediator would meet with the parties and would discuss their objectives and concerns. The mediator would help the parties parse their true concerns from their opening negotiating positions, and define clear criteria to measure a successful agreement. The mediator could focus discussions in such private meetings and point out extreme positions, offering creative solutions along the way.

A mediator's role often changes subtly in the course of a

negotiation. In the early stages, the mediator shuttles back and forth meeting with the parties, investigating issues, and reporting back to the conference. Later the mediator explores issues in greater depth, helps to draft an agreement, and proposes amendments. After ratification, the mediator oversees what Howard Raiffa calls, "post settlement settlements."[17]

There are various views on the proper role of a mediator. Some trained in labor relations believe that mediators should remain passive: any effort by the mediator to influence the style or content of the negotiations sacrifices neutrality. Others disagree and feel the mediator should be proactive as well as reactive. In general, the more experienced the parties, the less the mediator needs to interfere. The less experienced the parties, the more initiatives a mediator should take. The clearer the rules and the more institutionalized the negotiation, the less burden on the mediator. In the early days of negotiated industrial investment bargaining, a more proactive mediator will be needed.

With the appointment of a mediator, the next step will be to publish notice in the *Federal Register,* as well as in the major newspapers, trade journals, and other media of wide circulation. The notice should be written in plain English, and include the following: a description of the strategic industry(ies), a short summary of why it was designated and specifically how it satisfied the criteria; the names of the participating groups and their representatives; descriptions of the interests represented and the initial positions presented; the participating government agencies; the name of the proposed mediator; the issues the conference proposes to consider; and a proposed schedule for completing the work of the conference. The notice would invite members of the public to comment on whether a negotiation for the designated strategic industry is appropriate, whether all appropriate interests are represented, whether the members selected adequately represent their interests, whether the conference is considering the appropriate issues, whether agency representatives are appropriate, and other matters of interest. Comments would be due thirty to sixty days after publication of the notice. This procedure ensures that no group with a substantial interest is excluded.

The facilitator and the mediator next consider all relevant materials submitted in response to the *Federal Register* and other notices. No doubt at times someone will assert that he or she has been overlooked. This will require a determination of whether the new interest is sufficiently close to the issues under consideration that it has "standing." At times an interest group may be simply too remote to be included. In some cases even remote interests would be included and the determination guided by whether their petition was frivolous. Only those seriously interested in the outcome will normally seek to participate.

The second question is whether the proposed interest is different from the interests already represented. If it is virtually identical, there will be no need to include it. Sometimes parties will attempt to construct differences in order to secure a representative at a negotiating table. The facilitator and the mediator must determine whether the applicant's interests are really divergent from those proposed in the notice, and whether its interests are already adequately represented.

Third, even if an interest is already represented, in some cases duplication is desirable. In deciding whether to add a representative, the facilitator and the mediator must consider the number of representatives already present, the diversity of their views, and the importance of the new party to the negotiation.

In somewhat analogous situations, a mediator can seek the advice of the preliminary negotiators. The group as a whole is often in the best position to evaluate whether a sufficient nexus exists between the applicant and the subject matter. The final determination, however, is made by the facilitator and the mediator.

The sensitivity and importance of these opening moves should not be underestimated. In order to assure that the parties see the process as legitimate, each organization with a significant interest must be permitted to participate and no interest can be turned away unless its connection to the negotiation is remote. On the other hand, if every interested person, firm, or organization participated the process would soon become unwieldy.

One way of consolidating interests is for the facilitator to organize them into groups. The groups can then develop common positions and identify common representatives.

At this stage the negotiation is in danger of degenerating into a squabble over who gets to sit at the table. The facilitator and mediator must ensure that the process of assessing interests and assembling coalitions is of the highest integrity.

Judicial review is another issue. At this stage it would be most unwise. Permitting disgruntled parties to challenge a negotiation in court even before it begins will subject the entire process to delay and doubt and interfere disastrously with the fragile formation of trust. Judicial review needs to be deferred until the promulgation of a final agreement. This should not unfairly prejudice disappointed interests: they could still submit their views before such an agreement became final. They would still have ample opportunity to urge that it be renegotiated if they felt it was unfairly decided, and to upset it in the courts.

Illustration 1

Suppose the Semiconductor Industry Association, the Commerce Department, the National Academy of Sciences, or some other body nominates the semiconductor industry as a strategic industry. The OSI reviews this nomination along with other candidates and reaches the conclusion that the industry satisfies a sufficient number of the key characteristics to justify its being the subject of an NIIS. What would be some of the objectives and problems of this negotiation?

The basic threshold question for the captains of the industry is, would a negotiation be helpful, given the industry's structure, personalities, and technical needs? At this point in its development, semiconductor technology is turning over so rapidly and the applications of new innovations are so varied that no single firm can capture and control more than a few segments of the market for one generation. Success in this industry, perhaps more than many others, is determined not simply by inventiveness, but also by production skills and marketing finesse. There is a built-in incentive for firms to confederate.

For example, such alliances are important to a medium-sized, innovative semiconductor company with a relatively modest production capability and no marketing skills. Unaided, such a firm will not succeed; the competition is simply too ferocious. In order to secure contracts for its designs, or to identify its most profitable market niche, it must find partners. This will be a difficult decision for some corporate executives who want to do everything in house. Those with vision, however, will explore options.

A firm with strong production technology and marketing capabilities, but with a sluggish R&D division, may also perceive it in its interest to ally itself with the first firm. By doing so, it can benefit from the former's innovative design capabilities rather than itself pointlessly seeking to become the industry's leading inventor. Both firms have a natural incentive to find a cooperative solution, at times in cooperation with third parties, to capitalize on their collective capabilities.

But why should the semiconductor industry begin an NIIS when it may already enjoy ample representation through other channels? Why should a senior operating officer at Intel Corporation bother with an NIIS when the Semiconductor Industry Association (SIA) may be addressing Intel's problems over Japanese customs duties, the American Electronics Association (AEA) is already dealing with immigration issues, and the National Association of Manufacturers (NAM) is lobbying for R&D tax credits?

The answer may be that the NIIS can help Intel achieve its objectives more effectively and inexpensively than the existing fragmented structure. Within the NAM, Intel's interests must compete with a host of other diverse interests, some of which may not be familiar with or supportive of Intel's needs. The SIA, on the other hand, has proved itself most successful in dealing with relatively low-level and narrow issues. Intel and other corporations must pay excessive fees to lawyers and lobbyists who feed upon the food chain of special interests. By rationalizing the process by which Intel seeks the goals it cannot accomplish by itself, an NIIS may save time and money and increase the likelihood of success. Moreover, the NIIS would probably increase the visibility, membership, and political clout of the SIA, AEA, and other representative organizations.

The first procedural problem for the OSI will be the definition of the industry. The semiconductor industry today is particularly complex, consisting of: (1) small integrated-circuit (IC) "merchant" producers, such as Siliconix and Monolithic Memories; (2) large IC merchants such as Texas Instruments, Motorola, Intel, and National Semiconductor; (3) electronic systems manufacturers such as Hewlett-Packard; and (4) vertically integrated systems manufacturers such as IBM and AT&T. The structure of the industry is further complicated by its international character. Most of the major firms have cross-licensing arrangements with Japanese and/or European partners and in recent years there has been substantial foreign investment in U.S. companies.

The industry is also rapidly changing. The major merchant firms are consolidating integrated-circuit technology and emerging as a new generation of diversified electronics "systems" manufacturers. At the same time the smaller merchant firms are establishing themselves within niches of the rapidly segmenting markets for integrated-circuit components. "Captive" production—by acquisition or in-house start-ups—is also occurring as final electronic systems producers recognize the importance of integrated circuits to the development of future products and market growth.

The draftees of the initial offer need to consider whether they wish to restrict its terms to a part of the industry or to broaden it to apply to all these segments. Different segments of the industry today face different problems. Since the integrated-circuit industry is becoming more capital-intensive, finance will increasingly constrain the expansion of IC companies, particularly medium-sized firms. Medium-sized firms are generally unable to borrow heavily in a cyclical industry where debt represents a fixed cost, or to use profits from unrelated businesses, as larger integrated firms do. Start-ups sometimes find venture capital more easily.

A difficult issue will be whether foreign semiconductor firms are invited to participate. Many will question why Hitachi, Japan, should be invited to exert as much influence on U.S. domestic policy as Intel, U.S.A. On the other hand, under existing law it would be hard to ban Hitachi's American subsidiaries. The best solution is to deal with foreign firms through a separate negotiation as described in Chapter 11.

The plenary session's first task is to agree on the ground rules to govern the negotiations. A critical problem is privacy. There are strong reasons for assuring the privacy of the negotiation. First, a party may be reluctant to yield confidential data that can be useful to negotiations if doing so will destroy its confidentiality. The protection of trade secrets and other privileged information is an incessant concern for the semiconductor industry. Senior industry executives will hardly be willing to discuss their basic needs with their competitors if this means betraying corporate weaknesses or strategies. Some disclosure of course is a price in any concerted action, and the NIIS will not require any greater disclosure than already exists within the industry's trade association. Since the Semiconductor Industry Association has become increasingly active, many firms might elect simply to have the association represent them. The industry's firms—IBM, AT&T, and Texas Instruments—would likely wish to appear individually.

The parties may also be reluctant to bargain if they believe their tentative proposals might later be used against them in litigation, and some will be unwilling to bargain flexibly in an open setting. For these reasons, the negotiators should be permitted to close their meetings in appropriate circumstances. One way of striking a balance between the needs for confidentiality and disclosure is to require a majority vote with a clear statement of reasons before permitting the group to enter executive session. Without a convincing case, the negotiations would remain public. Since the draft agreement will be published, members of the public will in any event have an additional opportunity to check a decision that might be deemed adverse to their interests.

If the conference decides to go into executive session, a variety of additional problems need to be resolved. One is an agreement on how the group will make public statements. A basic requirement that no one may publicly characterize a position taken by another can prevent pressure from being applied on parties through press releases. Or, the committee could agree that no public statement will be made without review by all the parties.

A procedure must also be established whereby the parties' positions and the information exchange will not be held against them if negotiations are unsuccessful. This procedure is similar to the traditional rule of evidence that prohibits the subsequent use of offers for settlement.

Every negotiation is governed by several fundamental principles. The first principle is to focus on the interests of the parties, not on their positions. Philip Harter notes:

Parties develop initial positions for several reasons. They might be a package compiled by the representatives from the "wish" lists of the constituents. They might enhance the ultimate bargaining position. They might reflect the party's belief that the initial position is the only solution to the problem. Communications can quickly break down if the parties' initial positions are the focus of discussions because each side will dig in to defend its starting point, and antagonism will result.

The parties themselves do not always recognize what their interests are. They need to define what they really want, to sort out their priorities, and to define the criteria by which they will judge an ultimate agreement. Because the party may enter the negotiation with a particular position that does not reflect an interest analysis, the mediator or the parties themselves should probe to discover just what the respective interests are.

The second principle is to seek options that allow mutual gain. People enter into negotiations because they believe they can better achieve their goals through negotiation than through some other process. Agreement is more likely to occur if it can be cast in terms that permit each party to win since the negotiators can then view themselves as a collaborative group seeking a solution to a problem, rather than as combatants. To be sure, this goal is frequently elusive when the parties have conflicting interests that must be reconciled. The goal of attaining collaboration, however, can be borne in mind by the parties as they try to invent solutions that allow each side to win its important priorities. The parties must compare what is practically achievable in negotiations with what is likely to occur should negotiations break down.

The third principle is to define objective criteria. By agreeing during the negotiation to the objective criteria by which an ultimate agreement might be judged, the parties can facilitate negotiation. Once parties establish objective criteria, they can explore alternative ways of meeting their respective goals and measuring the proposed solutions against them.[18]

The art of negotiation offers various techniques to help the parties reach agreement. One is for the parties to develop a common data base by deciding to conduct research jointly. The parties preserve their option to disagree on the implications of such research. Each party can also review and comment on technical data possessed by another. This has often helped agreement on common principles. At times the parties will simply not be able to reach agreement on the interpretation of some data. The mediator can then help the parties reach a common interpretation.

It is likely that the circle of those involved will expand as a bargaining proceeds. For example, if the bargain contemplates legislation, it will be necessary to involve the key Congressional committees and their staffers; if local concerns are raised, state or local governments will become involved. If trade relief or other questions of foreign policy are deemed important, the State, Commerce, and Defense Departments, the Trade Representatives Office, and other government agencies will become involved.

Roger Fisher has proposed a sensible format applicable to most negotiations.[19] The first task is to focus on a manageable portion of work and to invent creative solutions. Next, the parties set objective standards to judge these options, and by their discussions, select the most promising alternatives.

A practical means of facilitating agreement is the use of a single negotiating text. By brainstorming with reference to a single document the parties can identify the critical issues involved and focus on potential solutions. By circulating the text for comment and revision, the range of consensus is thereby narrowed. No one is committed to these solutions. Rather, the goal is to define the contours of a possible agreement. No one is permitted to make adverse comments or criticisms. The function of the brainstorming is to develop as many ideas as possible. A mediator assists in developing a list and then the parties then begin weeding out the inappropriate issues and raising new ones.

Throughout the negotiation the elements of a strategic industry play a central role. As noted, the criteria define a strategic industry at the outset and thereby indirectly determine the critical interest groups. Since the elements of a strategic industry are "pressure points" for government action, they also have an important role in shaping and focusing the subsequent discussion. Moreover, they also help define new interests that ought to be involved. Although a given interest might not in itself be strategic, it could represent an important secondary beneficiary of government assistance to a strategic sector, or provide a strong domestic demand for a strategic industry's products. The revitalization of old industries by entrepreneurs with bold technological strategies is occurring in the United States today in autos, agriculture, consumer electronics, and other fields without government incentive. The negotiation could help accelerate this positive trend.

Although an intense engagement of interests will likely be crucial to the implementation of a stable and responsive agreement, the fray can also become overheated. At such times there is need for a cooler, longer-term, more analytic perspective and, perhaps most important, a perspective that does not demand any commitment from the parties. For this reason, the OSI with the aid of the staff of its advisory council can prepare a visionary agreement based on a deep probing and mapping of the interests of the parties. This detached, nonconfrontational counter draft would be circulated for comment and might prove particularly helpful in breaking logjams and in identifying solutions that the parties themselves might not easily discover.[20]

As the negotiations progress, the parties will begin to near consensus. There is no a priori definition of this term; thus parties must assure that it is properly defined and understood at the outset.

The most acceptable definition of consensus is a "general agreement." This means that no party dissents significantly from the shared position. General agreement does not necessarily mean unanimity, because even if someone disagrees, the dissent may not be significant enough, either in weight or number, to destroy the agreement. For example, a party may dissent on grounds that are generally viewed as irrational, or a party's interests may not be sufficiently affected to regard its dissent as significant. In group consensus dissenting interests that are not directly or immediately affected can be disregarded even on major issues without destroying the consensus. The dissent of a major interest, however, destroys a consensus even on a minor point. Positions are weighed, not counted. When deciding whether consensus has been reached, the nature of any dissent is considered, including the strength of the dissenter's views, the basis for the dissent, and the relationship of the dissenter to the issues.

How do the parties increase the likelihood of reaching consensus, and who decides when a consensus has been reached? There are several practical ways of proceeding. One is unanimity. Requiring unanimity ensures that no interest can be outvoted. Thus, when an agreement is reached, all interests have assented to it. Unanimity obviates the need for extensive fact-finding to legitimate a negotiation. Since unanimity grants a veto to every party, it transfers power to less powerful interests. This, however, is its chief defect. Often each party begins to worry that others will not agree and so attempts to preserve its ability to control the outcome.

Since in most cases unanimity will be regarded as impractical, concurrent majorities can serve as a simpler and more effective approach. If all interests concur, it may be unnecessary to obtain the agreement of each individual representative. Often in such situations members of various negotiating groups are identified by interest and caucuses are formed. Each caucus then supports the decision. It is not necessary that every member specifically agree. This procedure mitigates the potentially disruptive influence of an ideologue.

The final draft agreement would be published in the *Federal Register* and other relevant media. The notices would include the composition of the group; the nature of the consensus reached; the issues raised during the discussion; a short narrative about each section of the agreement; and data and other information considered by the group. As in other areas the purposes of publication are primarily to assure the broadest public support for the agreement and to permit dissenters an opportunity to register their opposition.

The notice will probably attract new interests and raise new issues that will compel the negotiators to return to the table. This is not a waste of time. With each cycle of bargaining the issues will likely become more clearly defined, the dissent less acute, and consensus more easily attained.

Closure in virtually all negotiations is a central issue. If left too open-ended, some of the participants might not take the proceedings seriously, while others with vested interests in the status quo might hold out, hoping to frustrate agreement.

Two techniques can be used to strike a balance between the need for resolution and the countervailing desirability of according all appropriate interests a fair hearing. First, a time limit will be needed. This issue can be negotiated by the parties at the outset or discussed throughout. If an agreement was not realized within the limit, the negotiations would either be abandoned or postponed.

Second, the facilitator needs some mechanism of helping to break a deadlock of interests, particularly when one group appears to be holding out until the time is exceeded. In such cases the facilitator might be given a limited authority to draft a solution to the deadlock that would bind the parties unless they countered with a better, more mutually agreeable proposal.[21] Such authority would have to be used subtly and sparingly so as not to replace a party's recalcitrance with governmental arbitrariness.

Illustration 2

How should the facilitator and the staff of the OSI mediate the attainment of joint gains in the semiconductor industry? Because of the multiplicity of interests and the ferocious competition in this industry, it might be unwise to urge face-to-face bargaining at the outset. A less threatening approach would be for the OSI to prepare a creative set of options and to circulate a draft to the initial participants for their comments. Although no company would obligate itself to any position by suggesting ways of improving the draft, its suggestions would help to get the process going.

Here are some of the proposed win-win solutions contained in the draft.

The protection of microcode is an issue of sufficient clarity and current importance to the semiconductor industry to command the parties' attention. Microcode is the operating program that runs a logic device. Although microcode in theory can be protected by a patent or copyright, in practice under existing law virtually anyone can escape liability simply by tweaking the system and running a slightly different program. As a result, firms that have expended substantial funds in perfecting and marketing the device are denied a substantial part of the fruits of their invention.

The facilitator will first map the respective interests involved. A leading firm like Intel has a strong interest in expanding current copyright and patent protection for its state-of-the-art device. It also has a subordinate interest in permitting a few firms to produce and sell the device under license. This enhances the market's acceptance of the device. Intel's smaller competitors, however, have an opposite interest. They will seek to limit Intel's copyright and patent protection in order to give them freest rein to experiment and innovate. Both Intel and its smaller competitors have a joint interest in reducing the existing uncertainty in the industry from the patchwork of contractual arrangments and unclear legal standards.

This coordinate interest gives the facilitator his target. His basic task is to devise a legal standard sufficiently clear that it protects Intel's innovation while still encouraging its competitors to innovate. In finding this middle point, the facilitator will need to explain the issue with the Patent and Trademark Office and staffers of relevent congressional committees, clarify their positions for the semiconductor firms, and help both sides formulate a strategy for implementation. The principal issue in these discussions is how to raise the value of license agreements. This might require stiffening the copyright or patent laws so that no one could reverse engineer, manufacture, or sell a device without a license. This could raise the value of second-source agreements and encourage their wider use across the industry. By encouraging broader use of such contracts, the OSI would help reward innovation, discourage theft, stimulate technological diffusion, and help reduce uncertainty.

What is the character of some of the other bargains that could be brokered by this process? In some cases the facilitator simply helps accelerate the rate of linkages, such as those between vendors and users of automated chip-design systems. In other cases, he or she encourages joint research on projects that might otherwise be abandoned. A leading semiconductor maker might reject a proposed project because the rate of return is too low, for example, 12 percent. A firm in a less vibrant industry, such as steel, however, might find a 12 percent annual return very attractive indeed. The facilitator would point out the potential gains to both.

In some cases the facilitator might even get the leading firms to consider collaborating with the industry's less successful companies. This constitutes the greatest challenge for the facilitator and staff because such alliances appear against the interests of the dominant firms. The joint development of "clean room" technology, however, would seem one case where although all parties will benefit by a concerted effort, the competitive position of the leaders would in no way be jeopardized. Clean room technology involves sanitizing the basic environment of semiconductor production. It is a crucial requirement for virtually all advanced work. Although the development of this technology will benefit the less competitive firms, the leaders would probably be able to exploit such advances more fully. The development of this technology will be a net gain to all.

The facilitator's role is not always so easy. We must not underestimate the fierce conflicts that a semiconductor industry negotiation can provoke. Although the semiconductor industry has not experienced the conflicts with labor that have beset other industries, such as automobiles, automation in the semiconductor industry will force automation in user industries that are already minimized. These unions might wish to intervene in the semiconductor industry negotiation.

Equipment vendors might also perceive a threat. As the semiconductor industry becomes increasingly dominated by larger firms, or by consortia of smaller firms linked by second-source agreements, over time the demand for equipment might be reduced. This would compel a shakeout in the vendor market that might be vigorously opposed by the weaker vendors.

Although not widely publicized, the manufacture of semiconductors requires the use of various toxic substances. Environmental interests might therefore insist on invervening in the discussions.

The advent of these interests will raise acute problems of legitimacy and administrative feasibility. From the perspective of the semiconductor makers, the petition by the environmentalists or the unions to intervene would seem like an irrelevant intrusion. The facilitator is immediately placed in the difficult position of balancing the virtues of opening the process to all legitimate interests against the desirability of preventing a breakdown in the discussions. The semiconductor firms, on the other hand, have to weigh whether the potential gains of continuing to negotiate are worth having to deal with issues that they feel could be more effectively checked by the existing political and legal process.

In riding herd over these discrepant interests, the facilitator and the core group do not have to deal with the unions, vendors, or environmentalists within a single discussion. Each issue can be segregated on a separate agenda with only those interests most concerned with that issue participating. The environmentalists might have no direct concern about the vendor's situation, and the vendors might see the unions' problem as a separable concern. The participating semiconductor firms might conclude that confronting all these interests head on in separate bargaining sessions would weaken these interests' political and legal clout outside of the bargaining room. By parsing out the interests, and by helping to keep the discussions focused on a narrow set of concerns, the facilitator is more able to move the parties gradually toward a tentative understanding.

The final agreement would have a hybrid status in law. Although the courts might decide otherwise, it would seem to be in part treaty, collective bargaining agreement, rule making, and private contract. It is like a treaty in its multilateral form and its principal reliance on government action for its implementation. It is like a collective bargaining agreement in that it is a mediated settlement in accordance with arranged rules. It resembles a rate-setting procedure in public utilities because parties are permitted to negotiate schedules under government supervision. It is like a private contract in that it is an agreement on specific terms and conditions.

The agreement might also include a number of private pacts and understandings contingent on future acts or circumstances for their performance. Like a contract or treaty, the agreement could contain specific provisions that address changes in circumstances, such as merger, bankruptcy, or an acquisition. The agreement could also contain severability

300

provisions so that its provisions could be applied independently.

Periodically the agreement would come up for review and it would have an expiration date. Where there was a change in administrations, the rights defined under the agreement would continue as in any other public contract, although they might be superseded by legislation. In cases of impairment of existing contracts, compensation would be required.

The flexible character of the agreement suggests how it might be enforced. For example, the agreement could grant the private signatories rights to enforce the government's contractual obligation of procurement. Some provisions, of course, could not be legally enforceable. No committee of the Congress can legally contract to enact legislation, any more than the State Department can contract to produce specific results in a negotiation with a foreign government. The best the government, or indeed any other participant can do, is pledge its "best efforts." In such cases the agreement would contain a skein of contingent promises. If X committee introduces A legislation and it passes, Y will perform B act, and Z will implement the program in this way. And so on.

To remind the parties of its binding character, the agreement would impose specific penalties for breach. And even if penalties proved too costly to enforce, a company's failure to comply would tarnish its reputation and create a precedent for its exclusion from future negotiations. Private enforcement of public obligations might also play a part. By its terms the agreement could subrogate the government's claim to specific aggrieved private parties.

The agreement would provide a framework for the specific tax, trade, and other incentives based upon it. Beyond this it would represent an important precedent that could shape the course of subsequent debate in a strategic industry and in future negotiations in other industries. It could also shape expectations and actions in the financial community and the securities markets that would compound its influence far beyond its original terms.

Illustration 3

What would be the character of a negotiated agreement in the semiconductor industry? In general format it might resemble that concluded on May 21, 1980, by federal, state, and local negotiators concerned with the overall development of Columbus, Ohio.[22] That agreement included a basic preamble stating the intent of the parties; an agenda of topics; the basic points of the agreement, covering transportation, human services, fair housing, historic preservation, displacement, leveraging private investment and intercity business development, unemployment, pollution control, and the management of urban sprawl; a detailed procedure for implementing and monitoring the terms of the agreement; and, finally, a list of the signatories.

The signatories to the semiconductor compact might include the representatives of major federal agencies, the pertinent Congressional committees, the chief executive officers, the vendors, unions, or firms in other industries, and various other special interests. One set of provisions in the agreement would involve the government's commitments. These would cover increased R&D tax credits; special grants to assess the industry's manpower needs; a detailed plan to negotiate the reduction of foreign customs duties; federal funding for the industry's think tank, the Semiconductor Research Corporation; more effective legal protection for industrial property rights; and assessment of the impacts of semiconductor production on employment and the environment.

The agreement might also address specific problem areas, for instance the Defense Department's Very High Scale Integrated Circuit (VHSIC) project. To date the project has had three purposes: to advance the date of common commercial use of VLSI; to increase the speed at which advanced circuit technologies are applied to military systems; and to assure the development of circuit speed and built-in verification. One of the industry's principal concerns about VHSIC has been its diversion of scarce resources away from the commercial sector. The agreement might contain new guidelines issued by the Defense Department, based on the negotiations, that reflected a more sensible balance between industrial and commercial needs.

Another issue might be wasteful reduplication of efforts. At present there are various special state and federal programs to promote research and development in the semiconductor industry. California, for example, has established the "Microproject" to support local firms and to attract out-of-state companies. A board of overseers screens research programs proposed by industry and university researchers. State funds are provided to match industry commitments up to a total of $1 million. Other states are following California's example. The final agreement might contain commitments or understandings among some states or communities to rationalize the use of funds in order to avoid waste.

The agreement might also serve as an umbrella for a variety of private pacts, commitments, and understandings covering the gambit of second source, joint research, acquisitions, and other collaborative arrangements already discussed. They might also involve compensatory schemes to special interests that had established they could be injured by the industry's activities.

The final agreement would reflect for the first time a coherent statement of the semiconductor industry's needs and the various trade-offs and sacrifices required in attaining them. Although there have been various studies of these needs, such as greater access to capital, liberalized foreign markets, removal of regulatory constraints, particularly export controls, and more effective legal protection of industrial property such as microcodes, there has never existed an effective process to integrate and implement these recommendations, nor one that would actually reward a confederation of interests. For the first time the key actors in the industry, the relevant Congressional committees dealing with finance, science, technology, the Commerce, State, and Defense departments, the USTR and the Patent Office would be forced to confront each other and come to some accommodation. Since the process would be very visible, these agencies would not be inclined to sabotage each other's actions. From the fray, an integrated strategy could emerge.

Among the virtues of a negotiated investment strategy is its flexibility and adaptability to the needs of the participants. It is important that these qualities not be lost with ratification. Thus the implementation of the agreement needs to be closely monitored. Just as interests changed before ratification, it is reasonable to expect that old concerns will change after ratification, and new ones will emerge. A mediator should be retained to assist where later conflicts arise or parts of the agreement cease to serve their original functions. To preserve its flexibility, it would be unwise to enact the agreement itself into law, even though many of the terms and conditions will

303

require legislative or administrative acts. In most cases the agreement would expire within a few years, and if necessary, the negotiation could begin anew.

Since the primary purpose of the NIIS is to promote economic growth in as fair, stable, and efficient a way as possible, it is very useful to build into the process a means of evaluating whether it achieved these objectives. For this reason, at the conclusion of a negotiation, a relatively neutral body, perhaps the Office of Technology Assessment (OTA), should be commissioned to study the impact of the targeted industry on growth. The review might cover a 5–10 year period, and analyze the specific pathways and patterns of technological change. OTA has already completed various reports on the electronics industry, but it has rarely focused specifically on the issue of economic growth. Such assessments would help significantly to refine the Trigger Method and strengthen other negotiations based on it.

Critics of the proposed mediated negotiation have already begun to raise serious fundamental objections.[23] Because no one has yet attempted a mediated negotiation for strategic industries, there is no way to disprove or corroborate the contentions of these critics. The analyst can only face their challenges head on.

As Ellis Hawley notes, the United States' past attempts at associationalism have almost invariably played into the hands of monopolists, the most high-spirited policies distorted to undemocratic, oppressive, and unresponsive ends.[24] Why should the NIIS, which appears to trample on the very spirit of antitrust, be different?

The NIIS is distinguishable from Hoover's associationalism or the excesses of the New Deal. The NIIS is not a scheme to bolster presidential power at the expense of the judicial and legislative branches. In fact, one of its principal virtues is that it takes the existing balance of power and governmental interests as given. The history of the implementation of the National Environmental Policy Act suggests the difficulties of forcing mission-oriented agencies to consider new interests or to amend their basic directions. This result would not be necessary in the NIIS, since each agency or division would need to represent only an existing interest or constituency.

Associationalism resulted in the circumvention of significant minority interests. By contrast, the NIIS is designed to assure the inclusion of most affected interests. Where decisions affecting these interests are today scattered and covert, the NIIS may force these decisions into the open. Moreover, a mediated negotiation involves clear procedures for participation, and opportunities to challenge an agreement before and after its ratification. Unlike the drafts of the industry committees in the 1930s, an agreement under the NIIS could not be imposed by fiat.

An NIIS also seems fair in substance. In theory the agreement will reflect as perfectly as possible the participants' best statement of their collective benefits. In other words, the parties should not be able to invent a better solution.

The NIIS may possibly also address the interests of future generations more effectively and at an earlier stage than the existing political process. Many observers fail to grasp how negotiation itself can actually help transform the negotiators' basic values. The participants' positions of course will reflect their perceptions of self-interest. Bargaining will force them to confront the social consequences of various options and work these options through to a reasoned consensus. In the past, law has had an analogous transformational influence. During the days of the civil rights movement, the courts not only helped to vindicate the claims of black Americans, they also incrementally transformed the values of the entire society by describing and expanding the social consequences of various actions.[25] The same transformation occurred in Japan during controversies of the 1950s and 1960s.

This creative function of the negotiations and the diverse number of participants can offer an effective means of facing the adverse consequences of a strategic industry's development. In this sense the negotiations will serve as a device for technology assessment. If part of the steel industry, for example, wants to introduce robots, it would no longer be a

305

foregone conclusion that many workers will need to be sacrificed. The NIIS could address this problem and a specific solution might be found. If other sectors demanded new jobs, the parties would labor collectively until they invented them.

It is true that the NIIS may override some interests, and here the critics may have a strong foothold. Not everyone can participate in all circumstances, not every claim can be honored, not every dissident appeased. For many, the NIIS will be able to offer only compensation. Yet this may be more than these interests receive under the existing political system. There is no way to give everything to everybody. This is the basic shortcoming of democracy.

The critics next assert that the NIIS is impractical for the following reasons: it is overly centralized; the process will become unwieldy by including so many interests; "losers" will sabotage the negotiations; partisan politics will engulf the proceedings; successful firms will ignore the negotiations; bargaining will be excessively costly; an unsuccessful negotiation will waste everybody's time.

As explained, the NIIS is presented as a first model of how bargaining might proceed at the national level. It would not be necessary, or even desirable, for state or local negotiations to be subsumed within the national negotiations. Indeed, these local discussions could complement national negotiations and offer a rich source of experimentation.

The NIIS involves a tension between administrative feasibility and equity. On the one hand, it is designed to include as many interests as legitimately seek to participate. On the other, the more interests that become involved, the more unwieldy the process becomes. The solution is that a balance can be struck by segregating the interests and focusing the issues. Not all interests need participate on every issue. Not every issue has to be discussed at the same time. By careful preparation of the agenda and by pyramiding and aggregating interests the problem of management can at least partially be addressed. Negotiations in other settings, involving even large numbers of participants, have proceeded smoothly.[26]

Because the NIIS appears so ambitious, some may wish to

test it. An initial negotiation could focus on the most immediate problems of a specific industrial segment; they need not encompass an entire industry. These early efforts would build trust and experience with the process that could support more elaborate future negotiations.

Few can hope to change human nature, and when issues are hard fought and defeat appears certain, losers often resort to sabotage. A democracy possesses ineffective means of preventing sabotage, although it does have ways of checking it. Disappointed interests have two basic ways of undermining the process, by law and by politics. If the NIIS offers a fair and open process in which all interests can participate, the claims of disgruntled interests will carry less political clout. The concerns of most similarly situated interests would be adequately addressed; others would be compensated. Only the most arbitrary claims would be dismissed altogether.

As noted, the NIIS would be supported by various procedural rules regarding standing to sue and judicial review. These are described below. In general, only those who actually participated would have standing. Those excluded would have to show that their exclusion was somehow arbitrary. In most other respects, the NIIS would follow existing administrative procedures.

Another objection is the process's vulnerability to partisan politics. If the Office of Strategic Industries were under the President, what would prevent the party in power from manipulating the process by controlling the appointment of the mediator, rigging the terms of the offer, or excluding disfavored participants? Although there would be no way to insulate the process entirely from politics—should this even be desirable—there is little chance that such actions could succeed. The AC could check the most rapacious of partisan gambits. More significantly, if the President, or his staff or party, excessively manipulated the process, this would be discovered, and it is unlikely that an agreement would be reached. A government that saw enough value in the process to initiate it would be less willing to engage in actions to subvert it.

Why should anyone take the NIIS seriously? It is relatively

easy to see why an unsuccessful firm might look anywhere for a handout, but what does the NIIS offer an industry's leaders?

If the country begins to experience serious economic difficulties, even the winners may recognize the need to secure special benefits and the process's appeal will increase. The industry's trust in the NIIS will also be enhanced, irrespective of the state of the economy, by the quality of the mediators, a presidential mandate, and the success of past negotiations. Each successful negotiation sets a good precedent for future action, and thereby providing stability.

In the end, however, as the illustration for the semiconductor industry suggests, the NIIS holds the leading firms in its grip only so long as they perceive it more in their interest to bargain than not. The incentive to participate comes from the prospects of additional gains, the reduction of existing costs such as lobbying or legal fees, or from the fear that competitors will somehow secure an advantage.

An unmeasured, empirical question is how administratively costly the NIIS process will be. The negotiations will demand time, energy, and resourcefulness, and the history of the labor field suggests that the administrative costs of bargaining often significantly exceed theoretical expectations. Yet the costs of NIIS may be less than those of adhocracy, proposals for comprehensive economic planning, or organizational changes in the American bureaucracy.

What if the parties to a negotiation fail to reach agreement? Although before abandoning the negotiations the parties may still have options, such as altering the format or replacing the mediator, failure is always a possibility.

It would be wrong, however, to conclude that even if the parties failed to reach consensus, the process wastes time. Bargaining helps the parties better understand the problems of their industry, exposes them to new opportunities, and prepares the government to take effective future action. The failure to reach agreement would also be an important signal that for the present, negotiation might not be an appropriate means of allocating resources to the designated strategic industry. This is the kind of market signal that many economists insist is necessary.

Difficult legal and other problems will also arise in the implementation of NIIS. The most obvious is antitrust. Apart from the serious antitrust policy questions the negotiations present, will the NIIS not greatly increase the likelihood of price fixing, territorial allocation, and other illegal anticompetitive practices? Since the parties to the negotiation will probably at times discuss competitively sensitive subjects like price, costs, and profits, it would seem appropriate for representatives of the Antitrust Department of the Justice Department to monitor the negotiations. Although the participants themselves would require a statutory immunity from antitrust liability, any such immunity needs to be limited. Given the many cultural, legal, and other differences between the United States and Japan, the de facto immunity conceded to the Japanese machine-tool cartel is a dangerously overbroad and unwise precedent for the United States. Since final agreement would need to be approved by the government, a substantial part of the constitutional problems arising within the bargaining sessions could probably be controlled.

A second issue is the limitations on agency participation in closed sessions. Under the Federal Advisory Committee Act (FACA),[27] the negotiating group would have to be established as an advisory group, notice of advisory committee meetings would need to be published in the *Federal Register* and other appropriate media, and the meetings would have to be opened to the public. FACA would require permission from the participating agencies every time the negotiators wished to convene in executive session. In the negotiated rule making currently underway with the EPA, the parties obtained FACA permission (called an FACA charter) only after great difficulty with the various limitations. If NIIS is to be implemented smoothly, FACA will need to be modified to provide less cumbersome procedures for closed meetings.

Judicial review is a third problem. Although the NIIS should reduce the need for judicial challenges, since those who are most likely to bring suit are the architects of the agreement, at some point judicial review must be available. As suggested, the point at which a final draft agreement is published seems appropriate. Any earlier point would doom the process to collateral attacks causing serious delays and undermining trust. In general, actions by the participating agencies based on consensus and within their jurisdiction should be sustained. Actions beyond jurisdiction or diverging from consensus would be subject to traditional standards of review.

NIIS also raises procedural questions and issues of delegation of power. The most serious procedural issue is whether the NIIS would be subject to various agencies' rule-making procedures that grant the public an opportunity to comment. If so, the notice and comment procedures could conceivably disrupt or delay the negotiations. Although in theory this constitutes a serious obstacle, in practice it is more likely that it would not. The NIIS could either entirely supplant the notice and comment process or, more simply, the draft NIIS agreement could serve as a draft for the agency's rule-making review.

In the past, the courts have ruled that it is inappropriate for an organization consisting primarily of private citizens to wield regulatory power. The starkest example of such hostility arose when the Supreme Court rejected many of the innovations of the New Deal. Since Roosevelt, however, there have been many examples where regulatory boards including private citizens have been upheld. Moreover, in an NIIS, since the governmental agencies and the Congress would retain final authority, delegation should not be a serious impediment.[28]

Conclusion

Declining rates of production, increased faltering competitiveness, and other economic ills will not be allayed, as the advocates of a national industrial policy allege, by more or better coordination of government. These will not be removed even by inspired leadership, much less by appeals to morality, generosity, or fellowship. Such views miss the more fundamental problem: how to construct a process that makes it in each person's perceived self-interest to seek joint gains by negotiating with his or her fellow. This awakened self-interest must begin at home, in communities, across industries, and throughout the society.

Chapter 3 pointed out the costs of adhocracy—the misallocation of public resources for R&D, the rising costs of capital, the ineffectiveness of current tax and other legislative remedies, the polarization of labor relations, the obstruction of innovation by haphazard regulation, the government's insensitivity to the uses of statistics, the importance of rapidly diffusing technological information in the promotion of strategic industries, and finally the waste of reduplicative state and municipal programs.

The NIIS may represent a viable means of addressing all these issues in the context of specific strategic industries. It is at least a worthy experiment. In place of adhocracy it would establish an overall framework: government R&D and procurement could be tailored to specific situations where they are most needed, rather than spread haphazardly over a range of industries. The rising cost of capital would be treated both as a generic problem as well as one that today is particularly onerous to specific sectors. The most irrational regulatory rules could be ferreted out and redesigned as they are in most other countries, to maximize protection of special minority interests with the overriding needs of the majority; new copyright, patent, and other legal regimes would be designed sensitive to the economic and technological conditions that exist in rapidly growing industries. The NIIS would encourage a depolarization of management and labor under more flexible, less adversarial conditions than obtain in the collective-bargaining structure of many industries. And it would also stimulate local communities and states to save scarce resources by realigning their interests. Lastly, public bargaining across a spectrum of strategic industries will accelerate the information exchange and technical diffusion

311

that we have seen throughout history have proved critical elements in economic growth.

These are formidable virtues, but the proposal is incomplete in one crucial respect. The United States can no longer plot such schemes in isolation, heedless of the interests of other countries, as it might have forty years ago. It is the wonderful paradox of the modern age that our adversary's loss is our loss, his gain, our gain. This principle gives insight into coping with the coming conflicts with Japan.

Part IV

A NEW CHARTER FOR A U.S.-JAPAN TECHNOLOGICAL PARTNERSHIP

Chapter 10
The Fourth Conflict

We are now in the third cycle of economic conflict with Japan in the last twelve years. The first involved wrangles over textiles. The second began with the "Nixon Shock" of August 1971 when the United States without warning threatened to embargo U.S. soybean exports to Japan. The third episode is the nastiest yet.[1] It involves more than thirty bills introduced in the 97th Congress urging government retaliation against nations that fail to accord U.S. firms reciprocal treatment. The principal target of this legislation is Japan. This chapter is concerned with the coming, more serious, fourth conflict.

I write as an American lawyer whose livelihood and life is in both worlds. I will describe faithfully the sources of discord, the coming fields of conflict, and the choices, both tragic and false, that will confront the leaders of the United States and Japan.

The Structure of the Trade Relationship

For some years the United States has been losing its share as an exporter of products to Japan. A comparison of the annual average of Japanese imports of basic materials and

315

manufactured goods from the United States in 1968–70 and 1976–77 shows that the U.S. is losing export shares not only in capital equipment, chemicals, and electronics, but also in materials, fuel, food, and coal. U.S. exports have largely been replaced by those from developing Asian countries.[2]

Japan's trade barriers do not adequately explain these data. The United States is supplying a smaller portion of Japan's overall imports despite the United States' long and close trading relationship, its domination of foreign investment in Japan, and the close defense alliance. Put starkly, Japan may need U.S. trade less. The trend of the 1970s continues in the 1980s.

Fred Bergsten, former Assistant Secretary of the Treasury, has advanced an important thesis of the relation of the yen-dollar exchange rate and the frequency of U.S.–Japan trade conflicts. Since the 1960s, he alleges, the yen has been significantly undervalued. During the late 1960s, the Vietnam war pushed inflation and the price of the dollar upward, at the very time that increasing productivity and expanding capacity in Japan drove the yen downward. This improved the competitiveness of Japanese goods, reduced the competitiveness of American products, and contributed to the first round of frictions. In 1975 and 1976 a renewed exchange-rate misalignment took place. The dollar appreciated substantially, due in large part to the 1975 recession and the resulting current account surpluses. At the same time Japan intervened massively in 1976 in the foreign exchange markets to block a significant strengthening of the yen. As a result the yen was again undervalued and there were massive Japanese surpluses in 1977–1978, including a five-fold rise in the U.S. bilateral trade surplus. This produced the second round of frictions in 1977–1978.

Beginning in early 1981, the Reagan administration's mix of policies drove interest rates upward. Huge amounts of yen were converted into dollars. At the same time, according to Bergsten, Japanese inflation ran well below U.S. rates of inflation. The price competitiveness of U.S. exports, particularly those aimed at Japan, deteriorated by more than 50 percent within three years. Bergsten and others attribute the current recession and the consequent frictions in trade to that cycle.

The exchange rate–trade friction thesis, however, must be qualified. It is less applicable to high-technology products that are not particularly sensitive to price (low price elasticities), such as computer aided design and manufacturing systems (CADCAMs), fiber optics, and microprocessors. These items are increasing objects of friction. The thesis would, however, apply to many other high-technology products that are price elastic and to the increasing range of industries dependent on these technologies. The evidence seems sufficiently compelling to consider ways of influencing a yen-dollar realignment.

As long as the Reagan administration and its successors run huge budgetary deficits, the government will have to intervene in the capital markets in competition with private borrowers. Given the low propensity of saving in the United States, funds for investment are already scarce. As a consequence interest rates will likely remain high, continuing to suck in huge foreign deposits and push up the dollar to even higher levels.

Bergsten offers four solutions, none of which in my opinion will prove effective. The first is direct administrative action by the Japanese authorities to control the outflow of capital. This runs counter to the moves toward capital liberalization recently introduced in response to U.S. pressure. It is unlikely that the Japanese government would suddenly reverse itself, even if this were desirable. The second is a form of interest equalization tax that would raise the cost of borrowing to foreigners to a level equal to, or above, the international level. This tax would be ineffective since most such funds are spent within Japan. Moreover, it would deny U.S. manufacturers a cheap and increasingly important source of financing. The third option, capital liberalization, Bergsten himself concedes will do little to allay the difficulty. Since the range of yen assets available to foreigners is much more limited than the range of dollar (and other foreign) assets available to Japanese investors, liberalization of capital into Japan

317

(inducing yen appreciation) will be more than offset by the flight of yen from Japan to the United States (stimulating dollar appreciation). His final recommendation of "an explicit endorsement by the [Japanese] authorities of an international key currency role for the yen" would be opposed by almost all informed sectors of the Japanese financial and government communities, if it would require a sudden, radical shift of policy. The sudden move to yen-denominated trade would exacerbate the Japanese government's already grave deficit and drive many exporters, security houses, and other firms dependent on cheap financing and accessible foreign markets, into bankruptcy. Very few in the Ministry of Finance and other powerful agencies could support such a policy.

Still a stronger, more stable international position for the yen is possible over time. Many Japanese companies prefer to negotiate in yen and a part of U.S.–Japanese trade is already in yen. Japan's efforts to induce foreign investment in high technology and other areas will also contribute. In the long run those trends may help resolve some sources of friction.

Another structural aspect to the conflict between the United States and Japan in high technology should be noted.[3] There are certain types of goods—for example, construction equipment, machine tools, office equipment (excluding computers), and color TVs—in which Japan's export growth has been greater than the average growth of Japan's exports, while import growth has been less than the average of Japan's imports. In other words, these are the products or, more precisely, product segments of major industries, in which Japan has been and is still strongest (and those which will be least affected over time by devaluation). They are sophisticated products, often requiring high levels of technology and investment. Another group—computers, autos, watches, IC engines—includes those products whose exports and imports have been growing faster than average. They appear on the whole to be even higher in technological content than the first group. These appear to be the current battleground,

318

where clear competitive advantage has not yet been gained either by Japan or exporters to Japan. The groups where export growth is larger or equal to import growth dominate the industries—such as textiles, shoes, chemicals, steel, toys— where very slow patterns of growth, or decline, are exhibited.

In James Abegglen and Thomas Hout's opinion, Japan's pattern of trade is rational and economically sound, even if the current levels and balance of trade are not. The trade pattern is shifting Japan's domestic production mix toward higher standards of living. Japan's exports of high value-added goods are rising faster than imports. To the extent that these are the same products in which U.S. producers believe they can dominate world trade, there is at least the potential for substantial conflict. The problem becomes more serious given the diverging perspectives of both countries.

The Premises of U.S. Postures and Positions

To Chalmer's Johnson, the United States is a "market-rational" state. A regulatory, or market-rational, state concerns itself with the forms and procedures . . . of economic competition, but it does not concern itself with substantive matters. . . . The developmental, or plan-rational, state [Japan], by contrast, has as its dominant feature precisely the setting of such substantive social and economic goals."[4]

Actually it is more accurate to describe the United States as a market-ideological state, since the free market, at least since World War II, has been elevated as an unassailable good in itself. The more competition the better, is essentially the credo of the Justice Department. U.S. law does not adequately concede that oligopoly may be essential for research in certain industries or that "excessive competition" may actually be destructive in others. The best example of the prevailing ideology is the outrage over derogations of free trade by foreign industrial targeting. A second example is the Treasury's sacrosanct position against encouraging or discouraging direct foreign investment in the United States.

The first corollary of market-ideology is an intense prejudice against government planning, since the reified market is seen as the best judge of virtually all decisions. The second corollary is that any governmental effort to distinguish between one technology or another, or one industry or another, is flawed, since these actions substitute an independent, perhaps contrary, judgment for the dictates of the market. My concern with strategic industries thus challenges the prevailing ideology.

Yet the landscape is littered with exceptions. Chapter 3 has already mentioned the hodgepodge of special dispensations to domestic industries, and in the international field there have been various "voluntary" restraint agreements and "orderly" marketing arrangements in textiles, steel, autos, motorcycles, and other products. The U.S. government is perfectly willing to abridge free-market principles when it deems it politically expedient. But such exceptions are always depreciated as insignificant deviations from the dominant ideology, irrespective of their actual economic consequences. The dissonance between ideology and practice makes U.S. positions seem to other countries uncertain, wavering, and unstable, and therefore hypocritical.

A country steeped in legalism, like the United States, will enshrine its dominant ideology in law. This propensity has two unfortunate consequences. It perpetuates an overwhelming righteousness. Since our positions are legal positions, they must also be just. More insidious, foreign deviations from our views and practices, such as foreign industrial policies that offend our ideological assumptions, are deemed vaguely immoral. Even if some Americans concede that other countries might reach different legal conclusions on similar problems, most Americans see foreign law as basically benighted. This allows us to mask our own deviations from the free market with legal legitimacy, while condemning the same practices in others.

The countervailing duty and antidumping laws are good examples. The most recent agreements of the Tokyo Round of the General Agreement on Tariffs and Trade (GATT) distinguish between "export subsidies" that are flatly prohibited and "subsidies other than export subsidies . . . which the signatories recognize as important instruments for the promotion of social and economic policy objectives."[5] The United States countervailing duty law treats many subsidies affecting the production, exportation, or sale of imported goods as potentially "unfair trade." Thus, under U.S. law "the provision of capital, loans, or loan guarantees on terms inconsistent with commercial considerations" is a potentially countervailable subsidy. The United States routinely provides similar subsidies to small businesses, minority businesses, rural businesses, and increasingly to giants like Lockheed and Chrysler.

The antidumping laws are also arbitrary. Dumping means selling in a foreign market below the prevailing price in the home market. Where price discrimination causes "material" injury to industries in an importing country, GATT permits the imposition of antidumping duties. Under U.S. law, imported goods sold at "less than fair value" that threaten material injury are subject to dumping duties. Fair value, however, is often extremely hard to define. Although sales in the home market provide a starting point, if the Department of Commerce decides that the data are not sufficient to form an adequate basis for comparison, it may look to third-country sales, or may construct a value, itself often arbitrary. In the present international environment such manipulations of law injure ourselves most because they fan a disproportionate sense of entitlement that blinds us to our true interests and those of others.

Since World War II there have been two forms of U.S. foreign policy: "high policy" has meant national security or defense; "low policy" has meant economic affairs. High policy has been determined principally by officials in the Defense and State departments, the National Security Council, and the intelligence community. Most of these people are specialists on strategic or military issues, and European, Soviet, or Chinese relations. Few have Japanese expertise or economic or business training. The regional bureaus of the State

Department, in particular the East Asian Bureau, sees itself primarily as the handmaiden, if not the architect, of high policy toward Japan. The overriding objective of various administrators has been the preservation and enhancement of the U.S.–Japanese alliance against the Soviet Union.[6]

As a consequence, U.S. policy toward Japan has proceeded on two tracks. In matters of high policy Japan is a trusted friend and ally; in matters of low policy it is often described as an unregenerate foe. High policy must be quarantined from low policy, lest the security relationship be jeopardized. Conflicts with low policy are generally overriden by security considerations. Bureaucrats who make their living on low policy must also devise ways of keeping their charges separate and unaffected.[7] This has been the situation during the last two decades, and such attitudes continue in large measure today.

Although the United States does not have a long-range plan toward Japan, one might say it has a long-range dream. It is a vision of an unremittedly anti-Soviet Japan, shouldering increasing burdens of its own defense and that of others, fully integrated into the western alliance, economically prosperous, but never quite as prosperous as the United States, to whom it is forever plighted. As with all such dreams, one often wakes to a contrary reality in anger, terror, and despair.

There is a political parallel in the U.S. government with the litter of adhocracy in the economic sector. It is most evident in the bureaus charged with formulating East Asian policy. The United States today has no Japan policy as it at least pretends to have toward the Soviet Union. Nowhere is there a clear statement of objectives, much less a systematic scheme to achieve these objectives. There are no long-range projections of future conflicts, even over high technology, and even less sense of how to manage them; no attention to the economic consequences of our exigent demands for rearmament and no evaluation of the deepest consequences of Japan's industrial strategies. Such indifference confuses our friends and makes them mistrust us. The unpredictability of our actions undermines respect. Such neglect is dangerous in the tempo of these times.

Divergent Japanese Perspectives

Chalmers Johnson notes that Japan's political economy, as that of many other countries, can be located precisely in the line of descent from the German historical school—sometimes labeled economic nationalism, *Handelspolitik,* or neo-mercantilism.[8] It is a Japanese interpretation of mercantilist thought, however, adapted to the modern age. Since the similarity is so striking, the subject of mercantilism itself deserves a brief discussion.

Mercantilism is best viewed as a phase in the history of economic policy dating from the late middle ages to the beginning of the age of laissez-faire.[9] The basic objective of mercantilism was to render all economic activity subservient to the needs and requirements of the state. Although it was primarily concerned with the unification of power over internal affairs, mercantilism came to regard protectionism as critical to this end.

Mercantilist attitudes foreshadowed later measures for favored sectors. In practically every known instance, Heckscher writes, "these French manufactures owe their rise to some interference by the state. It was a many-sided system of favours upon which the new structures were erected, such as subsidies, protection against foreign competition and other benefits to the undertakings themselves, besides personal privileges of different kinds for the managers and his subordinates."[10]

In addition to creating special favored sectors, the state intruded into most other aspects of economic life. "The state exploited for its own ends the monopolistic advantages which the guilds had secured for their own members or the owners of private privileges had secured for themselves. The state was brought, through this intervention, to acquire a financial interest in the existence and development of the system which had been taken over from the middle ages, and it thus became a new force in the preservation of municipal policy."[11]

One result was a proliferation of regulations designed to unify the treatment of industry over the whole country. For example, in France specific regulations were imposed on the manufacture of wool, the mixing of wool with textiles, the dye industry, and even on hosiery. "It was not so much perfect uniformity that was aimed at, as strict conformity with the rules which emanated from the central authority, though uniformity was the ideal."[12]

An important attitude toward monopoly underlay these regulations. To the English commentators of that age *monopoly* was "a word odious all over the world over," because it allocated to one the proper subsistence of many. Yet rather than encouraging unrestricted competition, this view fostered a spirit inimical to monopoly. On the occasion of the inauguration of a company of "Barbary" merchants it was remarked: "It may be beneficial that an indifferent proportion be appointed to every man, lest otherwise, the trade being not great, one, two, three or a small number may with their great substance overlay the younger and poorer sort and the greater number and so in the end attain monopoly."[13] This view led directly to the corollary that the best balance was achieved by a preestablished distribution of business opportunities among a certain number of people in a given trade. In other words, oligopoly based on a fair standard of living.

Policies toward trade were designed to reinforce mercantilism's domestic objectives. According to mercantilist axioms, the principal threat to economic policy lay in having too many foreign goods. The "fear of goods" rested on a popular prejudice that selling was somehow better than buying. Popular prejudice in turn was rooted in notions of economic self-sufficiency, or autarchy, that can be traced as far back as Aristotle.[14] Behind the prejudice lurked a cluster of assumptions. One was the idea of creating work at home and of taking measures against unemployment. The unemployment argument found a place of honor in virtually all proposals and demands aimed at restricting imports.

The second premise of the fear of goods concerned technical innovation and labor-saving machinery. Here the concern was that foreigners would get hold of the new discoveries, and that new avenues of employment could disappear if discoveries were not exploited within the country. Heckscher suggests, however, that the cause may in fact have lain much deeper. By the seventeenth century the mercantilists had already succumbed to the lust for enterprise and adventure and this, tied to the concern with the creation of employment, made production an end in itself.

In the practice of trade, the fear of goods has two practical consequences, the first on staple policy and the second in the monetary sphere. In its earliest form, staple policy referred to the practice of medieval towns of interrupting the flow of goods or trade from passing by a particular town with the intent of making the town the staple or entrepôt for the goods. Heckscher notes, "It was in fact through the organization of staple centers in foreign trade that trade was drawn to the place where the staple was fixed."[15] Venice always insisted that the city be the place of contract on the theory that "where the goods are, the merchants will gather."[16] "Passive trade" as it was called, sought to concentrate business within the city in the hands of native craftsmen, merchants, brokers, carriers. It was an effort to build infrastructure.

One corollary of staple policy was the treatment of "merchant strangers."[17] These were rules designed to bind the trade to the city and to limit the access and rights of foreign merchants. A second corollary was the policy of provision. Here too the primary objective was to ensure the greatest possible surplus for native consumption. Foodstuffs were everywhere the center of the policy. Trade in grains, meat, bacon, butter and cheese, as well as tallow and oil were often regulated.

More important than staple policy, however, were the consequences of the fear of goods on monetary policy. The result, of course, of the unwelcome acquisition of foreign goods was the loss of money, precious metals (gold and silver), and other treasure. The sixteenth century was the age of the conquest of Mexico and Peru when wealth and power were personified in gold and silver. The principal concern about a surplus of imports thus rested on the deeper fear of loss of wealth and power. The fear of surplus led to efforts to obstruct imports and stimulate exports, so that an "excess of exports" would lead naturally to a greater flow into the country of precious metals and money. In the balance of trade, the hunger for treasure was the reciprocal of the fear of goods.

Mercantilists, of course, were aware that the inflow of money would push up prices, which in turn would reduce exports and encourage imports. Under normal circumstances this would lead to a readjustment in the balance of payments in "favor" of the trading partner. The mercantilists sought to check a new equilibrium by restricting the outflow of precious metals, thereby undervaluing its currency. If a surplus of imports occurred, this would mean a corresponding surplus of debt abroad. Debt could undermine confidence in the native currency that could decrease its foreign value. But since an adjustment in the foreign exchange depended on an outflow of precious metals, the foreign valuation of the domestic currency would remain below the par of exchange. In consequence, exporters would receive more native units for every foreign unit, but importers would have to pay more units for every foreign unit. By this adjustment the balance of trade was corrected without the transfer of precious metals. This favorable situation would continue so long as the valuation of domestic currency remained below the par of exchange.

In curious ways mercantilism and laissez-faire overlapped. Both were ultimately concerned with liberty and freedom, the former for the state, the latter more so with the individual. And in mercantilism there is a strong recognition of economic interdependence. This led logically to a fervent regard for freedom of trade.[18]

Although the striking similarity of Japan's political economy and mercantilism has occasionally been noted, few have seen the link to Clausewitz. Karl von Clausewitz was a Prussian soldier, writer, and philosopher most famous for his treatise *On War*. Clausewitz's book is a theoretical treatise on war, based on Napoleonic experiences, and Napoleon's military strategies were essentially extensions in the military sphere of France's mercantilist policies. Only Britain at the time realized in laissez-faire its deepest mercantilist ambitions.

Clausewitz views war as a rational instrument of national policy, and in this sense he is part of a western tradition beginning at least as early as Machiavelli. The decision to wage war is rational in that it is based on costs and gains. War is never waged for its own sake, but rather to achieve some other goal. War's tactics are incremental, related, and multifaceted. Since war was "merely a continuation of political commerce," peace also is to be deployed to the ends of war. If one's enemy can be disarmed by trade and diplomacy, he will fall all the easier on the field of battle. War thus "becomes a game both objectively and subjectively, the element of chance only is wanting . . . and in that element it is least of all deficient."[19]

There is a disturbing parallel between mercantilism, Clausewitz, and the implementation of Japan's industrial policies to date, which has received little attention in either the United States or Japan. The concept of strategic industries itself derives from the Chinese military strategist Sun Tzu (in Japanese, Sonshi). Sun Tzu's classic, *The Art of War*,[20] contains prescriptions on estimates, plans and calculations, tactics for deception, recommendations for offensive strategies, dispositions, energy, analyses of weaknesses and strengths, and the deployment of secret agents. Sun Tzu's greatest insight, however, was that the various principles of war could be arranged systematically and that victory might be had by a method.

The art was dynamic and unfolding, and revealed by application to specific situations. It was an early form of technology. Griffith reports that in the thirteenth and fourteenth centuries Japanese samurai were well versed in Sun Tzu, even though only a few copies were in circulation and their contents guarded as secret weapons. Sun Tzu's method has continuously been linked in history with leverage and power. The greatest Japanese generals, Oda Nobunaga, Toyotomi Hideyoshi, Takeda Shingen, even Tokugawa Ieyasu[21] were profound students of the Master. In the Meiji period, Yoshida Shōin, the famous neo-Confucian, and through him Ito Hirobumi, the framer of the Meiji Constitution, and Yamagata Aritomo, the father of the modern Japanese army, were all schooled in Sun Tzu. Sun Tzu was regularly taught in military schools before the Pacific war, and an essay entitled "A Comparative Study of Sun Tzu and Clausewitz" was circulated in the upper eschelons of the Japanese military hierarchy.[22] It is said that there were over 100 separate editions of the Sun Tzu published in Japan before Pearl Harbor, including one devoted entirely to applying the principles of war to commerce.

Mercantilism and militarism were closely linked in Japan before World War II. The pioneers of modern Japan, Ito, Itagaki, Yamagata, and others were all samurai, who even when they were devoting their energies to the affairs of the state, saw themselves only temporarily away from military service. The prewar Ministry of Commerce was organized on the model of the German general staff, which in contrast to the Napoleonic structure stressed delegation, coordination, and close integration of personnel, intelligence, planning, and supplies. During the 1920s and 1930s the Japanese general staff and Japan's industrial planners tied the concepts of mercantilism and military strategy together in the "bloc concept." Originally this was conceived as a device to protect spheres of influence, particularly for defensive purposes, against the depredations of the western powers. However, in the dark days of the 1930s, the Greater East Asian Coprosperity Sphere increasingly served Japan's own expansionist aims in northern China and the Korean peninsula.

In the postwar period, the raw militarism of the prewar

era has been significantly replaced. Yet parallels persist. MITI retains the organizational structure of the German general staff. According to Chalmers Johnson, many of the architects of Japan's prewar industrial policies survived the war to continue to exert substantial influence well into the postwar period.[23] The fundamental mercantilist perspective continues today wrapped in new technologies and industries.

What then are the implications of the analogy with Clausewitz? I am not suggesting that Japanese government officials are avid students of Clausewitz. Many government officials, indeed perhaps most younger men, may not have read *On War*. Yet it may not be necessary for a writer to be in one's immediate consciousness to exert an influence. The emphasis on Clausewitz exposes unbound and in all its rawness the unstated struggle over power. Although Japan may not be bent on military confrontation with the United States, the next wars may not be wars involving gore upon the field of battle. They may be economic wars—but wars nonetheless—in their bounty of famine, pestilence, and suffering.

Like their American counterparts, Japan's leaders have a blind spot. To many, Japan's domestic industrial policies are ultimately rational. They are believed to be in the national interest, fair, and ethical. Most Japanese bureaucrats and businessmen believe that they are conducting themselves sincerely, in the sense that they are true to their highest principles. Most Americans, however, have no understanding of the subtleties of Japanese sincerity, and even less of the principles underlying it. In Japan the complaints of Americans and Europeans are often dismissed as peevish and unpleasant intrusions, and trivialized as evidence of foreigners' animus and incorrigible ignorance of Japan.

Since foreign grievances are seen as illegitimate, they are to be managed, not honored. Thus an artful political solution is found to every crisis. A game of mirrors results: each side is misread and misunderstood, and when the stakes increase, it becomes harder and harder to gauge the other's true intent.

The Spirit of Future Conflict

Japan and the United States today are proceeding on the assumption that neither needs respect the interests of the other. This is the classical zero-sum game. The Trigger Method, in somewhat modified form, can be used to predict some future economic conflicts with Japan.

The first step would be the conventional analysis of technologies and industries anticipated to grow rapidly and to trigger technological change or growth in other sectors.

The second step would examine the extent to which the same industries and the same technologies are major sources of present economic growth in Japan, and the extent to which they are anticipated to be significant sources of future growth.

The third step would assess the ways domestic U.S. law and practice selectively burden these sectors, particularly in comparison with Japan.

The fourth step would compare existing and projected U.S. world market share with that of Japan in these technologies and industries.

The fifth step would assess how trade with third-world countries will affect the competitive position of each country's industries.

The final step would determine how changes in the balance of technological and economic power will affect the military capabilities of the two countries.

Where two countries see the development of their respective industries as a zero-sum game, the chances for conflict should be greatest under these conditions:

1. Where both countries consider the same industries and technologies to be strategic for the present and the foreseeable future and where one or both perceive targeting by the other to be unfair or inappropriate.

2. Where there are substantial linkages to industries employing large numbers of people, and where government policy and/or industrial initiative is unable to facilitate rapid structural adjustment. (A good example is comparative

rates of automation and the American automobile industry.)

3. Where one country's international market share is beginning to decline and is forecast to continue to do so.

4. Where strong price elasticities exist so that forward pricing is common, and where shifts in the terms of trade are not set off by adjustments in exchange rates.

5. Where there is increasing recognition of the military applications of the technology or industry.

The following examples of possible areas of conflict satisfy some or all of these criteria.

Short-term conflicts

Semiconductors will most likely continue as an important field of conflict between the United States, Japan, and other countries. As of this writing, the U.S. industry is gearing up to challenge Japan's exports of the 256k RAM and other products, and the tensions increase monthly.

Telecommunications is another area of rising tensions. A recent example is the Fujitsu fiber optics dispute. In this case, American Telephone and Telegraph denied a contract to Fujitsu to construct an optical fiber network linking Washington, New York, and Boston on the grounds that a freight supplier would disrupt the integrity of the network, a potential threat to national security. Fujitsu had submitted the lowest bid. The contract was awarded to Western Electric Corporation. Fujitsu's subsequent appeal to the FCC was denied.

In a related matter ITT, RCA, and Western Union International in 1979 applied to the FCC for approval of new, specialized data services between the U.S. and Japan. Domestic subscribers would access the services through the facilities of TYMNET by TELENET through the domestic public switched telephone network and by private lines. Subscribers in Japan would access the services primarily through the public switched telephone network or through private lines between a subscriber's offices and the operating center of KDD, the foreign correspondent of the applicant.

On April 11, 1979, Control Data Corporation (CDC) petitioned the commission to deny these applications, reciting the difficulty the company had encountered in securing private line services for a subsidiary established to market its computer services in Japan. CDC alleged that its own service and others would be terminated after petitioners' services were introduced into Japan.

On December 14, 1979, the commission authorized the three applicants to initiate their packet-switched, usage-sensitive service between the U.S. and Japan for a one-year experimental period. Although the FCC has continued its interim approval, the factors that produced the controversy continue.

Closely related to telecommunications is office automation, a field that promises to become a multibillion dollar industry. Because of the intimate relationship of office automation to the enhancement of productivity in services, it is understandable that the Japanese government has sought to promote this industry. Because services are also an important U.S. export, however, it is likely that office automation will prove a source of conflict in the near future.

During the mid-1970s Japanese producers successfully exploited a niche in the world market for smaller, low-speed copiers. Copiers will also be a likely source of friction as Japanese manufacturers enter the medium- and high-volume areas at the heart of U.S. firms' current business.

Despite the fears of many U.S. manufacturers, Japanese makers have been unable to penetrate the U.S. market in minicomputers as successfully as in other areas. Establishing a distribution system has proved difficult and time-consuming and Japanese exporters have been slow to develop a distinctive software product. Analysts suggest that future conflicts will emerge in markets for minicomputers priced below $10,000, and between $10,000 and $15,000, where

Japanese advances in cathode-ray-tube terminals and non-impact printers may have their greatest impact.

In May 1982 Houdaille Industries, an American machine-tool manufacturer, petitioned the U.S. Trade Representative's Office to deny the investment tax credit to American users of Japanese NC machine tools, alleging that these exports benefited from an "illegal" cartel that dated from the 1950s. In April 1983 President Reagan, under substantial pressure from the Japanese ambassador, refused to exercise his authority to find violations of the U.S. trade laws, and denied the petition.[24] This has contributed to continuing U.S. perceptions of Japan's industrial targeting as an unfair trade practice.[25]

Intermediate-term conflicts

There is a strong possibility that biotechnology will become another area of contention in the 1980s. The reasons can be found in divergent national attitudes about the respective roles of industry and government, and in the specific circumstances of the genetic engineering industry.

Genetic engineering touches particular sensitivities in Japan because of its direct application to energy and food, two areas of Japan's greatest vulnerability. Although Japan's energy needs are well documented, most foreigners do not as readily grasp the sensitivities about agriculture. Agriculture is one of Japan's less efficient industries. As noted, historically it has deep religious significance.

Because of its intimate connection with agriculture, many Japanese believe genetic engineering to be more basic than other industries, and this perception of its fundamental importance awakens strong nationalistic feelings. Such nuances shape the attitudes of the Japanese bureaucracy, particularly officials in the Ministry of Agriculture, Forestry and Fisheries who today, and in the future, will rule on specific cases in trade in agricultural products between the United States and Japan.

The peculiar relationship of genetic engineering to political bargaining power will also prove a source of trouble. The enhancement of bargaining power is an explicit objective of the Japanese government's strategic planning. Some analysts suggest that Japan's increasing technological strength will be translated directly into political leverage in trade negotiations with the United States, in concessions in East-West trade, and in Japanese influence in the third world.

Genetic engineering will directly affect the third world because of its many applications to agriculture. The country that controls this core technology, Japanese analysts suggest, will be able to capitalize on food shortages in some of the poorer areas of the world and convert technological leverage to economic advantage. As in industries such as semiconductors, the increasing competition of Japan's genetic engineering companies will arouse the fear and distrust of powerful agricultural interests in the United States and abroad, which may militate for protection.

These general concerns could find expression in four specific fields of conflict. The most immediate problem is the perception and misperception on both sides about patent protection. On the Japanese side, many believe that U.S. industry is out to dominate the Japanese and world agricultural markets through its patent monopolies on the technology. Some Japanese policymakers view this as an issue of national security. On the U.S. side, many businesspeople are concerned that the Japanese Patent Agency will not grant appropriate patent protection.[26] Japan is under no international obligation to recognize the patentability of foreign inventions simply because an invention receives protection in the United States. As with other countries, Japanese law may differ on the patentability of a given application, and this is particularly true of new fields of technology. Moreover, an application may be denied if there is a conflicting claim. Many misunderstandings have arisen between U.S. and Japanese businesses over patents due to inaccurate translations. This is not the fault of the Patent Agency; it is often the responsibility of Japanese patent counsel or due to the vagueness in the original English application. Nevertheless, as frictions over new technological markets increase, many American businesses will view the decisions of the Japanese Patent Agency as underhanded.

Health and safety will be a second field of conflict. In recent years, there have been numerous clashes between U.S. commercial interests and the Japanese health or environmental authorities. In the mid-1970s, Japan's stringent auto-emission standards were the cause of a major bilateral imbroglio; this was followed by a controversy over Japanese delays in approving United States citrus fruits wrapped in containers impregnated with OPP, an allegedly carcinogenic fungicide. A third conflict concerned a noise pollution charge levied on foreign and domestic carriers to pay for the relocation and compensation of noise pollution victims living primarily in Osaka. A fourth matter involved the Ministry of Health's failure to expedite its approval of Abbott Lab's advanced radio immunology hepatitis test for use by the Japanese Red Cross. Since no effective bilateral agreement or means exists to handle such conflicts, it seems reasonable to anticipate similar trade-related conflicts in the even more politically charged field of genetic engineering.

A third area of coming conflict concerns the extraterritorial application of the U.S. antitrust laws. Since 1979, this has been the subject of discussion among the Departments of Justice and State, MITI, the Japanese Fair Trade Commission, and various other agencies in both countries. Japanese government policies toward the genetic engineering industry raise particularly difficult antitrust questions because of the number of firms involved (including many of Japan's leading corporations), the extent that information is shared, common goals identified, and resources allocated by mutual agreement. Structural differences between the two countries that create barriers to entry will exacerbate the problem. In the United States the major firms such as Genentech or Cetus are the brainchildren of academic entrepreneurs who were aided by venture capitalists and investment bankers. In Japan, many of the leading biologists and geneticists are legally barred from establishing their own private companies because technically they are public employees. Moreover, it is difficult for small firms to enter an industry whose domestic market is dominated by the giants. As the costs of financing research and development increase, it will soon be critical for Japanese firms to penetrate foreign markets in order to recoup their investments. At this point, the antitrust problem will surface as a significant issue.

A final problem is the increasing acrimony over the transfer of technology. Many Japanese now believe that because biotechnology is more basic than other technologies, some measure of autarchy is essential. One concern is that the United States will someday interrupt the supply of seeds or important technology. Such perceptions are reminiscent of the belief in the 1950s that the giant IBM would control the pace and direction of the Japanese computer industry. Although it is difficult to predict precisely which technologies will be principal objects of controversy, it is likely that technology transfer will surface as a significant issue as the general level of tensions in this industry rise.

Although U.S.–Japanese conflicts in commercial aircraft have not surfaced to any extent in the media, some in the U.S. industry are concerned over the Japanese government's promotion of an internationally competitive commercial aircraft industry. Although some American officials in the aircraft industry are as complacent about the industry's future as some major computer manufacturers may be about software, other aircraft makers are deeply worried. The first concern is simply that due to the dominant position of Boeing, other American manufacturers and suppliers to original equipment manufacturers (OEM) will be displaced in the world market.

A related problem is the weakening of the "gentleman's agreement" under which Japan, the United States, and Europe have agreed to harmonize interest rates on export credits. It is likely that the agreement will be undermined both by the U.S. government's reluctance to continue export promotion, and Japan's increasing need to find markets for high-technology exports.

A third area is the increasing frustration over lack of progress in negotiations on civil aviation, particularly concerning Japanese limitations on approved carriers, "beyond rights," and access to major cities.

Long-term controversies related to defense

I have suggested there is a sharp divergence of views between the United States and Japan regarding the relation of economic policy to national power. In the United States, power is identified with military muscle. Whereas the importance of a healthy economy is acknowledged, economic affairs are continually subordinated to military and security considerations. In Japan, economic policy has almost always been the cohort of the martial ambitions of the state. What are the long-term implications for these two countries, the one preoccupied with arms and defense, the other with economic strategies and logistics? The coming years will present five major classes of issues: the free ride; diversion; sale of arms; COCOM; and the defense build-up.

To many Americans Japan is not adequately shouldering the burdens of its own defense. An increasing number of Americans recognize that the United States can no longer independently shoulder its perceived global responsibilities—nuclear equivalence with the Soviet Union, access to international sea lanes, the defense of western Europe by NATO, bases in Asia, and the protection of its interests in the Persian Gulf[27]—thus criticisms of Japan grow sharper. The Japanese respond that defense expenditures have increased at more than 7 percent per year, and that the defense build-up already raises serious constitutional questions.

If the free-ride debate could stumble along only on the bone of fairness, it might not be a matter of great concern. But once the free-ride is linked to the idea that the United States is underwriting Japan's economic belligerency, it acquires a nastier turn because it feeds a sense of betrayal. Most Japanese may not even be aware of the implications of this harmful interpretation, but certainly many would feel deeply wronged by American retaliations motivated by it.

Military and civilian technologies mutually supplement and complement each other, and it is often impossible to quarantine one from the other. U.S. pressure on Japan to rearm, in particular coproduction programs, thus increases Japanese competitiveness across a whole range of industries. The F-15 built by Mitsubishi Heavy Industries Ltd. under license from McDonnell Douglas Corporation is a good example. In 1982 Mitsubishi introduced a nine-seat executive jet, selling sixty of sixty-eight planes in the depressed U.S. business-aviation market.[28] All these planes were designed and fabricated virtually under the same roof with an easy exchange of engineers and management. A U.S. Government Accounting Office (GAO) report cites various components, avionics, machinery, tooling, instrumentation, and propulsion technologies that Japanese industry has obtained through military coproduction. Similar commercial spinoffs can be found across a range of other industries.

Because most Defense Department officials are not accustomed to thinking in strategic industrial terms, there has so far been little awareness of the competitive impact of coproduction. Decisions on transfers of sensitive technologies follow the usual ad hoc pattern, negotiated by the Commerce Department and cleared by the Pentagon on a case-by-case basis. An underlying assumption is that the Japanese government will see the world as we do, and remain indifferent and slothful to the industrial applications of military technologies. Not surprisingly, as of 1983, no U.S. agency has kept comprehensive tabs on the transfer of defense-related technology to overseas companies.[29] There has been even less attention to the cumulative impacts of diversion.

Japanese officials are not constrained by American ideological divisions of high and low policy. In a country as focused on technological diffusion as Japan, a moment's reflection would suggest that every effort will be bent toward diverting useful technology to the civilian sector. The structure of the Japanese government and industry and the objectives of national industrial policy compel it.

As long as U.S. officials continue to refuse to think in strategic industrial terms, these practices will persist. And as long as they persist, there will be more and more cases of diversion. Japan's increasing industrial strength will feed with each step a greater sense of betrayal in the United States.

At present there is an unexamined contradiction between U.S. strategic and trade objectives toward Japan. On one hand the U.S. is pressuring Japan to invest in military hardware and to increase its commitment to self-defense. On the other, the U.S. has asked Japan, in effect, to check its headlong promotion of high technology. To the extent the contradiction is left unresolved, it will prove a source of conflict.

If Japan complies with U.S. pressure to rearm, it is natural that it will also begin to develop limited export markets initially for dual-use technology. This will be perceived in the U.S. as threatening the dominant position of the American industry in arms exports. As competition intensifies, the U.S. industry will increasingly be disturbed by Japanese restrictions on retransfer, while at the same time U.S. manufacturers will grow more reluctant to transfer technology through coproduction to potential competitors.

To date the United States has maintained its dominance in the Coordinating Committee (COCOM) by technological superiority, backed by the implicit threat of restraints on technology transfers to other COCOM members. Japan's increasing preeminence in high technology will erode the United States' present position of influence in the COCOM. This will exacerbate current disagreements on the administration and interpretation of COCOM rules relating to exports and reexports. On the U.S. side there may be an increasing tendency to use the COCOM system as a means of restraining Japanese competition in high technology, and on the Japanese side, to confuse legitimate U.S. grievances with spurious complaints.

Japan's defense build-up poses the final and most complex tangle of issues. In a sense the United States is pressing Japan into an impossible situation. Since the war, Japanese have been deeply pacifist and there has been strong public feeling against rearmament. Although such attitudes are beginning to change, many Japanese are sharply critical of American pressure, seeing it, as several U.S. Congressmen have stated, as a means of forcing Japan to spend resources on defense that could more productively be used for industrial development.

Most Americans, however, may not be so happy when they confront an independent and rearmed Japan. Consider a scenario where the Soviet Union offers to return the Northern Islands in exchange for Japan's agreeing to close American bases and cooperate in the development of Siberia.[30] How would an independent Japan act? Japanese neutrality would deeply disturb many American policymakers.

Moreover, there is no assurance that Japan's rearmament will be so benign. Although Japanese democracy is certainly flourishing, its past is deeply militaristic. And since even a limited Japanese nuclear capability could inflict serious harm on the United States, America's existing nuclear superiority over Japan may not be as significant as is generally supposed. Although a nuclear confrontation with Japan by the end of the century is highly unlikely, Japan's scientific and technological capabilities, as well as the spirit and organization of its fighting forces, would make it a redoubtable adversary in any conventional confrontation.

The Zero-Sum Solution

There is a structural propensity in U.S.-Japanese relations toward conflict. The U.S. approach is ad hoc and ideological, Japan's neo-mercantilist and unilateral. Together they offer a fading zero-sum solution.

Assuming this is what each side wants, what is the best way to proceed? U.S. leaders must understand that if present trends continue, U.S. bargaining power with Japan will become weaker not stronger. In military spheres Japan will become more independent, not less. It will produce what it wants, when it wants; divert technologies it finds useful; alter its relationships with the Communist bloc according to its interests, and less according to U.S. dictates; decide when and where it will deploy its powers (including troops) according to its own prerogatives, not ours. Japan will exert more control in trade negotiations; be less cowed by U.S. demands for market access, and keep its market closed should it desire; be more aggressive in third-world markets, and exercise far more financial, political, and legal muscle within the United States than it does today.

One appalling solution is for the United States to strike now, not later, to confront the inherent aggressiveness of Japan's approach not with anger, but with cold realism. What does "strike" imply? Demand absolute access in high technology, agricultural goods or whatever; sweep aside explanations with retaliation not procrastination; curtail coproduction; discourage rearmament; close off markets in high-technology products, monitor technology transfers; limit Japanese access to our centers of science and technology; and take every other action calculated to weaken, not strengthen, Japan's position toward ourselves and the rest of the world. Such actions will only widen the circle of enmity and mistrust.

How should Japan respond in a zero-sum world? Japan's position is weak in the short run but stronger in the longer term. By all means Japan should avoid confrontation with the United States and Europe; make minor concessions particularly in nonstrategic sectors, accompanying them with great posturings toward free trade; fancy the trappings of nonintervention; appear generous to the poorer countries; proceed silently and determinedly with the business at hand.

The more distant prospect, however, is not so clear. Japan's government deficit already exceeds that of the United States. It will increase if the government's promotion of high-technology industries proceeds on schedule. Softer values are replacing frugality. An aging population and rural stagnation will drive up welfare costs and reduce productivity. Japan's leaner and hungrier neighbors—Korea, Taiwan, Singapore,

341

and Hong Kong—will intensify their efforts to feed upon its shortcomings. Japan's leaders must run these shoals and keep American and European protectionist propensities at bay.

If the United States strikes now, Japan loses, but the United States also loses. It denies American users the world's technological advances; it props up inefficiency; it removes incentives from its most combative sectors; it undermines responsibility; and it rewards every nasty, small, bad-minded instinct that demands a hearing. The time is ripe for both sides to act, albeit for different reasons and from different perspectives, to seek a new approach.

Chapter 11

A Charter for a New U.S.-Japan Technological Partnership

There is a pattern to the disputes described in the previous chapter. The United States and Japan today are pursuing independent economic policies with little recognition of the gains from concerted action. Trenchant unilateralism is wasting resources and feeding conflict. The principles of action are ill-defined and in some respects unsuited to the needs of emerging technologies and industries. Existing bilateral institutions fail to offer an adequate structure for joint problem solving and effective communication. Any effort to forge a more productive partnership must thus begin with a coherent statement of better goals, principles, and procedures.

A New Goal: Joint Economic Growth

As discussed in Chapter 2, economic growth occurs when a society produces either additional quantities of the same goods and services or new goods and services. Growth is the result, at least in part, of an increase in inputs, physical or other capital, expansion of the supply of labor, or the discovery of new resources.

Customarily, growth is viewed and measured from a na-

343

tional perspective. But this need not be so. One might also view growth as an increase of technology, capital, labor, and national resources simultaneously in two countries, a region, or the entire world. For example, if economic growth is driven by convergence, complementarities, or synergism, another model would envision *joint* convergence, *joint* complementarities, *joint* synergism, *joint* linkages, feedback, and so forth.

I call economic growth driven by the coordinate development of strategic technologies and industries "joint economic growth." Joint growth differs significantly in character from growth occurring independently or in parallel within two countries.

Strategic industries can play as an important a role in joint economic growth as they do domestically. The basic theoretical justifications for governmental involvement are identical. As discussed in Chapter 2, markets function most efficiently when uncertainty is reduced, information is easily obtained, and all external benefits and costs are considered. Bargaining, whether domestic, bilateral, or multilateral, may be an effective means of compelling parties to confront the costs and benefits of their actions. By jointly reducing uncertainty, expediting the exchange of information, and by internalizing costs and benefits, two or more nations can assure that joint economic growth will proceed rapidly and at acceptable cost to others.

Why should the United States and Japan work together? The answer is not intuitively obvious in either country. Indeed, many people see very little gain and great cost in concerted action. The following are some of the principal American objections.

Working with the Japanese is politically unprofitable. As suggested in Chapter 10, there is an emerging albeit vague, view in the United States, particularly among businesses, that Japanese industry is baleful to U.S. interests, Japanese industrialists are duplicitous, and no real value can be had from closer cooperation. These are fundamental constraints, particularly in an election year, on an American politician's taking an affirmative stance on U.S.–Japanese collaboration.

The strongest political response is that an effective U.S.–Japan partnership is critical to U.S. national security; that the stability of the defense relationship will depend increasingly on the vitality of U.S.–Japan economic relations; and that a vital economic relationship must involve significant economic gains to both sides. The last point requires consideration of the more technical arguments against collaboration.

Because there are already many opportunities in the U.S. market, the U.S. does not need Japan. It is true that the U.S. domestic market is huge and that most firms can conduct successful business without any thought of Japan. Moreover, the theory of strategic industries suggests that an industry need not be internationally competitive to trigger economic growth. Possibly the United States could even survive if it sealed its borders.

The issue should not be cast in terms of survival, but rather in terms of growth and prosperity. By closing its border, the United States would significantly limit its growth possibilities. The market for strategic technologies and industries is not fixed but dynamically expanding. To realize the full advantages of these industries, the United States must capture bilateral and multilateral synergism, linkages, and feedback. Moreover, if U.S. industry is to compete effectively, particularly in these international industries, it must keep apace of new technological developments, find new markets, and the like.

To capture the benefits of strategic industries, protection is necessary, particularly in the early stages of their development. This is an empirical question. The history of the Japanese government's promotion of its strategic sectors certainly illustrates the uses of protectionism. It does not prove that all strategic industries must be protected. Since the Japanese economy is now far stronger than it was in the 1950s, one would suppose the need for protection would be less. Just as some industries may require a degree of oligopoly to provide sufficient incentives for innovation, so also protectionism may be necessary in the early stages of the takeoff of some strategic industries. Even so, protection may take place within the context of collaboration, just as Japan's domestic development demonstrates that competition and cooperation can be artfully combined.

Collaboration is impractical. If one believes that government has no useful role to play in the promotion of any industry, the argument seems even stronger in the case of joint action by two or many governments. Chapter 2 explained why government's involvement in the promotion of strategic industries may be appropriate in some cases. Although in theory joint action is also desirable, divergent national priorities, cultural and linguistic differences, and geographic distances might still render concerted efforts impractical. Yet such action has taken place between the United States and Japan in the military sphere throughout most of the postwar period. Since 1955 the two countries have conducted more than eighty naval exercises, and since the 1970s the Japanese ground forces have participated in Command Post Exercises (CPXs) with the U.S. Army in Japan. Joint military exercises and licensed coproduction are now well accepted. Outside of military cooperation, however, concrete examples of successful U.S.–Japan economic collaboration are extremely limited. It is these future cases with which the latter part of this chapter is concerned.

Closer U.S.–Japanese collaboration will lead to cartels and other anticompetitive actions injurious to other countries. In an interdependent world, many will argue that bilateralism solves few trade or growth problems; it merely shifts these problems onto others. Relief for one market translates into an import surge for another.[1] An international trading system based on bilateralism would set loose all the beggar-thy-neighbor practices of the unilateralism of the 1930s.

This argument is misguided. The following proposals for joint economic growth are not a new appeal to bilateralism. They are intended to show that orderly and sensible principles and rules can be devised to capture the gains inherent in almost all the new technologies. The basic ideas should be generally applicable.

Americans must not assume that Japanese do not also have grave misgivings about collaboration. Japanese concerns strike at the fundamental desirability of cooperation as well as the reliability of the American government.

Cooperation is excessively costly. For many Japanese, the economies of collaboration are far from evident. Japanese government officials recall how costly European efforts to coproduce aircraft, such as the Alpha jet, have been. The additional cost of manufacturing the Alpha jet is estimated at 10 percent; in some cases collaboration has required costs 40 percent above those of unilateral action.[2]

Will U.S.–Japanese collaboration be equitable? Japanese government officials note that close collaboration can actually depress trade or tilt the terms of trade against the weaker party. The proof, they note, is that U.S. arms sales to Europe and U.S. purchases from Europe actually increased from a ratio of 3.6:1 in 1976 to 9.4:1 in 1980. The increase occurred despite various memoranda of understanding pledging the United States to a "two-way street" in the arms trade with Europe.[3]

Such reports deeply concern Japanese government officials. Since many high-tech strategic industries touch sensitive defense issues, Japanese officials question whether the U.S. government can be trusted to share technology fairly.

Is the United States a reliable partner? This has been a long-standing Japanese concern. Many Japanese no longer believe that American leaders will provide adequate guidance, nor that U.S. government officials can competently conduct a program of close cooperation. Moreover, there are many disturbing precedents. Japanese government officials still smart from the vacillations of the U.S. government on the codevelopment of coal liquefaction and the embarrassment that other inconsistent U.S. positions have caused Japanese bureaucrats before the Diet.

None of these concerns can be dispensed with easily. The

reported costs of collaboration may not be entirely accurate, since they may not include the savings from avoiding reduplicative efforts. Moreover, the argument of excessive costs does not address the subject of additional benefits from collaboration.

In fact, there is already substantial international technical cooperation, particularly in the aircraft industry. The joint development, principally among European countries, of the Alpha jet, the Airbus, the Tornado aircraft, the EH 101 Helicopter, and the Boeing 767[4] are examples. Although the risks and costs of aircraft production have made such joint efforts necessary, the basic logic should also apply to other strategic industries.

Japanese concerns about the outcome of dealing with the United States are understandable given the relative sizes of the two countries. Yet such fears may be excessive. Collaboration should not be viewed as a means of altering the existing balance of economic power. Rather, it is one way for both countries to expand their production horizons. The continuing perception of many Japanese of themselves as a poor, isolated, and vulnerable people seems to me out of touch with the realities of Japan's present superpower status.

Americans may never be able to prove to the Japanese that we can be trusted fully. Yet this may not be necessary. If the U.S. competitive position in its major industries continues to deteriorate, America's leaders may begin to see that the past carefree approach to the nation's strategic industries is no longer acceptable. This recognition, coupled perhaps with greater Japanese appreciation of the virtues of the American political system—its encouragement of change, variation, and difference—may help to mitigate current acute concerns over U.S. reliability.

New Principles of Concerted Action

On February 10, 1983, the United States and Japan endorsed the recommendations of a bilateral working group

on the principles to govern the two states' actions affecting high technology. These principles were as follows:
The working group recommends that each government:

Goals and Means

- Recognize that high technology industries have been growing rapidly and that further expansion of these industries has the potential to open up economic frontiers, assist in the revitalization of the world economy and contribute to the elevation of the quality of life.

- Recognize the important role of government in improving the climate for private sector investment and research and also recognize its responsibility to minimize trade distortions and impediments to free and open trade, investment, and technology flows that may result from government actions related to domestic high-technology industries.

- Reaffirm the importance of the role of governments in vigorously safeguarding the rules of the marketplace and preventing anticompetitive or predatory practices.

Free Flow of Trade, Investment and Technology

- Undertake to ensure full mutual access to trade and investment opportunities in high technology industries.

- Work for the reduction and elimination of such impediments and distortions as may exist in high technology trade.

- Seek to ensure that opportunities to participate in each other's markets will be substantially equivalent. (With positive action on the part of the private sector and government, increased opportunities can be expected to lead to increasing participation in each other's markets which should be possible to assess.)

- Undertake to ensure that policies do not directly or indirectly discourage or impede government or private procurement of foreign high technology products or services, or bilateral transfers of technology.

- With a view to promoting free, fair, and open competition in high technology, undertake to provide that programs which provide particular advantages to enterprises in specific high-technology industries will be open to enterprises constituted under the laws and regulations of the one country and owned or controlled, directly or indirectly, by nationals or companies of the other country, on the same basis as to enterprises constituted under the laws and regulations of the one country and owned or controlled by nationals of that country.

International Cooperation

- Affirm the significance of exploring appropriate ways in which cooperative efforts, including cooperative R&D and technology exchange consistent with anti-trust laws and policies, could promote high technology industries.
- Undertake to ensure that participation in government-sponsored R&D projects will be open, in principle, to enterprises constituted under the laws and regulations of the one country and owned or controlled, directly or indirectly, by nationals or companies of the other country, on the same basis as to enterprises constituted under the laws and regulations of the one country and owned or controlled by nationals of that country.

Although this statement of principles is an important accomplishment, it is necessarily limited to the group's mandate to deal with high technology. From this book's perspective, it seems misguided in at least three important respects. The first relates to the relationship of government action to high technology. Although many high-technology industries may prove to be strategic industries, some may not. Government support to nonstrategic high-technology industries would be inappropriate. Conversely, although the working group's

350

mandate was limited to high technology, government support for strategic low-technology industries should be equally acceptable.

The second objection involves the reference to "free and open trade." This bias is reflected in the responsibilities to minimize distortions and impediments, to safeguard the "rules of the marketplace" and the various references to nationality treatment, a rule of international law requiring states to accord foreigners treatment essentially equivalent to that given their own nationals.

These principles are misguided because they fail to recognize the current needs and realities of government promotion of strategic high-technology industries. As I have suggested, in some cases nations may deem it necessary to subsidize these industries, restrict access to their domestic markets, or even support exports of their strategic sectors. Governments have longstanding working relationships with key suppliers. NTT is an example; the U.S. Defense Department is another. They cannot, and perhaps should not, be expected immediately to accord the same treatment to foreigners.

Although perhaps there is a political benefit for both countries in reaffirming the ideal of free trade, there is also a cost for each in committing to principles that neither side has any intention of honoring. Such actions undermine public trust and weaken other viable principles. It seems more sensible for both countries to concede the possible justification and necessity for some "anticompetitive" actions, but to require rigorous explanation for actions that are truly injurious.

Whereas in the above examples the principles are vaguely misguided, the requirement of substantially equivalent opportunity could be directly harmful. Given one interpretation, this principle suggests that competition across the two markets for high technology should be curtailed or expanded as both governments see fit. The principle seems to encourage voluntary restraints and other efforts to cartelize and balkanize markets that would be opposite to the principles of free trade the recommendations claim to espouse.

351

The recommendations proposed by the working group could usefully be supplemented by seven additional principles for joint economic growth.

The United States and Japan would recognize the desirability of harmonizing their policies toward strategic sectors to mutual advantage.

Both countries would agree to develop a common set of rules and procedures to govern the selection and support of their strategic industries. These would include a commitment to monitor the long-term impacts of strategic industries on economic growth.

Both countries would agree, wherever possible, to mitigate adverse consequences to third countries from their coordinate promotion of strategic industries.

Both countries would agree to share the surplus deriving from their concerted action under rules to be devised by them, and when appropriate, to dedicate a portion of this surplus to the needs of poorer countries.

Each country would endeavor to facilitate the adjustment of the other to the structural demands of new technologies and industries.

Both countries would assure transparency of policies, laws, regulations, and other measures, so that each might better understand the bases for the other's actions.

Finally, both countries would agree to discuss actions significantly affecting the other, before these actions were undertaken.

New Rules for Concerted Action

To be effective and to command respect, principles must be supported by rules that deal with the difficulties in applying those principles. Concerted action will require three classes of rules: international, bilateral, and unilateral.

On the international level, two of the most important questions are: Does a U.S.–Japan program for joint growth violate the most favored nation provisions of the GATT? Does the program violate the basic limitations on state support to industries contained in the Subsidies Code, negotiated under the GATT in 1979?

Article 1 of the GATT contains the basic principle of nondiscrimination:

With respect to customs duties and charges of any kind imposed on or in connection with importation or exportation or imposed on the international transfer of payments for imports or exports, and with respect to the method of levying such duties and charges, and with respect to all rules and formalities in connection with importation and exportation ... any advantage, favour, privilege or immunity granted by any contracting party to any product originating in or destined for any other country shall be accorded immediately and unconditionally to the like product originating in or destined for the territories of all other contracting parties.

The principle of "most favored nation" treatment is a basic element in most bilateral treaties dealing with friendship, commerce, navigation, and other international agreements, where it may be even more broadly and uncompromisingly stated. The principle of nondiscrimination is also applicable to the Subsidies Code.

The reason the MFN principle poses a problem is because it might be argued that a program of concerted U.S.–Japanese action would involve extensive "advantages," "favors," and "privileges" accorded to Japanese and American products. Another signatory of the GATT, such as one of the European powers, could challenge these measures on the grounds that they impaired or nullified benefits that they received under the GATT. The problem is potentially serious, because if the argument has merit, the United States and Japan would have to choose between flagrantly ignoring the GATT—an act that would invite retaliation and undermine the system—or renegotiating the entire agreement, a long and protracted process that would significantly retard the new initiative.

Although the legal issue is extremely complex, the United

States and Japan could make a strong case that concerted targeting was not contemplated by the GATT and therefore is not covered. MFN, they would suggest, applies to favoring products in trade. Concerted action to promote strategic sectors, they would contend, concerns economic collaboration and is analogous to the existing practice of countries in coordinating their monetary policies. New initiatives for joint growth would seem the 1980s equivalent to the earlier coordinating committees in the Organization for Economic Cooperation and Development (OECD) for steel and other depressed industries.

The Subsidies Code also presents a direct challenge to targeting itself. Both articles 10 and 11 include established principles against export subsidies and so-called domestic subsidies. Although signatories to the code recognized the importance of special programs to encourage research and development, especially in the field of high technology, the code continues:

Signatories recognize, however, that subsidies other than export subsidies . . . may cause or threaten to cause injury to a domestic industry of another signatory or may nullify or impair benefits accruing to another signatory under the General Agreement, in particular where such subsidies would adversely affect the conditions of normal competition. Signatories shall therefore seek to avoid causing such effects through the use of subsidies.

Here the response of both countries may be simpler than the MFN problem. Bilateral subsidies to strategic industries, they would argue, for the most part benefit other countries. Where there was a risk of harm, both countries would consult with third parties, as the Subsidies Code requires, and mitigate this risk.

A program of joint economic growth will also require new bilateral and domestic rules. One category will involve rules covering joint targeting. The main questions would be: which industries should be jointly targeted, what are the methods of targeting, and how should the fruits of targeting (the surplus) be measured and shared. These questions are discussed in the last section.

Rules to facilitate structural adjustment would also be needed. When MITI encourages the wide use of robots, this may increase productivity in Japan, but it also imposes strains on U.S. industries. In part these strains are beneficial: they stimulate technological change and innovation in the U.S. industry. But in part they cause injuries, particularly when U.S. laws constrain U.S. industry from adjusting as nimbly as Japanese industry. When these strains are felt, as they already acutely are, American businesses have a natural tendency to blame Japan and mobilize political pressure to sabotage what might otherwise be a salutary measure. Both countries should thus view adjustment as a common concern.

To forecast such problems, both countries must inaugurate impact studies of their various targeting practices. These studies would raise procedural questions as to who would perform the studies, how they would be financed, what would be investigated, who would review drafts, and how the findings would be distributed.

The third set of rules would address the critical problems of the new technologies themselves: the basics of technological information sharing, the protection of industrial property rights, limitations on the flow of technology and on investment, and restrictions on transborder data flows. Such problems are now so current and important they require some elaboration.

Protection of Industrial Property Rights

As we have seen, rapidly changing technologies pose difficult problems of legal protection. These are compounded where two countries like the United States and Japan are intensively competing for dominance of international markets. Here an overextension of monopoly protection through the patent or copyright laws, or a failure to enforce trade secret laws, can tilt the terms of trade. The advantage thus

355

secured may be multiplied across a spectrum of other industries.

Although patent and copyright protection for computer programs, genetically engineered microbes, and other high technologies are roughly similar in the United States and Japan, the area of greatest discrepancy is trade secret protection for unpatented know-how. The purpose of U.S. law is to provide a remedy for breach of faith, not to foster secrecy as an end in itself. Trade secrets are transferable by license, gift, or sale and are protected by civil, criminal, and equitable (injunctive) relief. In 1979 the Commissioners of Uniform State Laws adopted a Uniform Trade Secrets Act that codified the basic principles of the common law.

To date there is no provision under Japanese law that explicitly protects unpatentable know-how and trade secrets,[5] although theft of trade secrets is a criminal offense. As in the United States, industrial espionage flourishes. However, unlike the United States, in Japan most controversies in this area are settled privately.

The uncertainty in the law and the differences in social values underlying it were important elements in the Hitachi espionage case. In June 1982 the FBI arrested several officials of Hitachi and the Mitsubishi Electric corporations and charged them with conspiring to steal computer trade secrets from IBM. A federal grand jury subsequently indicted Hitachi, Mitsubishi, and eighteen individuals, most of them employees of the two companies. On February 8, 1983, Hitachi and two of its employees pleaded guilty in federal court to the charge of conspiring to transport stolen IBM material to Japan. Hitachi was fined $10,000, the maximum on the single count in the indictment. Two Hitachi employees were fined $10,000 and $4,000 and placed on five and two years probation.

Although the Hitachi case confirmed many Americans' existing prejudices about Japanese stealth and duplicity, the matter was viewed very differently in Japan. The Japanese press saw the arrests as "underhanded," "dirty," a "betrayal," and part of an overall conspiracy by IBM and the Justice

Department to damage IBM's chief foreign rival in the U.S. market.

Japan's failure to protect trade secrets is in many ways a vestige of an earlier age. The Meiji drafters of the Civil Code understood that weak protection was a useful device to acquire foreign technology and to diffuse information rapidly within the home market. Japan's patent law, which was originally modeled on the Spanish code, best illustrates this principle. The Hitachi case suggests some of the adverse consequences of a failure to reconcile domestic practice with international needs. The case stresses the importance of greater bilateral surveillance of trade secret misappropriation and of an alignment of the two countries' trade secret laws. Specifically, the two governments should clarify the ways in which protection reinforces or weakens existing plans to promote these sectors, identify specific barriers to the protection of these technologies, and finally, develop a common set of rules to deal with hard cases.

Both the United States and Japan impose restrictions on the free flow of technology. The inefficient, and at times unfair, administration of the U.S. export controls was discussed in Chapter 3. Japanese restrictions have focused on commercial and industrial as opposed to military technologies.

Since the early 1950s, Japan has closely supervised international technology licensing agreements. Under the old Foreign Investment Law[6] and the former Foreign Exchange and Foreign Trade Control Law, the Ministry of Finance (MOF), and the ministry with competence over the industry affected (usually the Ministry of International Trade and Industry, MITI) maintained plenary jurisdiction to validate, disapprove, or reform all technical assistance agreements. Prior to 1974, MITI officials often sought to influence the terms of these agreements, particularly royalty rates, grantbacks, and provisions for licensing to third parties.

By the mid-1970s the Japanese government had begun to liberalize and simplify the system. In December 1980 the

Foreign Investment Law was repealed and a new legal regime for the review of international license agreements was instated. All external transactions are now, in principle, unrestricted.

First, in lieu of validation, "technology induction contracts" are subjected only to reporting. Reporting applies only to inward licensing of technology by a Japanese resident from a nonresident. The conclusion or amendment of any such agreement involving the assignment or license of industrial property rights or know-how must be reported to the Bank of Japan.

Second, payments under inward technology agreements involving a "special means of settlement," such as offsetting debts and claims, must be approved by the government.

Third, the assignment and licensing of technology from a Japanese resident to a nonresident is in principle unrestricted with no report required. However, the competent ministry (in some cases MITI) must approve the assignment or license of technology (including grantbacks in connection with inward licenses) from Japanese residents to nonresidents when the technology involves: (1) nuclear fuels and raw materials; (2) space development; and (3) maintenance of international peace and security. MITI has designated the design, manufacture, and use by lease or license of about 150 items, 23 of which are nuclear- and military-related. Others include active circuit elements involving diodes, transistors, integrated circuits, and other semiconductor products having specified characteristics. The export controls on these technologies are divided into two geographic areas, covering most industrialized and semiindustrialized countries.

The restrictions on the outflow of technology may represent a shift in emphasis in Japanese government policy. Under the old law, validations focused on the inflow of technology. Regulations on retransfers of technology were strictly ancillary. The new provisions reflect the Japanese government's awareness of the growing superiority of some Japanese technology and its intent to subject (re)transfers of certain significant technology to specific terms and conditions.

The new technology licensing requirements are sure to prove a source of conflict, particularly if foreign firms perceive that these controls are being applied arbitrarily. Sensitivity is necessary on both sides. The United States must concede not only the right, but also the appropriateness, of the Japanese government's monitoring flows of strategic technologies. Although Japan's policies in this area may be similar to U.S. export controls on defense-related technologies, both sides should affirm the need for transparency.

Often the most efficient means for an American company to enter a foreign market is by the direct purchase of a controlling interest in a local company. This avoids the time, cost, and other risks of establishing an entirely new operation. Moreover, it permits the foreign party to hire skilled local scientists and executives, and to establish a major position in the local market. This is particularly necessary for foreign high-technology firms seeking to keep abreast of the rapid changes in the technology of their Japanese competitors.

The 1980 amendment of the Foreign Exchange and Foreign Trade Control Law (FEFTCL) still retains many burdensome reporting requirements similar to, but not as detailed as, those of the earlier law. Like the remaining restrictions on technology transfer, these rules cause delays and increase costs.

To the extent that Japanese high-technology companies are not similarly burdened in the United States, the FEFTCL and the administrative interpretations and practices that implement the law will continue as a source of bilateral conflict. The two governments should review the implementation of the new amendments, with particular sensitivity to their adverse impact on high-technology companies.

An increasing concern of many American companies involved in data-processing services is the interference with the flow of data across their boundaries. This is already a major concern of American companies in Europe. It should be an increasing worry for American companies operating in Japan.

The prior restrictions of MPT and NTT have been the source of three bitter controversies, the Tymshare, General

Electric, and Control Data cases discussed in Chapter 10. Although some of the restrictions that gave rise to these controversies have been informally set aside, various issues remain. The most important is the continuing discrepancy between the Japanese and U.S. interpretations of the Recommendations of the International Telegraph and Telephone Consultive Committee. The Japanese have contended that:

1. Their restrictions on data transfer between computer centers in the United States comply with the recommendations of the (CCITT) because these recommendations do not deal with situations in which international private lines terminate in more than one computer or data processing center.

2. The United States is requesting that Japan permit "incidental data switching," an issue not clearly resolved in the CCITT Recommendations, and one which should be discussed on a multilateral basis.

3. International regulations on telecommunications under the auspices of the International Telecommunications Union (ITU) permit each country to establish reasonable telecommunication systems in accordance with domestic law, and the Japanese telecommunications law reflects a reasonable application of this principle. The United States' position has been that incidental data switching between multiple computer centers should be permitted because to restrict this practice would constitute a non-tariff barrier.

To the extent that the two governments tolerate the existing state of legal uncertainty, conflicts over the basic rules will continue. Such conflicts will be aggravated by the incipient concerns in Japan over the protection of privacy and computer security. Such concerns, as in other countries, can be used to justify additional restrictions on the transborder flow of data.

The subject is currently being discussed in various international meetings, although with the exception of the CCITT guidelines no international rules exist to harmonize national practices. Japan and the United States must endeavor to mitigate the adverse impacts of such domestic regulations and to build on international data networks.

Many of the economic difficulties Americans are encountering in Japan can be reduced to the problem of access. On a superficial level this can be seen as the difficulty of gaining access to the Japanese market. On a deeper level, the issue is one of access to people's minds.

Joint research and development projects in Japan illustrate this problem vividly. Currently there are two problems: rights of foreigners to participate in the programs, and foreign access to the fruits of these projects.

Access to Japanese government research and development projects gives foreign firms a window on new scientific and technological developments, and also access to valuable opportunities for financing and technology transfer. In the past American high-technology firms appear to have been excluded from national research projects in Japan.[7] American subsidiaries of Japanese companies may not have been excluded from U.S. government-funded commercial programs, at least not to the same extent.

A more serious problem has been the restraints imposed on transfers of Japanese technology that originates in these programs. The principal difficulty arises from a discrepancy in U.S. and Japanese law relating to the treatment of jointly owned patents. Under Japanese law, patents owned by more than one company cannot be licensed without the consent of all co-owners. As a consequence, co-owned Japanese patents have not customarily been included in typical cross-licensing agreements. Co-owned U.S. patents are usually included. Until recently, this difference has not posed serious problems since U.S. technology was considered superior.

The situation changed with the advent of the VLSI program. The project yielded four categories of inventions:

1. Inventions by employees solely of one participant company (sole industry).
2. Joint inventions by employees of two or more participant companies (joint industry).
3. Joint inventions by employees of industry and Japanese government (joint industry–government).
4. Inventions made by employees of the Japanese government (sole government).

A problem arose over the manner in which subsequent patent applications were filed. About 1,200 Japanese patent applications were processed, most of which were filed in the name of the VLSI Association. A small number (about 4 percent) were filed in the joint names of the VLSI Association and the government. With the exception of those co-owned with the government, all patent applications therefore were directly controlled by the VLSI Association, which remained the licensor of the patents on behalf of all the participants. This directly abridged the rights of some American companies that claimed rights to grantbacks under existing cross-licensing agreements with the major participants in the VLSI project.

Under U.S. government pressure, the VLSI Association eventually permitted the industry participants to sublicense to third parties in categories (1) and (2) patents on a case-by-case basis, with the proviso that *MITI must be satisfied that adequate value be given in return.*

The VLSI incident raises three generic questions for American companies. First, as noted, the depositing of patents from joint research programs in the association diluted the existing rights of American firms under existing cross-licensing agreements.

Second, the practice increased the exposure of American firms to suits for patent infringement, since MITI, or more often the technology research association, often licenses and sublicenses many of the patents to a wide range of Japanese companies. At the same time, American firms had no channel to develop offsetting patents, since the technology research association itself does not possess a production base.

Third, the research association became a vehicle for controlling the outflow of technology. Although the Japanese government has emphasized that technology flows are no longer restricted, many American firms are concerned that the ownership of the patents by the association will be used as a means of affecting the timing or terms of transfer, especially royalty rates. The American party is usually in the position of licensing its portfolio of inventions, many of which were developed with U.S. government funding. Because of the association's control over patent rights and proprietary technology, the American party must negotiate not only with its licensee, but also with the Japanese government or the legal entity acting as a front organization. The interpolation of the entity at a critical moment can affect the terms of the bargain.

Today there are a number of projects that have followed the VLSI model. These include the development of technologies of the fifth-generation computer, the project on flexible manufacturing, and MITI's eight-year opto-electronic project discussed in Part II. Recently, however, the Japanese government has announced that in the future it will deemphasize the VLSI approach and will favor contracted research. Under this approach, patents would rest solely with the government; in the VLSI project, they were jointly owned by researchers and the association. Political tensions will probably increase even more, given the government's expanding control over international licensing.

The principles negotiated by the working group recognize the right of resident foreign firms to participate in joint research programs on an equal basis. Although as suggested this may not be practical, specific rules should be devised that will assure a fair level of participation consistent with the technical needs of each project. Deviations from this principle would be subject to discussion and mediation as will be explained.

Access is not solely a problem for Americans in Japan.

Japanese are often barred from working in defense-related industrial facilities in the United States, even though Canadian and British citizens are permitted to do so.[8] If both countries are serious about technological cooperation, they should at least consider developing sensible rules for reciprocal security clearances. This suggestion may raise serious concerns within the U.S. Defense Department where some will assert that the Japanese are less trustworthy than the Canadians or the British. But how long can American Presidents and others in high positions proclaim that the U.S.–Japan Security Treaty of 1953 is the foundation of U.S. security in the Pacific, yet distrust the partnership in its smaller substance? The U.S. double standard must also give American's some insight into the sensitivities of Japanese government agencies about permitting U.S. firms to participate in Japan's most vital technology development programs.

A program of joint growth would require other adjustments of U.S. law and policy. One issue would be the extraterritorial application of the U.S. antitrust laws to American participation in Japanese research and development programs. In the past, when joint research was more rigorously scrutinized, U.S. law might have presented a problem for the American participants, even though the research was conducted outside the United States. As noted, the Justice Department appears to be relaxing its standards for joint R&D within the United States and therefore the risk of prosecution seems minimal for research conducted abroad. Serious antitrust offenses such as price fixing, extraterritorial allocation, and other schemes, of course, would still subject the participants to criminal and civil liability. Although the law in this area appears more settled, it would be helpful if the Justice Department clarified and elaborated the guidelines in its 1977 international enforcement guide.

U.S. countervailing duty law is another problem. At present, U.S. countervailing law is far more stringent than the international rule. The United States allows countervailing against all subsidies affecting the production, export, or sale of imported goods, or the provision of capital, loans, or loan guarantees on terms inconsistent with commercial considerations. The International Trade Commission (ITC) has recently applied this standard to R&D subsidies in the Belgian Steel case.[9] Holding that support for research "on problems affecting only a particular industry or group of industries . . . and which yield results that are available only to producers in that country" is countervailable. If the U.S. position becomes the global norm, most nations will be countervailing against a category or subsidy that these same nations also judge appropriate.

To strike a balance between appropriate national actions and the interests of other countries, some analysts suggest distinguishing between "normal" subsidies and "excess" subsidies. Normal subsidies are those which, it is suggested, most countries will agree are necessary and appropriate. Excess subsidies are subsidies measured as either the difference between the countervailing country's own subsidies and the opponent country's subsidies, or between the foreign subsidy and some constructed global average.

Some analysts suggest that a critical measure of when a subsidy is excessive is when it is "long lasting." John Barton of Stanford University and others propose that when a subsidy is long lasting, it be exposed to treble damages, "probably best carried out by extending the period over which the countervailing duty is imposed." In the alternative, "an effort [is to be made] to capitalize the calculated future benefits to the foreign industry deriving from the subsidy's effect on its learning curve."

He continues:

To keep such damage calculations from affecting optimum allocation too severely, there would have to be ways to "buy out" from these remedies. Perhaps the foreign governments or industry could substitute damage payments by the foreign government or industry, or the government of the injured firm could, at its own option, substitute additional domestic R&D subsidies—a sort of high-tech adjustment assistance. Moreover, the risks of such enlarged countervailing might wisely be reduced by an international review and also by requiring the industry seeking protection to bear the burden of proving that it is affected by such a long-term learning-curve form of harm.[10]

Such proposals reflect a beginning awareness that U.S. law and policy is blindly self-destructive. Yet there are still problems. One is the difficulty of defining a "normal" subsidy. As we have seen, the requisite amount of subsidy will depend on the unique circumstances of each country. This can be determined only after analysis of convergence, innovation, diffusion, linkages, feedback, and many of the other indices described.

Linking the idea of excessive subsidies to the effect of their being "long lasting" may also be counterproductive. It is precisely because the effects of a subsidy will be long lasting, in that they will multiply over many industries, that nations will want to confer such subsidies.

The idea of an excessive subsidy seems, however, necessary. In cases of concerted action there will be a continuing risk that one side will oversubsidize. In theory, this is as inefficient as undersubsidization. Countries will want and need to retain this basic safeguard.

Strengthening Bilateral Institutions and Processes

Stronger bilateral institutions must be built on the foundation of a more viable working relationship. The most important ingredient of any good relationship is a sense of priority. Priority requires awareness of another's interests and implies consideration, an almost fundamental cultural value. At times it demands sacrifice. Priority means the parties will not threaten the relationship to coerce concessions, nor make concessions in order to purchase the other's good will. Such actions discredit and devalue a relationship.[11]

A second ingredient is effective communication. Effective communication requires frequent multilevel contacts, candor, and truthfulness. An identity of interests is not necessary, but each party must seek to understand what is being said and see the situation from the other's perspective. Effective communication may require acknowledging another's aggressiveness and telling the other party unequivocally that its actions hurt. There is little such communication today between the United States and Japan. There is much talk, many threats, much posturing, false premise, misrepresentation, but little clarity and less real interest in understanding and grappling with the other's true concerns or perceptions.

A final element is a recognition that nothing is fixed, everything changes. This implies resilience, flexibility, and compromise. A good relationship serves the interests of the parties at any time. The leaders of Japan and the United States must begin to face this evolutionary quality in all human dealings.

Not all couples want to be friends, nor are all unions bliss. Some may seek only a less lethal form of survival. This may also be so with nations. Ultimately the United States and Japan will have to decide how closely they want to labor together.

If in fact there still exists the possibility for effective collaboration, a program toward joint growth would involve Americans and Japanese in at least three kinds of activities in the coming years: jointly identifying strategic industries and devising methods to capture and apportion the gains; integrating state efforts to construct future cities of science and technology; and forecasting and settling significant disputes. Each activity will require new patterns of cooperation between government and private citizens.

Generally government plays its strongest suit when it writes the rules and keeps the peace. In societies like Japan, government is also an expert facilitator. Government is less effective when called upon to initiate creative action. Yet in the realm of strategic industries, government at times must be a legislator, facilitator, and initiator. This principle is equally true of joint government actions.

Fortunately, a part of an institutional framework to support joint economic growth already exists. In April 1982 the U.S. and Japanese governments established a joint working group on high technology, which has met several times and, as noted, has formulated a basic set of principles. Since 1973 the group has established various committees dealing with technical issues such as law and patents, and specific industrial sectors, such as semiconductors. Early reports suggest that the group has already begun to signal future disputes and help mediate existing tensions over high technology. The group could serve as the secretariat for a basic first step, the joint preparation of a series of bilateral studies on strategic industries and growth.

The purpose of the bilateral studies would be to pinpoint how joint growth might be engineered in a specific industry. The Trigger Method would be the primary analytic tool. The target industries, or industy segments, would be selected based on data collected by the OSI-AC, MITI, and other Japanese agencies on what strategic industries seemed most appropriate. This in itself would stimulate discussion, since each side may have different views of which industries are strategic. The selection of a strategic industry might also be integrated with the analysis of the industries that appeared headed toward greatest conflict. In this way the engineering of growth and the resolution of conflict could be combined.

The Trigger Method would need to be modified in other ways as well. As described in Chapter 9, after defining the targeted industry, the analyst next assesses the various economic indicators such as rates of growth, exports, productivity, innovation, investment in human capital, economies of scale, and the like. In the present case, the scope of inquiry will be expanded. The key questions will be what influence a given industry has on joint growth, joint productivity, joint research and development, joint invention, and so forth.

The technical analysis would be similar. The focus of inquiry will now be upon *joint* technological convergence, *joint* complementarities, *joint* synergism. Most important will be a consideration of secondary and tertiary effects, such as the multiplier effects in both countries, the forward and backward linkages, technological diffusion, and feedback loops. The joint research would culminate in a report, or series of reports, setting forth the conclusions of each step of the Trigger Method, along the lines of an environmental impact statement. The report would include an explicit set of recommendations and a scenario of action. For the reasons given in the discussion of the domestic NIIS, Japanese analysts must also examine growth in the United States and U.S. analysts would attempt to study the impact in Japan.

The mechanics of preparing the studies could proceed as follows. The secretariat would be the working group. It would be primarily responsible for reviewing the final document and for its release. Within the Japanese government, MITI, and the Industrial Structure Council, the Finance Ministry, and the Economic Planning Agency would be the most appropriate bodies to undertake responsibility for the preparation of a draft report. These drafts might usefully be circulated for comment to other concerned agencies, Diet committees, and existing task forces and study groups.

On the U.S. side, the Office of Strategic Industries and its Advisory Council would take primary responsibility for preparation of the first draft. Research on specific problems or aspects of the report could be consigned to the National Research Council, private think tanks, and universities.

After their completion, each side would circulate its draft to the other for review and comment. At this point it might be useful for the draft to be reviewed by a bilateral group of some of the leading entrepreneurs in the United States and Japan. As noted in Chapter 7, during the 1970s MITI established the Venture Enterprise Corporation to screen and support promising new enterprises. The steering committee has been headed by Soichiro Honda. Japan today, like the United States, is bubbling with creative thinkers like Mr. Honda, whose energies should be tapped. The convening of a bilateral group of inventors and innovators is something that can be undertaken effectively only by public-spirited private initiative.

After the drafts are reviewed and all comments analyzed, the findings would be compiled in a final report, a synthesis of the individual reports of each country. The final report would provide, a basis for specific joint tax and other incentives, as well as some of the other ventures discussed.

If the primary purpose of concerted action is to generate a surplus, the two countries will need ways of measuring and apportioning it. Since this is a complex task, and one where current analytic methods are inadequate, new tools will be needed. Only some of the important issues can be noted here.

The first task would be to define the surplus. The surplus for both countries could be determined by subtracting the sum of the net benefits of unilateral action from the net benefits of joint action. The key methodological problem then would be defining net benefits.

Fishlow's study of the development of the American railroads in the nineteenth century[12] offers one model of how to calculate the benefits of past strategic industries. Moreover, other analysts in MITI and elsewhere in the United States, Japan, and Europe have developed extensive data on the electronics and other strategic industries that could be used to predict future benefits. Ryūzo Sato and Gilbert Suzawa's important new book on modeling endogenous technical change will also be helpful.[13]

Assessing costs will be an equally difficult problem. There will be two kinds of costs: conventional costs like labor, capital, R&D; and external costs, such as pollution, and even arguably the costs of adjustment.[14] In theory, joint action should involve greater benefits and lower costs. Costs should be lower because reduplicative efforts and conflicts are mitigated and external costs are considered. Once benefits and costs are ascertained, the parties would be able to calculate the surplus by weighing the net benefits of independent action against the benefits of concerted action.

From a political perspective, the hardest issue will probably be how Japan and the United States would share the surplus. This problem would need to be negotiated. There is no a priori standard or solution.

Although some procedures exist for dealing with windfalls in other settings, such as the land use field, there are few rules in the international area for dividing such surpluses.

New procedures will need to be devised. One possible approach to apportioning the surplus is to recycle it in ongoing programs for joint growth. The same analytic approach could be used as was involved in the original targeting of strategic industries and in the design of specific incentives. In other words, the surplus could be treated as a revolving fund and allocated to new uses for joint gains.

Macroengineering projects offer a specific example of how the surplus could be deployed. Often the risks, costs, and time of these projects discourage individual companies or consortia from participating, even when national support is available. In such cases, or where mutual benefits justify spreading the financial burdens, bilateral and at times multilateral action is appropriate. From a technical perspective, such projects have the greatest chance of success where each party can benefit from a transfer of superior technology from the other. Where interests are thus allied, such projects turn political conflict to constructive ends. As noted, the aircraft industry affords several cases of successful, ongoing cooperation. Excellent future candidates could be the codevelopment of laser fusion, research on magnetic levitation rail technology, joint production of ethanol from natural gas using recombinant DNA technology, construction of a solar satellite, and cooperation on the Viking, Pioneer, and other deep probes of outer space.

Of all the unnoticed opportunities now present for fruitful U.S.–Japanese collaboration, Japan's technopolis program must rank close to the top. As explained in Chapter 7, foreign companies can now qualify for grants, special tax breaks, loans, guarantees, and various other incentives made available by various local governments. By participating, American firms will be able to gain access to the Japanese market, acquire a window on technology, build contacts and friendships, establish a reexport base and, in general, help shape Japan's industrial development. Recently a U.S. firm, the Materials Research Corporation, obtained a ten-year, ¥350 million ($1.5 million) loan from the Japan Development Bank to build a manufacturing plant in Ōita City in Kyūshū.

371

There is of course a cost to these new opportunities in the loss of American jobs. Although the Japanese government is opening its markets, it may also be encouraging U.S. firms to replace American workers with Japanese workers. This is a particularly sensitive issue today for many politicians who are already concerned about the flight of high-technology companies like Atari. For the United States the problem is how to capture the benefits of the new program while avoiding its costs.

One way would be for both countries to convert the technopolis into a bilateral program. States like California or Massachusetts with strong capabilities in high technology, or states like Hawaii that possess environmental resources needed by high-tech industries, might establish parallel programs to encourage a reverse flow of technology and capital. The High Technology Development Plan of the state of Hawaii is an early example. The Trigger Method could be used to help identify areas where an infusion of Japanese investment, technology, and managerial techniques could stimulate growth and create employment opportunities.

Often state government officials have higher priorities or are too busy to appreciate the gains from concerted bilateral action. Industry and other concerned citizens need not wait for government to take initiative. Rather than waiting for the governor to act, a group of informed and concerned private citizens could begin today to develop a program of incentives for foreign industries to locate in their state, particularly industries that would trigger growth. After composing a careful agenda, the group would assemble a high-level state delegation to visit Japan to meet with counterparts in the Japanese Ministries and Diet. The agenda would stimulate discussion and a joint working agenda would then be developed that would be the basis for subsequent action. No mandate is needed to get this process going. The visibility, debate, and negotiations surrounding the exchanges themselves make a bilateral technopolis program a self-realizing possibility.

Although discord may be part of all human affairs, most severe conflicts, particularly severe economic disputes, tend to be deviations from a relatively collaborative pattern. Strategic industries, however, pose distinct problems because of the stakes involved and significant costs and strains they impose on society. The possibility for conflict may be even greater where two nations like the United States and Japan perceive many of the same industries to be strategic.

Any appeal for a new institution to settle such conflicts, however, must first demonstrate why existing institutions are inadequate. For many disputes over contracts, the courts and alternative modes of dispute settlement, such as international arbitration, may in fact be more appropriate. It would be unwise for any new institution to attempt to duplicate or replace them.

A new institution, however, might be effective in dealing with other classes of disputes. The first class might be conventional disputes that are not being adequately handled by existing institutions. Protection of industrial property rights in advanced technologies may be one example. Patent counsel in various American and Japanese high-technology companies have said that they are reluctant to bring suit in the courts of either country. The issue is not only that in their view the courts may be biased. Jurists in both countries at times concede that the average litigant is "overdiscovered," "overinterrogated," "overdeposed," "overcharged," "overexposed," and "overwrought."[15] Although international arbitration appears to these men preferable to the courts, virtually all saw the importance of devising a more effective approach.

The second class of disputes would involve controversies over the rules of targeting, measuring, and dividing the surplus. There needs to be some mechanism to address such problems, lest concerted action spark more controversies than it settles.

The third class of controversies would involve disputes over governmental action. This is a category of disputes that private citizens experience particular difficulty in challenging. Attempting to address some of the problems of American businesses in Japan, the Japanese government in 1982 established a special Office of the Trade Ombudsman (OTO).

OTO's secretariat is the Coordination Bureau of the Economic Planning Agency. Within OTO there is a clearinghouse to promote settlement of grievances relating to the openness of the Japanese market.

A special headquarters is affiliated with the eleven trade-related ministries and agencies. The headquarters brings together the senior officers from the bureaus most concerned with trade. These include MITI, the Ministry of Finance, the Ministry of Health and Welfare, among others. Each of the eleven trade-related ministries and agencies has established a reception office to process incoming complaints. OTO provides the parties with a status report within ten days of receipt and monthly reports thereafter until settlement.

Although OTO represents a good start in addressing the overall problems of trade frictions with Japan, it may be too general to address the specific problems of conflicts involving strategic industries. Moreover, American firms do not regard it as sufficiently neutral to repose sufficient trust in it. OTO of course offers no solace to Japanese firms or individuals who may have significant grievances against the U.S. government.

Besides dealing more effectively with disputes, a new institution might help forecast future conflicts. In theory, this was part of the mandate of the "Wisemen's Group," a body of Japan experts established during the Carter administration. In fact, the Wisemen's Group has not become involved in the details of specific future conflicts, nor does it have the technical capability or staff to do so.

A final and important function of any new institution would be to help assure the uniformity, reliability, and predictability of the rules of collaboration. These include the rules of targeting, investment, and trade as well as those involved in the identification and allocation of the surplus. This is critical to the stability of any problem for joint growth.

For all these reasons, a new model must be found. The most appropriate would be a new U.S.–Japan Joint Commission for the Settlement of Disputes Involving Strategic Industries. Joint commissions have been established to deal with analogous kinds of bilateral conflicts over critical resources. The U.S.–Canadian joint commission on transborder pollution disputes is one example. Various joint fisheries commissions are another.

A U.S.–Japan joint commission could be most effective if it involved independent private citizens acting under a bilateral governmental mandate. Like other commissions, the members would require their own staff, funds, and supporting facilities.

The commission would have jurisdiction over complaints involving all classes of disputes. Its members would make use of various extrajudicial techniques including mediation, conciliation, and arbitration.

In investigating a dispute the mediators could call on a special team of experts to assemble and analyze facts and to prepare a record. The proceedings could be formal or informal depending on the circumstances. The existing OTO structure might be one useful approach. Another model would be the system established in Japan under the 1970 Law for the Resolution of Pollution Disputes.[16]

To assure that the commission actually performed its functions, a watchdog would be needed. This task could be performed by the industry associations in both countries. The details of working out a charter for the new commission would seem an important task for the Wisemen's Group.

Conclusion

The United States and Japan today face the twin problems of stagnant growth and rising conflict. This is the result of compartmentalized and countervailing national policies reflecting deeply divergent economic philosophies; of laws that restrict the flow of information, trade, and investment; and a poor process for dealing with our differences.

This chapter has outlined the elements of a new approach. First, the new goal of joint economic growth. Second, more effective principles and substantive rules to identify and share the surplus and to mitigate adverse consequences on other countries. And third, new institutions and procedures that will help both countries build a richer, more durable partnership.

The remaining years of this century need not be years of discord, want, and ignorance. It is possible to develop effective international rules and procedures to help us all find the way. This is the ultimate creative function of the law.

Epilogue

In his Nobel lecture of 1980, Lawrence Klein forecast global declining productivity and economic growth throughout the 1980s, basing his projection on the econometric models of seventeen OECD countries, eight socialist countries, and four blocs of developing countries.[1] Klein, however, did not account for the forces in the world that may compound the problem: continuing and rapid population growth, rising expectations and demands of entitlement, and national restrictions of all sorts on production, trade, and the transfer of technology. If such trends continue, disparities in world wealth will sharply increase and the plight of the poor countries will become more desperate.

There may still be time. If Japan and the United States could begin concerted action toward joint economic growth, other positive bilateral actions might follow. New regional blocs, based on 'clusters of strategic industries, might even emerge, perhaps growing first in areas of common culture, language, and national economic policy.

The east Asia edge—Japan, South Korea, Hong Kong, Taiwan, Singapore, perhaps some day even the People's Republic of China—are part of such a region, and all are growing swiftly. Moreover, all recognize the concept of strategic industries in one way or another and are vigorously pro-

377

moting these sectors. Irrespective of political ideology, these countries all also share a common Confucian respect for thrift, discipline, authority, obedience, and industry. Finally, intraregional trade has also grown in the last decade.

The theory of strategic industries suggests that there would be many advantages for these countries to set aside historic enmities and promote key sectors in common. Economies of scale would develop, opportunities for forward and backward linkages would expand, intraindustrial specialization could be promoted, legal, cultural, and institutional similarities might help marketing and stimulate innovation, political conflicts among existing policies could be harmonized, excessive competition adjusted, production rationalized, and dissemination of technical and scientific information diffused through a common communications network. In time similar associations might develop in Scandinavia, Canada, the United States, and Europe. The principles involved would grow like the common law, by experimentation and precedent. A general framework might eventually evolve as each region faced similar problems, tested new techniques, established common principles, created parallel institutions, and devised new systems of finance. The process of integration would itself be accelerated by the linkage of information networks in each region.

The promotion of such linkages is becoming an important objective of some international development organizations. A recent report of the United Nations Committee on Trade and Development focused on the cooperation among developing countries in strategic sectors and between developing and developed countries.[2] About half the exports of capital goods by developing countries are to other developing countries, the share being the highest in the case of India and Brazil. The report concludes that poorer countries should enter licensing arrangements with companies in the advanced developing countries; make greater use of the expertise of multinational firms; actively encourage technical exchange and joint research among themselves and with the industrially advanced countries; establish a supernational organiza-

378

tion of the major national associations of machining producers to negotiate subcontracting arrangements with machinery producers of developed countries; and conduct joint studies on the impact of the new technologies.[3]

The advanced or industrialized nations of Europe have also just begun to take an interest in devising a collective strategy for economic growth. Even as these words are written a working group established by the heads of state of the European community is issuing a manifesto on technology, growth, and employment. The report assigns specific national research tasks: photovoltaic solar energy (Italy, Japan); controlled thermonuclear fusion (European communities, the United States); photosynthesis (Japan); fast breeder reactors (France, United States); food technology (France, United Kingdom); acquaculture (Canada); remote sensing fom space (United States); high-speed trains (Federal Republic of Germany, France); advanced robotics (France, United States); biotechnology (France, United Kingdom); advance materials (United Kingdom, United States); biological sciences (European community); high-energy physics and exploration of the solar system (United States). Although the report does not adequately explain the bases for its assignments, it is at least a sensible first step around unnecessary and destructive political bickering.

The conclusion then is this: an era of rapid technological change demands legal, political, and economic innovators just as it does its creative scientists and technicians. A new breed of citizens must grow up who will dare to look across a tradition of sweeping half-truths, catechisms, and dogmas to the just essence of all things. These will be our sculptors of a better order.

Notes •

NOTES TO INTRODUCTION

1. Ira Magaziner and Robert Reich, *Minding America's Business: The Decline and Rise of the American Economy* (New York: Random House, 1983) and Robert Reich, *The New American Frontier* (New York: Times Books, 1983); Lester C. Thurow, *Dangerous Currents: The State of Economics* (New York: Random House, 1983); William Abernathy and Kim Clark, *Industrial Renaissance: Producing a Competitive Future in America* (New York: Basic, 1983); Bennett Harrison and Barry Bluestone, *Deindustrialization of America,* (New York: Basic, 1982); Amitai Etzioni, *An Immodest Agenda* (New York: McGraw-Hill, 1982); Seymour Melman, *Profits Without Production* (New York: Knopf, 1983).
2. Ronald Coase, "The Problem of Social Cost," *Journal of Law and Economics* 3 (October 1960): 1–44.
3. Richard Nelson and Sidney Winter, *An Evolutionary Theory of Economic Change* (Cambridge, Mass.: Harvard University Press, 1982).

NOTES TO CHAPTER 1

1. Lynn White, *Medieval Technology and Social Change* (London: Oxford University Press, 1962).
2. David S. Landes, *The Unbound Prometheus: Technological Change and Industrial Development in Western Europe from 1750 to the Present* (Cambridge, England: Cambridge University Press, 1969), pp. 41–42.
3. Ibid., p. 83.
4. Ibid.
5. Ibid., p. 84.

6. Ibid., pp. 84–85.
7. W. W. Rostow, *The Stages of Economic Growth: A Non-Communist Manifesto,* 2d ed. (Cambridge, England: Cambridge University Press, 1971), p. 8.
8. Ibid., pp. 52–53.
9. The following section relies extensively on Nathan Rosenberg, "Technological Change in the Machine Tool Industry, 1840-1910," *Journal of Economic History* 22 (1963): 414–43.
10. Ibid., p. 423.
11. Ibid.
12. George Stigler, "The Division of Labor Is Limited by the Extent of the Market," *The Journal of Political Economy* 54, 3 (June 1951): 190; quoted in Rosenberg, p. 424.
13. Rosenberg, "Technological Change," p. 425.
14. Ibid., p. 426.
15. Ibid., p. 429.
16. Ibid., pp. 430–31.
17. Ibid., pp. 437–39.
18. Albert Fishlow, *American Railroads and the Transformation of the Ante-Bellum Economy* (Cambridge, Mass.: Harvard University Press, 1965). Fishlow calculated that the social return of direct benefits to railroad investment in millions of 1860 dollars between 1828 and 1860 was as follows:

ANNUAL AVERAGES	NET CAPITAL FORMATION	DIRECT BENEFITS	NET EARNINGS	GROSS RETURNS	GROSS RETURNS LESS NET CAPITAL FORMATION
1828–1835	4.5	0.3	0.2	0.5	−4.0
1836–1840	14.0	3.9	2.0	5.8	−8.2
1841–1845	7.0	14.5	7.1	21.6	14.6
1846–1850	27.9	31.4	15.4	46.2	18.3
1851–1855	72.1	78.7	31.2	109.9	37.8
1856–1860	48.1	155.7	48.5	204.2	156.1

Source: Albert Fishlow, *American Railroads and the Transformation of the Anti-Bellum Economy* (Cambridge, Mass. Harvard University Press, 1965).

19. For a dissenting opinion see R. Fogel, *Railroads and American Economic Growth* (Baltimore: The Johns Hopkins Press, 1964), pp. 208–24. Fogel argues that if railroads had not appeared other industries, perhaps canals, would have taken their place. This, of course, would have

divided the country, and produced a very different configuration of transportation.

20. Nathan Rosenberg, "Technological Interdependence in the American Economy," *Technology and Culture* 20, 1 (January 1979): 27–28. Rosenberg notes: "Innovations leading to the reduction in high-voltage transmission costs have exactly the same effect. They make it possible to shut down relatively small, older plants and to exploit the economies of large-scale power generation in a limited number of localities" (p. 28, n. 3).

21. Landes, *Unbound Prometheus,* p. 275.

22. Ibid., p. 276.

23. The next section relies principally on Joseph Borkin and Charles A. Welsh, *Germany's Master Plan* (New York: Duell, Sloan and Pearce, 1943).

24. Ibid., p. 34. Like the terms "pool" or "trust," the term "cartel" is subject to various interpretations. As used herein a cartel means a combination or agreement, national or international in scope, in which the members, whether corporations or governments, seek to control one or more phases of the production, pricing, and distribution of a commodity. Most cartels of the modern type are trusts that govern whole fields of technology through patents, know-how, or control of facilities. World industries dependent upon localized raw materials are cartelized by similar methods. Cartels in democratic countries are formed for two purposes: to eliminate competition and to offset the hazards to vested interests that derive from technological change. In totalitarian states cartels are instruments of national policy, and in a warlike country, such as prewar Germany or Japan, cartels take their place in the scheme of warfare.

25. Ibid., p. 65. (Italics in original.)

26. Hearings, Temporary National Economic Committee, 75th Congress, Vol. 2, p. 1023. Quoted in Borkin and Welsh, pp. 24–25.

27. Ibid., p. 1024. Quoted in Borkin and Welsh, p. 25.

28. Paul Gibson, "How the Germans Dominate the World Chemical Industry," *Forbes,* October 13, 1980, pp. 155–64.

29. Lewis Mumford, *Technics and Civilization* (New York: Harcourt, Brace and Company, 1934), pp. 13–15, 17.

30. David S. Landes, "Watchmaking: A Case Study in Enterprise and Change," *Business History Review* 53, 1 (Spring 1979): 3.

31. Ibid., p. 12.

32. Ibid., pp. 12–13.

33. [Friedrich Osterwald], *Description des montagnes et des vallées qui font partie de la Principauté de Neuchâtel et Valangin,* 2d ed. (Neuchâtel, 1766), pp. 94–95; quoted in Landes, p. 25.

34. Landes, "Watchmaking," p. 34.

35. Ibid., p. 29, n. 59.

36. See G. G. Nash and E. A. Attwood, *The Agricultural Policies of Britain and Denmark: A Study in Reciprocal Trade* (London: Land Books, 1961).
37. Eric E. Lampard, *The Rise of the Dairy Industry in Wisconsin: A Study in Agricultual Change 1820-1920* (Madison, Wisc.: State Historical Society of Wisconsin, 1963).
38. Ibid.

NOTES TO CHAPTER 2

1. Carlo Cipolla, *The Economic History of World Population* (Harmondsworth, England: Penquin, 1965).
2. The physiocrats were a school of political economists in eighteenth-century France who believed that government should not interfere with natural economic law, and that land is the source of all wealth.
3. See W. W. Rostow, *The Stages of Economic Growth: A Non-Communist Manifesto* (Cambridge, England: Cambridge University Press, 1960), and W. W. Rostow, "The Take-Off into Self-Sustained Growth," *Economic Journal* 66 (March 1956): 25-48.
4. Edward F. Denison, *Accounting for United States Economic Growth 1929-1969* (Washington: Brookings Institution, 1974).
5. According to Alfred D. Chandler, Jr., in *The Visible Hand: The Managerial Revolution in American Business* (Cambridge, Mass.: The Belknap Press of Harvard University Press, 1977), p. 371, another economist, Robert Averitt, in *Dual Economy: The Dynamics of American Industry Structure* (New York: W. W. Norton, 1968), "has defined forty-one 'key industries'" which in 1963 had the maximum impact on the American economy. These were the industries that led in technological convergence, in investment in research and development, in production of capital goods, and in interindustrial dependence, involving extensive forward and backward linkages. Moreover, these industries had the greatest price-cost and the strongest wage-setting effects on other industries; they occurred in leading growth sectors; they displayed low employment and reduced employment in other sectors. Chandler notes that five were electronic and aircraft industries that were just getting started in 1917. Of the thirty-six in full operation at that time, all but three were in oil, rubber, chemical, and machinery and metals, two-digit SIC [Standard Industrial Code] groups. These three were scientific instruments, mechanical measuring devices, and sheet pipe and tube. All but four of these thirty-six key industries were concentrated ones, with the eight largest firms accounting for more than 48 percent of the total value of shipments. And in the remaining four, the largest eight accounted for between 32 and 42 percent of the total value of shipments.
6. Including increases in number of workers, hours worked, and education. See David Landes, *The Unbound Prometheus: Technological Change*

and Industrial Development in Western Europe from 1750 to the Present (Cambridge, England: Cambridge University Press, 1969).

7. Money and other forms of liquid capital are called financial capital. The role of financial capital is less well examined and thought to be a less significant factor in economic growth.

8. See R. M. Hartwell, *The Causes of the Industrial Revolution in England* (London: Methuen, 1967), and J. D. Chambers and G. E. Mingay, *The Agricultural Revolution, 1750-1880* (New York: Schocken Books, 1968). There was a symbiotic relationship between the two sets of technological advances, which has led to an important debate among historians. Some claim that the advances in agriculture led to a declining demand for agricultural labor and the enclosure movement forced peasants off the common lands. With no place else to go, peasants went to the cities where they formed an urban proletariat that was a cheap pool of labor providing a stimulus to the industrial sector. Others argue that technical change and advance in the industrial sector led to higher productivity of labor and higher real wages that attracted peasants from the countryside. Either way, the advances in knowledge were complementary and there were "forward linkages."

9. For a survey see Robert Solow, *Growth Theory: An Exposition* (New York: Oxford University Press, 1970).

10. For example, "disembodied" technical change simply shifts the whole function; "embodied" technical change is assumed to be introduced through new, more productive capital. It changes both the amount of capital and the relationship of capital to the productivity of other factors of production.

11. See for example the recent works of Martin Feldstein, Lawrence Summers, Lawrence Kotlikoff, and Adam Auerbach.

12. In 1970 IBM possessed $50 billion in card punching machines. In fact, the technology was already obsolete. An IBM employee at the time had invented a direct input device that would greatly have expedited information processing. IBM managers could not accept the financial dislocation the new technology would compel. It was suppressed and the employee later left to establish Inforex Corporation.

13. See Joseph Schumpeter, *Capitalism, Socialism and Democracy*, 3d ed. (New York: Harper & Row, 1950); Kenneth Arrow, "Economic Welfare and the Allocation of Resources for Invention," in *The Rate and Direction of Inventive Activity*, ed. Richard Nelson (Princeton, N.J.: Princeton University Press, 1962). See also Pankaj Tandon, "Optimal Patents with Compulsory Licensing," *Journal of Political Economy* 90, 3 (June 1982): 470–86; Richard Nelson and Sidney Winter, *An Evolutionary Theory of Economic Change* (Cambridge, Mass.: Belknap Press of Harvard University Press, 1982); Yoram Barzel, "Optimal Timing of Innovations," *Review of Economics and Statistics* 50, 3 (August 1968): 348–55; Partha Dasgupta and Joseph E. Stiglitz, "Uncertainty, In-

dustrial Structure, and the Speed of R&D," *Bell Journal of Economics* 11 (Spring 1980): 1–28; Jack Hirshleifer, "The Private and Social Value of Information and the Reward to Inventive Activity," *American Economic Review* 61 (September 1971): 561–74; D. G. McFetridge, *Government Support of Scientific Research and Development: An Economic Analysis* (Toronto: University of Toronto Press, 1977); Pankaj Tandon, "Aspects of Optimal R&D Policy," unpublished Ph.D. dissertation, Harvard University, 1979.

14. Jacob Schmookler, *Invention and Economic Growth* (Cambridge, Mass.: Harvard University Press, 1966), pp. 196–209.

15. Pankaj Tandon, "Optimal Patents with Compulsory Licensing," *Journal of Political Economy* 90, 3 (June 1982).

16. For an introductory discussion, see Kenneth S. Arrow, "Classification Notes on the Production and Transmission of Technological Knowledge," *American Economic Review: Papers and Proceedings* 9, 2 (May 1969): 29–35.

17. Ibid., p. 33.

18. Paul Samuelson, "The Pure Theory of Public Expenditure," *Review of Economics and Statistics* 36, 4 (November 1954): 387–89. The concept has been more fully developed by Richard A. Musgrave, *The Theory of Public Finance* (New York: McGraw-Hill, 1959) and Richard and Peggy Musgrave, *Public Finance in Theory and Practice*, 3d ed. (New York: McGraw-Hill, 1980).

19. Musgrave and Musgrave, p. 56.

20. Ibid.

21. Nelson and Winter, *An Evolutionary Theory*, p. 365.

22. But concentrated industries naturally impose social costs through restrictive competition. Firms in such sectors produce suboptimal levels of output and charge prices sufficient to generate monopoly profits by acting to prevent the entry of rival firms.

23. Robert Ornstein points out that the Hopi Indians, Trobriand Islanders, and other non-Western cultures have a very different time sense. See Robert E. Ornstein, *The Psychology of Consciousness* (Harmondsworth, England: Penguin, 1972), and *On the Experience of Time* (Harmondsworth, England: Penguin, 1969).

24. Marxist economists, of course, possess a clear bias in favor of linearity, because of Marx's interpretation of history as proceeding through defined stages of development. A part of the idea of nonlinearity is suggested in the simultaneous approach to causation in econometrics and in Arrow's writings on contingent commodities.

25. By this theory, all breakthroughs may be immediately possible because they inhere in the implicate order of things. A linear model would contradict this assertion because each step there will depend on a prior sequence of events. Refer to the discussion of stimulus diffusion in Chapter 5, pp. 199, for an insight into why a perception of the im-

minence of most technological breakthroughs has a subtle, although important, significance for government's promotion of technological change.

26. It should be noted that much current policy is directed at the existing tax code, which may overtax capital and discourage capital accumulation. It is directed at correcting an existing distortion, not on any need for an affirmative pro-capital policy.

27. Nelson and Winter, *An Evolutionary Theory*, p. 365.

28. Tandon, "Optimal Patents." Focusing on the problem of the tension that exists between the public benefits of sharing information and the incentives to produce it, Tandon has developed an integrated patent-licensing scheme. Under his plan patents would be granted but licensing would be compulsory. The patent life and the licensing royalty rate would be determined optimally on a case-by-case basis. Such a scheme steers toward the "best" middle position, but some incentive is lost and information is not fully exploited.

29. There is a large literature on measuring social benefits. One branch of that literature focuses on the difficulties that arise in the political process. An example is Arrow's impossibility theorem, which argues that rational social preference rankings cannot be achieved, in *Social Choice and Individual Values*, 2d ed. (New York: Wiley, 1963).

30. See Ronald Coase, "The Problem of Social Cost," *Journal of Law and Economics* 3 (October 1960): 1–44.

31. See generally Morton J. Horowitz, *The Transformation of American Law, (1780–1800)* (Cambridge, Mass.: Harvard University Press, 1977).

32. Paul A. Samuelson, "Presidential Address," in Samuelson, ed., *International Economic Relations: Proceedings of the Third Congress of the International Economic Association* (New York: Macmillan, 1969), p. 9.

33. The argument holds true even in the absence of war, embargo, or monopoly. It is all the easier in such cases, since vital supplies are interrupted.

34. T. M. Rybczynski, "Factor Endowments and Relative Commodity Prices," *Economica*, 22, 5 (November 1955): pp. 336–41.

35. See, for example, Bo Södersten, *A Study of Economic Growth and International Trade* (Stockholm: Almqvist and Wicksell, 1964), and Bo Södersten, *International Economics*, 2d ed. (New York: St. Martins, 1980), chap. 11.

36. The OECD's formulation of the polluter-pays principle was designed primarily to balance the costs of pollution equitably and with the least disruption to international trade.

37. In theory, it may not even be necessary for the second country's industries to be "linked" to the first for it to receive increased scientific knowledge and other benefits from the development of the first country's strategic industry.

38. A problem arises when theory is reduced to practice because, as noted,

economists do not understand why or how technological change occurs, the pathways it follows, or how to measure it. The emerging literature on comparative advantage suffers from the same biases as the rest of the economic literature on growth: it simply assumes that technological change occurs exogenously and then proceeds to analyze the consequences for trade.

NOTES TO CHAPTER 3

1. See "International Competition on Advanced Technology: Decisions for America," Office of International Affairs, National Research Council (Washington, D.C.: National Academy Press, 1983).
2. See *An Assessment of U.S. Competitiveness in High-Technology Industries*, a study prepared for the Working Group on High Technology Industries of the Cabinet Council on Commerce and Trade, May 19, 1982.
3. From 1962 through 1980 U.S. trade in high-technology products increased slightly while Japan's balance increased by 35 percent, and West Germany's by 13 percent.
4. *An Assessment of U.S. Competitiveness*, p. 9.
5. In "downmarket," non–technology-intensive products, U.S. losses were negligible and, as already noted, in textiles and apparel U.S. industries actually improved.
6. Arthur Neef and Patricia Capdevielle, "International Comparisons of Productivity and Labor Costs," *Monthly Labor Review* (December 1980): 32–39.
7. Bruce R. Scott, "Can Industry Survive the Welfare State?" *Harvard Business Review* 60, 4 (September–October 1982): 70–84.
8. Between 1970 and 1978 Japan and West Germany continued this rapid expansion.
9. Dr. George N. Hatsopoulos, *High Cost of Capital: Handicap of American Industry*. Study sponsored by American Business Conference, Inc. and Thermo Electron Corp., April 26, 1983.
10. The cost of capital services depends on the cost of fuels, increases in asset values due to inflation, tax credits, depreciation allowances, and the cost of asset decay (real depreciation).
11. Hatsopoulos notes that in 1979 the distribution of capital employed by Bethlehem Steel was 74 percent net fixed assets, 24 percent inventories, and 2 percent receivables, and for Digital Equipment, 41 percent net fixed assets, 39 percent inventories, and 2 percent receivables.
12. Hatsopoulos, *High Cost of Capital*, p. 120.
13. Ibid., p. 34. See comparable discussion on the semiconductor industry, chapter 5, pp. 113–114.
14. See "An Early Assessment of Three R and D Tax Incentives Provided by the Economic Recovery Act of 1981," Preliminary Report of the National Science Foundation Project, October 6, 1982.

15. 100 *Supreme Court Reporter,* 447 U.S. 303, *Sidney A. Diamond, Commissioner of Patents & Trademarks v̈. Ananda M. Chakrabarty et al.,* p. 2204. (1980).

16. *United States Law Week* 49, No. 79–1112, *Sidney A. Diamond, Commissioner of Patents and Trademarks, Petitioner,* v. *James R. Diehr, II and Theodore A. Lutton,* pp. 4194–4206, 3–3–81.

17. Karen Goodyear Krueger, "Building a Better Bacterium: Genetic Engineering and the Patent Law after *Diamond v. Chakrabarty,*" *Columbia Law Review* 81, 1 (January 1981): 159–78.

18. Richard Nelson and Sidney Winter, *An Evolutionary Theory of Economic Change* (Cambridge, Mass.: Harvard University Press, 1982). And see chapter 2.

19. Joseph F. Brodley, "Joint Ventures and Antitrust Policy," *Harvard Law Review* 95, 7 (May 1982): 1521–90.

20. Thomas W. Lippman, "Leaders of High Tech Industry Urge Hard Line Against Japan," *Washington Post,* February 3, 1983, pp. C11, C14.

21. The most recent Japanese input-output table is produced by the combined efforts of thirteen ministries under the general supervision of a committee of the council of ministers. For an interesting commentary see Wassily Leontief, "What Hope for the Economy?" *The New York Review,* April 12, 1982, p. 31.

22. E. Mansfield, *Federal Support of R&D Activities in the Private Sector* 106 (1976).

23. OMB, Budget of the U.S. Government: Appendix-FY 1983 (1982), at I-F8.

24. Office of the Federal Register, *The United States Government Manual* (1981), at 155.

25. In the 1970s there were severe shortages of specialists in high technology. Most prominent were shortages of computer specialists; others were reported for electronic specialists and chemical, electrical, and industrial engineers.

    The increases in salary levels in the private sector, which resulted from a tight labor market, seriously affected recruitment of instructors for U.S. engineering school faculties (currently there are 1,600 faculty vacancies) and for the armed forces (where pay scales did not keep up with the private sector). These increases also caused a sharp drop in the number of engineering Ph.D. candidates.

26. "America Rushes to High Tech for Growth," *Business Week,* March 28, 1983, pp. 84–98.

27. *Technology and East-West Trade,* Office of Technology Assessment. (Washington, D.C.: GPO, 1979).

28. See Richard B. Stewart, "Regulation, Innovation and Administrative Law: A Conceptual Framework," *California Law Review* 69, 5 (September 1981): 1256–1377; and Douglas H. Ginsburg, "Antitrust, Uncer-

tainty, and Technological Innovation," *Journal of American and Foreign Antitrust and Trade Regulation* 24, 4 (Winter 1979): 635–86.

29. 101 *Supreme Court Reporter, First National Maintenance Corporation* v. *National Labor Relations Board* (NLRB), p. 2573 (1981).

30. See "A Work Revolution in U.S. Industry," *Business Week,* May 16, 1983, pp. 100–10.

31. U.S. Congress, Senate, *Study on Federal Regulations,* Committee on Government Affairs, 96th Cong., 1st sess., December 1978, doc. no. 96-14; "Steel Trigger-Price Mechanisms," General Accounting Office rept. no. EMD-81-29 (Washington, D.C.: Government Printing Office, January 1981); U.S. Bureau of Economics, *Staff Report on Effects of Restrictions on U.S. Imports,* prepared for Federal Trade Commission by Morris E. Morkre and David G. Tarr (Washington, D.C.: Government Printing Office, June 1980).

32. Richard P. Nathan. "After Researching Early Reaganomics: Bad News for the Poor," *New York Times,* August 13, 1982, p. 14.

33. Congressional Budget Office, Human Resources and Community Development Division and Tax Analysis Division, "Effects of Tax and Benefit Reductions Enacted in 1981 for Households in Different Income Categories," special study, February 1982.

34. Robert Pear, "Poverty Rate Rose to Fifteen Percent in '82, Highest Level Since Mid-1960s," *New York Times,* August 3, 1983, pp. 1, 134.

35. The deprivation of a benefit is clearly not regressive in the same sense as the imposition of a disproportionate burden.

36. The computer industry remains complacent in its lead in software. Yet some researchers now acknowledge that Japan's software capability will equal or surpass U.S. capabilities within the next few years.

37. In the telephone communications industry after-tax profits increased steadily from $2.09 billion in 1965 to $11.90 billion in 1981. Expenditures for new plant and equipment in telephone communications have steadily increased from $43.3 billion in 1965 to $118.9 billion in 1975 and $187.4 billion in 1981.

38. Nathan Rosenberg, testimony in *United States v. AT&T,* November 1981, CA No. 74-1698, Defendant's Exhibit D-T-132, pp. 43–49.

39. George P. Sutton, "Technology of Machine Tools," vol. 1, Executive Summary, Machine Tool Task Force, October 1980, p. 6.

40. Ibid.

41. Ibid., pp. 6–7.

42. *The Machine Tool Industry* (McLean, Va.: National Machine Tool Builders Association (NMTBA), 1982), p. 250.

43. U.S. Department of Labor, Bureau of Labor Statistics, *Productivity Measures for Selected Industries, 1954–81,* December 1982, pp. 170–71. NMTBA statistics describe a greater increase in productivity than the Department of Labor statistics. However, the Bureau of Labor statistics

appear to be more accurate, for three reasons. First, the NMTBA chart begins in 1970, at a time when industry productivity was much lower than previous productivity levels (1970, 91.7, 1966, 111.7). Thus, the NMTBA chart distorts the productivity curve to appear as if it is rising when productivity is merely returning to 1965–1969 levels. Second, the NMTBA study is based on current dollar *sales* per production worker. Since dollar amounts, particularly in inflationary times, are increasing, the study adopts a bias toward increased production. Third, the Bureau of Labor study, published in December 1982, notes "because of periodic revisions in source data, the measures in this table may differ from those previously published." This study appears to be the most current.

44. *The Machine Tool Industry*, p. 252.
45. John P. Craven, "Industry/Government Relations in Offshore Resource Development," Paper no. OTC-1919, Offshore Technology Conference, Dallas, Texas 1973.
46. *An Assessment of U.S. Competitiveness*, Appendix, pp. 65–67.
47. *Aeronautical Research and Technology Policy*, Office of Science and Technology Policy (Washington, D.C.: Government Printing Office, November 1982); "International Competition in the Production and Marketing of Commercial Aircraft," Boeing Commercial Airplane Company, May 1982.
48. *Predicasts Basebook 1982* (Cleveland, Oh.: Predicasts, Inc., 1982), p. 642.
49. *Predicasts Basebook 1982*. Productivity increased in 1977, declined in 1978 and 1979, rose abruptly in 1980 and 1981, but declined by 4.7 percent in 1982.
49. 1983 U.S. Industrial Outlook, Department of Commerce (Washington, D.C.: Government Printing Office, 1983,); *Predicasts Basebook 1982*, p. 641.
50. See *An Assessment of U.S. Competitiveness*, pp. 14–15.

NOTES TO CHAPTER 4

1. This chapter is a synthesis of my own ideas and observations and those of Chalmers Johnson in *MITI and the Japanese Miracle* (Stanford: Stanford University Press, 1982). See also Miyohei Shinohara, *Industrial Growth, Trade, and Dynamic Patterns in the Japanese Economy* (Tokyo: Tokyo University Press, 1982).
2. For an in-depth discussion of this period, see Julian Gresser, Koichiro Fujikura, and Akio Morishima, *Environmental Law in Japan* (Cambridge: M.I.T. Press, 1981).
3. Shinohara, p. 26. Johnson suggests that the Japanese approach shows Soviet, French, and Germanic influences. Ueno emphasizes the continuance of French influence in the postwar period.

4. Ibid.
5. Saburo Okita, "Short and Long Term Economic Planning—Outlook of the Japanese Economy," unpublished manuscript, 1982.
6. Industrial Structure Council, Ministry of International Trade and Industry, Japan, *Japan's Industrial Structure: A Long Range Vision* (Japan: Japan External Trade Organization, 1975).
7. Johnson, MITI, p. 17.
8. Ibid., p. 18.
9. Ibid., p. 19.
10. Hiroya Ueno, *Nihon no Keizai Seidō* (*The Economic System of Japan*) (Tokyo: Nihon Keizai Shimbun Sha, 1978).
11. Johnson, MITI, p. 104.
12. Weber, of course, was concerned with industrial development in Europe. It should be noted that virtually all the principal Meiji legislation was imposed from continental Europe.
13. Johnson, MITI, pp. 109–110. Johnson notes: "The Important Industries Control Law was a short statute of only ten articles. According to its terms, when two-thirds of the enterprises in a particular industry agreed to a cartel, MCI would examine its contents and, if it approved, then authorize the cartel. The government could also change the terms or nullify the agreement. And it could force nonparticipants in the cartel agreement to abide by its terms if they did not do so voluntarily. As a result of an MCI-sponsored amendment to the law (introduced in the Diet during September 1932 and passed during 1933), the ministry obtained the powers to approve investments that would expand facilities by cartel members and to approve members' decisions to curtail production. Needless to say, all members of an industry were required to submit frequent reports on their investment plans and activities to the government. It is in this law that we find the origins of the government's licensing and approval authority and of the practice of 'administrative guidance,' which together became the heart of postwar industrial policy. To assuage skeptics in the Diet, the law had a five-year limitation written into it; on August 15, 1936, it was extended for another five years but it was superseded by the National General Mobilization Law before the second time period expired."
14. Based on personal discussions with Roger Fisher on the elements of crisis. See also Chapter 9.
15. Naohiro Amaya, "A Look at Knowledge Intensification from the Viewpoint of Cultural History," *Japan Reporting* JR-5 (75-3) (Japan: Ministry of Trade and Industry, February 1975).
16. Ibid., pp. 4–5.
17. Ibid., p. 7.
18. Ibid., pp. 5–6.
19. Ibid., pp. 15–16.

NOTES TO CHAPTER 5

1. Thomas S. Kuhn, "What Are Scientific Revolutions?" *Occasional Paper #18*, Center for Cognitive Science, M.I.T., n.d., p. 25.
2. Toshio Sanuki, *An Analysis of the Structure of the Japanese Economy* (*Nihon Keizai No Kōzō Bunseki*) (Tokyo: Keizai Shinbunsha, 1980).
3. Julian Gresser, Koichiro Fujikura, and Akio Morishima, *Environmental Law in Japan* (Cambridge, Mass.: M.I.T. Press, 1981).
4. This case study is based on Eugene J. Kaplan, *Japan: The Government-Business Relationship,* prepared for U.S. Department of Commerce (Washington, D.C.: GPO, 1972), pp. 103–107.
5. Kaplan notes that repatriation was permitted only if investment in production facilities contributed to the development of the domestic industry.
6. Kaplan notes that in addition, the tax base on imports was landed value while for domestic cars it was ex-factory price.
7. Kaplan suggests that it is surprising that not a single U.S. producer negotiated an equity position before 1971, since at least one foreign company was explicitly invited. MITI's chief objection was not that such investment was foreign, but rather that it was not easily controlled.
8. Kaplan notes that as early as 1952 MITI had subsidized specific parts producers and over the next few years had recommended that the Japan Development Bank extend long-term credit to the large, viable parts suppliers of the four major producers.
9. In JFY 1977 the Hitachi *keiretsu* consisted of forty consolidated subsidiaries (with Hitachi holding over 50 percent equity) and 434 non-consolidated subsidiaries (with Hitachi holding 20 to 50 percent equity).
10. Michael Burros, James Millstein, and John Zysman, *U.S.–Japanese Competition in the Semiconductor Industry,* Policy Papers in International Affairs, no. 17, (Berkeley: Institute of International Studies, 1982), p. 68.
11. Ibid., p. 67.
12. Ibid., p. 69.
13. Julian Gresser, *High Technology and Japanese Industrial Policy: A Strategy for U.S. Policy Makers,* paper prepared for Subcommittee on Trade of House Ways and Means Committee (Washington, D.C.: GPO, 1980), p. 13.
14. By the end of 1979 the VLSI Association had succeeded in developing 700 patentable technologies. They included electron beam lithography using variable shaped rectangular beams (April 1977), multiple walls with self-aligned manufacturing technology (November 1977), and a faster-scan electron beam exposure system (March 1978). Some of these generic technologies have already been commercially exploited.
15. Burros et al., pp. 75–76.

16. MOS are metal oxide semiconductors. RAM means random access memory. Ibid., pp. 150, 152.
17. Ibid., pp. 80–81.
18. Japan Information Processing Development Center, *Computer White Paper, 1981 Edition: A Summary of Highlights compiled from the Japanese original*, trans. Richard Foster (1981).
19. Special Taxation Measures Law, Articles 20–2 and 56–9.
20. For a confirming Japanese commentary, see Fumio Kodama, "Puru Seisaku ni Kansuru Kenkyū" (Research Concerning Pull Policy), NCB 8101 Materials of the Japanese Institute of Systems Engineering, July 21, 1981.
21. Burros et al., p. 56.
22. Ibid., p. 88.
23. Andrew Osterman, personal communication.
24. This flexibility, however, was itself offset somewhat by compensating balances maintained with the city banks by these same firms.
25. Two recent important articles are Richard R. Nelson and Sidney G. Winter, "The Schumpeterian Trade-off Revisited," *American Economic Review* 72, 1 (March 1982): 114–32, and "Simulation of Schumpeterian Competition," *American Economic Review* 67, 1 (February 1977): 271–76.
26. In economists' jargon, price is set above marginal costs resulting in a gap that reflects the social cost.

NOTES TO CHAPTER 6

1. Akira Nishii, "Towards an Advanced Society Evolving from Communications," paper presented at the Japan–U.S. Office Automation Forum '82, November 1982.
2. Some of these examples are drawn from Masakazu Kuranari, "Liberalization of Data Communication in Japan," unpublished paper, M.I.T., December 1981.
3. Ibid.
4. In mid-July NTT announced that it would begin selling LAN (local area network) products. No time frame for actual sales was given but the announcement was quickly followed by the denunciation by officials at Nippon Electronic Corporation (NEC), who decried the formation of an office within NTT to evaluate the possibility of sales of NTT LAN equipment. What sort of LAN products might NTT sell? The products would be digital PABXs, not optical fiber LANs. If NTT goes ahead and sells its own products it will have markedly changed its policies. There has been talk in the Japanese press routinely for quite a few years that NTT might become an independent, private corporation in competition with the major Japanese corporations. The announcement of an office to handle sales of digital PABXs might well be the first step in this direction.

5. See "Concerning the Promotion of Technology for the Optics Industry" (Hikari Sangyo Gijitsu no Shinkō Shisetusu ni Tsuite) Tsusanshō Kōhō, September 26, 1982.
6. The location of computers within the network is of course also critical to the allocation of cost, for those controlling the computer facilities basically pay less for uses of the circuits relating to data processing.
7. The basic software system consists of three subsystems to include problem solving and inference, knowledge base management, and an intelligent interface.
8. The system provides the human designer intelligent functions to support systematization work based on the knowledge base contents and it consists of three subsystems of intelligent programming, knowledge base designing, and intelligent VLSI designing.
9. This system has such functions as to permit the user easy use of the entire computer system and make the system highly reliable. These include programs to support the portability of software and data base from other machines, use-guidance functions, and automatic inspection and repair functions for the prevention and detection of failures.
10. The basic knowledge base supports the operation of the system itself in addition to containing the accumulated valid and universal knowledge necessary to the user. Generally, there are three types: the general knowledge base that mainly relates to the understanding of natural languages, the system knowledge base related to the system itself, and the applied knowledge base containing specialized knowledge for various applications.
11. Five types of basic application system can be cited: machine translation system, question-answering system, applied speech-understanding system, applied picture- and image-understanding system, and applied problem-solving system.
12. The following systems can be thought of as examples of knowledge information-processing application systems: intelligent CAE/CAD system, intelligent CAI system, intelligent OA system, and intelligent robot.
13. PROLOG, or Programming Logic, was developed in Europe in the late 1970s. It is used in artificial intelligence because its basic terms express logical relationships among objects, not just equations. Very few systems now use PROLOG; most are programmed in a less precise language called LISP (for List Processing).
14. Japan Information Processing Development Center, *Computer White Paper*, 1981 ed. A summary of highlights compiled from the Japanese original. Trans. Richard Foster. (1981), p. 66.
15. *Computer White Paper*, p. 67.
16. Kenichi Hirai, "Some Proposals Concerning Japan's Telecommunications Strategy," Institute of Business Research, Hitotsubashi University, September 1982.
17. This section relies extensively on Houdaille Industries, Inc., Petition

to the President of the United States Through the Office of the United States Trade Representative for the Exercise of Presidential Discretion Authorized by section 103 of the Revenue Act of 1971, 26 U.S.C. § 48(a)(7)(D), 1982. In September 1983, the United States International Trade Commission (ITC) issued an investigative report under section 332 of the Trade Act. It found minimal subsidizing of the machine tool industry by the Japanese government, as follows: 1978-$499,000; 1979-$319,000; 1980-$472,000; 1981-$322,000. See U.S. ITC publication no. 1428 (1983).

18. Houdaille Petition, p. 97.
19. Other tax incentives included incentives introduced in the 1950s; reserve for bad debts, reserve for retirement allowance, reserve for price fluctuation, accelerated depreciation programs, including "normal" depreciation methods and "special" depreciation.

    Export tax incentives include tax exemption for export income, special reserve for export losses, and accelerated depreciation for overseas offices.

    Incentives introduced in the 1960s: accelerated depreciation programs; export tax incentives, including special depreciation program for export, reserve for overseas market development, and tax exemption on entertainment and social expenses for export; tax credit program for scrapping machines and equipment; and tax credit for increased research and development cost.

    Incentives introduced in the 1970s: accelerated depreciation program for machines and equipment used by small and medium-sized businesses, and accelerated depreciation program for high-efficiency machine tools.
20. Opposition briefs on the Houdaille petition directly challenged the accuracy of these and related data.
21. Interviewees also challenge the accuracy of this allegation.
22. "Linking System for Compensating Sacrifice Exports," appearing in Japan Machinery Exporters' Association 25 Year Annuals, noted in Houdaille Petition, pp. 112–13.
23. These include:

Toshiba Machine	Aida Engineering
Toyota Machine Works	Mitsubishi Electric
Makindo Milling Machine	Toshiba Corp.
Hitachi Seiki	Nippon Electric
Yamazaki Machinery Works	Matsushita Research Institute of Tokyo
Okuma Machinery Works	
Yasukawa Electric Mfg.	Horiba
Ishikawajima-Harima Heavy Industries	Sumitomo Electric Industries
	Oki Electric Industry
Kobe Steel	Fujitsu Fanuc
Mitsubishi Heavy Industries	Shin-Nippon Koki

24. "The Race to the Automatic Factory," *Fortune*, February 21, 1983, p. 64.
25. See, generally, Stanley B. Gershwin, "Material and Information Flow in an Advanced Automated Manufacturing System," LIDS-P-1199, Laboratory for Information and Decision Systems, M.I.T., May 1982.
26. This study relies in part on the work of the author as a member of the advisory committee to the Office of Technology Assessment, and on the office's final report, "International Competitiveness in Biotechnology," draft, July 1983.
27. "Special Issue: Research on Biotechnology in Japan," *The Japan Industrial and Technological Bulletin* 14 (1982). (Japan External Trade Organization.)
28. In October 1981 the Japanese Fair Trade Commission initiated an investigation into an alleged cartel among pharmaceutical manufacturers.
29. The discussion of emerging government policy relies on Masami Tanaka, "Biotekunoloji no Shinkö ni Tsuite" (Concerning the promotion of biotechnology), *Hakkō to Kōgyō (Fermentation and Industry)*, 40 (1982).
30. See Jöel de Rosnay, "Biology, Computer Sciences, and Automated Control Engineering: The Dawn of the Biotic Age," unpublished paper, n.d.
31. For a brief review of Defense Department interest see Jim Ostroff, "Biochips," *Venture* 5, 2 (February 1983): 65–68.
32. Shinohara, *Industrial Growth*, pp. 41, 43.

NOTES TO CHAPTER 7

1. There is a substantial literature in Japanese on Japanese environmental law. The principal text in English is Julian Gresser, Koichiro Fujikura, and Akio Morishima, *Environmental Law in Japan* (Cambridge, Mass.: M.I.T. Press, 1981).
2. The history of the auto emission case is discussed in ibid., pp. 268–74.
3. See ibid., chaps. 3–7. These agreements were at times negotiated on a tripartite basis among citizens, companies, and the government.
4. The story of how Japanese society went about making this adjustment is told again in ibid., pp. 29–51.
5. The best-known series of books on this subject are by Jon Woronoff: *Japan: The Coming Social Crisis* (Tokyo: Lotus Press, 1981); *Japan: The Coming Economic Crisis* (Tokyo: Lotus Press, 1981); and *Japan's Wasted Workers* (Tokyo: Lotus Press, 1981).
6. Kenji Miyamoto, "What Is Happening to Japan's Industrial Structure?" *Journal of Japanese Trade and Industry*, 1, 3 (May 1982).
7. See Kisō Sōzai Sangyō no Tenbō to Kadai (Perspectives and Themes of the Basic Materials Industries), MITI, 1982.

8. Tokutei Fukyō Sangyō Antei Rinji Sochihō, Law. no. 44, 1978.
9. See MITI, Regional Development and Pollution Industrial Relocation Office, Outline of Industrial Redistribution Policy (Kōgyō Saihansei Shisaku no Aramashi), July 1982. Also Dario F. Robertson, "Planning for the Technopolis: Regional Development and Foreign Investment," *East Asian Executive Reports* 4, 10 (October 15, 1982): 6–7, 18–19; Justin Bloom and Shinsuke Asano, "Tsukuba Science City: Japan Tries Planned Innovation," *Science,* 212, 4500 (June 12, 1981): 1239–47; Hidetatsu Furutake, "Technopolis Construction Concept," *Journal of Trade and Industry* vol. 1, no. 5 (September 1982): 10–13.
10. MITI, *Venture Businesses in Japan and VB Promotion Policies,* B1-19, 1975.
11. *Venture Businesses in Japan and VB Promotion Policies* (Tokyo: Ministry of International Trade and Industry, November 1975), B1-19. See also *VEC '80* (Tokyo: Center for the Development of Research and Development Enterprises, 1980).
12. See "Report of the Research Committee on the Promotion of Research and Development Enterprises" (Kenkyū Kaihatsukei Kigyō Ikusei Shinkisaku Kenkyūkai Hōkoku Shō), November 4, 1981.
13. Even today the Tax Reduction Act, 1980, the Research Revitalization Act (18.2.6632), and the Small Business Investment Company Act, 1980, evidence continuing congressional concern about these issues.
14. In addition to NTDA's technology diffusion programs, various other services are provided by the government's Small Business Promotion Corporation (SBPC) and the Small and Medium Enterprise Agency (SMEA). SMEA administers a nationwide technical information service network that features twenty-one regional centers. Interested firms and individuals can readily obtain scientific reports and technological data from these convenient locations. The centers also serve as a valuable communications channel for the NTDA.

    SBPC administers a network of 128 prefectural research institutes. These institutes perform a variety of services for smaller firms, which are the hotbed of innovative activity. One of those services is the provision of technical guidance during the implementation of new technology. An itinerant technical consultancy service is maintained, and technical training courses are provided. The research institutes also provide laboratory facilities that may be used by a small firm for independent research, or for joint research on a project sponsored by the institute. The research results generated at one of these prefectural institutes can be considerable. NTDA assists with the necessary patenting and acts to publicize the innovations.
15. See Prime Minister's Office, "An Investigation on the Protection of Privacy" (Puraibashi Hōgō ni Kansuru Seron Chōsa), May 1956.
16. See Gresser et al.
17. The Environment Agency has currently budgeted ¥ 10 million for FY

1982 to perform an assessment of the environmental impact of DNA research.

18. A complete translation of this important case appears in Gresser et al., pp. 105–24.

19. Barbara Bialick, "Can You Live With the Computerized Office?" *Whole Life Times,* March 1983, pp. 33–37, 58, 59.

20. Tamotsu Sengoku, "The Mismatch in Japan." Preliminary Report to the Jobs in the 80s Project, Japan Youth Research Institute, September 1980.

21. See N. Maeda, "A Fact-finding Study on the Impacts of Microcomputers on Employment," Ministry of International Trade and Industry, Special Committee on the Impacts of Microelectronics on Employment, November 10, 1979.

22. *Research and Study Concerning Influences of Microelectronics on Employment: Results of the Survey on Labor Statistics by Occupation in Fiscal Year 1980* (Tokyo: Ministry of Labor, June 12, 1981), pp. 3–4.

23. Ibid., pp. 5–6.

24. Ibid.

25. Based on private discussions and film interviews of Asahi's workers.

26. Wassily W. Leontief, "The Distribution of Work and Income," *Scientific American* 247, 3 (September 1982): 188–99.

27. Based on Mark J. Ramseyer, "Letting Obsolete Firms Die: Trade Adjustment Resistance in the United States and Japan," *Harvard International Law Journal* 22 (1981): 595–619.

28. *Tokutei Fukyō Gyōshū Rishokusha Rinji Sochihō,* Law No. 95, 1977.

29. Haruo Shimada, "Perceptions and the Reality of Japanese Industrial Relations: Role in Japan's Industrial Success," unpublished paper, 1982.

30. Tadashi Hanami, "Worker Motivation and the Japanese Industrial Relations System," paper presented at workshop on Capitalist-Socialist Dialogues on Organizational Behavior, European Institute for Advanced Studies in Management and the Helsinki School of Economics, Helsinki, May 26–28, 1981.

31. Joseph Weizenbaum, *Computer Power and Human Reason* (San Francisco: W. H. Freeman, 1976), p. 261.

NOTES TO CHAPTER 8

1. I am indebted to Professor Harvey Brooks, personal correspondence, July 22, 1982, for this observation.

2. Richard Davies, "Is Nuclear Power a Strategic Industry?" unpublished paper, MIT, Program in Science, Technology and Society, 1982.

3. William J. Abernathy and Balaji S. Chakravarthy, "The Federal Initiative in Industrial Innovation: The Automative Case," *Sloan Management Review,* 20, 4 (Spring 1979): 3–18.

4. Nørregaard P. Rasmussen, *Studies in Inter-Sectoral Relations* (Amsterdam: North Holland Publishing Co., 1956), p. 142.

5. The proposed method of identifying, assessing, and negotiating benefits for strategic industries is summarized in its entirety in Chapter 8.

6. Arthur D. Little, Inc., "Patterns and Problems of Technical Innovation in American Industry," report to the National Science Foundation, September 1963, p. 181, quoted in Nathan Rosenberg, "Technological Interdependence in the American Economy," *Technology and Culture* 20, 1 (January 1979): 46–47.

7. Ibid., p. 41.

8. Ibid., p. 43.

9. Nathan Rosenberg, *Perspectives on Technology* (Cambridge: Cambridge University Press, 1976), p. 102.

10. Jacob Schmookler, *Invention and Economic Growth* (Cambridge, Mass.: Harvard University Press, 1966).

11. For a discussion of the importance of the learning curve in the aircraft industry, see John Newhouse, "A Sporty Game," *New Yorker* magazine, June 14, June 21, June 28, July 5, 1982.

12. An important additional index of technological capability may be the number of parts.

13. See Chapter 5.

14. See Chapter 5.

15. A related factor may be "reciprocity." Reciprocity is similar to synergism except that the latter emphasizes the effects of interaction while the former stresses design. Rosenberg describes how the machine tools that manufactured the Colt revolver copied the operation of the revolver, and the revolver mimicked the tools that made it, and similarly in the automobile and other industries. Reciprocity may well be a special case; the subject deserves further study.

16. Joji Arai, "The World Is Divided into Three Technological Parts," *World Paper* 4, 10 (October 1982), p. 11.

17. Raymond de Roover, *Money, Banking and Credit in Mediaeval Bruges* (Cambridge, Mass.: The Mediaeval Academy of America, 1948).

18. David Landes, *The Unbound Prometheus: Technological Change and Industrial Development in Western Europe from 1750 to the Present* (Cambridge, England: Cambridge University Press, 1969).

19. Germany well understood the strategy of total war. Karl von Clausewitz (1780–1831), the father of German militarism, set out the major premise when he said, "War is no independent thing; the main elements of all great strategic plans are of a political nature, the more so they include the totality of War and the State." To Clausewitz, peace was a continuation of war by other means. To Germany he said: "Disarm your enemy in peace by diplomacy and trade if you would conquer him more readily on the field of battle." Quoted in Joseph Borkin and Charles A. Welsh, *Germany's Master Plan: The Story of In-*

dustrial Offensive (New York: Duell, Sloan and Pearce, 1943), p. 16. For an extended discussion of Clausewitz see Chapter 10.

20. I am grateful for these insights to John Craven of the University of Hawaii. For a similar discussion, which however does not use the term "scale ratio," see Donald A. Schon, *Beyond the Stable State* (New York: Random House, 1971).

21. Albert O. Hirschman, *The Strategy of Economic Development* (New Haven: Yale University Press, 1958), p. 117.

22. James M. Utterback, "The Dynamics of Product and Process Innovation in Industry," in *Technological Innovation,* ed. Christopher T. Hill and James M. Utterback (New York: Pergamon Press, 1979), p. 49.

23. Julian Gresser, Koichiro Fujikura, and Akio Morishima, *Environmental Law in Japan* (Cambridge, Mass.: M.I.T. Press, 1981).

24. See J. W. Lozier, "The Forgotten Industry: Small and Medium Sized Cotton Mills South of Boston," *Working Papers from the Regional Economic History Research Center,* 2, 4 (1979); J. W. Lozier, "Rural Textile Mill Communities and the Transition to Industrialism in America, 1800–1840," *Working Papers from the Regional Economic History Research Center,* 4, 4 (1981): 78–94.

NOTES TO CHAPTER 9

1. Simon Kuznets, "Modern Economic Growth: Findings and Reflections," *American Economic Review* 63, 3 (June 1973): 253.

2. Joseph L. Badaracco, Jr., and David B. Yoffie, "Why a U.S. Industrial Policy Will Fail," Harvard Business School Working Paper, 83–20.

3. I am indebted to Lawrence Susskind for many of these observations.

4. Lawrence Susskind and Anne Aylward, "Comprehensive Planning: A State of the Art Review of Concepts, Methods, and the Problems of Building Local Capacity," draft prepared for the Advisory Commission on Housing and Urban Growth, American Bar Association, January 29, 1976.

5. Ellis W. Hawley, "Herbert Hoover, the Commerce Secretariat, and the Vision of an 'Associative State,' 1921–1928," *Journal of American History,* 61, 1 (June 1974): 139–140.

6. George C. Lodge, *The New American Ideology* (New York: Alfred A. Knopf, 1980).

7. See Bruce R. Scott, "How Practical Is National Economic Planning," *Harvard Business Review* (March–April 1978).

8. Most commitments have been honored, the promised funds have been allocated, and implementation is progressing. The change in leadership in the White House has made implementation more difficult. See "A Negotiated Investment Strategy for Columbus, Ohio," in Lawrence Susskind and Frank Keefe, *The Negotiation Process* and *The Agreement,*

Report of the Negotiated Investment Strategy Project, Columbus, Ohio, May 1980. Also based on discussions with Lawrence Susskind.

9. This discussion relies in part on Philip J. Harter, "Negotiating Regulations: A Cure for Malaise," *Georgetown Law Journal* 71, 1 (October 1982): 1–118.

10. To assist its functions, the OSI could draw extensively on the experience of the Office of Management and Budget (OMB) and the Federal Mediation and Conciliation Service (FMS).

11. Such broad circulation is assumed wherever *Federal Register* appears in this text.

12. I am indebted to Lawrence Susskind for this idea.

13. This procedure is based on discussions with Lawrence Susskind.

14. Ralph L. Keeney and Howard Raiffa, *Decisions with Multiple Objectives: Preferences and Value Trade Offs* (New York: John Wiley, 1976).

15. In the National Coal Project it was $400,000 for two years.

16. These steps are close to those contemplated by Philip Harter in his description of negotiated rule-making. See Harter, "Negotiating Regulations."

17. Howard Raiffa, *The Art and Science of Negotiation* (Cambridge, Mass.: Harvard University Press, 1983).

18. Harter, "Negotiating Regulations," pp. 86–88.

19. See Roger Fisher, "Ten Steps to Move from a Conflict to a Solution," Harvard Negotiation Project, September 11, 1982 (draft).

20. This suggestion is based on a discussion with Howard Raiffa.

21. For a relevant precedent see Japanese law for the Resolution of Pollution Related Disputes in Julian Gresser, Koichiro Fujikura, and Akio Morishima, *Environmental Law in Japan* (Cambridge, Mass.: MIT Press, 1981), pp. 325–48.

22. Lawrence Susskind and Frank Keefe, "A Negotiated Investment Strategy for Columbus, Ohio," May 1, 1980.

23. The following discussion is based on critical comments by Professors Abram Chayes, Milton Katz, and Howard Raiffa.

24. Susskind and Keefe.

25. For a discussion of law's similar function in Japan see "The Transformation of Values and the Legal Process," in Gresser et al., *Environmental Law in Japan*, pp. 29–51.

26. Larry Susskind reports that the Columbus negotiation involved over forty-five active participants and their supporting staff. In the Osaka airport noise pollution case, over 10,000 persons participated in a mediated settlement. See Gresser, *Environmental Law in Japan.*

27. Harter, "Negotiating Regulations," pp. 22–23, n. 128.

28. Similarly, since the negotiation would actually serve the objectives of Executive Order No. 12,291, 3,3, C.F.R. 127, 128–30 (1981), a regulatory impact analysis should not be required.

NOTES TO CHAPTER 10

1. See, generally, C. Fred Bergsten, "What to Do About the U.S.–Japan Economic Conflict," *Foreign Affairs* 60, 5 (Summer 1982): 1059–75.
2. James C. Abegglen and Thomas M. Hout, "Facing Up to the Trade Gap with Japan," *Foreign Affairs* 57, 1 (Fall 1978): 146–68.
3. Ibid.
4. Chalmers Johnson, *MITI and the Japanese Miracle: The Growth of Industrial Policy, 1925–1975* (Stanford: Stanford University Press, 1982), p. 19.
5. See, generally, Carl J. Green, "The New Protectionism," *Northwestern Journal of International Law and Business* 3, 1 (Spring 1981): 1–20.
6. The following is based on my own observations as special advisor to the Assistant Secretary of State for East Asian Affairs during the Carter administration.
7. As concern about the economy increases, just now there is a recognition that economic policy *is* a matter of national security.
8. Johnson, *MITI*, p. 17.
9. Laissez-faire dates generally from the publication of Adam Smith's *An Inquiry into the Nature and Causes of the Wealth of Nations* (New York: Random House, 1937). See Eli F. Heckscher, *Mercantilism*, translated by Mendel Shapiro, revised edition edited by E. F. Soderlund. Vol. I and II. (London: Allen & Unwin, 1955).
10. Ibid., Hecksher, vol. I, p. 187.
11. Ibid., pp. 178–79.
12. Ibid., p. 158.
13. Ibid., p. 270.
14. Ibid., p. 130. Autarchy, however, should be distinguished from mercantilism in that the former sought to limit or abolish all trade relations with other communities, not imports alone.
15. Heckscher, *Mercantilism*, vol. II, p. 61.
16. Observation by the historian of Venice, E. F. Brown. Quoted in Heckscher, vol. II, p. 61.
17. Ibid., p. 73.
18. Ibid., pp. 316–324.
19. Karl von Clausewitz, *On War*, ed. Anatol Rapoport (Harmondsworth: Penguin, 1982), pp. 116, 119.
20. Sun Tzu, *The Art of War*, trans. Samuel Griffith (Oxford: Clarendon Press, 1963).
21. Founder of the Tokugawa Shogunate. See Ibid., Appendix 2, "Sun Tzu's Influence on Japanese Military Thought," pp. 169–78.
22. Written by Lieutenant-General Muto Akira, Ibid., p. 177.
23. Johnson, *MITI*, p. 37.
24. The Cabinet was concerned about the effect on other countries' practices of a U.S. determination that income tax–related levies were exempt from GATT sanctions. The Cabinet was reluctant to grant the

specific relief requested, although it was prepared to find a basis for relief under section 301 of the trade laws.

25. See also *In the Matter of Foreign Industrial Targeting and Its Effects on U.S. Industries,* transcript of the Proceeding before the U.S. International Trade Commission, June 15, 1983.

26. This fear may be groundless. The Japanese Patent Agency was apparently prepared to recognize the patentability of the plasmids in the *Chakrabarty* case exactly at the time that the General Electric patent was denied by the U.S. Patent Office. G.E., however, decided not to process a patent application in Japan.

27. See Michael Nacht, "When Worlds Divide: Diverging Conceptions of the National Interest in the United States and Japan," unpublished paper, October 1982.

28. See special report, "Rearming Japan," *Business Week,* March 14, 1983, pp. 110–11, 114, 116.

29. Naturally, the Japanese government, highly aware of the industrial importance of these technologies, keeps statistics. According to *Business Week* Ibid., p. 110, MITI officials report 2,000 deals signed in 1981 involving license fees of $1.7 billion, more than half of which was paid to U.S. companies.

30. According to Professor Michael Nacht, the Soviets flirted with this idea in 1956.

NOTES TO CHAPTER 11

1. Carl Green, "The New Protectionism," *Northwestern Journal of International Law and Business,* 3, 1 (Spring 1981).

2. *Wing Magazine,* September 28, 1982, Chōkan, no. 1326, p. 9.

3. *Aviation Week and Space Technology,* May 30, 1983.

4. The Boeing 767 is currently being developed by a consortium involving Mitsubishi, Kawasaki, Boeing, and Italian interests.

5. A number of scholars have argued that unpatentable know-how can be protected under the Japanese Civil Code.

6. See Foreign Exchange and Foreign Trade Control Law, Law no. 228 of 1949, arts. 42–43, and subsequent amendments in Law no. 65 of 1979, and Cabinet Order, no. 260 of 1980.

7. This statement is based on interviews with U.S. companies operating in Japan. I have no evidence, however, that any U.S. company actively made a formal request to the Japanese government to participate. Such discrimination, if it does exist, may violate Japan's treaty obligations to the United States. See U.S.–Japan Treaty of Friendship, Commerce, and Navigation, April 2, 1953; Japanese Treaty, no. 27 of 1953.

8. I am indebted to Carl Green for bringing this example to my attention.

9. See John H. Barton, "Technology Trade," paper presented for the

Trade Law Panel, American Society of International Law, April 14, 1983.
10. Ibid.
11. I am indebted to Roger Fisher for some of these insights.
12. See Chapter 1.
13. Ryūzo Sato and Gilbert S. Suzawa, *Research and Productivity: Endogenous Technical Change* (Boston: Auburn House, 1983).
14. Some economists may question whether a cost of conflict is an externality, since technically it is not an actual cost of production. Some will also argue that cooperation will dampen initiative and innovation, and that this cost must also be considered.
15. Communication from Alvin Issacs, Patent Council for The Polaroid Corporation.
16. See Julian Gresser, Koichiro Fujikura, and Akio Morishima, *Environmental Law of Japan*.

NOTES TO EPILOGUE

1. Ray Hofheinz Jr. and Kent E. Calder note these other common elements:
   Government policies that promote savings and investment, rather than consumption.
   Control of economic policy-making is in the hands of an elite corps of bureaucrats.
   Relatively equitable distribution of income among the population.
   Control of some key sectors of the economy by large corporations or industrial groups that are unfettered by American-style antitrust laws.
   An emphasis on educational programs to train skilled workers.
   Political control by a single party, which provides stability for long-term economic planning.
   Regulating yearly wage increases for workers so that they do not fuel inflation.
   The Eastasia Edge (New York: Basic Books, 1982).
2. See "Problems and Issues Concerning the Transfer, Application and Development of Technology in the Capital Goods and Industrial Machinery Sector," and "The Capital Goods and Industrial Machinery Sector in Developing Countries: Issues in the Transfer and Development of Technology," study by the United Nations Conference on Trade and Development Secretariat, TD/B/C.6/AC.7/2, May 3, 1982.
3. The UNCTAD report neglects the International Agriculture Research Centers (IARC). IARCs are islands of high technology in lands of stagnancy and desolation. In some cases their libraries keep abreast of current literature and they maintain sophisticated equipment. They engage in cooperative experiments with researchers at other institutions, sometimes located halfway around the globe and in places even

404

harder to reach than their own headquarters. IARCs serve in many countries as the principal bulwark against famine. At a nominal cost of $150,000 a computer polling system could be introduced that would permit all these centers to send and receive seventy-five typewritten pages per day. The benefits to inhabitants of these remote enclaves would be reaped a thousand fold. See Ithiel de Sola Pool, Elliot Friedman, and Colin Warren, "Low Cost Data and Text Communication for the Less Developed Countries," MIT Research Program on Communications Policy, January 1976.

Index

407

409

411

412

413

417

419